www.wadsworth.com

www.wadsworth.com is the World Wide Web site for Wadsworth and is your direct source to dozens of online resources.

At *www.wadsworth.com* you can find out about supplements, demonstration software, and student resources. You can also send e-mail to many of our authors and preview new publications and exciting new technologies.

www.wadsworth.com
Changing the way the world learns®

Counseling Adolescents and Children

DEVELOPING YOUR CLINICAL STYLE

DEANNA S. PLEDGE

THOMSON

WADSWORTH

Australia • Canada • Mexico • Singapore • Spain • United Kingdom • United States

Executive Editor: Lisa Gebo
Acquisitions Editor: Julie Martinez
Assistant Editor: Shelley Gesicki
Editorial Assistant: Amy Lam
Technology Project Manager: Barry Connolly
Marketing Manager: Caroline Concilla
Marketing Assistant: Mary Ho
Advertising Project Manager: Tami Strang

Project Manager, Editorial Production: Katy German
Print/Media Buyer: Jessica Reed, Karen Hunt
Permissions Editor: Sommy Ko
Production Service: Carlisle Publishers Services
Copy Editor: Karen Bankston
Cover Designer: Blue Bungalow Design
Printer: Transcontinental Printing

Printed in Canada
2 3 4 5 6 7 07 06

For more information about
our products, contact us at:
**Thomson Learning Academic
Resource Center
1-800-423-0563**
For permission to use material from this text, contact us
by: **Phone:** 1-800-730-2214
Fax: 1-800-730-2215
Web: http://www.thomsonrights.com

Library of Congress Control Number: 2003106896
ISBN 978-0-534-57379-9
ISBN 0-534-57379-7

Brooks/Cole—Thomson Learning
10 Davis Drive
Belmont, CA 94002
USA

Asia
Thomson Learning
5 Shenton Way #01-01
UIC Building
Singapore 068808

Australia/New Zealand
Thomson Learning
102 Dodds Street
Southbank, Victoria 3006
Australia

Canada
Nelson
1120 Birchmount Road
Toronto, Ontario M1K 5G4
Canada

Europe/Middle East/Africa
Thomson Learning
High Holborn House
50/51 Bedford Row
London WC1R 4LR
United Kingdom

Latin America
Thomson Learning
Seneca, 53
Colonia Polanco
11560 Mexico D.F.
Mexico

Spain/Portugal
Paraninfo
Calle/Magallanes, 25
28015 Madrid, Spain

DEDICATION

For Mom, Dad, Kate, and Hildi
Your joy and support in my life, and in watching
this book come together, make it all the more satisfying.

Contents

Chapter 3

Theory Into Application   43

Part Two

APPLICATION   67

Chapter 4

Initial Stages of Counseling   69

Chapter 5

Working Stages of Counseling   88

Chapter 6

Final Stages of Counseling   *120*

Part Three

SPECIFIC PROBLEMS AND DISORDERS   **135**

Chapter 7

Mood Disorders   *137*

Chapter 12

Professional Issues Across Treatment Settings   220

References   237

Index   285

Preface

The impetus to write this textbook and the accompanying workbook arose from my teaching experience with graduate students in a counseling program. The program was originally designed as a training program for school counselors; however, in teaching the courses, I found a paucity of materials directly related to counseling skills with children and adolescents. Initially, this did not present a problem, as I could bring examples from my practice to the course. However, as students addressed their assignments, I often heard comments and complaints that the case examples would be more helpful if they addressed issues with children and adolescents.

Couple that experience with a bias of mine in education, training, and practice, which is the importance of self-awareness for those in our profession. I am a believer in the psychoanalytic approach to training that requires students to engage in their own therapy. Despite that bias, I understand personal therapy may not always be an option for students. The workbook that accompanies this text combines case examples that provide an opportunity for application and practice of skills, with personal exercises designed to push students to explore individual biases, prejudices, or hidden fears. The exercises and case examples relate to the topics covered in the text and other issues encountered when working with children and adolescents (e.g., biases toward or against children or adolescents, feelings about certain disciplinary approaches, and expectations about child, adolescent, and parental behaviors). I strongly believe that a lack of awareness regarding personal biases can be one of the more destructive forces in therapy, so I hope the workbook exercises provide a helpful complement to the topical content in the text.

The text is designed to provide a combination of information for practical application, embedded within empirical knowledge regarding various aspects of working with children, adolescents, and families. Work with children and adolescents occurs within a family context; therefore, the text offers a child-centered family approach to therapy. Interaction between family members is a critical aspect of treatment, and family factors related to treatment are addressed throughout the text. Specific protocols are provided for the initial interview, a mental status exam, referral procedure, and suicide assessment and response. A sample treatment plan and no-harm contract are also included as practical guides. Specific treatment techniques are outlined throughout the text as well. My aim is to convey the feeling of sitting with a good supervisor as you read this text and I hope you will keep it handy for reference as you approach your practice.

ORGANIZATION OF TEXT

The text is organized into four major sections, addressing crucial aspects of working with children and adolescents within a family treatment context. Part One addresses underlying developmental theory (Chapter 1), family factors in treatment, including resiliency and multicultural factors (Chapter 2), and application of these theories and concepts in practice (Chapter 3). Part Two addresses the process of therapy or counseling, including attention to specific aspects in each "phase" of therapy. Part Two is organized by the general headings of three major aspects of counseling: development of rapport (Chapter 4), the working stage of counseling (Chapter 5), and termination issues (Chapter 6). Part Three addresses specific disorders, normal developmental challenges, and appropriate techniques for those presenting problems, again within a family context. Part Three explores mood disorders (Chapter 7), externalizing disorders (Chapter 8), and developmental disorders (Chapter 9), and normal developmental challenges (Chapter 10). Part Four addresses professional developmental issues related to specific treatment settings, professional ethics, and management of the therapist's biases. Part Four examines bias and ethics (Chapter 11) and professional issues related to different treatment settings (Chapter 12).

Acknowledgements

In many ways, this textbook and workbook are a culmination of my own professional training experiences, and a way to give back to the profession. One of the major points I took away from my training was the importance of self-knowledge in ethical practice. As I've gained experience, I have been able to enjoy the process of developing rapport and helping clients in their therapeutic work. So, of course, I want to acknowledge the contribution of my professors, mentors, colleagues, and students for the opportunities and experiences that have helped me grow professionally. And I want to thank my clients for the privilege of working and learning with each of them.

I want to acknowledge the contribution of each member of the publishing team who helped make this idea become a reality. Julie Martinez supported the idea from its inception, and helped shepherd the project to its completion. Janet Kiefer was instrumental in the final editing process. My thanks to each of the following reviewers for their time and comments in the early stages: C. Timothy Dickel, Creighton University; Robin Carter, California State University, Sacramento; Susan W. Gray, Barry University–Ellen Whiteside McDonnell School of Social Work; Denise Worth, California State University–Chico; Sarah M. Toman, Cleveland State University; Donna Henderson, Wake Forest University; Michael Baltimore, Columbus State University; Elisabeth Bennett, Gonzaga University, School of Education; Teresa Christensen, University of New Orleans; Ann Bauer, Cleveland State University; Peggy Kaczmarek, New Mexico State University–Las Cruces; John C. Worzbyt, Indiana University of Pennsylvania.

Finally, I want to thank my friends for their feedback and support of this project, particularly Mandy and Jeanne. Their shared enthusiasm helped make the process fun.

THEORY

This section is intended to help readers understand the experience of being a child or adolescent at particular ages in order to

- *enhance rapport*
- *understand how to tailor the intervention to this child at this time/phase in his or her life in this family/life context*
- *to "get inside the child" to understand what she or he believes at this age and what she or he thinks at this age*

A basic challenge of working with children and adolescents is understanding the developmental level as part of the process of determining what's "normal" and what's not. Children and adolescents do not develop at the same rates or in the same ways. General developmental considerations and differences in physical, cognitive, emotional, and social development will be reviewed in Chapter 1.

All of us are embedded within a family. Without some understanding of the powerful influence of the family, our work will be incomplete. Chapter 2 will address family factors to consider in the context of therapy with children and adolescents, including resiliency, different family belief systems and structures, and multicultural factors. Interactions of these factors within the context of family life cycle will be reviewed.

Chapter 3 discusses how to get started. Starting therapy can feel like jumping into the abyss, particularly for beginning level therapists. Application of developmental theories to interview and diagnosis will be reviewed in this chapter. A sample report illustrates the integration of factors discussed in the first three chapters and its use as a guide for intervention and treatment.

DEVELOPMENTAL FOUNDATIONS OF COUNSELING WITH CHILDREN AND ADOLESCENTS

INTRODUCTION

This chapter reviews and highlights developmental considerations in tailoring effective counseling interventions for use with children and adolescents. Although a foundation of developmentally appropriate expectations is needed for assessment and treatment, this chapter does not purport to offer the depth of knowledge a human development text might. Rather, this chapter will provide a developmental perspective for working with children and adolescents that can be applied to the assessment and treatment process presented in later chapters. Information about working within a family context will be addressed in Chapter 2.

This chapter reviews theoretical perspectives on physical, cognitive, social, moral, and emotional development. Although developmental issues factor into treatment with individuals of all ages, developmentally appropriate interventions are especially critical for children and adolescents. The "normal" developmental frame provides expectations for behavior and functioning at various ages. When certain behaviors, thoughts, or reactions are deemed outside "normal limits," appropriate interventions can be applied. If we attempt to work with children or adolescents without appropriate developmental expectations, our hypotheses and interventions are likely to be ineffective, perhaps even harmful. A sound understanding of what is considered normal functioning provides direction for our later interventions.

The ability of a child or adolescent to respond to therapeutic intervention is found in the context of their level of developmental functioning (Kazdin, 1989). Although the process of therapy may feel like stretching toward that next developmental level, we as therapists cannot push our young clients beyond their current developmental functioning. To do so is to do harm. Take the simple example of learning to ride a bike. If we place a 3-year-old on a 14-year-old's bike, tell her to "go for a ride and have fun," and let go of the bike, what happens? The bike and the 3-year-old will fall to the ground. Why? Because the 3-year-old was not developmentally ready physically (her limbs are too short), cognitively (she may not understand the directions), and emotionally (the task may seem scary and overwhelming). Similarly, we cannot push children beyond their developmental level in our work with them (Mahoney, Robinson, & Fewell, 2001). If they are only ready to play with toys on the floor or express their feelings through markers, we cannot make them fit an adult model of talk therapy. Even many adolescents are not developmentally suited for talk therapy (Campbell, 1993). Children rarely just sit on the couch and tell us their problems. We must use empathic abilities—the childlike and adolescent parts of ourselves—to understand their thoughts, beliefs, and experiences at each developmental stage within the context of their family, community, culture, and individual characteristics to help them understand, heal, and grow (Aponte & Winter, 2000).

Current models of development emphasize the actions of the individual in her own development (Steinberg, 2001), a change that has been consistent with many techniques in the popular culture to provide a more stimulating environment for children. Despite the general notion that we cannot push development, you may witness attempts by parents and caretakers to do so. Although some interventions may attempt to bring clients to a level of functioning more consistent with general expectations for their developmental level, we must remember not to push them beyond their current physical, cognitive, and emotional levels of functioning.

ASSUMPTIONS AT THE FOUNDATION OF WORKING WITH CHILDREN AND ADOLESCENTS

Some professionals, primarily interpersonal psychoanalysts (Lionells, Fiscalini, Mann, & Stern, 1995), argue that premature insight introduces thoughts and fantasies that are not part of the child's normal developmental process. Attempting to facilitate academic and physical skills before a child is developmentally ready may hinder or delay appropriate development by pushing the child beyond developmental readiness (Gartner, 1995).

Meeting clients where they are ensures we are setting aside our own, sometimes subconscious, agendas as we work with clients (Marlatt, 1998). Problems arise when we are unaware of these personal biases (Aponte & Winter, 2000; Bermudez, 1997; Bowling, Kearnery, Lumadue, & St. Germain, 2002); the workbook accompanying this text is intended to guide students in working through potential biases to increase professional effectiveness.

Children and adolescents can be even more acutely aware than adults if the therapist is not fully present during sessions (Bowling et al., 2002). If you find yourself doing your grocery list in your head or replaying a movie from the weekend, they'll know. Any of these therapeutic lapses can "tear" the therapeutic alliance, decreasing the effectiveness of the work (Sugarman, Nemiroff, & Greenson, 2000).

Working with children and adolescents requires you to be in touch with your "inner child," combining childhood memories with your knowledge of appropriate developmental levels in a productive way. A competent child and adolescent clinician must be able to effectively connect with childlike qualities within oneself to truly establish rapport. This often involves the use of developmentally appropriate play (Campbell, 1993). To let your young clients know they are being heard and un-

Remembering How to Be
Human 101

Use your emotions to
connect with your clients:

child: wonder, joy, anger,
confusion

adolescent: rebellion,
masked insecurity, false
bravado, "the imposter
syndrome," compassion,
beginning mastery and
independence

derstood requires respect and understanding not often experienced by children or adolescents in their daily lives. Part of the healing process of the therapeutic relationship is the respect the child or adolescent experiences in the collaborative professional relationship. This ability to alternate between various perspectives is not required in the same way when working with adults. Perhaps this is why many people find working with children and adolescents to be so challenging, but it is part of the pleasure as well. This juggling act can be difficult at first, but it comes more easily over time. It offers one of the joys of the profession.

As a professional entering a session with an adult client, many beginning therapists find themselves feeling anxious about their level of skill; however, children may appear less intimidating initially. In many ways, working with children can be more challenging because of the complicated layers of development, family influence, and pathology that present to the clinician (Aponte & Winter, 2000).

DEVELOPMENTALLY APPROPRIATE INTERVENTIONS

A central challenge, especially for beginning therapists, is learning to distinguish between what's normal and what's not for the children and adolescents with whom you'll be working. Initially, it can seem overwhelming to learn how to identify what's normal across the entire developmental range for children, adolescents, and even parents with whom you'll be working, but many frameworks and developmental guidelines can assist with this process. During the first few years of practice, you may want to keep your human development text handy. Even Einstein used the phone book as a reference, so there's no shame in supporting your body of knowledge. Generally, developmental guidelines include physical, emotional, social, and intellectual or cognitive growth. Our discussion will also touch on moral development and aspects of identity development. The interaction of individual development for the child or adolescent within the family's developmental stage will be addressed in Chapter 2.

Normal Development or Abnormal Presentation? Developmental Considerations in Working With Children and Adolescents

Recent views of development emphasize (1) the individual's active participation in her own development and (2) the role of interaction between various aspects of development in that process (Jackson & Bosma, 1992). This shift in perspective recognizes that the developmental process differs from person to person, even within the limits of normal development. Development may be "uneven" within the same individual as well as in comparison to others of the same chronological age. *Uneven development* refers to varying rates of development across physical, cognitive, emotional, and social domains (Neubauer, 1996). Of course, environmental and genetic factors influence these individual differences (Silva, 1996). What this means for the clinician is a need to attend to detail in teasing out behavior, thoughts, and reactions that are considered within normal limits from those that are not (Neubauer, 1996). Our diagnoses arise from this distinction between normal and abnormal behavior. Differential diagnosis, the process of distinguishing between diagnoses, is covered in Chapter 3.

Physical Development

Physical development is often the most obvious or striking aspect of child and adolescent growth. The overt signs of physical development become most obvious at puberty, when secondary sexual characteristics develop. The rate of development can create challenges in adjustment for both males and females. As might be expected, gender differences exist in relation to the rate of maturation.

Females who develop early experience less support and more negative attention in comparison to those who develop "on time" (Jackson & Bosma, 1992). Girls who mature early also are more likely to report concerns about their weight, a potential early entry point for the development of eating disorders (Williams & Currie, 2000). Increased tension in relationships with mothers and teachers has also been reported for girls who mature early (Jackson & Bosma, 1992). Greater tension in mother-daughter relationships may be attributed to the increased attention that early-maturing females receive from boys and sometimes from men inside the family. Some theorists suggest that the daughter's physical maturation brings up issues regarding the mother's own attractiveness and sexuality (Boyd, 1989; Neubauer, 1996; Ruiselova, 1998). The increased tension present in family relationships of girls who mature early may also be affected by the tendency of those girls to engage in more delinquent behaviors and to withdraw from family and friends (Laitinen-Krispijn, Van der Ende, Hazebrock-Kampschreur, & Verhulst, 1999).

Generally speaking, early maturation is a more positive experience for males than females. Cultural emphasis on size that is often associated with physical strength carries a positive halo effect for boys who mature early. They are often treated as though they are older than their chronological age by adults and peers around them (Jackson & Bosma, 1992). The assumption of being older often leads to greater responsibilities and freedoms for the early-maturing boys. A decrease in social and attention problems has also been associated with early maturation in boys (Laitinen-Krispijn et al., 1999).

Both girls and boys who mature early are reported to be at greater risk for engaging in unhealthy behavior, such as smoking or drinking at a young age (Wiesner & Ittel, 2002). The literature also suggests that family, cultural, and community factors may interact with the "timing" of puberty. Researchers found a higher frequency of externalizing or acting-out behavior among both males and females who matured early when their parents tended to use harsher or inconsistent disciplinary measures with them in comparison to families using a more nurturing and involved parenting approach (Ge, Brody, Conger, Simons, & Murry, 2002). The youth who matured early also tended to associate more frequently with peers considered "deviant" or marginal, those peers who engage in high-risk behaviors, tend to make poor choices, and may display poor impulse control and judgment. Living in an economically disadvantaged neighborhood was identified as another factor associated with externalizing behavior for those who mature early. Additionally, these risk factors were reported as consistent across gender for early adolescents (Ge et al., 2002).

Conversely, late-maturing boys are more likely to experience teasing from peers and experience self-doubt because they don't physically resemble their peers (Jackson & Bosma, 1992). Later maturation has also been associated with attention problems in boys (Laitinen-Krispijin et al., 1999). Thus, boys who mature later in both social and academic realms may experience challenges.

The challenges for females who mature late are similar to those of boys. Peer rejection and teasing are frequent occurrences (Jackson & Bosma, 1992), and withdrawal from peers can be a factor for certain personality types. Some young women who are active in sports and view themselves as less like the mature female in our culture may actually enjoy or be comfortable with delayed maturation (Crisp, 1997; McNab, 1983) and engage in anorexic behavior to maintain the role of a child within the family. In those cases where disordered eating patterns do not develop, acceptance of the rate of physical maturation can represent a positive coping strategy; however, for others, such an approach may precede the later presentation of anorexia. Participation in gymnastics or other sports that emphasize small physical size has also been associated with development of eating disorders to maintain a slower rate of physical maturation (Sherwood, Neumark-Sztainer, Story, Beuhring, & Resnick, 2002).

Late-maturing boys and early-maturing girls struggle with similar challenges (Alsaker, 1992). Both feel different from their peers on the basis of appearance and may be subjected to ridicule as a result. Additionally, the physical differences made obvious by the varying rates of maturation heighten adolescent insecurities and self-doubt that are already present. Many adolescents feel they are "on display," a condition that would call attention to these differences from peers. The adolescent may perceive the differences as greater than they actually are or may experience concern that others are talking about her.

Social Development

Psychosocial Stages   Because of the extremely social nature of most adolescents and the desire for popularity and connection, Erikson's (1964) *psychosocial stages* can serve as a helpful backdrop for our interactions with children in terms of diagnosis, identification of target problems, and implementation of appropriate interventions. Understanding the psychosocial challenges in each stage of development can provide a frame of reference for the novice counselor and a helpful reminder for more seasoned professionals. Application of Erikson's (1964) model to a sample of elementary and secondary school students in China was conducted by Wang and Viney (1997), who found general consistency in terms of stage-relevant experience. The study serves as a template for use of Erikson's model with children across cultures. Initial results suggest such application is appropriate.

ERIKSON'S PSYCHOSOCIAL STAGES
- trust vs. mistrust (birth to 1 year)
- autonomy vs. shame and doubt (1 to 3 years)
- initiative vs. guilt (3 to 6 years)

- industry vs. inferiority (6 to 12 years)
- ego identity vs. ego diffusion (12 to 18 years)
- intimacy vs. isolation (18 to 40 years)

Using a deficit model, we can identify the challenge for the client. This identification can pinpoint the developmental stage at which the individual is fixated, allowing the clinician to refine and tailor the intervention to best strengthen the client's underdeveloped skills. Erikson's stages can be applied across the life span to identify areas of deficit to tailor interventions for specific clients. If the chronological age does not match the psychosocial stage in which the client is functioning, we cannot push the client's developmental level to fit neatly into theoretical categories or models. Rather, we can use those theories to guide our interventions to fit the client.

Erikson's model provides a range of "normal limits" to use in determining where upon that continuum a client is currently functioning. In addition, it provides an anchor for placing specific developmental issues. For example, if you are working with a 10-year-old who is struggling with issues of trust and mistrust, you can make an initial hypothesis that your client is "behind" from a standpoint of psychosocial development. Such a determination can give you a place to start in tailoring your interventions. Look for triggers that may have precipitated such a "regression." Has there been a recent family move? A death in the family? A close friend who moved away? The loss of a pet? Any of these events may be interpreted by the child as a betrayal of trust, pushing the ability to cope at a psychosocial level back to that of a much younger child. An alternative approach might include reviewing family history to determine if a similar traumatic change occurred when the child was at the age when trust and mistrust is a primary focus, between birth and one year. These are examples of how you might use Erikson's psychosocial stages to plan and implement your interventions.

Peer Relationships   Although the impact of parents is being accepted as more influential over teens than was once the case, interactions with peers continue to influence social development. As children and adolescents continue to define themselves and forge their individual identities separate from their families, both positive and negative aspects of friends can define the quality of the friendship. The interactions between friends and the activities in which they engage influence the client's self-esteem, social behaviors, and psychological adjustment (Berendt, 1998). A more positive perception of the friendship is associated with a healthier self-esteem, better psychological development, and more prosocial behaviors. Specifically, close friendships have been shown to ameliorate tendencies toward shyness and facilitate more active engagement with peers (Berendt, 2002).

However, specific environments and availability of positive peers is also a factor in social development. For example, in certain inner city neighborhoods, gangs may represent one of few choices for social interaction among peers. For children and adolescents growing up with exposure to gang culture, contact with other peers may not be an option, or they may actually be snubbed in favor of allegiance to neighborhood gang members. Of course, in the context of individual differences, some children and adolescents who grow up in such neighborhoods choose not to be influenced by these environmental factors. Regardless of the specific choice, it is clear that the context in which one lives has a major effect on social development (Cadwallader & Cairns, 2002).

Emotional Maturity/Development

An important component of emotional development is attachment, as it relates to feelings of security and insecurity. For young children and even into adolescence, attempts to compensate for feelings of insecurity are often displayed in aggressive behavior. Aggressive behavior has been associated with poor social skills, increased family stress, and higher levels of anxiety (Schmidt, Demulder, & Denham, 2002). A relative lack of awareness in younger children is within normal limits. Thus, the use of aggressive behavior as an attempt to compensate for lack of skills or insecurity is generally viewed as normal. However, a lack of self-regulation with such behaviors in middle childhood through adolescence is viewed as outside the context of normal limits (Grolnick, Kurowski, & Gurland, 1999). The presentation of such behaviors in later age ranges would be an appropriate area for intervention aimed at increasing social skills and basic knowledge of emotions and their regulation or management, such as coping with typical feelings in new situations. Bullying is an example of this behavior that has been pushed to an extreme; it has been identified as a significant factor associated with school violence (see Part three).

Development of empathy is another integral aspect of emotional development that normally begins at a fairly young age, usually in the early elementary years. Factors that impede the normal developmental process with regard to empathy are similar to those identified in the development of aggressive behaviors. Insecurity, primarily with regard to attachment to primary caregivers, and a more shy or fearful temperament have been associated with an inability to develop empathic skills (van der Mark, van Ijzendoorn, & Bakermans-Kranenburg, 2002). The ability to be empathic toward others requires the regulation of one's own feelings of anxiety or fear related to a specific situation. Additionally, being empathic requires that one be able to "get out of oneself," imagine how another person feels, and be concerned about how that individual is feeling. These fairly sophisticated skills are blocked by overwhelming emotions of fear or insecurity in those children and adolescents who may be somewhat delayed in their emotional development.

Conversely, a secure attachment to parental figures is associated with positive self-esteem and self-efficacy (Leondari & Kiosseoglou, 2002). Disruptions to the development of a secure attachment can come in the form of physical separation such as abandonment or prolonged illness of the parental figure. However, emotional unavailability in the form of parental depression (Herring & Kaslow, 2002) or neglect can mimic physical separation and present similar challenges for the young child or infant. Bowlby (1969) proposed that a secure attachment forms on the basis of the caregiver's consistent responses to the young child, thus forming a bond of trust that positively influences later relationships. The consistent interaction between child and parent is thought to form a foundation of positive expectations, allowing more open interactions with others throughout life.

Attachment Styles   Distinct attachment styles have been identified empirically (Ainsworth, Blehar, Waters, & Walls, 1978) that allow us to differentiate between various presentations of this important indicator of emotional development. These specific patterns have been labeled insecure/avoidant, secure, and insecure/resistant. An insecure/avoidant attachment style is described as the avoidance displayed by an infant toward her parent upon the parent's return. Typical presentations can range from completely ignoring the caregiver to a more ambivalent response, including a combination of greeting and turning away from the parent. Upon separation, young children with this attachment style display less distress than those with a secure or resistant attachment. A secure attachment is characterized by the child who actively seeks and maintains contact with the parent. Little avoidance is observed upon reunion, and a clear preference for the primary caretaker is noted. The insecure/resistant attachment is characterized by significant resistance to interaction upon the parent's return. A more punishing or angry presentation toward the caregiver is often observed.

A fourth attachment style has been identified by Main and Solomon (1986), characterized by "disorganized or disoriented" reactions. As the label suggests, there is little consistency in the response of these young children upon separation or return. Some describe their behaviors as contradictory, confused, and apprehensive.

How does this information about attachment styles help us to determine normal or abnormal emotional development? The quality of the attachment essentially provides a firm base from which the child can explore herself and her surroundings. For those who have developed a secure attachment, it is easier to forge new relationships and explore new situations. A secure attachment facilitates normal development and the ability to form a strong therapeutic alliance.

Goleman (1995) also proposes a measure of emotional intelligence, emphasizing the importance of these skills in the success of a normal life. Goleman suggests that emotional intelligence comprises a set of skills and perceptions related to interpersonal relationships, understanding others, and empathy. He describes the development of depression as a result of deficits in emotional intelligence. Seeking to meet needs through maladaptive strategies highlights apparent deficits in emotional knowledge and understanding.

In addition to psychosocial stages, we need to be attuned to traditional models of development with regard to physical, intellectual, and emotional development to help make the distinction between "normal" developmental limits (e.g., areas where the child might "outgrow" certain behaviors or exhibit behaviors considered developmentally normal) and those that might be considered consistent with pathology. For example, nightmares are normal at age 2 and unusual at ages 10 or 16. If nightmares occur outside the times normally expected according to developmental guidelines, some questions to explore include trauma, abuse, challenging life transitions, and fears. Exploring the environment by putting things in one's mouth is normal for infants, not for middle school students. What about a need for routine or difficulty with change? Is this a child who has features of obsessive compulsive disorder (OCD) or not? What about a fascination with taking things apart? Is this a normal curiosity or attention deficit/hyperactivity disorder (ADHD)? Finding the answers to these questions usually occurs over time working with the child and family.

Cognitive Development

Let's briefly review the traditional cognitive developmental theories (consult a human development text for more in-depth information). The major influences regarding cognitive development include Piaget (1963), who outlined the stages of development as sensorimotor, pre-operational, concrete operational, and formal operational, while Kegan (1982) outlined incorporative, impulsive, imperial, interpersonal, institutional, and inter-individual stages. An information-processing approach has been suggested as an alternative perspective of learning. These perspectives are also being expanded in terms of the general understanding of intelligence, a concept that is more broadly approached by Gardner's model of multiple intelligences (1983). Gardner originally identified seven areas of intelligence, including logical-mathematical, linguistic, spatial, musical, bodily-kinesthetic, intrapersonal and interpersonal. Gardner purported that the various intelligences function together, although people display varying strengths in each of the areas. Regardless of intellectual strengths or weaknesses, underlying processes of memory and attention are necessary for information to be processed or encoded, manipulated, and used.

Attention   The ability to attend or focus the attention on specific stimuli is necessary for learning to occur. Therapy has a psycho-educational component; therefore, the client's ability to attend—both in and out of session—becomes a necessary prerequisite for successful therapy as well as success in many other areas of life. Influencing the young client's identity and beliefs in a positive way may involve interventions aimed at attention and memory, common problems for many children and adolescents who come into treatment.

Our ability to intervene will be limited by the client's current level of development and directly linked to attention, memory, and motivation (Lewis, 1995). Because different memory functions are performed in different areas of the brain and development occurs at different stages across and within individuals, all clients will present slightly differently from others and from themselves on previous occasions. Many who work with children and adolescents in settings as varied as school to scouts fall into the trap of social comparison, but this is generally not productive. Variable presentation is often part of normal development. It is important for the clinician and for parents to be aware that children and adolescents often present with varying responses, even on tasks they were able to perform just a few days earlier, because of the uneven nature of human development. Over time, most developmental tasks become more predictable and more routine in their presentation in normal development. Such routine and predictability will not be achieved in abnormal development.

Interaction of Memory and Developmental Level in the Therapeutic Process

One of the challenges of working with children and adolescents is sifting through a body of clinical knowledge, interweaving that with an assessment of your clients' developmental stages, and adapting this information to your clients. Many layers contribute to the process, making it more challenging and more exciting to sort out your clients' level of functioning and readiness to engage in the change process. Just as parents find that life changes daily with a child, so your approach as a clinician may need to change daily to match the current developmental level of the child or adolescent with whom you're working.

An important way that information about client readiness, particularly at a cognitive level, is synthesized is through the client's learning style. A client's learning style will also help direct the optimal approach for interventions. Learning styles take a similar perspective as Gardner's multiple intelligences in identifying the mode in which the client will be most receptive and responsive as an intervention. For example, a visual learner may respond most readily to an imagery technique.

Learning Style

Just as the developmental process is highly idiosyncratic, so is the process of learning. Analyzing the individual's process of learning and memory may be helpful in identifying the optimal intervention for each client. Part of this process can focus on the client's learning style; for example, many children are comfortable with a kinesthetic or active manipulation style. Certain individuals maintain greater comfort with a kinesthetic learning approach from young childhood throughout adult life. Some children may appear to be more adept at verbal skills, though their cognitive abilities may be developing at a slower pace. Young children with a large vocabulary may not fully understand the meaning of the words they use. Many adults are drawn in by the verbal fluency of young children and forget about the likelihood of uneven development in other areas, sabotaging effective treatment due to faulty developmental assumptions.

Auditory and visual learning styles are also common and often fit better with our traditional public school approach to learning. Part of the challenge when reviewing academic problems along with social or emotional concerns is that our schools are geared toward auditory and visual learning styles. Although this approach may have been traditional, the auditory and visual emphases effectively leave out many learners. Obtaining permission to speak with teachers, counselors, and other school personnel will help you understand the child's learning style outside of a more controlled setting, such as a practitioner's office. As an example of short-term memory skills, pay attention to whether the child uses information in an action setting (e.g, dialing a phone) but seems unable to express the information through language or writing. Notice if the child blurts out information unrelated to the question being asked. This may give a clue as to the chunking strategies or associations used in learning. For long-term memory skills, observe the client's ability to relate detailed information about topical areas covered in class as compared to strengths in procedural knowledge, such as tasks involving motor skills (Lewis, 1995). After determining a general learning style and possible knowledge deficits, interventions can be tailored to the developmental level and individual differences of each particular client.

Identity Development

As Lewis (1995) notes, memory contributes to one's sense of identity, yet many of our younger clients choose not to remember misbehaviors, embarrassing deficits they have observed in themselves when compared to others, or simply the usual awkwardness of normal growth and development. Taking Lewis's observation a step further, it is no wonder that our clients face confusion in trying to make changes within themselves given the combination of their typical "forgetting" coping skill and the developmental process over which they have no control. Forgetting is often manifest in "I dunno," heard by so many teachers, therapists, and parents. The lack of control inherent in normal growth and development appears to be a strong factor in the motivation of many misbehaviors or distracting behaviors. These behaviors often serve the purpose of attempting to distract others from a more embarrassing truth that the youth wants to hide, whether consciously or not. Take as an example the proverbial class clown; an underlying motivation for clowning around is to distract attention away from an academic skill deficit, thus avoiding the discomfort of not knowing how to do something everyone else magically seems to understand. Other children may attempt to compensate by "losing" their assignments or the materials necessary to complete the assignments. Both of these are examples of a choice (that is most likely unconscious) to be labeled "disorganized" or "funny" to gain a reprieve from doing work they may not know how to do. Many children and adolescents choose a relatively negative label to conceal the confusion or hurt from what is perceived as a significant deficit when compared to peers. In other words, it's better to be known as funny than dumb.

A commonly held assumption among today's youth is that of needing to know how to do something before they receive any instruction on the topic. This belief ties directly into a child's self-esteem and identity. Part of our task is to help these clients accept that it's normal not to know everything, that asking for help may not hurt so badly, and that everyone has their own set of strengths and things that are difficult for them. Children and parents need to understand the impact of development on their ability to learn and perform certain tasks. They may need to develop an understanding—and be given permission—not to "know it all" and to feel secure in their own developmental path. Unfortunately, comparing themselves to others can often leave children and adolescents feeling frustrated, inferior, and hopeless. Although psycho-educational interventions can help turn those beliefs around, many young clients will turn to others around them to help figure out their identity through social comparison and through feedback from peers and adults.

External Feedback and Identity Development

As children and adolescents grow, change, and develop, they are not always certain about their own perceptions and thoughts and remain vulnerable to suggestion from others (Cohen and Harnick, 1980; Goodman, Ruby, Bottoms, & Aman, 1990). In other words, young clients may question their own knowledge base or ideas about how to proceed in social situations even though their understanding of certain concepts may rival that of adults (Johnson & Foley, 1984; Loftus and Davies, 1984). Children normally listen to adults around them, initially for reasons of survival, which leaves a strong imprint to continue this behavior. This expectation is often a factor in the power abusers hold over their young victims, for example. What once was a survival mechanism can work against young people at other points in their lives or in new situations. Old responses may not adapt well to new life challenges and may be reinforced within the child or adolescent's memory due to repetition by others.

A negative effect from the repeated messages of parents or adults may contradict children's or adolescents' perceptions of reality (Lewis, 1995), leaving them confused. Such confusion can create conflicting reports of a young client's own experiences. The inability to organize seemingly unrelated elements makes recall of specific incidents difficult or developmentally impossible (Johnson & Foley, 1984). This recall is hampered by the young client's confusion over what aspects are her own thoughts and perceptions and which are those of someone else. In enmeshed families, for example, such confusion is typical due to the lack of clear role differentiation and boundaries between family members. Kobasigawa (1974) noted that prompting may facilitate recognition of details, but rote recall is generally insufficient to facilitate change, because children have not been able to make the connection between behavior and affect for themselves. Child recall ability continues to be an issue within the legal system (Lewis, 1995); it is often even more complicated by the interaction of emotion and trauma on memory functioning.

Self-Observation Skills

A complicating factor is that many children and adolescents have incomplete self-observation skills. These too are still developing. Accurate self-observation requires application of both short- and long-term memory skills, depending on the individual circumstance under scrutiny. Some younger clients may lack the ability to remember certain details of their own experiences, and they may not attend to others, simply because those details have not become important in their definition of themselves. As their identities develop and become more crystallized, children and adolescents (sometimes even adults) attend to information that reinforces their developing view of themselves. During the process of identity formation, which lasts until late adolescence or early adulthood, a client may be overwhelmed by information that supports and refutes the developing self-image, creating confusion, internal chaos, and conflict from the cognitive dissonance experienced as a result. When external stimuli contradict the developing internal self, frustration usually results. Not attending to those confusing, conflicting stimuli helps decrease the internal discomfort; as a result, those experiences may never reach the child's or adolescent's memory.

Sexual Identity Formation

Over recent years, our profession has become increasingly aware of the difficulty facing many gay, lesbian, or bisexual adolescents. The rate of suicide associated with these young people has been reported as significantly higher than the general teen population. Isolation and lack of support have been cited as two primary factors contributing to suicidal ideation. Understanding some of the challenges facing these teens can increase their sense of support and decrease isolation.

The process of sexual identity formation can be complicated for gay, lesbian, or bisexual youth, particularly in smaller communities where less support is available. Lack of role models has often been identified as a particular challenge for youth. Troiden (1988) has suggested stages of development for homosexual identity formation:

- *Sensitization,* defined as a sense that one is different from peers; may include initial recognition of attraction toward same-gender peers.
- *Sexual identity confusion,* characterized by confusion and angst over the recently recognized attraction; may include a sense of panic, disbelief, or denial regarding the sexual identity due to concerns about potential negative reactions from others.
- *Sexual identity assumption,* which often includes a period of experimentation and consideration of a gay or lesbian self-identity and lifestyle.
- *Integration and commitment,* characterized by positive self-acceptance and relative openness about one's sexuality.

The sense of being different and feeling isolated have long been identified as risk factors for suicide or self-destructive behaviors in gay, lesbian, or bisexual teens. A higher level of risk exists regarding suicidality and general health risks in this population (Lock & Steiner, 1999; Remafedi, 1999), as compared to a general population. Learning about students' experiences can also be a wonderful way for school counselors to become more sensitive and gain ideas about how to approach change at their schools (Harris, 2000).

Moral Development

Gilligan (1982, 1994) proposed a model of moral development, including two gender-related moral orientations: (1) justice and individual rights, and (2) ethic of care. The first is described as more consistent with male ethical judgment, while the second is purported to be more consistent with female ethical judgment. Gilligan's theory of moral development was tested by Skoe (1998) through her instrument, the Ethics of Care Interview (ECI); her findings suggest the importance of care-based morality across gender. The ECI parallels Kohlberg's (1981) stages of justice-based moral development, measuring hierarchical levels of development in the care ethic, according to Skoe.

Gilligan's Ethics of Care emphasizes a relational component in women's orientation as compared to that of men. For example, her model compares caring, responsibility, and concerns about getting hurt or feeling disconnected for women with a sense of fairness, independence, and a concern about conflict of rights and being too close in relationships for men. The differences highlighted in Gilligan's ethics of care are consistent with general adult models of human development. Current level of moral development often impacts the child or adolescent client's decision-making process. Knowledge of the current level of moral development provides a foundation for interventions as well.

SPECIAL CONSIDERATIONS IN CHILD AND FAMILY WORK

Most children and adolescents come to us for services because someone else thinks they need to be there. This child's behavior is creating problems for someone else, and that adult probably has concerns about the child's well-being and future on the basis of current behaviors. Although this is the typical progression into therapy for our clients, it brings with it an inherent difficulty in the child's level of self-awareness, ability to self-monitor, and potential animosity and/or shame about being brought in for treatment. The normal challenges and limitations of development in childhood may be exacerbated by family dynamics or the simple fact of seeking treatment. These limitations include a lack of ability to self-reflect and self-monitor, preconceived notions about authority figures and fear of "getting in trouble," family beliefs and rules about talking (either inside or outside the family), pent-up animosity within the client or family prior to coming in for services (particularly with adolescents or when there has been a history of abuse), and the limitations in expression that are part of normal development, as when children have difficulty expressing themselves or understanding the ramifications of their actions.

Developmentally, the ability to self-monitor does not usually develop until elementary age and, due to individual differences, often not until later. For others, such as those with ADHD, the skill may never become fully developed. Most children who come to us for treatment are not good self-observers; they simply don't engage in this behavior, or their ability to do so is skewed (e.g., eating disorders). Thus, our challenge in helping clients become successful includes developing a positive and productive strategy for observing and intervening in their own behavioral patterns. Obviously, if the child does not view a behavior as problematic, enlisting her aid and motivation will be difficult, and depending on the nature of the relationship with the parent, a certain level of resistance may have already developed that could interfere with therapy. Parents, likewise, may have formed rigid perceptions of their children that may be difficult to influence in a positive way.

Children often lack self-awareness of problems or concerns. Parents, particularly when they don't have a full understanding of the mental health problem or disorder, often try to use an authoritative role in parenting to push for compliant behavior or, at the other extreme, to act as a friend in an attempt to persuade the child. Either presentation creates potential difficulty for the clinician in potential transference issues—not to mention the potential to be drawn into the maladaptive family system. The child or adolescent client will have formed certain expectations about interacting with adults. Those expectations may be influenced by interactions with teachers, coaches, or other family and community members. Young children are often more reserved in initial meetings with new adults, while adolescents may present as surly and uncooperative. The need to meet the clients where they are cannot be overemphasized. Adopting an approach that emulates the parent-child relationship is not productive as it draws the therapist into the maladaptive family system. Early interactions provide another opportunity to demonstrate to the young client that these sessions and the therapeutic interactions will be different from those with other adults in the client's environment. This is a strong and powerful message that is necessary for successful child and adolescent therapy.

For some children in the early elementary years, the lack of self-awareness is developmentally appropriate but can hinder the therapeutic process. For this reason, special techniques and exercises in cultivating self-observation skills are often necessary. We must look to what motivates the child or adolescent client. A common motivation is decreasing the negative consequences or increasing freedom, particularly for older children and adolescents. Another motivation is *secondary gain*, the unidentified gain from the behavior. For example, a child with attention deficit disorder may act out in the classroom to gain the attention of other students and feel more positively about themselves. The secondary gain in such a situation often involves feeling relief from the discharge of excessive energy or avoiding academic work they don't know how to complete. For many of these children and adolescents, it is less embarrassing to "get in trouble" than to admit they don't know how to do something their peers have already mastered. ADHD often makes it difficult for children to attend to and learn some of the basics. Unlike adults, children may accept their symptoms as part of life or exhibit a tendency to attribute their suffering to external causes (i.e., blaming others). Helping children and adolescents accept responsibility for their own behaviors and decisions is one of the major challenges of our therapeutic work with them.

THERAPEUTIC RESPONSE

A balanced approach is required from the therapist, focusing on empathic responses to the child's description of her emotional experience of various aspects of her life, including counseling, learning, parenting, or peer interactions. Additionally, we need to look at our own theories surrounding behavior and motivation. For example, if we believe that children are motivated by M&Ms, then we are likely to focus solely on a strict behaviorist approach. Most professionals today accept a more eclectic approach to theories of personality and behavior. They tailor their interventions to the client's motivation, level of development, and readiness. Crespi and Generali's (1995) developmental counseling theory matches the stage of client development with appropriate counseling strategies, an important aspect of tailoring treatment to the needs of the client. As with any approach to intervention, the clinician must be aware of her assumptions and their potential impact defining the "problem," understanding the client, and selecting a form of intervention.

For example, the general assumptions underlying Adler's (1982) theory of personality are that people are responsible, creative, unified, social beings whose behavior is purposive and goal directed.

- The fundamental motivational force underlying all behavior is a striving from a feeling of inferiority to a feeling of significance, completion, and perfection.
- Human behavior is purposive and goal directed (although children may be unaware of their specific goals).
- Personality is organized in a unified, holistic, and self-consistent fashion.
- Behavior occurs in a social context and therefore has social meaning.
- Behavior is assessed and evaluated within the social system.
- The actions of an individual are best understood by the application of idiographic laws. Assumed goals may be at the root of most children's behavior based on Adler's concepts of attention seeking, power, revenge, and assumed disability.

Children who engage in attention seeking often feel that they are insignificant and unimportant unless at the center of adult attention. Children and adolescents may seek to make themselves feel better through others. The attention may be gained through appropriate or inappropriate actions. For example, a child asks an inordinate amount of questions or asks for help she doesn't need, or an adolescent frequently drops by the nurse's or counselor's office. These children/adolescents have fragile ego strength and often feel insecure unless shored up by an adult. Children dominated by the goal of power demonstrate an aversion to control by adults and authority figures. Such children gain a sense of significance and self-importance by showing adults they will not be controlled by rules or adults; they often engage adults in power struggles. Revenge is characterized by behavior designed to inflict hurt back onto adults or onto the society those adults represent. Acting-out behaviors are often directed toward the perceived vulnerabilities of parents or family values. Finally, children may assume disability, replacing conflict and acting-out behaviors with inactivity and passivity about friends, family, and activities.

Our perspective becomes fuller when we realize that most children and adolescents have far fewer coping resources than we do as adults. Most children attempt to manage emotional energy via discharging it, usually through physical or verbal acting out. Understanding that this type of response is normal for children due to their developing intellectual capacities helps us to respond at an empathic level. Just as some adults become incapacitated by the overwhelming nature of their emotional experience and resort to more limited and "primitive" coping skills, children often regress when the strength of their rage, sadness, or other emotional response is too great for them to comprehend, or they have limited knowledge for dealing with the challenge. Uncertainty about appropriate responses often pushes children back to known behaviors that may appear regressive. Education regarding more appropriate skills is often at the heart of interventions in such instances. By giving the client alternative response, you are helping them to grow and change old habits that are no longer effective for them at the current developmental stage.

Mosak and Maniacci (1993) outlined six principal goals of the therapeutic process for Adlerian therapies:

1. strengthen client's social interest
2. diminish client's feeling of weakness, inability, and inferiority
3. recognize client's strengths and resources, develop courage
4. alter client's lifestyle, change faulty assumptions and beliefs, replace big distortions with relatively smaller distortions
5. change mistaken goals (motivation)
6. help client become more cooperative and contributing in social relationships, adopting an attitude of social equality

With adolescents, we may employ their "private logic" or internal dialogue about personal values and convictions. Regardless of age, use of language consistent with developmental stages is necessary. This is an important part of rapport building essential to being effective with children and adolescents. Often a difficult aspect of working with children and adolescents is treading the balance between being accepted (getting in touch with one's own inner child) and being an authority figure. If we relate to children as teachers or pseudo-parental figures, we may have lost them and are not doing our jobs. If we are able to establish an appropriate relationship with our young clients, we can use the therapeutic alliance, the working relationship, to therapeutic advantage. We can use the vehicle of the relationship to stretch the child's ability to begin to recognize her own behavioral problems and decision-making process.

Developmental experiences of children and adolescents can be influenced by the ways in which they spend their leisure time. Despite increased demands for school projects and homework, there appears to be a wide range of parental response to these stressors. As parents withdraw their structure and attention, children and adolescents tend to focus more on friends and television. Spending time in this type of activity when compared to more structured activities such as sports, clubs, or the arts appears to provide little for the child or adolescent in terms of positive development (Larson, 2001). Structured activities appear to provide opportunities for successful completion of positive developmental tasks such as a healthy self-identity, the ability to motivate oneself, and individuation.

For those children and adolescents who may have less success in meeting these developmental outcomes, therapy and counseling can help clients develop tools to successfully meet developmental milestones. Helping children and adolescents understand the impact of their actions on others as well as themselves is often a focus of such developmental approaches. Group interventions offer a unique opportunity for young clients to gain feedback from peers about others' perceptions of them and a chance to "practice" behaving in different ways (Brown & Prout, 1999). Providing feedback about feelings and perceptions toward other group members is an important skill for many young children to develop. An open style of communication may be foreign to them because their family does not interact in this way, but therapeutic interventions can help them develop this important skill. As with any developmentally focused intervention with children and adolescents, clinicians must be cautious not to push clients beyond their normal developmental stages (Jackson & Bosma, 1992).

Interventions focused on motivation development and positive self-perception help build a sense of self-efficacy in children (Wigfield & Eccles, 2002). Opportunities to do so need to include plans to perform the targeted behaviors due to the kinesthetic nature of learning in most children. The success of interventions will be enhanced through the repetition of these newly learned behaviors. Groups and school settings offer the opportunity for "practice." Enlisting parents' aid can also provide opportunities for children to implement and practice new behaviors, increasing the likelihood of lasting change. The success of such endeavors enhances the child's sense of self-efficacy, providing the motivation to move forward, and commitment to remain in therapy.

DISCUSSION QUESTIONS

1. How does developmental level impact work with children and adolescents? Are there any ethical issues involved in not using a developmental approach with this population?
2. What issues are important to consider in working with early- and late-maturing males and females?
3. How does one engage in a child-centered family approach to therapy?
4. What type of interview approach is optimal for each developmental level?
5. Apply Mosak and Maniacci's six principal goals of the therapeutic process to a specific treatment goal. What type of intervention might be suited to each of your goals?

FAMILY INFLUENCE ON DEVELOPMENT

INTRODUCTION

In Chapter 1, we explored aspects of individual development that will shape your interventions and interactions with children and adolescents. Your clients also function within the context of a family. In fact, their influence is so strong that your client relationship may extend to family members as well. Your success will hinge on your ability to understand the child or adolescent, members of the client's family, interactions and relationships among family members, and the impact of community and culture.

Within the family, myriad influences affect individual functioning for all family members, not just the child or adolescent client. The dynamics of family interactions may be represented in the child's behavior and actions. Even though the child or adolescent is identified as the client, the entire family may benefit from intervention, although some parents may resist. In terms of effectiveness, our efforts are enhanced or stymied by the involvement of family or lack of participation, respectively.

Within a family, many factors have a direct impact on the child or adolescent: the personalities of parents and their respective life experiences, the family life cycle, family composition, socioeconomic issues, family belief systems, social support system, community, extended family relationships, life events, and cultural influences. These factors will be reviewed in this chapter to provide the family context necessary for treatment of children and adolescents.

FAMILY DEVELOPMENTAL PHASES

Families undergo developmental changes throughout a "life cycle," similar to the process discussed in Chapter 1 on the development of children and adolescents.

Phases of the family life cycle (Cowen & Hetherington, 1991; McGoldrick, Heiman, & Carter, 1993) are identified as:

1. between families: the unattached young adult
2. the young couple: the joining of families, most often through marriage
3. the family with young children
4. the family with adolescents
5. "launching" children and moving on
6. the family in later life: extended family issues and new roles once again

Adjustment to transitions within the family life cycle may be especially challenging when other life events occur simultaneously—for example, the birth of a child when the older child is starting school. Individual expectations of family members can also influence the adjustment process, such as the stressors created for parents expecting their adult children to move out when that may not be financially possible. Some things remain constant throughout the family life cycle: The family's belief system and "identity" typically do not change. As we discuss additional aspects of the client's family in the context of our treatment, we must remain cognizant of where the family is with regard to its life cycle.

CONTINUING TO INVOLVE THE FAMILY

From a therapeutic perspective, it becomes important to engage all family members, particularly parents, early in the process. Some family literature states that the father can play a key role in the success of therapy (Walsh, 1993): Once the father is engaged, the rest of the family can feel free to be committed to the process as well. Anecdotal data not only support the literature, but also indicate that many fathers hold a fairly skeptical view of the likelihood of success from therapy. Any of these contradicting displays of support will allow children and adolescents the room they need to dismiss therapy. Looking for early signs of discontent about the therapeutic process and confronting parents, children, and adolescents about their true goals can sometimes make a difference in turning things around. Once a greater level of investment is obtained, the chances of a successful outcome are again enhanced.

While active involvement of the parents is an important component of therapeutic success, one must remember the balance between engaging parents and the child or adolescent client (see Chapter 4). Increasing parent participation in therapy is part of the goal of the child-centered family approach; yet if it is done in such a way that the child or adolescent feels slighted, left out, or minimized, parents' increased participation may have a counterproductive effect.

THERAPIST ROLE IN FAMILY THERAPY

Our role in the family system is to help ensure the family is not knocked off balance by life stressors. This may require us to remind them of their strengths or to help them identify those strengths. Mobilizing the resources and support available to them is another task to help families embrace their own competence. Reducing conflict by implementing positive communication and coping strategies is another intervention that will stay with the family as a tool long after the initial crisis.

FAMILY STRUCTURE AND FUNCTION

Connectedness exists on a continuum within most families. At one end, we observe *enmeshment,* in which there is little differentiation between members' identities, life goals, or even daily activities. Being too close does not allow for healthy individual development. In these families, members may develop internalizing disorders, such as anxiety or depression. Turning inward may feel as if it is the only way to gain personal space and emphasize boundaries in response to uncomfortably close relationships within the family. At the opposite end of the spectrum, we observe *disengagement,* in which there is almost no contact between family members and a great degree of individual differentiation. Here, family members function almost completely independently, except that they share a common living space. Members of a disengaged family are more prone to develop externalizing disorders, such as aggressive behaviors as a compensatory attempt to gain support and attention from outside the family. Neither of these extremes promotes flexibility or healthy functioning. Attempts to promote more healthy functioning will most likely be experienced as stressful by family members. Instructing family members about the process of change and the likelihood that they will experience some anxiety or awkward feelings in the process helps them be aware of what to expect, and increases the opportunities for successful change.

FAMILY-CENTERED INTERVENTIONS

Ooms and Preister (1988) have suggested a family-centered model to guide these interventions:

1. Identify and build on family strengths and resources to empower families.
2. Approach individual problems with a family-centered perspective to enhance family cohesion and increase a sense of support within the family.
3. Be flexible in your provision of services, and help the family access a broad range of resources.
4. Emphasize prevention and early intervention, not letting stressors accumulate and overwhelm the family.
5. Foster collaboration among community agencies and families.

FAMILY BELIEF SYSTEMS AS LEVERAGE FOR CHANGE

A key to effective change within a family system is the family's belief system, similar to an individual's self-image. If the family views itself as effective, relatively well in control of the environment, and possesses a positive outlook, the family is more likely to be resilient and able to meet challenges effectively. Resilient families can confront a challenge, manage it, buffer the effects of stressors, effectively reorganize after stressors, and move forward.

Family Factors/Beliefs

Family beliefs form the foundation for the identity of the family. A colloquial way of thinking about family beliefs is that of the "family motto," often reinforced by cultural, community, and religious values (McGoldrick, 1993; McGoldrick, Pearce, & Giordano, 1982; Spiegel, 1971). Although these beliefs contribute to cohesiveness of the family group, they also can confine individual members to roles adopted within the family. Such limitation can constrain healthy development of the family and its individual members.

Family factors impeding rather than facilitating the process of change include unspoken family expectations to keep a "stiff upper lip," not to "air the family's dirty laundry," or not to ask for help (Jackson, 1965). For some families, not talking about negative events is a way of attempting to control those events. These behaviors and beliefs become the family norm and guide repeated relationships and patterns among family members (Constantine, 1986; Rolland, 1988). They also maintain family culture (Lyons & Kashima, 2001). The norm may be their family strategy for coping or part of their approach to resiliency. If that mechanism works for this family, the clinician needs to take a cautious approach in removing that response before replacing it with another. Respecting what works for the individual and the family and learning how to build on their strengths is a necessary part of becoming a healthy part of the family system, as opposed to becoming enmeshed in unproductive roles (Kraemer, 1994). It is also necessary to explore whether this response is consistent across all situations or only for certain sensitive issues, such as sexuality, death, or finances. Finally, determining whether there is a cultural component is an essential part of the assessment, aimed at tearing apart family beliefs, patterns, and individual roles.

Certain cultural/family factors work against the normal process of therapy. Each family essentially develops its own "culture," either building on ethnic roots or forming a new system quite separate from family history. Attempts to move away from one's native culture can be part of the immigration process or an attempt to "blend in." This type of response is commonly associated with adolescents. Such attempts to move away from one's culture can create conflict within the family.

In a similar way, attempts to "socialize" clients to the process of therapy can create conflict as well. For example, a clinician's assumption that expression and talking about thoughts and feelings is healthy and positive may be at odds with the family's beliefs. The client's family may believe talking "airs the dirty laundry" and should not be done. Encouraging, gently pushing, or directly confronting clients from such a family could create significant discomfort and certainly would work against any rapport that had already been established. Many individuals, be they adults, adolescents, or children, will experience conflict when placed in a situation that encourages them to behave in a way that is inconsistent with their family norms. This conflict may manifest in anxiety, possibly pushing the client to withdraw or to respond in anger as a distraction that covers their true, uncomfortable feelings. Our attempts to engage clients in therapy may create discomfort around cultural expectations in addition to family belief systems.

MULTICULTURAL FACTORS

Multicultural differences affect individual experiences and perceptions in such a way that our work with persons from other cultures may become harmful if we are unaware of those differences or attempt to push clients beyond their usual patterns and norms too quickly. Establishing strong rapport becomes even more important when multicultural issues are part of the therapeutic relationship. The strength of the therapeutic relationship may need to withstand even greater "tear" (Greenson, 1965) because of potential misunderstandings on the basis of cultural differences.

This is true for work with individuals as well as families. A multicultural approach includes a necessary sensitivity on the part of the therapist to differences in family belief systems, grieving processes, gender roles, discipline approaches, beliefs about ancestors, ability to cope, expectations, and relationships. The impact of cultural factors will vary based on such concrete factors as the length of time the family has been in the new country, and more individual factors such as personality characteristics. The process of adjusting to life in a new culture or country, following immigration, has been labeled *acculturation*.

Impact of Immigration on Families

The impact of migrating to another country is hard for many people to imagine. Any differences in culture and language experienced while on vacation hardly replicate the upheaval and strangeness people encounter when moving to a new culture or community. For many families with elder members, there may be restrictions on the use of the new country's language or other accommodations to the home country's culture (Chun & Akutsu, 2003). For many teens, an elder's reaction to the new country may feel stifling and unfamiliar. Over time, the constraints may feel confining to the teen, who may wish to rebel but faces too much pressure from family and cultural constraints to do so. Such internal conflict can lead to behavior that may be viewed as disrespectful by adult family members (Santisteban & Mitrani, 2003).

Factors influencing the adjustment or acculturation process include length of time in the new country, family's overall acceptance of the teen reaching out to others, and expectations for the teen to use a native language or dress in specific ways (McLatchie, 1997). Montague (1996) identifies four types of acculturation experiences of which to be aware when working with clients from diverse cultures: (1) "immigrant unacculturated," referring to those coming from outside the current country, (2) "indigenous unacculturated," referring to those born in the current country who retain traditional values, behaviors, and attitudes consistent with their ethnic background, (3) "indigenous acculturated," referring to those born in the current country and following the majority culture, and (4) "immigrant acculturated," referring to those coming from outside the current country who embrace the majority culture.

A truism offered by Montague (1996) that supercedes individual differences, whether due to multiculturism or other influences, is to treat all clients with respect for who they are, trust, and understanding and acceptance. By approaching each child, adolescent, and family as unique in their own right, we are offering the respect these individuals and families require and deserve. This type of humanistic approach is a large part of a multicultural perspective—valuing each person for his individual differences.

Valuing each client as an individual and approaching him with respectful and appropriate curiosity or a desire to learn about this person does much to foster a multicultural approach in treatment. In fact, one must be cautious when learning specific characteristics of various cultures not to perpetuate stereotypes from the cultural generalities usually reviewed in such coursework (Shih, Pittinsky, & Ambady, 1999). As such, multicultural information can be viewed as a tool to help define what is considered "within normal limits" for various cultural experiences, similar to our developmental expectations for children and adolescents. Thus, we have multiple templates to consider in working with special populations: developmental expectations, multicultural experiences, family system, and individual differences.

Multicultural Aspects of Behavior

Multicultural issues have been included in counseling curriculums for quite some time now; however, application of findings, or extending research efforts to work with children and adolescents, has been lacking (Liu & Clay, 2002). A few studies have identified trends in behavioral expectations for children across cultures. For example, internalizing problems appear to be more frequently reported in African and Asian cultures, while externalizing problems seem to be more frequently identified as problems in Australia, Europe, and the United States (Kagan, 1984; Ollendick, Yang, King, Dong, & Akande, 1996). However, individual differences exist and must be respected.

In order to be effective, clients must be understood within the context of their personal culture as well as within the context of the majority culture in which they find themselves. As Sue and Sue (1990) note, "Counselors who hold a worldview different from that of their clients and are unaware of the basis for this difference are most likely to input negative traits to clients" (p. 153). These findings are similar to the studies reviewed on the impact of bias on professional work with gay and lesbian clients, reviewed in Chapter 11. These "hidden biases" are the very reason that therapists and counselors are encouraged to participate in their own counseling and to explore personal beliefs and potential biases. Failure to do so is likely to influence therapeutic relationships in a negative manner.

Racism and other biases have been identified in several studies as a potentially harmful dynamic in the therapeutic relationship, from the therapist as well as client reports (Casimir & Morrison, 1993; Grier & Cobbs, 1980; Helms, 1984; Jenkins-

Hall & Sacco, 1991; Ridley, 1995) and in family therapy (Boyd-Franklin, 1988; Falicov, 1983; Hardy & Laszloffy, 1992; McGoldrick, 1998). Gamst, Dana, Der-Karabetian, and Kramer (2001) found that clients participated in a greater total number of sessions when client and counselor were "matched" for ethnicity (Asian American in this study). Kurasaki, Sue, Chun, and Gee (2000) found that Asian American clients reported poorer outcomes and less satisfaction with treatment when therapy was not experienced as culturally responsive. Some clients describe the therapeutic relationship as hostile, which would, of course, make effective therapy difficult. Other studies report positive counseling effects from matching client and counselor (Sue, Fujuno, Hu, & Takeuchi, 1991; Takeuchi & Uehara, 1996; Yeh, Eastman, & Cheung, 1994).

Often, the biases and negative stereotypes of therapists were developed early in childhood (Bigler & Liben, 1993). As a result of early belief formation, biased perceptions may be used to make judgments about others outside of the conscious awareness of the individual (Devine & Elliot, 1995). The potential harm results not only from the tendency to make judgments based on biased information, but perhaps more importantly, the resistance of the beliefs to change (Butcher & Scofield, 1984; Strohmer & Shivy, 1994). Examples of therapist biases from the literature underscore the necessity for each professional to engage objectively in personal exploration to become aware of these potential obstacles within the self of the therapist to good work. The accompanying workbook expands on these opportunities.

Additional examples of these concerns are in the findings of Tomlinson-Clarke and Camilli (1995), who report a greater number of diagnosable disorders of mental illness for African American clients and different treatment interventions when compared to European American clients. A tendency to overdiagnose psychopathology in minorities by not giving credence to cultural factors has been noted by others (Lopez & Hernandez, 1986; Lopez & Nunez, 1987; Rollock & Terrell, 1996; Sue & Sue, 1987; Sue, 1988; Westermeyer, 1987), as have differences in parenting practices (Taylor, 1991). Multicultural awareness or training can help the therapist in maintaining a balance between cultural differences and a tendency toward personal bias. For example, parenting practices of African American families have been noted to involve more physical discipline as compared to Caucasian families, possibly pushing more African American children into the foster care system (Pinderhughes, 1991). Because of prevailing differences between the majority culture's definition of acceptable disciplinary practices when compared to practices of other ethnic groups, certain families may become labeled as abusive, unfit, or unhealthy if the therapist is not attuned to cultural differences (Hampton, 1991). Such differences do not condone violence in the family; interventions involving the entire family, such as in revising parenting techniques, should be incorporated into therapy. Basic differences in family practice or disciplinary approaches can create conflict and distrust between the African American community and social service agencies. We will discuss the potential impact of suspicion of outside agencies in Chapter 6, as it relates to premature termination.

In addition to a tendency to overdiagnose certain segments of the population, failure to recognize mental illness in African American families and juvenile offenders has also been identified (Lewis, Balla, & Shanok, 1979; Lewis, Feldman, & Barrengos, 1986), preventing families and individuals from receiving appropriate treatment. The behaviors that were framed as normal by counselors working with African American juvenile offenders included identifying hallucinations as part of the youth's culture, defining extreme paranoia as an adaptive response, and labeling grandiosity as "streetwise" (Lewis et al., 1979). These examples represent an extreme form of misunderstanding on the part of counselors (Sandhu & Brown, 1996) and may serve to isolate and harm individuals, in opposition to professional codes of ethics.

THERAPEUTIC APPROACH IN THE CONTEXT OF CULTURE

Each family has its own culture and expectations regardless of ethnic background. It is necessary to be aware of these differences even if a client's family experience appears to be quite similar to the majority culture or that of the therapist (Alessandria, 2002) and to be certain as a therapist of one's own awareness of self, value system, possible biases, and potential interaction of these personal issues in the professional relationship (Lefley, 2002). In many ways, Rogers's (McDougall, 2002) person-centered approach may have much to offer in terms of application to a multicultural approach. Rogers emphasized accepting the client, providing unconditional positive regard, and practicing empathy. At some level, these techniques translate to acceptance. Although as McDougall (2002) notes, each approach needs to be evaluated for its appropriate application to diverse clients, Rogers seems to provide a reasonable starting place of acceptance.

A simple, practical approach to increase one's awareness of multicultural issues in counseling is suggested from the training literature of recreation specialists. Sheldon and Datillo (1997) suggest that professionals examine their biases, learn about the community in which clients live, remain sensitive to the client's and their own language, observe how families within the community interact, and be open to learning about diverse experiences from various sources.

Not only is there a potential interaction between the therapist's personal experiences and biases, but also between the therapist's multicultural counseling training, theoretical orientation, and empathic abilities. Constantine (2001) found that those counselors who were more effective in their ability to conceptualize culturally diverse client's mental health issues had received more formal training in multicultural issues, adopted a more eclectic therapeutic approach, and displayed a better empathic understanding of clients. An important part of the family's cultural experience may include aspects of acculturation or becoming part of a new majority culture for immigrant families as well as families who move to a new community.

Family Factors

The individual experience of immigration, or even moving to a different part of the country, stretches the family's resources. The number of simultaneous adjustments to be made is similar to the divorce process in terms of the stress from the timing of myriad changes (Ben-Sira, 1997; Pledge, 1992). Clinicians must consider the level of acculturation in the client's family and specific factors defining various cultures for those families who are immigrating. In addition, the factors surrounding a family's immigration may cause the family to turn to each other for support or may create such high levels of stress that outside support may be needed. A family approach can be more effective in helping the family as a unit, and as individuals, begin to build their own support network within their new community. Members of the professional network (possibly yourself) can become even more important as the family begins to form their own support network beyond initial contacts (Pipher, 2002).

Awareness of specific challenges that may be associated with the experience of families from various cultures can help ease anxiety for family members and increase comfort and a sense of community (Cornille & Brotherton, 1993; Falicov, 1995; Gopaul-McNicol, 1995; Levenbach & Lewak, 1995). The process of immigrating includes the equally challenging, simultaneous tasks of separating from the family's country of origin and adapting to a new country (Mirsky & Kaushinsky, 1989). Being aware of technological differences, language differences, varying food preferences, and different social norms are all equally important in your ability to be supportive of clients, and be efficient in your work with them.

Exploring the family's reasons for immigration, length of time in the country, individual family member's adjustment, and the family's experience of the immigration process are important factors to consider when beginning work with families who have immigrated (Slonim-Nevo, Sharaga, & Mirsky, 1999). Those authors also suggest the therapist attempt to determine whether the presenting problems are "universal" or are better understood in the specific cultural experiences of the family. Attributing the etiology of the presenting concern to the immigrant experience helps normalize feelings and behaviors for the family (Slonim-Nevo et al, 1999) and as such may help empower the family and strengthen its resiliency. In working with immigrant families, the therapist may take on the role of "culture broker," assisting the family in its assimilation process or facilitating the process by helping the family make connections within the community with someone who can help familiarize the family with cultural norms (Pipher, 2002).

As Marcia (1994) suggests, the acculturation process includes a progression of identity formation that is dependent on the length of time the family has been in the "host" or new country. Marcia's process of identity development as applied to acculturation includes the following stages: (1) foreclosed, limiting self-exploration and options, (2) identity diffused, resulting in lack of direction and/or commitment, (3) moratorium, or taking a time-out and not addressing the issue of identity formation, and (4) identity achievement, the successful resolution of identity conflict and healthy commitment to goals. Understanding where the individual and family are with regard to the process of identity development is an important component of tailoring effective interventions.

A relatively common immigrant experience for families who have recently relocated is for the children in the family to become liaisons between the family and the new majority culture (Fuligni, Yip, & Tseng, 2002). Although this takes advantage of an increased flexibility and ability to adapt in younger people, it can put the child in an untenable position, lodged between the exciting aspects of the new culture and maintaining traditional aspects of the family's home culture. Factors to consider in supporting your young client and helping the family adjust include the reasons for the immigration and feelings about "fitting in" to the new culture. Children or adolescents may be eager to become part of the new culture for many reasons—because they want to fit in, because it is fun and exciting, or because they have become the translator of the majority culture for the family. Older members of the client's family may not embrace the culture or may fear losing their family's ethnic roots if the acculturation happens too quickly.

Parenting Differences

Parenting differences are not just observed between families of recent immigrants and those who have lived in a country for many years, even for generations. Differences are noted across ethnic groups, varying socioeconomic levels, and family types. Making comparisons to the majority culture and then determining what the other styles are lacking is the crux of the deficit approach. Parental involvement and parenting styles have traditionally been noted in the literature using a deficit approach by comparing parenting styles of all social, economic, and ethnic groups with that of European American styles (Bradley, 1998; Peters, 1985; Spencer, 1990; Vega, 1990). This approach sometimes produces deleterious results, or at least inaccurate perceptions, for the children of such families. However, increased attention to the social and political factors that may have influenced different parenting approaches is contributing to greater understanding of the need for diversity with respect to parenting practices (Hossain & Roopnarine, 1994; Ogbu, 1981).

Parents' ability or willingness to provide support to their children struggling with mental illness is also influenced by their culture's orientation toward mental illness. Stigma often prevents parents from obtaining services for their children (Tung, 1980). For example, Vietnamese parents may expect their children to manage anxiety or depression silently and on their own; the perception of more severe mental illnesses, such as schizophrenia, had historically been believed to be the result of evil spirits (McKelvey, Sang, & Tu, 1997). However, an almost equal number of Vietnamese parents in a more recent study of families living abroad (McKelvey, Baldassar, Sang, & Roberts, 1999) identified the cause of mental illness as a biological or chemical brain or spiritual imbalance. In this study, more than 60 percent of parents identified suicidal behavior as a symptom of mental illness; however, other behaviors commonly accepted as symptomatic of mental illness by Western standards, such as cruelty to animals or impulse control problems, were endorsed by less than 40 percent of the sample, and eating disorders by only 8 percent. Less than half of parents in the sample indicated they would seek services from a psychologist or similar mental health professional.

The impact of ethnicity on parenting practices varies widely. Higher levels of verbal and physical expression of affection and nurturing are noted in Puerto Rican and Latin American parents (Escovar & Lazarus, 1982), including a desire for being close and feeling responsive within families (Harwood, 1992). Clear structure within these families, including more frequent use of directives and modeling, appears to have been misinterpreted as authoritarianism in the past (Mirande, 1991). African American families appear to have a stricter parenting approach, including respect for authority with a simultaneous display of support and emotional expression (Bartz & Levine, 1978; Rashid, 1985; Taylor, Chatters, Tucker, & Lewis, 1990).

Although less research has been conducted on parenting styles across cultures and the impact on child behaviors, some studies have focused on maternal interactions. Steinberg, Mounts, Lamborn, and Dornbusch (1991) report a stronger relationship between an authoritarian approach and positive school performance among European American and Latin American adolescents than among Asian American and African American adolescents. Simarily, Deater-Deckard, Dodge, Bates, and Petitt (1996) reported that physical punishment was associated with increased acting out and aggressiveness for European American children, but not for African Americans. Any of these factors may be tempered by gender effects between parents that may become confusing for the children in the new culture (Darvishpour, 2002). No significant gender effects across ethnic groups or culture have been identified, other than observing a strong same-gender effect in early childhood (Isley, O'Neill, Clatfelter, & Parke, 1999), a factor that is relatively consistent in human development across cultures. Fagan (1998) found few differences between parenting styles for mothers and fathers within the same family among African American or Puerto Rican families.

Part of the challenge for children and adolescents is making sense of gender roles that may be at odds with the traditional culture and that of the new culture. Conflicting gender roles within the respective cultures may make adjustment more difficult for adolescents and engender additional conflict between parents and children, based on the adolescent's perception of acceptable parental practices. Despite this possibility of differences and conflict, an interesting study was completed in China questioning adolescents regarding their perceptions of parenting styles that indicated less difference in parental perception across cultures than one might imagine. Shek (1998) found that adolescents perceived mothers as using more positive parenting approaches than fathers. Fathers were perceived as "less responsive" and "less demanding," with more of a laissez-faire approach to parenting. Interestingly, although the sample for this study was Chinese, some of these general parenting characteristics are similar to general perceptions of Western parenting and consistent with other studies (Forehand & Nousiainen, 1993; Shek, 1995). For example, adolescents' perceptions are consistent with the role of the mother in Chinese culture and in many Western cultures in monitoring the daughter's activities more closely in the charge to maintain the daughter's chastity (Shek, 1998).

Parenting styles influence family experiences and are important in shaping child and adolescent development (Shek, 1989, 1993), regardless of cultural differences. Specifically, empirical evidence links parenting style and adolescent development in several areas, including academic achievement (Dornbusch, Rotter, Liederman, Roberts, & Fraleigh, 1987; Paulson, 1994), problem behaviors and psychosocial adjustment (Lamborn, Mounts, Steinberg, & Dornbusch, 1991), general well-being (Fine, Voydanoff, & Donnelly, 1993), self-concept (Mboya, 1995), delinquency (Conger & Conger, 1994; McLeod, Kruttschmitt, & Dornfeld, 1994), and drug abuse (Baumrind, 1991; Johnson & Pandina, 1991). Evidence has also been accumulated about the associations between family functioning and other areas of adolescent psychological well-being and problem behavior, including identity formation (Bosma & Gerrits, 1985), suicide (McKenry, Tishler, & Kelley, 1982), psychopathology (Prange, Greenbaum, Silver, & Friedman, 1992), and proneness to delinquency (Tolan & Lorion, 1988). Poor family functioning has been associated with elevated levels of substance abuse (McKay, Murphy, Rivinus, & Maisto, 1991; Smart, Chibucos, & Didler, 1990), and smoking (Doherty & Allen, 1994). However, little support has been found for any association between adolescent somatic complaints and family functioning (Hundert, Cassie, & Johnston, 1988; Walker, McLaughlin, & Greene, 1988). These findings highlight the importance of reviewing parenting styles, family discipline, and the child or adolescent's role in the family's acculturation during the assessment and treatment of children and adolescents with their families. Family conflict is often an indication of dysfunction or a need for intervention.

Although parent-child conflict is often present in families throughout the family life cycle, it has also been viewed as a potential stressor for adolescents, specifically regarding adolescent adjustment and well-being (Shek, 1997). Some data shows an association between parent-adolescent conflict and injuries (Bijur, Kurzon, Hamelsky, & Power, 1991) and problems in identity development (Peterson, 1989). Tomlinson (1991) has identified parent-adolescent conflict as a "major influence" in the presentation of maladaptive behavior in adolescents. It is important to note that in most studies completed to date "adolescent well-being" has been defined in terms of the presence or absence of psychiatric symptoms, academic performance, self-esteem, history with juvenile authorities, or other measurable concepts. Through these behaviors, the child or adolescent may be acting out part of the family conflict.

By definition, you may be working with children or adolescents in your practice; however, pragmatically, you are working with families. As such, you may need to work with parents on issues of discipline and technique. In Yang's (1986) review of Taiwanese studies on family, he concluded that parental attributes of acceptance, positive regard, proper restraint, love, reward, and reasoning intended to induce positive self-concept, self-assertion, and internal locus of control may reduce delinquent behavior. These findings appear relatively consistent with findings from Western research and can become part of your arsenal to help train parents in appropriate skills. Perhaps, in the context of parenting skills, certain approaches universally achieve positive results, similar to a universal approach to counseling skills (Garfield, 1994).

Although the findings about potential influences and interactions between adolescents are quite interesting, our discussion would be incomplete if the general issue of family systems was not addressed. As you may recall, systems theory proposes that individuals do not exist in isolation but continually interact with and are influenced by others within their system. The system can include immediate family as well as the larger community of neighbors, friends, school, and others. It would be naïve to review the findings about parent-child interactions without being aware of the potential bidirectional influence in such relationships. Parents are influenced by children, and children are influenced by parents. Additionally, research supports the importance of such systems in the influence of behavior across cultures (Rothbaum, Rosen, Ujie, and Uchida, 2002).

Family Dynamics and Communication

Just as interactional styles within families have been found to be a factor in adolescents' mental health, general adjustment, and academic performance, so have family dynamics been identified as a contributing factor in the presentation of certain types of mental illness. *Expressed emotion* (EE), defined as hostile or critical comments made to or about a family member, has been heavily researched with regard to prediction in the course or severity of many illnesses, behaviors, and life events, including depression, schizophrenia, bipolar disorder, anorexia, relational control, and communication (Bebbington & Kuipers, 1994; Friedlander & Heatherington, 1989; Goldstein, 1992; Kershner, Cohen, & Coyne, 1996; Raymond, Friedlander, Heatherington, Ellis, & Sargent, 1993; Wuerker, 1994; Wuerker, Haas, & Bellack, 1999). The majority of these studies have focused on Caucasian samples.

In addition to critical comments, the component of emotional overinvolvement is often described as intrusive or "mind-reading" statements directed toward the client (Miklowitz et al., 1989; Strachan, Leff, Goldstein, Miklowitz, & Nuechterlein, 1989). Because of varying communication styles among families in different ethnic groups, it is important to review the findings across cultures with regard to this important factor of expressed emotion in order to avoid making assumptions about the impact of EE on the prediction of mental illness or in the complication of adjustment. Lower EE levels were observed in Mexican American families (Karno et al., 1987) and Indian families (Leff et al., 1987), as compared to families in the majority of studies (i.e., Caucasian families). Although expressed emotion has been associated with a desire for interpersonal control in relationships, no significant findings have been reported from the few cross-cultural studies completed to date. Gender roles have been found to be relatively consistent (i.e., father as traditionally more dominant in communication style) across ethnic groups (Wuerker et al., 1999). The level of conflict in families can also be related to the psychological well-being of various family members.

Other Family Considerations

Parents with a chronic mental illness present a challenge for children as well as professional caregivers (Bell, 1992; Chi & Hinshaw, 2002; Solantaus-Simula, Punamaki, & Beardslee, 2002). Unfortunately, many children and adolescents in these family situations take on a much more active role in the family's daily functioning and maintenance than is appropriate for their age and development. The demands of this dual role place additional strain on them and may prevent them from engaging in age-appropriate activities or in completing their academic work. The additional strain also pushes them beyond their developmental level, which may create other acting-out behaviors. The acting-out behaviors may be their way of expressing feelings about the demands being placed on them, when they are unable to do so verbally. Possible interventions include family sessions, appropriate care for parents, enlisting community resources and aid to decrease the load on the children (or parents), and encouraging age-appropriate activities and boundaries for parents, children, and adolescents. Placement may be necessary in certain cases if the parents' functioning is significantly impaired; however, such placements can also create stress despite efforts to improve the situation.

Children and adolescents in foster care are faced with significant uncertainty about themselves and their place in life. Many times, this uncertainty has a negative effect of interfering with their ability to pursue the same types of academic goals or extracurricular activities as other children of a similar age and socioeconomic status (Farmer et al., 2001). These stressors may remind a client of the losses he has experienced, interfering with current functioning. Such issues as anger or sadness regarding his family situation, feelings that life hasn't been fair to him, and a need for positive mirroring and knowing someone cares about him, are appropriately addressed in therapy. Collaboration with the case manager to encourage the child or adolescent's involvement in extracurricular activities is usually in the client's best interest in addition to addressing issues of adjustment to placement as well as any trauma that may have preceded placement.

FAMILY DYNAMICS

When working with families and children, it is often necessary to help families regulate distance and identity in the relationship. For some families, the interactions are too close, while there may be too much distance in others. This disengagement or enmeshment may be part of the dynamic that brings the family in for treatment. Repetitive patterns of communication and behavior between parents and children can come to define the relationships and confuse roles (Brafman, 2001). Role-plays in which roles are reversed between children and adults can be a powerful intervention to initiate change. Parental attempts to maintain control sometimes take an authoritarian bent, leading to negative interactions between parent and child (Barber, 2002); this dynamic may be associated with marital conflict as well (Buehler & Gerard, 2002). These patterns become more destructive over time, particularly as children approach adolescence. Parental work stress may be a factor in some families. Although effects may be indirect, conflict does appear to increase between parent and child related to increased work stress for parents (Crouter & Bumpus, 2001).

Violence can erupt out of frustration from repeated family patterns over time. Children, adolescents, and even adults may feel there is no other option or hope for change unless physical measures are taken. Family factors associated with aggressive behavior include loss of one or both parents to death or lack of interest/attention toward the child, cold or distant family interactions, greater degree of family conflict, severe behavior problems (e.g., fire setting or violence), or lack of commitment to education. Substance abuse and behavior problems at school are not associated with aggressive behavior (Seifert, Phillips, & Parker, 2001). Luthar and Burack (2000) note the importance of reviewing the impact of individual experience interacting with development for inner city youth and across distinct ethnic groups. Brooks-Gunn, Duncan, Klebanov, and Sealand (1993) also found powerful effects on several developmental factors associated with the child or adolescent's neighborhood. A positive outcome was noted on IQ and decreases in teen births and school dropouts. Other authors describe family factors such as economic status and positive attachment as important in the development of resiliency, positive self-esteem, and coping skills (Cairns & Cairns, 1994).

INDIVIDUAL DIFFERENCES IN RESILIENCY

Individual differences within clients and families affect any adjustment process. If a family is generally optimistic and shares a supportive outlook on life, the client has a positive foundation for making good adjustments. However, any individual differences, such as repeated losses (even including loss of pets or frequent moves) can make a transition more difficult. Repeated losses can create a situation of cumulative stressors that beat down a family's resiliency. Some families develop a pattern similar to learned helplessness (Seligman, 1975), where they begin to doubt their own ability to influence the environment. Such a perspective becomes almost a self-fulfilling prophecy if the family adopts this as part of its family belief system. This type of response can be observed even in strong, healthy families who have experienced multiple losses or deaths within a short time. A difficult aspect of responding to repeated stressors is the toll it takes on the individual's and family's self-image. As they begin to feel less effective in "bouncing back" from these repeated stressors, some clients may internalize a negative view of themselves, assuming that they "just can't do it anymore." Lamentations such as "What's wrong with me?" convey the angst of such experiences and the depth of pain associated with such a shift in self-perception. A simple, but effective initial intervention is often to assure the client that his response to the repeated stressors is normal—what he's had to endure is abnormal. In other words, anyone faced with similar stressors would have responded as he has. Such a psycho-educational intervention can reassure the client that this is not a permanent condition. There is hope that he will return to his previous level of functioning and outlook on life. This provides hope and the knowledge that the experience is in some ways universal. This hope can help the client retrieve his formerly positive attitude. If a positive attitude did not exist previously, the case conceptualization would be quite different. In that case, we would probably be working with someone with a level of chronic depressive symptoms and would need to tailor our interventions accordingly.

DIVORCE

Divorce can be an extremely traumatic experience. Although not physically life threatening, the process of divorce can be just as damaging to one's worldview and self-image. Although much more common than in previous generations—current estimates are that half of marriages will end in divorce (National Center for Health Statistics, 2003)—the process is painful for all involved. At one level, the divorce is unexpected, just like an accident or natural disaster. The fact that something unanticipated is happening to members of the family experiencing divorce is stressful. It doesn't fit with expectations about how life was supposed to progress. Dashing this expectation affects all family members, including a ripple effect on extended family and sometimes friends. Part of what's hard about the initial realization is the emotional vacuum that accompanies it for some adults and children. The vacuum arises out of the lack of expectation for experiencing divorce, which signifies to some that the life they have known has ended. The finality of this change can be felt in the previous statement. Divorce can feel like a death to some family members, because it is a death of dreams, hopes, and lifestyles.

Parental Behaviors

Parents can help children adjust by not placing them in the middle of any negative interactions. As a therapist working with families, part of your role may include providing specific instructions to parents. For many parents, their own "emotional meltdowns" or distraction with newly single life may make them unavailable for their children's emotional needs. This leaves an even larger void and task of adjustment for children. Parents need to manage their own emotional concerns separate from their parenting and their relationship with their children. Instruct them about how to act in the best interest of their children. For example, emotionally troubled parents may need to be reminded not to pump their children for information about their ex-spouse and not to expect their children to act as messengers. Helping parents be available for their children is one of the more positive interventions you can make for children and adolescents at this point.

Sessions with children or adolescents need to allow them the space to talk or act out their feelings in a manner that feels comfortable to them. If a child or adolescent is feeling badgered or focused on too much in the divorce process, therapy can replicate those feelings if you are pushing too hard. Take the child's lead and allow him to grieve, be angry, feel uncertain, and wonder about aspects of daily life in ways he may not be able to do elsewhere. Give him permission to express his conflicted feelings and his questions about where he'll live, if he'll have enough money to buy a stereo, and what will happen to the family dog. These may be the burning questions on your client's mind. Helping him talk with his parents about those and other issues may be an important part of the healing process.

Blended Families

Challenges in coping with change due to a parent's remarriage can be challenging for children of any age. For many children, it seems that the longer they enjoyed having a single parent as a companion, the more difficult it is for them to accept changes in that relationship. In many cases, a parent's remarriage brings up basic issues about sharing one's parent and questions about where the child (even an adult child) fits into the parent's life. This transition can bring up unexpected feelings of jealousy, anger, and betrayal the child or adolescent may be reluctant to express because he understands at an intellectual level that the change is good for his parent. At an emotional level, however, the response may feel like a toddler's tantrum. Helping clients and families understand these competing responses is a challenge in their acceptance of this life change. Many remarriages end in divorce because the family was not able to meet the challenge of sorting out emotional and intellectual responses.

Factors to be aware of in working with blended families include: divided loyalties, feelings of being left out or treated differently, complications of changing family composition as various children transition in and out of the family home, different parenting styles, the need to build new relationships and maintain existing ones simultaneously, and differences in daily life, such as different kinds of foods, schedules, chores, and strong feelings. Many clients and families expect that they will immediately become a family after the parent remarries and that the children will automatically get along.

Phases of Adjustment in Becoming a Blended Family

Families begin in *fantasy,* defined by Papernow's (1993) integration process for blended families that consists of seven stages of development. The second stage is *immersion,* which may feel like a cloaking, dunking, or euphoric embrace of the new family situation. As the label implies, reactions to this stage are somewhat overwhelming and may feel like a continuation of the fantasy in that the perception is not yet accurate. That more objective perspective is associated with stage three, *awareness.* During this phase there may be a tendency to split along biological lines, reverting to former alliances between parent and child, or with the parent who is out of the home, depending on the relationship between former spouses and stepparents. During this phase family members may begin to feel or recognize a possible need for change. Phase four is termed *mobilization,* a time when family members may begin to think more concretely about the need for change, identifying a desire to work toward stronger relationships in this new family or recognizing that the differences and conflict may be too great. During phase five *action,* tensions may become overwhelming and divorce may occur. If the decision during the mobilization phase was to work on issues to enhance adjustment, seeking counseling may be the action that occurs in this phase, rather than divorce. In phase six, *contact,* relationships continue to be sorted out, including contact with the former family, managing visitation schedules, and adjusting boundaries between the former and current family members. The final phase is *resolution,* which Papernow warns may take as long as five years as the new couple achieves a stable bond strong enough to withstand the stress and demands of complicated family relationships. A significant accomplishment in this final stage is that family now defines itself as a family, emotional bonds feel strong, and there is a sense of stability and security. Tensions have decreased and been replaced by warmth and support.

Grieving the "Original Family"

In order for a positive resolution to occur, family members must have a chance to grieve the loss of the former family, any dreams about reunification, or the loss of a particular lifestyle. Realistic expectations about the quality of relationships within the blended family are also an important aspect of a positive adjustment. Assumptions that a stepparent will instantly be treated in the same way as the biological parent are obstacles to a healthy blended family. Likewise, expecting children and adolescents to immediately begin acting as if they are siblings, perhaps by pushing them together, will likely result in conflict. Parents need to be advised to give relationships time to develop on their own; otherwise, the only aspect of true sibling relationships that will be seen is that of conflict. A strong bond between the new parents—a kind of "united front"—is also beneficial to the strength of the blended family. Helping the family work through their own experiences in the adjustment process will involve satisfactory resolution of similar issues, depending on individual differences within each family.

DEATH

The best ways to help someone who has lost a close friend or relative to death vary by age. For young children, our goal is to help them understand that grandma won't be coming back anymore. Adults around the child may be emotionally unavailable as they struggle with their own grief. When adults are unavailable for support, children and adolescents are left to figure things out for themselves. Unfortunately, they usually don't have the life experiences or support to determine what's going on. Their way of "filling in the blanks" may be inaccurate, but they may not recognize this until years later. If you are working with a family at the time of a death, you have an opportunity to support your client through your sessions. In addition, some schools have grief groups that may be beneficial in providing support and working through these feelings.

Common strategies for coping with such loss in children and adolescents include journaling, maybe even writing a therapeutic letter, particularly if there was not an opportunity to say good-bye. Encouraging young children to make a memory book or a collage about the person can help provide closure as well. Some young children and adolescents describe having dreams about the deceased or even seeing them around bedtime or other quiet times of the day. These are not cause for alarm if they occur on just a few occasions. If the "visits" become more regular, additional work may be necessary as you take a more active role in helping the client work through his grief. Such experiences generally indicate difficulty letting go of a special person. Children may want to hang on to the experience because it helps them feel connected to the deceased and helps them to feel special. Facilitating communication between family members about the deceased may help the child feel supported and more grounded. Adjustment for all family members will likely be more challenging if the death was unexpected or accidental. Seeking out the support of a group may help all family members feel more supported by being able to meet with others who may have had similar losses. As with most therapeutic issues, cultural factors affect how families grieve. For some families, grieving may be a private process, while others prefer to reach out. Remain cognizant of these differences when applying interventions and working to build up a support system.

TRAUMA

Although most of us have a general definition of trauma, this term represents a significant range of individual experiences. What is considered traumatic for one person may be less so for another, and similar experiences may even affect the same person differently at different times in their lives. For children and adolescents, developmental stage is a critical aspect of the effect of experience, which will be addressed further in Part three. Because of the range of reactions to traumatic events, one must remain nonjudgmental during all stages of treatment, but particularly during the early stages of assessment and rapport building. If, for example, you do not define a particular event as traumatic and convey that to the client early in therapy, you may lose the opportunity to establish rapport and help that individual. The workbook accompanying this text provides additional opportunities to explore potential personal reactions to client trauma, allowing you to be more present to the client.

Healing involves feeling safe or being able to trust again after trauma. That safety may come from your therapeutic relationship with the child or adolescent. This is no easy task, but generally involves helping the child, adolescent, and family members adjust to a new reality—a new view of themselves, those around them, and their worldview. The expectation that the world is a safe place or that everything happens for a reason may be temporarily shattered, as the individual approaches the healing process. For those suffering from abuse, the healing process is likely to be longer and more involved, depending on the manner in which they coped. The more layers that have been built up to protect themselves from "danger," the more difficult will be the recovery process.

Even with something as commonplace as auto accidents, part of the challenge is returning to life and routines with a different understanding of expectations and reality. Our challenge is to help clients get back into the car again and go through the daily routine that so many of us take for granted, instead of expecting the fear and anxiety of an accident.

Some symptoms of trauma blend with those of depression or anxiety. Distinguishing characteristics include the presence of intrusive or repetitive thoughts in compulsive features, or extreme worry in cases of anxiety. If accompanied by irritability, sleep disruptions (too much or too little), or self-destructive tendencies (e.g., drinking, drug use, or sexual acting out), there may be a mixed presentation of depression and anxiety. Chapter 7 helps identify these differences.

Post-Traumatic Stress Disorder

Post-traumatic stress disorder (PTSD) can result from various life events, ranging from a fire in the home to being abused. Thus, it is important to consider developmental limitations when tailoring interventions for children and adolescents. Specific developmental differences to consider when planning interventions include varying abilities to regulate affect and understand relationships and causation. Interventions for PTSD symptoms include training in coping skills, managing emotional triggers, and cognitive-behavioral strategies designed to restructure responses to the trauma (Vernberg & Johnston, 2001).

SAMPLE QUESTIONS TO EXPLORE REACTIONS TO TRAUMA

THERAPIST: *Do you have thoughts that just pop into your head sometimes, like at school or when you go to bed at night?*

THERAPIST: *What are those thoughts about? Do they keep you from doing your work, or being able to go to sleep?*

THERAPIST: *What changes have you noticed about sleep or appetite?*

Emotion and Trauma—Effect on Development

As young clients reconstruct the events of their day, they may not differentiate between what they actually did and what they thought about doing. This can create significant problems for clinicians who elect to approach sessions with children and adolescents in a similar talking and questioning mode as one might with adult clients. For this reason, it may be helpful to anchor details of the child's life with holidays, seasons of the year, special occasions, or favorite television programs (Hudson, 1990). These idiosyncratic aspects of developing memory take on additional significance as we look at evaluation in the context of therapeutic work around traumatic incidents (Terr, 1988) or in investigations of abuse (Schetky & Green, 1988). For example, Terr (1983) has found that children primarily under the age of 8 have been found to distort their perception of time, particularly with regard to estimates of duration for a traumatic event. Her research also notes that there may be some lapse or misperception of memory over time, part of which may be self-protective (Terr, 1980). Being unable to recall details of a traumatic event may serve a purpose in helping the individual move forward in his adjustment. Memory of trauma is also affected by the age at which the trauma occurred. For example, if a trauma occurred when the individual was at a preverbal stage of development, verbal memories will not be available (Engel, 1962; Terr, 1985). However, if some memory exists, the child or adolescent will change his perception and understanding throughout his life as he continues his growth and development. This describes the phenomena seen in abused individuals who may continue to have a reaction at significant developmental stages throughout their lives (e.g., dating, leaving home).

Developing Client Insight Within the Context of the Family

When the client develops understanding, it is truly an "aha" moment, like a flash of insight. However, until that point the client might have described therapy as if it were torture. Close parental and teacher involvement are critical to provide the structure that is not yet developmentally present for the young client or older clients for whom the emotional conflict is too intense. Complications arise when emotions become involved in the interactions (almost always in families), so part of a successful approach in child-centered family work is guiding all members of the family to interact in more positive and supportive ways. Helping the child or adolescent feel safe and supported is necessary before progress can be made. Although making therapy a safe place is part of your professional role, much of this support will come from the client's family and support system. You can help the family be supportive by reviewing appropriate expectations, which will prevent setting the client and family up for failure. Important aspects of your role as a clinician include being a supportive guide, educator, and advocate. Your role will include directing attention toward and away from issues that are unproductive, potentially damaging, or poorly timed. Timing and titration of interventions are equally important for the client and his family to achieve change.

POSITIVE LIFE EVENTS

Stress exists in all aspects of life. Normal transitions include positive events and accomplishments as well as negative influences. Positive events may provoke some stress simply because they represent change. Such a positive change as graduation from elementary school or high school can create some self-doubt and performance anxiety: "Can I make it?" "What if nobody likes me?" "What if I can't get my locker open?" "I don't really want to go to college." These responses are normal fears and anxieties, although the specifics may differ slightly for each client.

DISCUSSION QUESTIONS

1. Discuss how stereotypes have influenced diagnosis and treatment of cultural groups.
2. What factors might influence a family's process of acculturation in their new country?
3. What role might a cultural stigma play in a family's willingness to seek mental health services?

4. What type of sensitivity does Montague suggest with regard to multiculturalism in one's practice?
5. What is the therapist's role in family therapy?
6. What phases are involved in the adjustment of the blended family?
7. What is the role of the family belief system in resiliency?
8. What effect does family structure have on a family's ability to change?

THEORY INTO APPLICATION

INTRODUCTION

Our discussion in the first two chapters focused on the impact and interaction of individual development and family factors in therapeutic work with children and adolescents. Translating theory into practice is the focus for this final chapter in Part one. Ivey's (1986) framework on the application of developmental level to therapeutic approach will be reviewed. Approaches to gathering information, including structured interviews and choice of assessment measures, will be discussed in the context of developing an individual style as a beginning professional. Finally, we will examine the process of assimilating the information gained from an initial evaluation based on interviews and family history into a report, and we will review a sample report.

The client, family, and therapist—and the interactions among them—all influence the therapeutic process. From a psychodynamic perspective, transference and countertransference can impact the process. Individual biases and personal history of the therapist can affect interactions and interventions. From a systems perspective, all of these factors and the interaction of the client and community can affect change. The community can become an integral part of healthy interventions. However, how the "problem" is defined will impact the direction of your interventions. The initial section of this chapter will focus on helpful therapeutic perspectives for self-exploration to address potential biases, integrate community support into your interventions, use loss as a therapeutic concept for managing interventions, and consider general issues regarding work with children and adolescents.

HELPFUL THERAPEUTIC PERSPECTIVES

Concept of Loss as a Therapeutic Framework

It is often helpful to conceptualize many of the challenges our clients, or ourselves, face in the context of loss. We must first come to understand that loss takes many forms—physical, emotional, psychological, and ideological. With the example of divorce, the loss of the family unit as it had previously been known may bring on additional significant stressors as well, including changes in housing, family routine, and economics. Additionally, parents may lose their perception of themselves as capable, competent, and attractive, which often filters down to their interactions with their children. Children and adolescents may struggle with unfulfilled hopes and desires as well, harboring dreams that the parents will reunite, perhaps to the point of manipulation. They may also blame themselves.

Children are not, and should not be expected to be, aware or conscious of the various challenges that make their adjustment difficult. That's where the real work of therapy begins and the challenge to help clients with little awareness express their concerns. Unlike adults, where some level of insight is assumed to facilitate the healing process, insight may not be a viable mechanism or mediating principle for most child and adolescent clients. As such, we have to look to less direct techniques to help them alleviate their concerns.

Indirect Communication

For children and adolescents, direct communication about such issues is often too difficult, and they may revert to expression of such conflicts through behavioral means. This is the normal way for children and adolescents to express conflicted feelings before they develop the intellectual capacity to do so. Helping parents, teachers, and others who work with children to understand this basic concept can contribute much to facilitating the healing process by reducing the negative consequences in the child's/adolescent's environment. In other words, as authority figures in the child's life begin to understand that her behavior is a means of communicating her inner emotional state, the consequences can be altered to provide a learning experience for the child who is not able to fully understand her own actions. The process of therapy can assist in working through these issues, at times without directly discussing the issue at hand, for some of our young clients.

Unique Aspects of Therapy With Children and Adolescents

We must remember what a privilege it is to work with our clients and to be allowed into the intimate aspects of their lives. By maintaining this degree of respect for our clients, we can be more effective for them. One of the hallmarks of successful therapy is the recognition that these interactions must be different from other social interactions in the child's life. Therefore, if we find ourselves replicating other relationships in the child's life, we must stop and reassess our own direction. If we are reiterating the "rules" as laid down by parents, teachers, or the Juvenile Office, then we are interacting in the same way as others do with this young person, and we can expect nothing new in terms of her interactions with us or others. The corrective emotional experience provides a new response from an old stimulus, allowing the client to experience a positive change.

We must keep in mind the premise that therapy provides a "corrective emotional experience" (Yalom, 1983) for our clients. Granted, we must remember that children by definition do not have the same level of ego strength, superego functioning, or ability to self-monitor as adults. If we are not providing a different type of relationship—an opportunity to explore their choices, identity, relationships, future, and behavior—then how are we providing an opportunity for growth to our clients? In my perception, we are not, and if we are not, then we are unsuccessful. One of the wonderful and challenging aspects of our profession is that we are continually stretched. Most professions require some type of continuing education; ours occurs at an internal and external level in order for us to be truly effective.

Coping With Transitions

Another helpful perspective for viewing life transitions as well as trauma is that the individual's coping response can be considered a normal response to an abnormal life event. By normalizing our clients' responses to their life stressors, we help them regain a stronger, healthier sense of themselves, thus building a foundation for future work. Maladaptive coping mechanisms can include any number of different responses to life transitions or stressors. A common example of maladaptive coping skills is using a mechanism the individual has "outgrown." These coping mechanisms were developed in childhood and worked then because the child had limited skills and awareness about the situation. Out of habit and because it worked in the past, the client maintains the defense mechanism until it becomes clear that the mechanism is no longer working. It is as if a 16-year-old is trying to stuff her feet into a pair of toddler shoes. They just don't fit anymore! The therapist's job is to help the client fashion a new pair that fits.

Examples of outgrown coping skills might include overeating, using comfort foods, blaming others, or withdrawing. More healthy choices might include getting exercise, talking, drawing, or writing about the transition or stressor. Even practicing responses in front of a mirror might be a helpful strategy for some. In examining maladaptive responses, we first help the client recognize that her current choices for coping are no longer working, if she hasn't already realized that. Secondly, we identify typical coping strategies and begin to try them on. There is an element of trial and error in finding interventions that "fit" the client. It's often a good idea to suggest the client try one or two new coping skills each week, until she finds the best substitutes for the old behaviors. As therapy continues, each coping skill will be fine-tuned or discarded until effective strategies are found. This process is not as time-consuming as it may sound, and helps the client feel involved.

Resistance

If the client has continued complaints about the interventions or nothing seems to work, you are probably dealing with some resistance from the client. A resistant presentation may mean that you are getting closer to the true, underlying issues, and the client is experiencing discomfort about moving toward the painful feelings and beyond to new choices and behaviors. Anxiety may impede progress for the client. Recognize the therapeutic dilemma, give it a name, and let the client know you empathize with her. The support, safety, and consistency of your working alliance will give the client the necessary space to work through these difficult issues.

Connecting With Clients—Identifying Concerns

Reviewing a typical day with your client may begin to provide clues to potential areas for change of which the client may be unaware. Working through this lack of awareness is particularly important for children, for whom such lack of insight is developmentally appropriate. As therapists, we help filter the information about coping and healthy responses in ways that do not interfere with their developmental growth. A common mistake for many who work with children and adolescents is attempting to use traditional talking therapy or assuming that gaining insight will be helpful in moving toward change. Children are egocentric, a developmentally appropriate orientation for many until late adolescence. This perspective precludes them from being able to self-observe or monitor at a level necessary for change. Additionally, many children, partially due to their egocentricity, are unmotivated to change, regardless of insight. Their base of operation stems from the arena of immediacy.

Deficits in Planning and Organization

Many children, particularly those who come to us for services, have limited ability to plan and organize their thoughts and actions. This type of limited response is developmentally appropriate until early adolescence, after which time we may expect an enhanced ability for our clients to consider the potential consequences of their actions. We need to remain cognizant, however, that certain disorders preclude the ability to perform these basic cognitive functions well into adulthood. ADHD is a common example of a disorder that makes such forward planning difficult. Regardless of etiology, our task is to help clients form, and respond to, structure in a way that facilitates change.

Tools for Clients

A basic tenet of counseling psychology is to give our clients the tools to make changes for themselves and to foster self-growth and exploration. With children and adolescents, this approach is even more critical in light of meeting the goal of not moving our clients too quickly along the developmental pathway. We must remain sensitive to issues of willfulness or resistance and to a skills or knowledge deficit. A defined deficit requires that we respond by providing the necessary information or skill base to our clients; however, willfulness requires a firm, consistent response, with exploration of motivational factors. It suggests an external structure that will probably involve the parents.

Avoiding Pain

People of all ages attempt to avoid pain by distracting themselves and others from their perceived deficit or shortcoming. Young clients' behavior may represent an attempt to "cover up" an academic or social deficit, of which no one else is aware. They may have been performing the cover-up for most of their lives. If so, their awareness of the initial reason for the cover-up behavior may be long buried and hard to identify. If the cover-up behavior has become a pattern, we are actually helping the client to change at two different levels—the current behavioral level and the original behavior as well. With such clients, part of the hard work of counseling may include identifying these problem areas, grieving for the difference from peers, and forging ahead with a new plan, which may involve such complicated therapeutic work as helping them experiment with a new self-concept and new behaviors and coping skills. It may require some clients to stretch from being the class clown or someone who doesn't care about school to a more dedicated and involved student. We must remain aware how difficult this shift will be without other changes to the environment. Just as drug and alcohol treatment relapse is more likely when no changes have been made to the external environment, our clients will face more obstacles when there have been no changes in their peer group or academic environment. It may be necessary to work with the school counselor or academic team to help foster an environment in which students can feel free to change their behavior or make more positive choices at school.

Psycho-Educational Approaches

An effective intervention will include psycho-educational components as suggested when handling life transitions to help clients understand that their responses are normal. Such information can help ground clients and their families again. Typical client responses to anxiety may be to foresee catastrophes and get lost in fear of those unlikely occurrences. Emotions cloud their thinking, and they may not be able to use their normal coping skills or even think clearly enough to recognize they are engaged in what may be a repetitive pattern. Increasing awareness of their emotional state, potential choices, and realistic outcomes can help them manage their anxiety. Borrowing a technique from group approaches, the therapist can challenge clients to live in the "here-and-now." Such an approach helps ground many clients in the present and prevents future-directed forecasts of doom. Other approaches that can achieve similar results are traditional relaxation strategies, such as deep breathing, large muscle tensing and relaxing, and visual imagery. The goal for all these approaches is to keep the client grounded in the present rather than "getting lost" in their thoughts and fears about the past or future.

Resiliency and Family Beliefs

Family beliefs and approaches will affect the client's ability to remain in the present and explore new coping strategies. A family intervention, during which parents can hear for themselves your recommendation for a different coping approach than they are used to, can help give your client permission and space to try something different and not feel guilty for breaking any unspoken rules. Part of the therapist's role is to increase the strength of the client's resiliency, which may involve family and community resources as well as family legacies, such as personal beliefs about being strong and capable. Genograms (see Part three) can be used to identify these family patterns if the client is unaware of them.

Adult and Community Support

Support from adults within the child or adolescent's community can be a significant factor in the individual's ability to be resilient and develop the strength to cope with life challenges (Wolkow & Ferguson, 2001). Ideally this support will come from parents, but not all parents can provide this level of support. In those cases, encouraging contact with a mentor or through community involvement is suggested as a possible resource. Support in the community broadens the resources available to the youth at times of stress.

Significant variability is observed regarding individual reactions to stress, and those youth without family support or with diminished family support are likely to be more vulnerable to negative life influences and stressors. Community programs can sometimes help bridge this gap and provide necessary support. Examples include Boys and Girls Clubs, Scouts, church groups, and school clubs. These programs all offer an adult mentor or positive role model who can be supportive and available to the child or adolescent.

Another important aspect of such community programs is the opportunity for altruism. This is a long-standing therapeutic factor in groups (Yalom, 1983) that is now being recognized as a positive factor in helping young people make more positive choices in their lives when faced with stress. Engaging in altruistic acts helps children and adolescents feel more positively about themselves, develop a healthy self-esteem, and build empathy skills and the ability to cooperate (Canale & Beckely, 1999).

Pets as Support

Pets can often help bridge this gap between the social areas where some youth feel uncomfortable with people to the special connection between animals and children. Family pets can serve as a source of unconditional support and a confidante within the family at those times when conflict may be heightened between parents and children. Having a pet won't prevent a child from reaching out to undesirable peer groups, but an animal's presence in the family may help the child or adolescent remain connected to the family rather than seek outside sources of social support. In a more structured approach to using animals to help children and adolescents feel better about themselves and feel supported, pet therapy fills this niche in treatment programs such as residential centers and inpatient programs (Nebbe, 1991).

On the converse side of relationships with animals, it is important to note that animals can become the target of aggression, a "red flag" behavior for intervention by professionals, particularly when the behavior is repeated or severe (Flynn, 2000). Early violence toward animals may signal potentially serious problems with anger management, possibility of violent behavior toward family members or peers, a lack of empathy, and a potential disregard for societal norms. Social skills groups within the school may be the best intervention for such children and adolescents, providing an opportunity to build a base of support through group membership at the school and to practice social skills, receive feedback from others, and develop empathy. Volunteering at a local shelter, with appropriate supervision, may be another way to develop empathy. For those who seem unaffected by these interventions, more intense services and assessment for more serious problems is probably warranted.

Risk Factors in Abuse

Victims of abuse often experience negative psychological and emotional outcomes. Some may act out their experiences on others, becoming offenders themselves in a misdirected effort to work through their own issues. Although it is difficult to identify all factors that may predispose abused youth to abuse others, it appears that exposure to adult caretakers who have a history of abusing others could be a factor (Lightfoot & Evans, 2000). It's possible that having the role model of a known individual close to them who has chosen to abuse himself or others makes the behavior feel more like a viable option. An adult caretaker who has engaged in abuse may set up expectancies about gender role models or even be perceived as giving permission to engage in such behavior. Factors that might predispose abused youth to abuse others include distorted perceptions about caring relationships, a common fear of letting others know about the abuse, and feelings of isolation from the support of others. Victims of sexual abuse often have experienced other forms of abuse or coercion as well, leaving them feeling even more defeated and worthless. When compared to children with behavior disorders, the potential risk factors differ for victims of abuse, including having a parent with a psychiatric illness and increased parental conflict in the home.

Abuse experiences are often traumatic, and when experienced early in life, can serve as precipitators for later substance abuse (De-Bellis, 2002). Abused and traumatized children are at risk for processing problems on the basis of early trauma. In certain cases, abusers will even include alcohol or other substances in the abuse process to induce compliance. Thus, the use of alcohol or other substances may begin as a habit or may continue as a result of impaired judgment and decision making in the wake of the traumatic experience. Age is also a factor in the severity of symptoms, with more severe symptoms consistently noted for younger children (Rossman, Bingham, & Emde, 1997).

Resiliency Factors

Children with physical disabilities, chronic illness, and more challenging temperaments are at greater risk for emotional disorders, behavioral problems, school-related adjustment problems, and abuse in their own families, due to their behaviors and the strain of caring for them and providing structure (Askildsen, Watten, & Faleide, 1993; Coyne & Anderson, 1989; Ievers et al., 1994). Stressors often precipitate a change in family dynamics toward more structure, with decreased communication and less warmth (Wamboldt & Wamboldt, 2000). Positive family factors, such as increased family cohesion and organization, have shown improvement in control of some medical conditions, such as asthma (Meijer & Oppenheimer, 1995). Creating meaning out of the experience helps the family maintain a sense of mastery and control that enhances coping responses (Rolland, 1993).

Characteristics of healthy and resilient families can work against the stresses and strains of daily life and special challenges. Social support and flexible responses of family members can buffer against the eruption of violence. Mary Catherine Bateson (1990) describes this healthy quality of families nicely as "improvisation." Families can indeed take their cues from improvisational troupes such as Second City or the Groundlings in being able to respond capably, spontaneously, and with humor to life challenges.

Different Types of Families

A more flexible perspective with regard to the definition of a "family" is already occurring as family structures become increasingly diverse. Walsh (1993) notes the importance of ex-spouses, extended family, and even pets in providing different types of support to families. Although this may appear nontraditional, a more fluid definition of family is becoming more descriptive of people's day-to-day lives. A "family" is no longer defined as simply those who live under the same roof, but can reach around the world with the connections available through technology. Helping children, adolescents, and families identify members of their own far-reaching support network can increase their sense of self-efficacy, groundedness, comfort, and confidence within themselves.

Rolland (1993) identifies family variables that may also interact to affect the family's response to illness and other stressors. These include the family life cycle (e.g., childbearing phase or middle childhood), individual life cycles (including developmental levels as well as the phase of onset for the disorder—prior to diagnosis, early in diagnosis, or during treatment), and family beliefs and responses to illness and loss. When family members take on too active a role in the care of an ill family member, they often inhibit normal developmental patterns (Campbell, 1993). Although this may be a common response of parents in situations of acute or chronic illness, a balanced approach allowing caretaking and independence is probably more healthy for the child or adolescent.

Specific "shock absorbers," or buffers to stress, that Walsh (1993) identifies are flexibility, connectedness, and social/economic resources. She describes each of these as providing part of a necessary balance for families to meet life's challenges. A colloquialism often used to describe being surprised or temporarily defeated by an unexpected event is "being knocked off balance." Walsh's (1993) approach recognizes this in her suggestion of balance, almost as part of a paradoxical continuum.

Flexibility provides stability. Connectedness allows us to develop as individuals. Resources are best shared among family members. She suggests these buffers will strengthen family bonds.

Family History

Family history is important in determining the family dynamics, beliefs, and expectations for each child as well as any genetic predisposition toward certain disorders. Family influence in the child's growth and development cannot be overemphasized. This is true regardless of the family's presence or absence in the child's life on a daily basis. In families with absent parents due to divorce, death, or adoption, children tend to idealize the absent parent. In younger children, these desires to idealize the parent work in concert with age-appropriate magical thinking, to possibly create additional stress or an unrealistic view of their lives. A systems perspective is the best general rubric for understanding the various stressors and factors of influence in a child's life.

Family factors and involvement are critical components of treatment for children, adolescents, and their families. Family history commonly provides information that may be helpful in diagnosing mental illness. A history of affective illness, alcoholism, or drug abuse may predispose children to experience mood disorders (Schraufnagel, Brumback, Harper, & Weinberg, 2001), and developmental stages appear to interact with regard to specific presentations. Manic features are more likely in younger children, while depressive symptoms are more common in conjunction with adolescence (Cole et al., 2002). Bipolar disorder appears to be a factor in increased conflict between adolescents and parents, when compared to those without a diagnosis or those with depressive symptoms alone (Robertson, Kutcher, Bird, & Grasswick, 2001). Greater family conflict is often associated with adolescent depressive symptomatology (Puig-Antich et al., 1993; Sheeber, Hops, Alpert, Davis & Andrews, 1997).

As you might have gathered, diagnostic skills, which include gathering information, are different from counseling skills. Diagnostic skills include more direct questioning and use of more close-ended questions, with the therapist more clearly directing the topics being discussed. During initial information gathering and diagnostic phases, the therapist is in more of the "expert" role, which can sometimes be uncomfortable for novice therapists. Gathering information often occurs prior to the initiation of counseling sessions; that is, many professionals will structure their sessions to begin with evaluation during the first or second meeting and begin actual counseling interventions after completion of the evaluation. Other professionals will complete a preliminary evaluation and then continue an ongoing process of evaluation.

Thus far, we have considered important family information to which you must be sensitive as you gather information. There remains the nagging question of how to gather information. Many clinicians develop their own internalized standard interview over time, partially drawn from instruments, partially from supervisors, and guided by interactions with the clients themselves. However, structured interview instruments are available and may decrease your level of anxiety by ensuring that you're not going to miss any key points during the diagnostic interview. In addition to using a structured interview to assist with your assessment, you will need to develop a mechanism to recall and apply basic developmental information to your practice.

DEVELOPMENTAL THEORY INTO PRACTICE

The importance of integrating developmental theory into practice has been suggested for some time (Erikson, 1963; Gilligan, 1982; Ivey, 1986, 1991; Kegan, 1982; Kohlberg, 1981; Piaget, 1963). Indeed, after working with children and adolescents for some time, it is apparent that anyone who does not bring developmental theory into their counseling with young clients will be practicing unethically, perhaps even dangerously, by failing to identify certain aspects as outside the normal developmental range. The result is missing the opportunity for treatment or identifying a behavior as pathological when it is actually within normal developmental limits. Another danger is identifying too strongly with parents, thus losing touch with your important role as advocate, and perhaps interpreter, for your young client. All stage theories, regardless of specific content, assume a process of sequential development or progression through identified stages. Ivey's (1986) approach, however, attempts to apply aspects of developmental stage theory by linking developmental level with specific interventions tailored for each client (Ivey, Rigazio-DiGilio, & Bradford-Ivey, 1991). Linking theory and intervention through application offers a significant contribution to our work with children and adolescents. Ivey's approach provides an integration of developmental theory and application and can be used as a working guide for novice therapists.

Ivey's Cognitive-Developmental Levels

Ivey (1986) proposes four cognitive-developmental levels, an extension of Piaget's work, through which all individuals progress: (1) sensorimotor, (2) concrete, (3) formal, and (4) dialectic or systemic. No age ranges are provided, because Ivey (1999) did not consider the stages hierarchial. The levels are outlined in the following sections with specific suggestions for intervention at each.

Work With Clients at the Sensorimotor Developmental Level   The client's behavior at the sensorimotor level is often random and disorganized. Magical thinking may be observed; however, most of the client's descriptions are fairly tangible or can be directly experienced (e.g., events that can be seen, heard, or felt). The client experiences and organizes her world through visual, auditory, and/or kinesthetic processing of the stimuli around her. The experience can be described as one of relatively immediate gratification and living in the present. Conversely, relatively immediate bursts of anger or frustration may also be observed, giving the impression of unpredictable or immature responses. Interventions focused on

helping the client gain some distance from the intensity of her emotions are appropriate for the sensorimotor cognitive-developmental level (Crespi & Generali, 1995).

Work With Clients at the Concrete Developmental Level   Ivey (1986) describes clients at the concrete cognitive-developmental level as more focused on specific details, moving beyond the immediacy of the sensorimotor stage. This orientation to detail allows the client to be aware of antecedents and consequences to events and behaviors, a strength that may be used to facilitate therapeutic work around self-observation. Self-observation at this stage is not likely to include reflection of feelings but rather the linear description of events and emotions. Many clients at this level tend to get lost in the details when describing situations, which keeps them from being able to examine feelings, motives, or other aspects that might facilitate change. Granted, this type of storytelling is similar to that observed in resistant clients, but it may have a developmental component as well. If you determine the storytelling behavior is simply developmental, then redirection is an appropriate intervention. However, if the storytelling is more consistent with resistance, more challenging or confrontational interventions may be more effective. With children and adolescents, a skill deficit approach can be helpful in identifying resistance. That is, if you explore the client's knowledge base and affective response for performing a certain task and determine that the necessary knowledge base is absent, the specific skill is absent, and the motivation is present, you are probably working with a client who requires a psycho-educational approach. Conversely, if knowledge and skills are present yet motivation absent, you are probably facing some resistance to the therapeutic work. Regardless of the presence of resistance, general interventions for clients at the concrete level of cognitive development include social skills training, communication skills, and emotion identification (Crespi & Generali, 1995).

Work With Clients at the Formal Developmental Level   Self-observation skills are present in the client at the formal operational level. Clients are able to analyze situations, recognize behavioral patterns, and compare behavior across settings (Ivey, 1986). Therapy with clients at this developmental level will begin to resemble traditional talking therapies as a result of their skill, understanding, and abilities. A level of abstraction is present in the client's thinking, as is the ability to think about oneself and others. The ability to self-observe and abstract allows for a greater range of interventions for clients at the formal cognitive-development level. Interventions requiring the recognition of patterns can be applied to many aspects of a cognitive-behavioral approach, for example.

Work With Clients at the Dialectical Developmental Level   A client operating at the dialectical level is able to integrate the various aspects of her experience across developmental levels. The client becomes aware of the interaction and influence of various life systems and events on choice and behavior. Ivey (1986) describes the individual at this level as being able to observe herself and the perspectives of others. The client can be an active participant in thinking about herself, thinking about thinking, and thinking about behavioral change (Ivey, 1986). The client has the ability to fully participate in therapy from a developmental perspective. Thus, it is more likely that resistance will be a part of therapeutic impasse at this level. However, other cognitive deficits, such as memory and information processing skills, may also interfere with the client's ability to engage in the therapeutic process, and these deficits should be ruled out as well. If prior testing has been completed at the school, for example, those results can be reviewed as part of your initial assessment.

Structured Interviews

Some clinicians, particularly in their early years of practice, are more comfortable with a structured interview format, such as the Structured Diagnostic Interview for Children and Adolescents-Revised, or DICA-R (Reich, 1997, 2000). Such a structured interview not only provides a format for the therapist to follow, but also assists with diagnosis. Using diagnostic and screening instruments such as the DICA-R or the Child Behavior Checklist (Achenbach, 1991) provide validation of developing diagnostic skills. Such confirmation is important in the continuing process of developing the ability to differentially diagnose various conditions and concerns fairly quickly.

The anxiety associated with diagnosis is often quite high for new professionals and those in training; however, structured interviews and checklists provide objective validation and may sometimes offer additional information that was overlooked. In order to be comprehensive in the diagnostic process, it is often helpful to use instruments or a structured process to decrease distractions and omissions. The Child Behavior Checklist provides a structured, efficient way to obtain information from other sources that is so vital in child assessment. Parent and teacher forms are available and can be computer scored to provide an overall diagnostic impression in such areas as social interaction and level of behavioral activity. Another instrument that produces diagnostic information is the Child and Adolescent Psychiatric Assessment. The instrument also assesses demographic factors specific to family, school, and peers (Ezpeleta, Keeler, Alantin, Costello, & Angold, 2001).

Although instruments may provide support and structure for the traditional initial interview or for those times when additional information is needed after initiation of therapy, crisis intervention usually involves no instruments other than the therapist's expertise. This situation invokes significant anxiety for some clients and therapists (Van Ornum & Mordock, 1990). Review of instruments, notes highlighting possible important areas to include, and possible developmental markers can provide essential support for those first few interviews.

SELECTING DEVELOPMENTALLY APPROPRIATE DIAGNOSTIC AND ASSESSMENT INSTRUMENTS

If prior assessment or testing has not been completed, you will need to determine the need for additional assessment beyond your initial interview. Part of this decision may be based on the constraints of the setting in which you are working, which is addressed more fully in Part three of this text, and part of the decision may be based on the clarity of the initial diagnostic impressions obtained solely on the basis of interview and history. Although each of us eventually develops our own style, it usually is adopted from a blend of what we were exposed to during our training, perhaps lifting some items from a structured interview and mixing this with our own intuitive sense and specific testing or checklists. Many people come into the field because of a desire to work with children, a basic empathy or intuitive sense. Training provides an empirical base to refine and support those intuitive senses with research and long-held applications that work. Regardless of the specific format you develop, it is critical that you remember diagnosis is a fluid process when working with children and adolescents. The diagnosis may change as the client continues to grow and develop across intellectual, physical, emotional, and social spheres. Thus, your initial assessment will provide a clinical "snapshot" of the client at that specific time, at that particular stage of development, and in her current circumstances. Changes in any of these areas will likely alter the diagnosis.

Initial diagnostic efforts will include gathering information from the child or adolescent and parents during the initial session. You may also have access to classroom observations from teachers or day-care providers and other testing that has already been completed. Parents will provide their observations about the child's behavior and information about developmental level, family and peer relationships, and medical and family histories. It is important to obtain medical history due to the biological basis for many disorders with which we work. Depression, anxiety, ADHD, conduct disorder, and oppositional defiant disorder have all been shown to have a relatively strong genetic component (Goldsmith, Buss, & Lemery, 1997; Goldsmith, Gottesman, & Lemery, 1997; Nigg & Goldsmith, 1994; Thapar & McGuffin, 1994).

Mental Status Exam

A *mental status exam* is a focused interview intended to determine the level of psychological and emotional functioning for the client at that point in time. Typically, mental status addresses such factors as the client's mood, thought capacity, and demeanor. A sample report is provided later in this chapter.

Mental status exams are used to review various systems for clients of all ages: (1) sensorium, (2) perception, (3) thinking, (4) feeling, and (5) behavior (Robinson, 2001). The exam is usually included as a separate portion of the initial interview or assessment. Specific subcategories obtained by interview and history are as follows:

- intellectual functioning
- memory and judgment
- thought content
- verbal skills
- social skills
- eye contact
- changes in sleep, including nightmares, dreams, sleepwalking or talking

- appetite disturbances
- somatic complaints
- substance abuse
- unusual thoughts or behaviors
- imaginary friends/hallucinations
- suicidal/homicidal ideation or actions
- mood/affect
- fears/worries
- behavioral concerns
- insight into behavior/problems
- peer/family relationships
- satisfaction in daily life
- strengths/assets

Accuracy in Diagnosis

In order to increase the accuracy of diagnosis with children and adolescents, it is necessary to gather information from multiple sources such as school, parents, other caregivers, and professionals. Ideally, this information gathering would involve multiple assessment measures (Essau & Petermann, 1999), but due to excessive cost and time, such a detailed and involved procedure is generally not implemented. Most professionals working with children and adolescents gather information from parents, the client, and school at a minimum.

Most standardized interviews that are available are designed and validated for children age 7 or older (McClure, Kubiszyn, & Kaslow, 2002). Examples of available interview schedules include:

- National Institute of Mental Health (NIMH) Diagnostic Interview Schedule for Children Version IV (NIMH DISC-IV) (Shaffer, Fisher, Lucas, Dulcan, & Schwab-Stone, 2000)
- Children's Interview for Psychiatric Symptoms (ChIPS) (Weller, Weller, Fristad, & Rooney, 1999)
- Schedule for Affective Disorders and Schizophrenia for School-Age Children (K-SADS-Epidemiological Version) (Orvaschel, 1995) or (K-SADS-PL-Present & Lifetime Version) (Kaufman et al., 1997)
- Anxiety Disorders Interview Schedule for DSM-IV: Child Version (ADIS for DSM-IV:C) (Silverman & Albana, 1996)
- Diagnostic Interview Schedule for Children and Adolescents-Revised (DICA-R) (Reich, 1997)
- Children's Depression Inventory (Kovacs, 1992)
- Conners Rating Scale (Conners, 1997)
- What I Think & Feel (Reynolds & Richmond, 1985)
- Wechsler Intelligence Scale for Children (Wechsler, 1991)
- Child Symptom Inventory (Sprafkin, Gadow, Salisbury, Schneider, & Loney, 2002)

Although each instrument provides structure, the level of structure and length varies by instrument. All require training, but highly structured interviews require less. Computerized versions are available for most of the instruments.

Rating scales are sometimes used as self-report measures, for parent or teacher report, or for use by the clinician. Examples include:

- Beck Depression Inventory, Multidimensional Anxiety Scale for Children (March et al., 1997)
- Eating Disorders Inventory (EDI) (Garner, 2002)
- Parent and school input through the use of the Child Behavior Checklist (CBCL) (Achenbach, 1991) and the Conners' checklist focusing on ADHD symptoms

These instruments can be helpful, particularly if a comprehensive or multidisciplinary evaluation is planned. However, most practitioners develop their own version of a structured interview or diagnostic schedule. The BEACON approach, discussed in Chapter 4, is a model offered by the author to provide guidelines for developing your own approach. The goal of assessment, interviews, or evaluation is to provide adequate information to make a clinical determination of the presenting problem. This case conceptualization will guide your hypotheses and interventions; however, coming to a conclusion is not always straightforward or direct, particularly with children and adolescents. The individual aspects of development can cloud the diagnostic process, as can cultural and family issues.

DIFFERENTIAL DIAGNOSIS: FIGURING OUT WHAT'S GOING ON

Between family concerns, developmental issues, and personality characteristics, sometimes it's challenging to come up with a diagnosis. Even ADHD symptoms can mimic a residue of emotional concerns. Teasing out differences from memory or concentration problems associated with ADHD versus emotional concerns or abuse can be a challenging differential diagnosis. *Differential diagnosis* requires an understanding of the nature of possible disorders. It is helpful to think of the manifestation of the disorder as being on a continuum. For example, picture the classic symptoms of attention deficit with hyperactivity at the center of a continuum; at one extreme is attention deficit without hyperactivity or behavioral concerns, and at the other extreme is attention deficit with hyperactivity and impulse control problems so severe that the behavioral component is approaching that of conduct disorder.

Using the concept of a continuum of symptoms for varying presentations of the same disorder can help you be more clear in your definition of a disorder. A flexible view of diagnosis is one that combines the "essential" features of a disorder with those that may vary. For example, with ADHD, the essential feature is that of inattention. Additional symptoms include behavioral components, such as impulsivity, acting out, defiance, a feeling that the rules don't apply to them or that they don't need to be bothered by consequences, or a feeling that they are somewhat equal to adults in their environment.

History provides another important frame for defining "essential" features. How long have parents noticed the behaviors or symptoms about which they are concerned? In most cases of organic or classic ADHD, the symptoms will have been present since the child's matriculation into the public school system, although such presentation may occur earlier if children are enrolled in preschool or day care. Usually, the clash of a need for structure and self-control with the child's idiosyncratic need for following her internal rules is observed at this time.

However, if the symptoms don't manifest until fifth grade or junior high, the history needs to be viewed in terms of other types of life experiences that may have changed the child's behavior. This is not to imply that a traumatic event must have occurred if these symptoms begin to manifest at this age, but a close examination of history will be helpful. The child could have experienced something of which the parents are unaware or a shared life event, such as a family move, in a completely different way than other family members have.

Another potentially confusing aspect of differential diagnosis is the shared presentation of many types of symptoms. Just as emotional disorders can mimic ADHD symptoms, keep in mind that other disorders may have a similar overlay. Many disorders "cluster" together: Components of obsessive compulsive symptoms may also be present in other forms of anxiety. For example, features of autism, typically social components, may coexist with ADHD. Features of ADHD may be mimicked in children or adolescents who are feeling depressed or anxious or are experiencing post-traumatic stress disorder (PTSD). The intrusive thoughts associated with PTSD may provoke a reaction consistent with an attention deficit.

Pushing Through

When dealing with co-morbid disorders, it is generally necessary to identify each symptom of concern and understand the diagnosis in order to design our interventions. Differential diagnosis helps identify specific components or areas of concern in treatment planning. Treatment planning and diagnosis are ongoing aspects of therapy for children and adolescents. Additional information is likely to come out as you continue working with a child or adolescent and her family. The additional information often requires that you modify your initial diagnosis or differentiate between two or more diagnoses. The *Diagnostic & Statistical Manual* (DSM) (American Psychiatric Association, 1994) is a wonderful resource for differential diagnosis, however the following process may be helpful in distinguishing between disorders.

The key to making a differential diagnosis is distinguishing between behaviors that are "hallmarks" or identifying features of a disorder from those that may be lesser symptoms of another disorder or simply developmental presentations that are normal markers within the life of a child or adolescent. Even with normal developmental markers, the timing and intensity of the presentation can vary, requiring attention to both the details of development and the definitions of disorders.

A helpful outline for making distinctions of differential diagnosis includes:

- a careful history (including behavior and family)
- sensitivity to onset of symptoms
- severity, consistency, and duration of symptoms
- significant changes within the individual's life and family
- medical conditions

Obviously, gathering information is an integral component of determining current level of development, family relationships, and appropriate interventions. A developmental perspective can be applied to this phase as well.

Gathering Information for Differential Diagnosis

It may be helpful for beginning clinicians to use objective measures to help learn to identify appropriate developmental expectations for children and adolescents physically, emotionally, intellectually, and socially. It is always best to determine if any physiological or organic bases can explain abnormal behavior in children; however, one must first determine what is considered abnormal. As part of the initial intake process, information should be obtained from the parents/guardians and other caretakers such as grandparents, babysitters, or teachers about the child's general functioning in other settings. The most recent physical exam may also provide crucial information.

History   As we have noted, attention to family history provides helpful information about potential predispositions to certain disorders. Be aware of those disorders for which there is a strong body of support for genetic predisposition (e.g., mood disorders, ADHD, substance abuse). Although we are not defined by our history, genetic or otherwise, it is a factor to be considered in differential diagnosis regarding the likelihood for presentation of certain disorders when the individual is confronted with stress, for example, or at certain developmental stages.

Onset   The presentation or onset of disorders can be sudden or gradual. In working with children and adolescents, both presentations can be challenging for differential diagnosis due to the similarity with the presentation of developmental changes. Compare the details of the client's history and onset of symptoms with the guidelines listed in the current edition of the DSM.

Severity, Consistency, and Duration of Symptoms   If symptoms are variable in their presentation, it is more likely they are related to a developmental wave or change than a specific disorder, but this is not always the case. Inconsistent presentation of symptoms is typical of some disorders, such as ADHD. Consistency of presentation also refers to consistency across settings, so your questioning will need to address the antecedents of symptoms and the settings in which they occur.

Symptoms consistent with specific disorders are usually more intense or severe in their presentation than developmental symptoms. For example, many adolescents experience crying spells. However, daily crying spells are more likely consistent with a depressive disorder than normal adolescent behavior.

Duration is related to onset in terms of how long the symptom has been present but also can refer to the duration of each episode. To use our example of crying spells, each occurrence may last one hour, but the onset was only last week, and frequency has been only once a week. Contrast that with one-hour crying spells that have occurred almost daily over the past month. These examples illustrate the process of differential diagnosis on a small scale.

Accompanying Trauma or Life Events   Determining whether a response is stable over time or has presented after specific changes within the individual's life is an important determinant in the process of differential diagnosis. When inquiring about symptom onset, ask about other life events, trauma, or changes in the family around the same time. Clients and family members often have difficulty making these connections because the particular trauma may have affected others in the family as well. If the presentation of symptoms can be linked to specific changes within the individual's life, such as the death of a grandparent or a family move, the symptoms are more likely a reaction to loss or trauma. That information provides the focus for your initial intervention. If those factors have been addressed without result over a reasonable amount of time, the possibility of a disorder needs to be revisited. Perhaps the trauma or loss served as a trigger or catalyst for a particular disorder.

Medical Conditions   An essential step in differential diagnosis is to rule out the possibility of symptom presentation as part of a medical condition (Cummings & Wiggings, 2001). General categories of medical conditions that may affect emotional or behavioral functioning include: (a) neurological conditions, such as a brain tumor or infections to the nervous system, including HIV, (b) systemic conditions, such as hyperthyroidism, (c) side effects of prescription medications, or (d) substance abuse.

It is necessary to understand the etiology of the disorder, just as it is necessary for us to be aware of our underlying theories and assumptions that are moving the therapeutic work forward. Look for the presence of risk factors associated with the development of certain disorders. For example, risk factors for the development of anxiety disorders include a shy or quiet temperament, particularly in conjunction with anxiety in the family, avoidant coping mechanisms, or extremely stressful life situations (Dadds & Barrett, 2001). Carefully designed interventions that are tailored to fit the specific origins and symptoms will increase our ability to be effective in making changes, despite the increased challenge inherent in working with co-morbid disorders.

PHARMACOLOGICAL AGENTS/TREATMENTS

A variety of pharmacological agents are used with children. This review is not intended to be comprehensive but offers an overview of considerations regarding medication referral. Common conditions for which medication may be recommended include:

- attention deficit disorder
- childhood depression

- anxiety disorders, including separation anxiety, generalized anxiety disorder, obsessive-compulsive disorder, and/or tics
- eating disorders
- impulsive behavior

Referral to the child's pediatrician, the family's primary care physician, or a psychiatrist are the common sources to obtain assessment for medication. The more complicated the clinical picture, the more appropriate is referral to a psychiatrist in order to obtain the most effective intervention. With co-morbid or coexisting conditions, it may be necessary to use a combination of medications to treat severe, debilitating symptoms. The psychiatrist will have knowledge of the interactions between medicines and the most effective combination for resistant symptoms. The psychiatrist will also involve the family in order to obtain adequate history for medication assessment. In addition, family history may provide a clue to the most effective medication for a particular child or adolescent, based on the relative success or ineffectiveness of various medications for the parent or other family member. It is important to remember the potential interaction of other medications, other medical conditions, and stress on the effectiveness of medications. Some families also have a bias against the use of medication, which may interfere with the young client's compliance. Children and adolescents often take their cue from parents regarding feelings about medication and therapy in general.

Additionally, if a child or adolescent is not diagnosed with a condition that may benefit from medication until long after the initial onset, the client may have become used to compensating for the disorder in a specific way. She may feel uncomfortable about using medication because she does not like the way it makes her feel. A similar complication in the use of medications is that of tolerance developing to its effects. Anecdotal reports and clinical studies report relative ineffectiveness of certain medications, particularly stimulants, over varying amounts of time, ranging from one month to a few years. The general response to tolerance is to increase the dosage or add another medication in combination with the initial dose; however, resumed effectiveness is also noted after a medication hiatus or following a switch to another medication. In certain cases, the effectiveness is increased after these modifications to the regime, and the original effect is regained (Ross, Fischhoff, & Davenport, 2002).

Commonly used medications for ADHD include stimulants; however if accompanying depressive symptoms are present, an antidepressant may be added or may be selected as a first choice, aiming for a combined effect. In some younger children who may still be experiencing enuresis (bed-wetting), imipramine is often selected as a first choice because of the combined effect on attention, enuresis, and depressive symptoms.

Commonly prescribed antidepressants for children and adolescents include selective serotonin reuptake inhibitors (SSRIs), such as Paxil and Zoloft as first-order interventions. For clients with more complicated biochemistry or recalcitrant symptoms, Prozac, Effexor, Celexa, or.Wellbutrin may also be used. Anxiety disorders may also be initially treated with SSRIs, depending on the severity of the symptoms. Sertraline, an SSRI, has been recently tested to be effective in children as well (Rynn, Siqueland, & Rickels, 2001). Fluvoxamine has been used in trials of several anxiety disorders, including obsessive compulsive disorder, social phobia, separation anxiety disorder, and generalized anxiety disorder, with positive results (Cheer & Figgitt, 2002). As with most disorders, the optimal treatment intervention uses a combination of medication and therapy to achieve the most enduring results. The medication provides a "window of opportunity" for the child or adolescent to learn and implement other coping and management skills.

Anorexia and bulimia have been shown to respond positively to pharmacological intervention in certain individuals, including children and adolescents. Diagnosis is an ongoing process with eating disorders to assess the impact of developmental changes and the ongoing effectiveness of medication interventions. Bulimia nervosa symptoms decrease in frequency and intensity with the use of antidepressants in short-term treatment (Kotler & Walsh, 2000). As with mood disorders and most other problems, the most effective treatments combine the use of medication, as needed, and psychotherapy.

SSRIs are also helpful in treating OCD. In studies, this class of medication has been effective with few, if any, side effects. Sertraline, fluoxetine, and fluoxamine also produced positive results in studies. More positive and enduring results were observed in those clients who participate in cognitive behavioral therapy in addition to taking medication. Long-term follow-up indicated medication cessation after one or two years without negative effect (Thomsen, 2000). Fluoxetine has also been studied with regard to its effectiveness on PTSD symptoms in children and adolescents. Even in relatively short duration (30 to 76 days), significant improvement in symptoms was reported. Reduced frequency and duration of symptoms was observed in clients taking fluoxetine. Specifically, reexperiencing, avoidant behaviors, general affective numbing, and arousal were decreased (Yorbik, Dikkatli, Cansever, & Soehmen, 2001). Tegratol is sometimes used for control of seizures and behavior in resistant cases.

Risperidone is sometimes used in cases where other pharmacological treatments have been unsuccessful. Although its primary use has been identified as an atypical anti-pychotic medication, its use has also been associated with ADHD, conduct disorder, oppositional defiant disorder, autism, Asperger's syndrome, pervasive developmental disorder, anxiety, depression, dysthymia, schizophrenia, adjustment disorder, OCD, and other unspecified behavior disorders (Simeon, Milin, & Walker, 2002).

Legitimate concerns exist on the part of parents and professionals regarding the use of psychotropic medication with very young children. However, the severity of the presenting concerns for many young children warrants some type of intervention for various reasons. Developmentally speaking, children of this young age are often unable to control or even monitor their own behaviors simply because it is beyond their developmental level to be able to perform such sophisticated functions. Many parents hold unrealistic expectations about a child's level of functioning, and effective therapy may require psycho-educational intervention in addition to the medication or other therapies that have been prescribed. Parents may need to maintain a more active role throughout the life of a child who has difficulty providing her own structure and appropriate direction. Whether the family chooses to use medication and whether the medication is ineffective or a positive adjunct to other therapeutic interventions, parents remain the primary force in their children's lives (Cummings & Wiggings, 2001).

INITIAL TREATMENT PLAN

Name: _____

Date of Birth: _____

Dates of Evaluation: _____

Intake Screening: _____ (if you were assisted by another individual)

Reason for Evaluation/Identifying Data: _____

_____

Client is a _____-year-old Caucasian male, from (geographic location), who was referred by (referral source and geographic location) for evaluation. The family had sought services from our office in the past; however, had transferred care to another physician due to insurance constraints. Client was accompanied by his parents/foster parent/guardian, (parent(s)'s name). Client had difficulty identifying a reason for the evaluation/stated the reason for evaluation as _____. Parents expressed concerns about _____ (e.g., his inability to control his impulses at home, with peers, and in the classroom).

Client attends regular/special service classes at (name of school) in (geographic location). Parents report that he may not be able to return to the school, due to his behaviors. Client is in the custody of his biological parents/describe other custody arrangements.

Procedure

Evaluation included interview/mental status examination with client (name), and history provided by parents (name) (include information from other sources as well, e.g., school reports, previous psychological or achievement testing, medical information, or reports from social service or juvenile authorities).

History of Presenting Problems

Parents described being frustrated and uncertain regarding how to handle client (name) in the last few weeks preceding the evaluation. They reported increased aggression at home and school. He has become increasingly verbally and physically aggressive toward siblings, including a reported threat with a knife when he became angry. Parents report that he has been throwing objects in the car while parents are driving. Client has received three after-school detentions this academic year due to fighting. His

Continued

grades are steadily decreasing, despite initial efforts to improve earlier this academic year. Parents reported that client does not complete his homework. Conduct problems are reported in all classes, according to the parents. They indicate he has few friends at present.

Parents are concerned regarding client's increasing fascination with guns and knives. Client is reported to have begun playing with matches and firecrackers indoors over the past six months. He is also reported to have begun smoking. However, when parents impose limits on client (e.g., not allowing him to attend group activities), he is not affected. Frequent "blow-ups," described as angry verbal and physical outbursts, are reported by parents. Client is becoming increasingly oppositional against parents' attempts to redirect him. He frequently refuses to complete chores and often lies to parents in an attempt to "get out of" consequences or responsibilities. Family life was described as "disrupted" by parents. Communication is poor at present.

Parents described client's sleep as restless. He experiences initial insomnia and "talks" in his sleep. No concerns described regarding appetite or somatic complaints.

Prior Psychiatric History

Parents reported that client is being maintained on (medications) at the time of the evaluation, prescribed by Dr. _____. He has been receiving the current combination and dose of medications since (date). No other medications noted. Neither client nor the family is participating in any outpatient therapy at present, although a history of previous family therapy three years ago is noted. That therapy was provided by Dr. _____ and continued for (number) sessions. The family chose to terminate the services due to a change in their insurance plan.

Medical/Developmental History

Parents reported that client has a history of frequent ear infections as an infant, and had three surgeries to implant eustachian tubes. Delays noted in social skills; however, parents identified no other developmental concerns. He did receive screening at the Autism Clinic at the University Hospital and Clinics in (date). Parents report the diagnosis was "behavior problems." A neurological exam is scheduled for (date), which the family is encouraged to keep.

(For females, include information about menses and birth control here.)

Family History

Client was living with his biological parents, (parents' names), and his (list any siblings), at the time of the evaluation. (Include any information regarding custody or visitation here.) Significant problems were reported in all family relationships. No family history of mental illness or substance abuse noted.

Mental Status Examination

Client was observed to be an average nourished, _____-year-old boy, with a stocky build who appeared his stated age. He presented with flat affect and congruent mood. Client's activity level was within normal limits for his age and development. Slight distractibility was observed. Speech production and quality were generally within normal limits for his age and development.

Client appeared to be functioning in the average range of intelligence, based on his verbal skills, reasoning abilities, and general fund of knowledge. His memory for immediate, recent, and remote events was intact. Client was oriented to person, place, and time within appropriate limits for age and development. Client's judgment and insight are impaired at present. He is minimizing his angry outbursts and current academic difficulties.

Client did not evidence psychosis, thought disorder, or obsessive patterns. He denied suicidal or homicidal ideation, plan, or intent. He also denied hallucinations, and no delusions were elicited during the mental status interview. Client denied any fears or worries. He reported decreased satisfaction from daily activities over the two weeks preceding the evaluation. He has also noticed that he easily becomes angry "over nothing"; however, he denied his acting out angrily toward others. Client was able to recognize the problems created for him by his decisions to act as an adult in many situations (e.g., making decisions about whether he chooses to follow school rules). He continues to have great difficulty in recognizing the consequences of his actions and problems associated with many of his decisions.

Client reported difficulty settling down for sleep due to ruminations about the next day and described feeling tired. No problems reported with appetite or somatic complaints. He denied any history of stealing, fire-setting, cruelty to animals, or thoughts of running away, despite parental report to the opposite with some of these behaviors. He did admit to lying to "get out of trouble."

Asset

Client identified his strengths as helping his parents and playing baseball. His parents are supportive of him.

Diagnosis

Axis I   Major Depression, Single Episode (296.21)
Attention Deficit Disorder/Hyperactivity Disorder, NOS (314.9), by history Relational Problem, NOS

Axis II   No diagnosis
Rule in/out Autistic Features

Axis III   History of ear infections as an infant

Axis IV   Psychosocial stressors are moderately severe. These include conflict at home and school, declining grades, little social support.

Axis V   Current GAF: 65
Highest GAF during last year: 65

Recommendations:

The following recommendations were provided to client's parents (and client consistent with developmental level) on the final date of the evaluation.

1. Recommend outpatient, child-centered family therapy.

2. Recommend medication consult with family's primary care physician, pediatrician, or psychiatrist to determine appropriate medication intervention.

Parents were/were not in agreement with the recommendations, which were implemented upon completion of the evaluation.

_____

Deanna S. Pledge, Ph.D.

Date of Report: _____

SAMPLE REPORT: PUTTING IT ALL TOGETHER

A typical report incorporating the information gleaned from interviews is provided on pages 63–65.

This sample report is typical of that produced in an outpatient or inpatient setting. It is used as a snapshot in time for clients and their families. The report documents the rationale for the diagnoses and treatment plan, documents further action, and assesses level of commitment to the treatment by parents. Thus, the report is an important initial document, guiding the early therapy sessions.

DISCUSSION QUESTIONS

1. How might you handle the question of medication with your clients?
2. What factors are important to consider in applying developmental theory to practice?
3. Review several structured interview instruments and compare them to a general mental status exam. Formulate your own approach from this comparison.
4. Walk through your first meeting with a family. What will be important factors to remember?

APPLICATION

This part examines the phases of treatment: establishing rapport, engaging the child or adolescent in the working phase, and "sending them on their way" with their new skills (termination). Readers will learn much about application, as this part draws more heavily on clinical experience than Parts one and three.

The initial stages of counseling present many challenges for beginning and experienced therapists. Each client and family bring unique problems and perspectives that the therapist must identify and find productive ways to intervene, and interact within that system. Important aspects of that process early in treatment include establishing rapport, engaging the client and his parents, and managing multiple levels of therapeutic relationships, including confidentiality. Those aspects will be reviewed in Chapter 4.

Therapeutic work develops on the strong foundation of the relationship established in the early phases of counseling. In Chapter 5, the process of change will be discussed within the context of various therapeutic approaches. Interventions to work toward therapeutic goals will be reviewed, including expressive approaches, games, genograms, and drawing.

Finally, Therapy comes to a close in either a planned or unexpected way. Termination issues are addressed in Chapter 6, including reactions of therapists, clients, and parents, factors contributing to early termination, recognizing when the work is complete, helping the client and parents assimilate and maintain gains made in therapy, and productive ways to end the counseling relationship.

INITIAL STAGES OF COUNSELING

INTRODUCTION

This chapter explores the initial stages of counseling, including establishing rapport, engaging the child or adolescent client, managing confidentiality within a child-centered approach, establishing norms, and using play early in the therapeutic relationship. In essence, when working with a child or an adolescent within a child-centered family orientation, you are establishing parallel therapeutic relationships with the young client and his parents simultaneously. There is a balance in engaging members as equally as possible in these early stages to establish the necessary rapport. All relationships may be strained at some point during therapy, and you will need a strong alliance in order to continue therapeutic movement. Before any therapeutic movement or work can occur, rapport must be established.

GETTING STARTED WITH YOUNG CLIENTS

In a typical first interview with a child or adolescent, it's important to focus on less sensitive topics initially to help ease anxiety. Exceptions to this include those children or adolescents who obviously do not want to be in the session. For those clients, start with the resistance. This is a specific example of meeting clients where they are. You state the obvious, that the client doesn't want to be there. One essential concept communicated to the client through this direct approach is that you will behave differently than other adults in his life. The therapeutic relationship will rely on collaboration, not authority. As the therapist, you must foster the client's active participation. You respect their perspective and strive to understand their experience and their view of the world and themselves. You are an advocate for them when appropriate; however, you also hold them accountable. Such an approach fosters a more authentic interaction between you and the client, helping to establish the norm that your conversations can be different (Feldman, 2002). The client is given implicit permission to be different in the therapeutic relationship, exploring new ways of behaving. All of these underlying messages are essential. Regardless of the client's level of readiness or cooperation, these implicit messages build a strong rapport.

If the client's opposition over being present is not obvious, begin the interview by focusing on less sensitive topics, such as school, friends, pets, special interests, or leisure time activities. It is also acceptable to begin an interview by asking the child or adolescent client if he knows the purpose of the interview. If he knows—his parents have spoken with him, or he has an idea on his own—then start there. By asking about the client's understanding of the purpose of the visit, you learn about family dynamics, the client's level of self-awareness, and his readiness for change. The client's answer can guide you toward the next phase of your interview.

PRODUCTIVE PROBES: WORKING TOWARD CASE CONCEPTUALIZATION

Regardless of the level of self-awareness or age, a useful probe is that of "three wishes." You may liken it to the child's story of Aladdin, to which most clients positively respond. They are familiar with the story, boosting their level of comfort and confidence during the session. The three wishes probe is designed to explore the client's fantasies and desires. The probe is another projective technique in that the client's answer provides a good barometer of self-awareness. For example, if the family is going through a divorce, but the young child mentions nothing about the divorce in his wishes, requesting material items instead, you have information to use as you formulate your clinical hypothesis. Two possibilities are that the child is not bothered by the divorce or is denying stronger feelings.

In another example, if an adolescent wishes for more free time with friends but neglects to mention the behavioral problems that parents identified, you have received a clear message that the client is not interested or motivated in changing the behavior. Alternately, the client may not trust you enough in the first session to go into further detail. He has, however, identified an incentive for changing behavior. Spending more time with friends can be negotiated with parents as an incentive when the client shows improvement in the target behavior. You are probably beginning to notice that seemingly simple probes and questions provide a wealth of clinical information to be used throughout therapy, not just in the initial session (Feldman, 2002). You can begin to form a thread of common issues and responses to reflect back to the client during the process of developing insight.

In continuing the interview, explore fears, worries, anger, sadness, and things that make the client feel confident or happy. Identify heroes, discuss relationships with family members, and list somatic complaints, or any problems with sleep, nightmares, or eating habits. You'll want to rule in or out any suicidal ideation, mood changes, repetitive thoughts or rituals, and indications of auditory or visual hallucinations. Review feelings about school and leisure activities. Try to follow a generally logical approach and not skip around too much, as this can become confusing for the client.

Interview Techniques
Use open-ended questions whenever possible. As you become familiar with the hallmarks of various disorders or problems, your interview technique will evolve, and you will know more intuitively what questions to ask. Initially, it is best to ask a broad range of questions, allowing you to collect a great deal of the information from which to form your case conceptualization. Following the format in Chapter 3 or a structured interview format will help you develop your own approach to information gathering.

LESS VERBAL CLIENTS/NONVERBAL TECHNIQUES TO ESTABLISH RAPPORT

Younger children and those with social deficits, processing problems, or "an attitude" may not be able to express their specific concerns clearly. Such a presentation is within normal limits for younger children but presents a challenge in therapy. In these cases, verbal interactions yield little information and can serve to make the young client more uncomfortable and less likely to cooperate. You may want to supplement your interviews with drawings from the child. Prompting the client to draw a picture of family or favorite activities can provide good places to start (Veltman & Browne, 2001).

Early in one's profession, there can be some pressure to fill in silences that occur during a session. Silence can move the client toward sensitive issues in a therapeutically productive way. However, for some children or adolescents, silence can also feel uncomfortable and create distance in the relationship. Drawing or playing games can help direct therapeutic interventions, without falling into a style of communication that is similar to informal relationships in other areas of the client's life. Your discomfort with silence may also prompt you to talk about yourself, distracting the focus from therapeutic tasks. Responding to such pressure can move the interactions toward an informal style of communication that is more consistent with personal relationships. You may find that you are self-disclosing without thinking about the therapeutic impact of such statements. Although self-disclosure is used more often and is generally more straightforward with child and adolescent clients, such "sharing" can have unexpected and powerful effects on therapy (Hill & Knox, 2001; Psychopathology Committee of Group for Advancement of Psychiatry, 2001). When using self-disclosure, be certain to consider its therapeutic rationale and impact. Some minor sharing (e.g., about enjoying drawing or pets) can enhance rapport with less verbal clients.

With a less verbal and more reticent client, you will certainly need to obtain information from parents and school personnel about functioning in those areas (Thuppal, Carlson, Sprafkin, & Gadow, 2002). Similar to adults with a change in work habits, you'll want to know what changes have been observed in the child's behavior. Is the ability to perform academic tasks at the usual level? Are grades dropping? What about behavioral changes in the classroom, during recess, or with peers? Does the child continue to be involved in extracurricular activities as before? What changes are noted in behavior at home? Is the child more isolated at home, staying in his room? Is the adolescent away from home more often? Is the child or adolescent more secretive about activities and more irritable about sharing almost any kind of information? Any of these can be indications of serious concerns guiding your interview with the client and parents. Managing information during these parallel interviews is also an important part of the process.

CONFIDENTIALITY WITHIN FAMILY WORK

Limits of confidentiality need to be explained to the child or adolescent client and to the parents (Andreozzi, 1996). Parallel conversations are held with the young client and the parents addressing the limits of confidentiality (Sargent, 1997). Child and adolescent clients need to feel that they can trust the therapist and may have difficulty doing so when a child-centered family therapy approach is used (Smith, 1995; Tickle-Degnan, 2002). In this approach, the therapist meets with the child or adolescent individually but also spends time with parents individually. The purpose of this parallel process is to work with the parents on parenting, developmentally appropriate expectations, and general family issues. The focus while working with the adolescent is on individual coping skills, decision making, and perceptions (Kaslow, Smith, & Croft, 2000). Family sessions are always an option, as needed. However, if the level of conflict or hostility is too high for productive sessions, it is better to postpone joint sessions (Bale, 1993; Uribe, 1988).

Limits to confidentiality in therapy include the need to report suicidal ideation to parents and the obligations of a mandated reporter to report suspected abuse to authorities. Therapists, counselors, psychologists, teachers, school administrators, and physicians are among professionals who are mandated reporters, obligated by law to report suspected abuse to social service agencies and authorities (Foreman & Bernet, 2000). Clients need to be informed of these limitations in the initial session.

RAPPORT BUILDING WITH CHILDREN AND ADOLESCENTS

Getting in Touch With Yourself to Get in Touch With Your Clients

Part of the challenge of working as a child/adolescent therapist lies in the ability to flexibly and successfully negotiate between various aspects of yourself (Evans, 1988). For this reason, attention and awareness of personal boundaries is necessary to be effective. The age-old adage of engaging in your own personal therapy is an important component of your training (Hofberg, 2001; Mace, 2001; Williams, Coyle, & Lyons, 1999). By learning how to recognize your own boundaries, limitations, and biases, you can be a more effective clinician. The accompanying workbook provides opportunities to explore these personal issues so that they don't become an obstacle to your ability to use your internal tools to the best advantage of your clients and your work.

This "internal" work (Evans, 1988) will allow you to move more fluidly between relating and identifying with your young clients and drawing on the adult side of your training and expertise simultaneously. This challenge separates the more successful clinicians from those for whom establishing rapport is difficult. Just as with parent-child, authoritarian relationships, young clients usually don't respond well to authoritarian counselors (Grolnick & Farkas, 2002). Part of this balancing act involves being able to identify and relate just as well with parents as with the children. A definite challenge for many clinicians is the ability to shelve personal biases about parenting and being children (Andreozzi, 1996; Sargent, 1997; Tickle-Degnan, 2002).

Initial work with children can often be challenging, particularly for novice counselors. Being honest with yourself regarding your concerns and fears will make you a better therapist. Explore these feelings and concerns in the workbook to help you work through them. Familiarity with the discomfort in exploring personal issues can help make child and adolescent clients feel more at ease, thus facilitating a positive working alliance to make counseling more effective and productive. Many child and adolescent clients often don't want to be in the office in the first place. By recognizing and connecting with their discomfort, you can begin to establish rapport by building on the discomfort rather than allowing this to work against therapy before it has even begun.

Setting Expectations

Another aspect of the comfort issue relates to those children or families who may have participated in previous therapies and come to therapy with preconceived notions or expectations (Roberts, 1998). These expectations can enhance work with clients, or they may work against therapy in that setting (Borgers & Tyndall, 1982). For example, let's say a therapist begins work with a 10-year-old boy who had previously been in therapy with another counselor; the majority of their sessions were based on playing battle bots or games on the therapist's computer. If the therapist assumes that his work with this young man will begin with simply sitting and talking (as many beginning therapists assume), his task of establishing rapport is off to a difficult start from the first session. To avoid these pitfalls, it is often helpful to assess the type of previous work addressed in therapy and how the child felt about that work. If a child or adolescent comes to you thinking therapy is playing games—with no therapeutic work—reorientation becomes the first task of therapy. You must help set the norm in individual sessions similar to group work. Ask what the client liked or disliked about previous therapy. Ask what made him feel comfortable and what felt like work. All of this information can help you tailor your work to meet clients where they are. This basic premise of good therapy is even more critical in your work with children, in which you must also assess developmental level when tailoring your interventions for optimal effectiveness.

Younger Children

For most children under the age of 10, the level of comfort can be maximized by providing a warm, child-friendly environment. It's OK to set expectations around behavior, such as putting away one toy before getting out the next. This often includes toys and games; however, it is often best to set a limit around using these games in the first session. Games can be distracting before rapport and therapeutic norms are established, but you may want to use simple toys to help establish rapport (Campbell, 1993; Schaefer, 2000). This ties directly into the child's expectations about sessions. We know that most children do not request therapy themselves. This reality can set up a level of animosity between the child and the therapist even before the first session (Bale, 1993). The therapist can be labeled as the "enemy," often becoming the target of the child's anger that may have been previously directed at the parents. As soon as you begin therapy with children, you become part of their community and their family. You must exercise caution not to get pulled into unproductive roles within the family (Minuchen, Rossman, & Baker, 1978). It can be more difficult to recognize countertransference with child and adolescent clients than with adults, especially if you gloss over your own issues concerning children and families. These strong influences can be detrimental to therapy if you try to ignore them.

Multiple Levels of Rapport

The dual balancing act of establishing rapport with young clients and their families can be challenging (Feldman, 2002). We must be able to stretch ourselves, yet remain authentically present with our child clients, their parents, and all family members when in conjoint family sessions. It can be helpful to use our own perspectives from childhood, reviewed through the lens of adult experiences and professional training. Our experience, our emotions, our intellect are our tools (Bennett-Levy et al., 2001). The ability to honestly address our own issues is a key factor to achieving this stance and enhancing our own effectiveness (Hofberg, 2001; Mace, 2001; Williams, Coyle, & Lyons, 1999).

As with children in any setting, our clients can sense whether we are being authentic with them. Often the basis of such authenticity is our ability to be truly respectful of young clients. Children today receive mixed messages about their worth and value. As our society has become increasingly child-oriented, children have become more aware of their rights but less accepting of their responsibilities, creating a huge rift in many families (Ruck, Keating, Abromovitch, & Koegl, 1998). For example, it is not uncommon for children to call the child abuse hotline themselves or report on their perceptions of being abused at the hands of their parents, when no abuse has occurred. Unfortunately, for those children who are being abused, the fear of repercussion is so great that they generally do not contact authorities about the abuse (Sedlak & Broadhurst, 1996). Such life experiences can make establishing rapport more difficult.

Rapport With Children and Adolescents

Establishing rapport, whether through talk or play (Campbell, 1993), employs a similar perspective from the therapist. If you begin engaging in "nonclinical" talk with children and adolescents, you can learn many things about them: how they see the world, how they see themselves, how they feel about coming to see you, how they view their parents, what their general mood is, and what obstacles they typically face in their daily lives. In an initial session, you can see how the child reacts to new situations in his daily environment as well. As one assumes in a psychodynamic approach, the client's world and usual patterns of interaction are re-created in the therapy session. These observations begin to form the basis of your case conceptualization. Although they may not be comfortable enough to display all these patterns, attitudes, and behaviors in early sessions, young clients will likely expose certain aspects of their personality in that initial session.

Helping child and adolescent clients feel comfortable in the session is critical. Ways in which rapport may be facilitated include drawing pictures of one's family or any subject of the client's choosing if he does not wish to draw a picture of his family. Drawing a picture of the family serves a dual purpose. It not only aids in the client's level of comfort, by giving him something to focus on and keep his hands busy, but it also provides a view into the child's world. Here you may apply some of the principles of art therapy and borrow from the forensic field in helping to interpret the meaning of these drawings. Although you can make interpretations about the meaning of the drawing, check it out with the child (Dunn, O'Connor, & Levy, 2002; Veltman & Browne, 2001). Ask him to talk with you about the drawing, explaining the drawing and its meaning. When interpreting drawings, as when using any projective technique, you should err on the side of caution in making your interpretations.

For example, placement in family drawings is assumed to have some meaning about the level of closeness in relationships (Dunn, O'Connor, & Levy, 2002), similar to assumptions about where clients choose to sit during a family session. However, if a child leaves a family member out of the drawing, puts him or her in at a distance from himself, or draws a family member as an afterthought, you need to bolster your hypotheses about distance in the relationship with information from child and parent interviews. You cannot assume an omission from the drawing reflects a wish for that person to be absent, although it might. When making such projective interpretations, you must be cautious not to overinterpret (McClure, Kubiszyn, & Kaslow, 2003).

Cautionary Notes

Projective interpretations leave a lot of room for the therapist's biases to become embedded in the treatment and interpretative process (Garb, Wood, Lilienfeld, & Nezworski, 2002; Lee & Hunsley, 2003; Veltman & Browne, 2001; West, 1998). The exercises in the workbook serve as a precautionary mechanism to avoid bias in your work, helping you to make more conscious than unconscious interpretations of the child's drawings and preferences. The child may have misunderstood your directions and drawn only those persons who physically live in his home in the case of a divorced family, for example. Such a misunderstanding of directions could lead to a significant misinterpretation.

Children's minds, bodies, and emotions work differently than ours do as adults. Some of the more successful child and adolescent therapists exercise some fluidity in their ability to move back and forth between those aspects of themselves that allow them to connect with children and adolescents. Using ourselves as a tool—a vehicle for therapy—allows us to be effective. In doing so, we enhance our ability to establish rapport, to suggest appropriate interventions, and to provide genuine empathy to the young clients with whom we work. As therapists, we may be among the few adults who can make a positive connection with some of the youth with whom we work. If a client is feeling suicidal, for example, we may be the sole source of support at this moment (Garmezy, 1991; Ness & Pfeffer, 1990). For many children, particularly adolescents, feeling misunderstood and marginal is a common experience that we can turn around in therapy.

In order to connect with clients and make accurate diagnoses, we must be aware of the general development process.

DEVELOPMENTAL CONSIDERATIONS IN TREATMENT

This text is not designed to provide a comprehensive developmental overview, but it does recognize that further attention to developmental levels within the context of information gathering may be helpful. This section discusses typical expectations across age groups.

Infancy Through Age 5   Realistically, it is quite difficult to conduct therapy with children under the age of 2. For this age group, gross screening measures and physical examinations often provide the most accurate clinical picture of basic developmental functioning. The Denver Developmental Screening (Frankenburg & Dodds, 1969) is one source for determining developmental levels in this young age. For those children who may be more advanced in terms of language and fine motor skills, drawing and play therapy can provide appropriate interventions.

A common problem for beginning clinicians working with young children is to emphasize language interactions too strongly. In observing the pretend play of this younger group, caution must be taken not to overlay adult expectations or meanings onto the child's play (Watson & Guajardo, 2000). The child's motivation or understanding of the play during this time of early learning and role exploration often differs from the more directed play of later years.

For this age group, traditional language interactions are ineffective and may confuse the young client, making the child uncomfortable and rapport difficult. Some clinicians include parents as a compensatory mechanism for the lack of language development; however, if parents are included in the interview situation, the child's behavior will likely be influenced by their presence, altering the diagnostic outcome. Altering the child's behavior by involving the parents can become an issue in interviews assessing abuse, in particular, although it is important to remember that children of any age are more likely to act differently when with parents than with another adult.

Ages 5 Through 8   Most children of this age have been exposed to the school system and have become comfortable meeting with new adults or individuals to whom parents might introduce them. They also have a concept of doctors' visits from well-child appointments and of school counselors that can help them understand the interaction. These factors make it easier to begin establishing rapport early in the therapeutic relationship. Children of this age are often attracted to various toys and therapeutic items in the professional's office, and these items can also be used to increase the child's ability and willingness to engage in the therapeutic process, although certain limitations and directions are appropriate in the first few sessions. These limits help set the expectations for therapeutic interactions within the session.

Ages 8 Through 12 Children of this age may vary greatly in their presentation to a new adult, depending partially on the quality of their interactions with other adults in their environment. What types of socialization experiences the child has had should become apparent as the sessions progress. Through the child's interactions with you, his assumptions can be observed. In other words, if the child is generally successful in school and has experienced positive interactions with adults, the likelihood of establishing a positive rapport with him is increased, simply because of a history of positive relationships with adults. The expectations of these children are consistent with a positive outcome, and they will likely be able to establish a good rapport. Conversely, the task of establishing rapport is more difficult with children for whom adults represent authority figures and negative interactions or with adolescents who have frequently experienced defensive responses. Because of the astute nature of children's and adolescents' perceptive abilities, it is important to be authentic with them. Being honest and open in the therapeutic setting can provide another indication that the therapeutic relationship will be inherently different than other relationships in their lives. That assumption is a necessary foundation for rapport, as it becomes a positive tool to enhance the effectiveness of therapy.

Ages 12 Through 16 Additional resistance can be observed in children of this age group, particularly if their behavior or grades are identified as part of the presenting concern. The client's negative attitude may be compounded if he has little investment in change or is hypersensitive to it. Many adolescents develop a rebellious attitude and feel intruded upon when others identify concerns for them. They will likely become defensive as these sensitive issues are raised. It is unfortunate at one level that adolescents adopt a rebellious attitude because it can cut them off from the support they need in addressing the myriad life transitions associated with this phase of life; however for many adolescents, the rebelliousness serves to help them begin to separate from their family. Gilligan (1982) notes that for many young females, sexual activity is viewed as a means to achieve separation from the family. However, if pursued prior to completion of a healthy individuation process, the sexual relationship or resulting pregnancy can become a substitute for the incomplete separation from the parents. Ivey (1991) notes similar pressures for young men as they approach separation and individuation, describing the push to "become a man" in sexual, emotional, and financial terms before being psychologically prepared to do so. The ambiguity experienced as a result can lead to unhealthy expression of concerns through conflict or destructive acting out. Ivey (1991) suggests that these extreme feelings of discomfort and inner conflict often lead adolescents to experiment with drugs and alcohol, almost as a form of self-medication. Those adolescents who are less healthy respond to the development challenge of separation and individuation in ways that often set the stage for serious problems due to an inability to make mature decisions when faced with major life choices (Crespi & Generali, 1995). Typical adolescent behaviors that are examples of unhealthy responses include defensiveness, rebelliousness, or excessive conformity.

Ages 15 Through 19   Mixed reactions continue to be seen in late adolescence, dependent on the adolescent's progression through the separation/individuation process. Ivey (1991) highlights the critical importance of a solid developmental foundation of connections and attachments in order to facilitate the separation and individuation process. Individual differences are a crucial part of clients' responses in therapy as well as in their daily lives. For example, if significant animosity has built up in the client's family and social support systems, the adolescent is much more likely to be suspicious of therapeutic interactions with them. Obviously, establishing rapport can be more difficult in these cases, and you may need to remind yourself and your clients' parents of the time it can take to establish a working alliance.

The client's personal experience can be a factor in establishing rapport, but many adolescents feel good about the opportunity to come in for sessions. As a result of their continued intellectual development and increased self-awareness, adolescents can be ideal clients with whom to work, despite anecdotal reports to the contrary.

DIAGNOSTIC CONSIDERATIONS WITH CHILDREN AND ADOLESCENTS

After establishing rapport, reviewing confidentiality, and completing the interview, you will assimilate the information for the initial diagnosis. A working diagnosis is usually provided in feedback to the family at the end of the initial session, providing a starting place for therapy. As noted in Chapter 3, diagnosis is an ongoing process with children and teens, primarily due to their continuing growth and development. For this reason, you may revisit the diagnostic process at times during the course of therapy. Usually the ongoing diagnostic process is less formal and may involve only a few questions, updating specific symptoms or behavioral changes. Other ethical issues around the diagnostic process with children and adolescents are addressed in Chapter 11.

Diagnosis in children and adolescents is best approached conservatively. Due to the ever-changing nature of the level of functioning for children and adolescents as a result of their ongoing development, it is best to approach diagnosis, or "labeling" a child, with caution. In order to follow the professional adage to "do no harm," it is necessary to think about the process of labeling a child with a serious disorder that may follow him throughout his academic career and have potential effects on the rest of his life. Of course, the application of accurate and appropriate diagnoses can help a child receive the care and special services he needs. However, being too quick to provide a diagnostic label for a condition that may also be influenced by development and situational factors—and therefore, subject to change—can prove detrimental for the child and exemplifies unethical practice with this population of clients.

Developmental Considerations

Diagnosis in children and adolescents (and even adults at certain life stages) can be affected by developmental level. In addition, due to the close interactive nature of family relationships and the suggestibility of children, their behavior and choices may also be influenced by parents' behaviors or expectations (McClure, Kubiszyn, & Kaslow, 2002). Although the use of a joint interview or interactive assessment session between parents and child or adolescent is often suggested in the professional literature to observe and assess potential interactive effects within the family, few standardized procedures exist for implementation (Mash & Foster, 2001; Zeanah, 2000). The same rationale underlies most family therapy approaches, suggesting that counseling sessions replicate interactions from the home (Sugarman, Nemiroff, & Greenson, 2000). Thus, our observations of parent/child interactions will usually provide information regarding potential problems with communication, parental emotional support, and levels of enmeshment and distance.

Another important nonverbal aspect of observing clients is attention to discrepancies between verbal and nonverbal presentation. For example, a child may say there are no problems as he sits alone with arms crossed, head down, and a scowl on his face. Similarly, a client may smile as he describes a sibling getting hurt or a pet dying. Whenever behaviors are incongruent with the words the client is using, you have an opportunity to gently confront these discrepancies. By doing so, you are helping the client connect with his affect or emotions and giving him permission to recognize and work through issues he may have been hiding, denying, or uncertain of how to manage.

Accuracy in Diagnosis

To increase the accuracy of diagnosis with children and adolescents, it is necessary to gather information from multiple sources such as school, parents, other caregivers and professionals and ideally to involve multiple assessment measures (Essau & Petermann, 1999). However due to excessive cost and time, such a detailed and involved procedure is generally not implemented. Most professionals working with children and adolescents gather information from parents, the client, and school, at a minimum.

The instruments outlined in Chapter 3 can be helpful, but, most practitioners develop their own interview style. The BEACON approach offers guidelines for developing your own approach to initial interviews and to providing a focus to initial sessions.

BEACON APPROACH TO THERAPY WITH CHILDREN AND ADOLESCENTS

Managing the cues from your clients and their parents during the initial session will guide your rapport building and provide clues for the state of the therapeutic relationship throughout treatment. The BEACON model is provided as a general guideline for your clinical work. We'll talk first about what to look for generally and then review a specific example of parts of an initial session.

Using Your BEACON to Manage the Initial Session

BEACON is an acronym representing cues to watch for in an initial session with a young client. Carefully observe these aspects of presentation.

Behavior Assess the client's behavior/activity level. Is it normal, excessive, delayed, or slow? At the same time, consider the child's presentation and demeanor. Would you characterize it as sullen, shy, or anxious, for example? Finally, pay attention to the child's general appearance.

Eye contact Too much or too little? Some "looking away" is normal in the first session.

Attitude Would you characterize the client's attitude as cocky, confident, troubled, or indifferent?

Comfort and cooperation How does the client respond to a new adult, an authority figure? In terms of cooperative behavior, does the client try to pick a fight or, conversely, seem too compliant? Would you describe the client as cooperative or uncooperative?

On task Rate the client's ability to participate in the session. Consider the combination of eye contact, demeanor, attitude, talkativeness, self-awareness, attention span, and ability to focus.

Nuances of nonverbal cues, mood, and affect The appropriate range for an initial interview may vary from quiet or shy to smiling and talkative. Try not to confuse sullen with depressed affect.

How to Respond Based on a BEACON Assessment

Behavior Considering the young client's behavior, this initial observation is focused solely on whether the activity level is within normal limits, excessive for the interview, delayed, or too slow for the developmental level and situation. As a clinician, you must remember the context for these conclusions is drawn from an artificial first meeting with a professional the child or adolescent does not know. In the school or home setting, his behavior may be quite different (more distracted or more attention-seeking, for example). Although a more typical presentation will develop in your sessions over time, it will take a few sessions before the client's behavior is more consistent with his behavior in other settings. For some young clients, it may be even longer before that presentation develops, if at all. This is part of the value of natural observation. Although natural observation may not be an option for you in some treatment settings, at a minimum, information can be obtained from teachers or others who are working with the child in that setting.

In responding to a child's presentation and demeanor, consider these common presentations:

- *Sullen* The sullen adolescent may also present as surly. You may encounter negative attitude that is overlaid onto you from previous interactions with other adults. In this first session, the power of first impressions is palpable. You must try to connect, but don't try too hard—he'll sense that, too. Confront the adolescent regarding his feelings about the session. Explore his perception of why he is in your office. By recognizing the "elephant in the room," you can defuse some of the client's anger by encouraging him to talk. Granted, it may be the only session you have with the adolescent if he is truly reticent, but perhaps a seed has been planted. For the sullen child or adolescent client, there may be an association between a counselor's office and getting in trouble. The parents may have presented coming in for counseling as an idle threat long before their feet crossed the threshold of your door, giving the child a preconceived expectation about your interactions. Explore the child's expectations. He may fear consequences, testing, or being asked things he doesn't know (which may include motivations for the behavior that brought him to your office).
- *Shy* Don't come on too strongly. Suggest and offer adjunctive activities for the child or even some adolescents to "fiddle with" while talking with you. By providing a physical or kinesthetic focus, some of the client's nervous energy is dispelled appropriately. He can focus on the ball, pin sculpture, or drawing while talking less self-consciously about what he's thinking and feeling. Talk with both children and adolescents about favorite things or pets to help them become more comfortable. If all else fails, simply follow your structured interview after an initial conversation.
- *Anxious* It is important to help the client feel comfortable in your office. Similar to the shy client, giving an anxious client something to do can be helpful in discharging his anxiety. It is also helpful to explore specific fears or concerns the client may have. He may be afraid of being tested or about what he'll be asked to do, for example.

Eye Contact   Too much eye contact in the form of frequent staring may suggest that the client is intrigued or has poor social skills. Conversely, too little eye contact may indicate that the child may be nervous around new people, may be uncomfortable socially, or may have autistic or attention deficit features, or some form of developmental delay. In some cases, the young client may be simply distracted by the toys and new items in the office. Some "looking away" is normal in the first session as the client checks things out.

Attitude   A young client's attitude in the initial session offers several clues on how the therapist should respond:

- *Cocky*   This attitude is often seen in adolescent clients during the initial presentation and sometimes throughout treatment. The cocky attitude can provide a psychological defense for the adolescent, protecting him from taking responsibility for behaviors that may be extreme from his usual responses or from the knowledge that his current choices and behaviors are hurting the parents he loves and respects (even though those feelings may not be apparent at present).

- *Confident*   These clients appear to feel good about themselves and how their life is going at present. This attitude may be consistent with concealing the truth of the problems from themselves and their parents, or it may be consistent with the parents erroneously identifying the child or adolescent as the "problem."

- *Troubled*   This attitude may indicate true concern about their behaviors, relationships, and current situation, or it may be consistent with confusion about the consequences of their actions.

- *Indifferent*   These children or adolescents may be aware of concerns but show little remorse or concern for their actions or the consequences of their actions. This attitude is consistent with clients who lack the skill or ability to observe or monitor themselves, their behavior, and their choices.

Comfort and Cooperation   Comfort levels with a strange, new adult, an authority figure, may vary widely. Some gifted children are more comfortable with adults than peers and may not present with any apparent problems to you in the first few sessions. Gathering additional information is even more critical with this group. Children who have a history of problems at school, at home, or in the community will have a more difficult time establishing rapport, which may be due to a cumulative distrust of authority figures from previous experiences.

In terms of cooperative behavior, some clients may be genuinely cooperative. Other factors observed in such a genuine presentation include an honest representation of presenting concerns (at an age-appropriate level) and an ability to engage in some discussion of attempts to change or a desire for change.

Many clients who present in an uncooperative fashion are actually angry with their parents for bringing them into the session. In this presentation, the technique of directly addressing their concerns about being in the office is usually the most effective way to establish rapport.

Some child and adolescent clients may present as angry, defiant, or challenging in order to distract from sensitive issues or real concerns. Conversely, some young clients may seem too compliant. This type of behavior can be consistent with children or adolescents who use a "good" presentation to avoid confrontations about their misbehaviors. An overly compliant presentation can be similar to "faking good" on an instrument such as the Minnesota Multi-phasic Personality Inventory (MMPI) (Graham, 2000). The behavioral overcompensation essentially serves as a distraction from the concerns at hand. Exploring interactions with peers by talking with parents or teachers may provide a more realistic presentation of the client's general demeanor. Information gathered from these additional sources may be used in the working phases of treatment as a confrontation of the discrepancy between the client's demeanor with you and reports from other sources.

On Task   The combination of eye contact, demeanor, attitude, talkativeness, self-awareness, and respect for boundaries can help you assess the client's ability to participate in the session. Is the child distractible and unable to attend to you? Is the child more interested in objects than in you? Do you find yourself feeling frustrated with the child? These feelings are probably consistent with the feelings and reactions of other adults in the child's life. Remember that part of your role is to respond differently than other adults in the client's life. Is the child wandering around the room or able to sit and talk (relative to age)? This could be a display of anxiety or resistance.

Nuances of Nonverbal Cues, Mood, and Affect   The appropriate range for an initial interview may vary from quiet or shy to smiling and talkative. Confusing sullen with depressed affect could have a profound impact on the course of therapy. Explore the client's perception of why he is at the interview and how he feels about it to help make this distinction.

An effective approach is to explore with the child or adolescent client things that make the client feel happy, sad, mad, scared, or worried. Exploring each emotional state and what the client is able to identify (or not) can provide a sense of the client's self-awareness and understanding of consequences and give some indication of potential prognosis or success in treatment.

PROCEDURES FOR THE INITIAL SESSION

It's best to begin with the basics when approaching the initial interview. Just as we observe our clients' behaviors, they are likely to make assumptions about therapy from our behaviors. A first step is to determine who will go first. Clients and their families may make assumptions on the basis of your choices about the structure and order of the interview.

Generally speaking, it is best to have separate interviews with the parents and the child or adolescent. Having separate interviews serves several purposes. Parents and young clients will feel more comfortable and be more likely to speak without feeling the need to censor themselves in this setting. However, if you plan to work only in a family mode, you may want to have the entire family come in initially so that you may observe their interactional patterns and roles with one another. When using a child-centered family approach, it is not necessary to bring everyone together initially, and separate interviews can actually provide you with a clearer understanding of the parents and the client from the outset.

You may want to choose the order of interviews in certain cases. For example, if the child is very young and uncomfortable meeting alone with new people or if the presenting issue centers on separation anxiety, it is best to start with parents and the client. The parents can be excused once the child becomes comfortabl new setting. With children or adolescents whose acting-out behavior has become problematic and may include control issues within the family, some therapists will elect to have the parents come in first to send a subtle message of alliance between the therapist and parents. Others will elect to have the young client come first to send a positive message about his role in therapy, in the hopes of enhancing rapport.

Within a child-centered family approach, as an example, the author divides the use of the initial session relatively equally between the parents and the child or adolescent in individual sessions. In other words, the sessions are approximately 30 minutes each, with additional background having been provided by the parents during an initial phone call. The intake form is completed by parents with younger children and often is completed jointly by families with an adolescent. Even the manner in which the family chooses to complete the information can begin to provide early diagnostic observations. The family's behavior in the waiting area can often be the closest you will come in private practice to naturalistic observations of family interactions. For counselors in other settings, such as schools, residential centers, and home-based treatments, more opportunity for such observations is provided.

Noticing Nonverbal Behavior in Families

As you observe, remember the basics of naturalistic observation embedded within your clinical skills of observation. What is the body language between the parent and child or adolescent? Do they choose to sit together or apart? Is it obvious they are together as a family, or does it appear that no apparent connection exists between family members? In the latter instance, review the family dynamics. If there is a divorce in the family and both parents have chosen to participate for the session, what is the apparent relationship between the parents and between each of the parents and the child or adolescent? In the few minutes before you begin the formal session with the family, you can glean a wealth of information that will provide a framework regarding family dynamics. It may prompt specific questions that you would like to ask or add to your own interview approach.

Additional aspects of the naturalistic observation include general demeanor, general level of comfort with a new individual, level of anxiety or other feelings about the session, gait, and level of engagement in the session.

SAMPLE INTERVIEW PROCEDURE WITH AN ADOLESCENT CLIENT

The following is provided as a typical example of an early interview.

To begin the interview, invite the adolescent to make himself comfortable in the interview room. Allow him to sit where he likes and observe his demeanor. Does he "plop" or "sprawl" on the furniture? Does he seem anxious or angry, closed or open? Notice if he waits for you to sit down. All these observations offer clues to the client's understanding of relationships with adults and authority figures. As noted elsewhere, if the adolescent appears sullen or angry, start there.

> THERAPIST: *How did you feel about coming in today?*
>
> CLIENT: *(shrugs shoulders)*
>
> THERAPIST: *Well, it seems like you're not feeling very happy about being here. I can understand that. There are probably lots of other things you'd rather be doing than sitting in some stranger's office, talking about things you may not want to talk about. Whose idea was it to come in today?*
>
> CLIENT: *(not quite so slouched—a bit more eye contact—checking out the therapist). My mom—it was a stupid idea. There's nothing wrong. Coming to a counselor is so stupid. I've done it before, and it doesn't do any good.*
>
> THERAPIST: *It's hard to come in and talk about things. What did your mom want you to talk about?*
>
> CLIENT: *She's always getting on me about something. I don't know why she thinks talking to anybody else is going to do any good. They just have all these stupid rules.*
>
> THERAPIST: *Oh, so you guys sometimes fight about the rules?*
>
> CLIENT: *Yeah, the rules. Like getting home on time and doing chores and homework.*
>
> THERAPIST: *Yeah, that happens in lots of families with whom I work. The parents see things one way and kids see things another way. It makes it really hard to talk, and sometimes just feels bad, especially if it feels like you used to get along.*
>
> CLIENT: *Yeah, they never used to get on me like they do now. It feels like I can't do anything right and they don't care anymore. (tears up)*
>
> THERAPIST: *Seems like it hurts, too.*
>
> CLIENT: *Yeah, makes me mad, too—like they don't trust me.*

At the end of the session, the therapy concludes with this comment: "Seems like you've talked about some pretty hard things today. How would you feel about coming back for another session?"

NONDIRECTIVE APPROACHES AND NONVERBAL BEHAVIORS IN CHILDREN

To begin the initial session with a younger child, invite the child to make himself comfortable. Observe his reaction to any toys, games, or interesting objects you have in the room. Does he sit and direct attention toward you, at least initially, or does he immediately begin roaming the room and begin picking up objects? You may want to place a limit on use of toys during the initial interview to avoid distractions in the brief time available for assessment. In lieu of freely exploring the toys, you may offer younger and older, fidgety children the use of a "fiddle basket" containing such items as a stress ball or Slinky to occupy his hands and attention as he talks (Schaefer, 2000). It can be extremely uncomfortable for young children to just sit and talk. This is a common mistake among some therapists in terms of professional expectations about the child's ability to engage as if he were an adult. The compromise of offering small objects for busy fingers or the opportunity to draw a picture of his family usually works best in the initial session. This approach offers a blend of structure and limits in some areas—establishing initial norms—while providing freedom and exploration at another level, that of personal and emotional expression. Such a blending allows a frame for work to begin even from the first session. With active children, you may need to redirect them.

Excerpts From Sample Confidentiality Discussions

THERAPIST: *The things we talk about are confidential. Do you know what that means? . . . Yes, like private. It means that I'm not going to tell your parents everything we talk about. Now, I will tell them if you talk about ideas of hurting yourself or others, or if someone is hurting you. It's kind of a safety thing. We want you to be safe, and your parents need to know. Sometimes other things come up that I might think are important to talk with your parents about, and I'll tell you that's how I feel. Then we can decide how to talk with them about it. It's usually best if we all sit down together and talk about it. I know that might seem kind of hard or scary right now, but that's why I'm here to help with those hard conversations—to help you learn how to have those conversations with them on your own. Because I'm not part of your family and won't always be there to help with those conversations.*

I'll be telling your parents the same thing, so they understand what's going on, too. It's completely your decision if you want to tell them what we talk about any other times. Usually I will meet with them a few minutes at the beginning or the end of each session, too—for scheduling and to let them talk with me about how they're seeing things because we know parents see things differently than kids. But I won't be telling them what you said when I meet with them. I'll be giving them ideas for themselves and let them know generally how things are going. Usually, we meet for three or four sessions and decide how it's going. That gives us time to get used to each other and see if meeting helps things improve or feel better.

How does all that sound? Does it make sense?

The parallel conversation with parents covers the same basic issues: limits of confidentiality, the parameters and goals of the child-centered family approach, and the general time frame for the general treatment plan. A balance is needed for this discussion and in general throughout the course of treatment, when using a child-centered family approach (Evans, 1988).

PRESSURES OUTSIDE THERAPY ON CLIENTS

In certain families and communities, children or adolescents may be required (due to circumstances beyond their individual control) to take on adult responsibilities such as watching younger siblings after school or taking a job to help with expenses. While such arrangements have been common in families for generations, what has been overlooked is the ambivalent experience for the child or adolescent. That ambivalent experience is one of being required to act as an adult—being pushed beyond their normal developmental level when it is convenient for the parent—and then being asked to shrink back to the role of a child, being controlled instead of being in control. The elasticity required of children in such situations is far beyond what their normal developmental resources can handle, and as a result, we often see increased acting out or negative attitude.

For children, talking directly about their feelings is often not an option, and even if they are able to do so, it may be acting in direct opposition to family rules and expectations, thus creating additional anxiety. Parents may not understand or recognize this difficult process for children. As a result, children in these situations can find themselves feeling stuck with feelings and reactions larger than they can comfortably handle. Parents are often unaware of the challenges being placed on their children by chores or family requirements, such as sibling supervision. It is often part of our role to help parents understand the quandaries into which they place their children and to work to extricate all family members from these conflicting roles.

DISCUSSION QUESTIONS

1. What important factors must be considered in diagnosis with children and adolescents?
2. Discuss the process of multiple rapport building when working with children and adolescents in a child-centered family approach.
3. Apply the BEACON model to a case example of your own.
4. What factors around structure and order are important to consider when initiating a session?
5. How do personal biases work against authenticity in sessions?

WORKING STAGES OF COUNSELING

INTRODUCTION

This chapter reviews the process of using the therapeutic alliance established in the initial phase of counseling to maintain engagement with the client and facilitate the work of counseling. The *working phase* of counseling generally refers to the mid-portion of therapy. The client has become comfortable with the therapist and feels safe enough to begin looking at difficult issues or make a commitment to behavioral change. It is that time following the initial rapport-building stage and evaluation, beginning at approximately the third session and continuing until prior to termination, approximately the final two sessions. In certain treatment settings or with certain clients, however, you may only have one or two sessions, if there is a drop-in format or premature termination. Issues involving termination will be addressed in Chapter 6.

The working stage requires that the client and parents are engaged in the process of therapy, meaning that goals have been identified and agreed upon. This chapter presents techniques to address various problems using the therapeutic alliance to facilitate that process. We begin by discussing the client's motivation to participate in ongoing sessions.

MOTIVATION AND INVESTMENT FOR TREATMENT

A general assumption in working with adults is that the pain created by symptoms and current circumstances is sufficient to motivate them to work in session. This assumption is often inaccurate for children and adolescents who become our clients (Berns, 2001). First, most children and adolescents do not ask to come for treatment, and choice can be an important component of motivation (Enright, 1975). Secondly, for children and some adolescents who often cope by "forgetting" about concerns, the therapeutic process, which calls attention to matters they would rather forget, can be more stressful than the consequences of the behavior itself. This conflict is evident in the example of a child who "chooses" to be the class clown rather than admit to a learning problem. Child clients may manifest these concerns by acting out in session or resisting coming to the appointment. They may become destructive during the session when anger has not previously been part of their play themes. Some child clients may clam up in an attempt to control or "punish" the therapist or their parents by being uncooperative in session. Adolescents may "forget" appointments. An oppositional young client, regardless of age, may take the bus home or go to a friend's to avoid the appointment even when she's been reminded of it. All of these acting-out behaviors convey the young client's true feelings about the sessions; that is, their behavior conveys their anger, their lack of investment in the therapeutic work, or their discomfort with the content of the sessions.

These examples represent various types of resistance. Just as there are varying motivations for committing to treatment, there are just as many reasons for resisting therapy. Miller (1993) offers five reasons for resistance: (1) shyness, which results in a silent client who simply doesn't talk or participate in sessions; (2) efforts to preserve self-esteem, similar to our "class clown"; (3) the "yes-but" response of rejecting interpretations and interventions that prevents treatment from proceeding; (4) lack of a working relationship or resistance to establishing one; and (5) "character" resistance, similar to the example of the client who will not or cannot participate in the sessions at any level. Any of these types of resistance can stop therapy, although some are more amenable to treatment than others. Using the strength of the therapeutic alliance and the resources of the parents can help move through these resistances.

If a positive initial rapport has been established, the process of moving into the working phase of counseling will be facilitated. If not, however, the level of resistance needs to be addressed and communicated to the parents. If resistance is too great at a given time, little therapeutic progress will be made. You have an ethical obligation to communicate this to the parents and recommend other treatment options. These options could include continuing work with the parents around management skills, enlisting the aid of the school counselor or other community resources (e.g., the juvenile office or other structured programs), depending on the severity of accompanying behavioral concerns. In some cases it may not be possible to establish a therapeutic rapport.

THERAPEUTIC/WORKING ALLIANCE

The therapeutic relationship or working alliance is the primary mechanism facilitating treatment (Sugarman, Nemiroff, & Greenson, 2000). The *working alliance* refers to the positive relationship established between the client and therapist. It is the vehicle that facilitates change. If rapport becomes diminished or is never adequately established, the therapeutic relationship is probably not strong enough to withstand the tension experienced when challenging clients or helping them push through difficult issues. The authenticity and empathic presence of the therapist invites clients to engage in therapy, to participate in the relationship by being honest and by allowing themselves to be vulnerable and perhaps different from how they are in other aspects of their lives. This difference will facilitate a point of growth for the client.

Part of the challenge in the therapeutic relationship with children and adolescents is the necessity of establishing a similar alliance with the parents. There is a necessary balance between the two therapeutic relationships, and the therapist must be careful not to become triangulated in existing family dynamics (Bowen, 1972). It is just as important not to skew family dynamics by your presence in the family system. You want to effect change within the system, so your presence needs to have some impact, but the impact must be therapeutic for the client and her family. Being aware of your own reactions and biases can diminish the likelihood of these potential pitfalls.

Countertransference is easy with children and adolescents, particularly if you have not fully sorted out your own issues. Therapists can overidentify with clients, taking on a strong advocacy role on their behalf with parents. Such an approach may be counter-therapeutic, though in cases involving abuse, such a protective role may be warranted. Some therapists may identify more strongly with the parents if they hold more traditional views of discipline or authority. In the vast majority of cases, a more balanced response is the most effective therapeutic approach for your child or adolescent client; it allows the entire family to feel supported by the therapeutic efforts.

MOVING TO A DEEPER LEVEL

If the initial work of establishing a positive rapport, working alliance, and goals has been successful, the next step is to move on to the working stages of counseling. With the establishment of positive rapport, there is genuine hope for a good prognosis or outcome. During the working phase, you will be stretching the fabric of the relationship to help your young client understand herself better, develop positive coping strategies, master the ability to monitor herself and her choices, and move gently toward the next developmental phase. Work with parents during this phase will focus on helping them provide developmentally appropriate supervision and structure for their child or adolescent, understand appropriate family boundaries and roles, and receive guidance about the family life cycle and their role in the eventual process of separation-individuation.

Moving to a deeper level cannot occur unless appropriate rapport and trust have been established in the early stages of therapy. A basic level of development is necessary in order to move forward as well. You will recall this from the discussion in Chapter 1 that counselors cannot push their clients beyond the limits of their current developmental level. Developmental limits do not preclude a skills training or behavior modification approach, but these goals must fit with current limits of the client. A parent training model may be a more appropriate intervention if the child or adolescent is not able (or willing) to participate in therapy.

Moving to a deeper level with children and adolescents will not be routinely achieved in the same manner as insight is developed with adults. For example, insight-oriented approaches are ineffective with a majority of younger clients but might be helpful when working with older adolescents. Reaching a different level of communication and understanding with clients can help produce this deeper change (Murray, 2002). Metaphors are often an effective tool to help children and adolescents increase understanding of themselves, others, and life situations (Close, 1998). Children and adolescents are often more comfortable with these "stories" that are easier for them to understand than complicated verbal explanations. Metaphors are developed through talking, drawing, games, or play. They provide a much more effective intervention for most child and adolescent clients, because the metaphors are more consistent with developing levels of cognitive and emotional skills.

Metaphors with children and adolescents may feel more like fables or fairy tales in that they allow an objective identification with a character other than themselves. Mutual storytelling and therapeutic games provide opportunities to influence the direction of such stories so that the therapist can insert appropriate examples into the discussion. Even with non-therapeutic games, like checkers or Connect Four, the therapist can make observations about missed opportunities or being unaware of choices, making the game a metaphorical vehicle for decision-making and self-awareness.

Regardless of how any therapeutic technique "fits" your client's developmental level, the process of change is not constant. It's typical for clients to pull back to a more superficial level of play or interaction following a major insight or behavioral change. As you gain experience, you will recognize the needs of the client with regard to when to push and when to allow the client some space to assimilate new changes.

Monitoring the Pace With Children and Adolescents

The ebb and flow of therapy has a different rhythm for each client embedded within the context of family, culture, developmental level, and the specific presenting problems. It is often necessary to slow the process or to engage in what may feel like circular progress when following the child or adolescent's readiness or lead during therapy. You may need to adjust your expectations and help parents set realistic expectations as well. Conversely, you may also need to push the process along with some clients.

It is important to remember that the process of change is not linear (Mahoney, Robinson, & Fewell, 2001) and is often more effective when combined with self-reflection (Carey, 2001). Therefore, it can be a challenging process to match the pace and timing of the child or adolescent client. Therapists may experience the process as slow and laborious. They may feel pressure from parents, agency constraints, or managed care to rush the process, and it may be difficult to restrain from pushing therapy. However, it is just as critical with children and adolescents as with adults to maintain an appropriate pace that does not feel pressured to the client. Even if the process feels particularly slow with child clients, we need to respect their pace and, at times, communicate with adults in their environment information about appropriate pacing.

As noted, it can feel even more complex to determine the appropriate pace (Wrenn, 1988) when working with child and adolescent clients due to the added dimension of developmental level interacting with the family system issues in identifying what's appropriate and what's not for each particular client.

Balancing Between Young Clients and Parents

Early issues over who initiated therapy and how invested the client is will resurface throughout therapy, often when the adolescent is angry, feels badly, or is going through a stressful time. If the adolescent client, in particular, perceives that the therapist is more closely aligned with her parents, the therapeutic alliance may become damaged beyond repair. Normally, the working alliance undergoes "tear and repair" (Sugarman, Nemiroff, & Greenson, 2000) during the working stages of therapy. Stretches and strains to the working alliance arise out of challenges and confrontations the therapist provides to the client to induce responsibility and insight, depending on individual therapeutic issues. The strength of the rapport provides the space for strain to occur in the relationship without severing or breaking the alliance, an event that usually precedes early termination. The adolescent's level of suspicion can be an obstacle to the working alliance, particularly if she is uncertain about the depth of your relationship with her parents. Many adolescents also question how confidential the sessions are, particularly when using a child-centered family approach. This type of client requires more initial and ongoing attention to maintaining the therapeutic alliance and ensuring confidentiality.

In some settings, the adolescent's concerns about confidentiality may be well founded. Clients may have already experienced a rupture in a previous therapeutic relationship before coming to work with you. Other situations in which confidentiality may have been breached in the eyes of your client include academic situations or forensic settings in which the client may not have fully understood the limitations to confidentiality. Any of these experiences can have a strong ripple effect and may impede your initial efforts to build trust and rapport.

Maintaining a balanced relationship simultaneously with parents and adolescents is a challenge. In addition, personal biases may influence you to favor, albeit slightly, either the parents or the client. Adopting the perspective of either the parent or the young client too strongly is a potential pitfall when working with children and adolescents. Although these complications of mixed alliances are more problematic when working with adolescents, they are also encountered with younger children. The challenge of maintaining a balance arises out of the same approach that also serves to make child or adolescent therapy successful—a child-centered family approach (Andreozzi, 1996; Kaslow, Smith, & Croft, 2000; Sargent, 1997). This approach involves the client and parents from the beginning in an almost separate but equal, or parallel, manner. The message is sent from the first meeting that everyone is involved in treatment, but still allowed individual time in session. That time and space become critical for self-exploration, venting, and exploration of family dynamics. Of course, maintaining the flexibility to hold joint or family sessions is an important aspect of treatment as well.

The prospect of family sessions can feel overwhelming or just "bad" for many children and adolescents. Again, there is the possibility that past counseling may influence perceptions for the current sessions. Exploring previous counseling experiences in terms of what felt helpful and what was not helpful can convey the message that the current alliance will be collaborative, and different, from previous work. Conversely, there may have been a strong alliance previously that could interfere with current attachments or provide information about client strengths and coping mechanisms. These potential obstacles may prevent the child or adolescent from experiencing the sessions as a safe place, but they can also provide direction for you to help the client feel comfortable using sessions to vent and explore emotions, personal identity, and potential dreams and plans.

The importance of a balanced approach cannot be overemphasized in terms of its contribution to the success for this complicated work. Subtle factors can influence outcome at this working stage. A stronger alliance (real or perceived) with either the child/adolescent or the parent can upset the necessary balance to move forward in therapy. Parents may feel left out or "ganged up on," just as children and adolescents might. The risk when parents feel this way is that they will prematurely terminate treatment. If adolescents sense a stronger alliance with parents, they may simply refuse to participate in sessions. They may continue to attend, because they usually don't have a choice, but they may refuse to speak or engage while in session.

Additionally, if the alignment is too close with the parent, there is the risk of pushing the child past her current developmental level in order to meet the demands of the parent, laying the foundation for therapeutic failure because the child is developmentally unable to meet the demand. Similarly, if the alliance with the parent is too strong, the rapport with the child/adolescent may be lost, precluding any further therapeutic work. The child may experience the therapeutic relationship as coercive, similar to her perception of other relationships with adults, such as in parent-teacher conferences. It may be helpful as you move into the working stage of treatment to revisit the limits of confidentiality with the child, adolescent, and parents just to reinforce what can and cannot be shared. Parents often have to be reminded of the limits as well, particularly if a level of enmeshment exists in the family dynamic.

Sharing Information With Parents Without Breaching Confidentiality or Damaging the Therapeutic Alliance

Some parents push to gain information about their child from the therapist and must be gently reminded of the boundaries. You will share general information about how the sessions are going and discuss helpful parenting skills and approaches, and of course, you'll share information regarding the child's intent to harm herself or others. However, you cannot become a spy within the family ranks, divulging information from parents to child or from child to parents. That is the purpose of family sessions—to discuss those important issues that have come up in other contexts and to help the family develop communication skills. Reminding all family members of that early discussion about confidentiality may make more sense when they are experiencing the situations you have already described to them. The reminder can also serve as an invitation for them to meet together and discuss sensitive issues. During the working phase you will have established rapport to such a level as to be able to risk some "tearing" in the alliance that can often occur during a family session.

Facilitating communication among family members is an important role for you as therapist, but family members will need to be able to continue to communicate once your therapeutic relationship ends. Emphasizing a goal of keeping the family connected and communicating after therapy ends is empowering because it reinforces your belief in their ability to solve their own problems, and it communicates to the child or adolescent client that therapy will not continue indefinitely. Even if you have positive rapport with them, many young clients continue to experience some stigma, or at least internal conflict, about their participation in therapy, and they often are curious about how long therapy will last.

The risk of losing the therapeutic balance is even more real when working with children who experience uneven development, such as gifted children or those with ADHD. It can be easier to make a judgmental error if the true developmental level of the child is somewhat unclear or uneven (refer to Chapter 1). For example, gifted children and those with ADHD both can experience poor peer relationships. For gifted children the social development may be commensurate with peers but below the intellectual level of development. Many adults assume that gifted children should be functioning at a higher level in all areas, setting the stage for potential conflict in the parent-child relationship, depending on parental expectations. It is critical not to push clients beyond their developmental stages in the name of change. Although such efforts may benefit others (e.g., those who brought the child or adolescent in for treatment), the stress and frustration experienced by the young client is likely to create more chaos within the family system. Your role during family sessions may be compromised if you have had trouble maintaining a balance, thus decreasing your ability to be effective.

CHALLENGES TO THE THERAPEUTIC RELATIONSHIP

Difficulty maintaining balance within the family system is just one example of a challenge to the therapeutic relationship. You may be tempted to approach your therapeutic relationship in the same way that a special teacher or coach of yours did, but that will be counterproductive. It is important to remember to forge a different type of relationship therapeutically with the child or adolescent than in other areas of her life. In order to effect change regardless of treatment modality, you must work to provide a "corrective emotional experience" (Yalom, 1983), and part of facilitating such a change is fostering a different type of relationship than the client has with others. The foundation of such a relationship allows your client the freedom and support needed to explore alternative ways of being, coping, thinking, and behaving. That is the crux of a corrective emotional experience. Warmth, acceptance, and support allow the child to explore the emotional pain that may accompany the realizations that her choices are creating problems for herself, that they may be disappointing important adults and caretakers in her life, or that there may be limitations for herself that she has been denying.

The child's natural inclination to please her parents and other important caretakers continues into adolescence and can be one of the few areas of leverage to allow for change to occur. This bond or attachment may provide the only source of motivation for change. Difficulty forming attachment, or discomfort being emotionally close to others, are specific instances when such motivation is absent. Despite emotional boundaries in the therapeutic relationship, attempts to be authentic in that relationship can also make these clients feel uncomfortable or resistant.

Overwhelming the Client With Affect/Closeness Attachment Problems

Part of the strength of the therapeutic alliance is the combination of authenticity without the emotional overlay of close family relationships. The lack of long-standing patterns of interactions provides some emotional distance for the client to explore new responses and behaviors. Although this emotional distance can facilitate change in the therapeutic relationship, the lack of an emotional bond can be an obstacle with certain clients. For example, working with adopted children, particularly those who suffer from reactive attachment disorder (American Psychiatric Association, 2000), may be challenging because of the difficulty in forming an emotional bond or working alliance. In a chameleon-like fashion, some of these children adapt to what they perceive are the desires of the adults around them. This achieves a false sense of connection and allows the child or adolescent a greater measure of freedom on the basis of her "good behavior." The facade is broken when a conflict or disagreement occurs, and the child or adolescent's lack of remorse becomes apparent.

Children or adolescents who suffer from this disorder have difficulty forming important emotional attachments, as the name would imply. For these young people, the closeness and positive feelings associated with emotional intimacy and caring relationships are extremely uncomfortable, actually creating stress from the excessive stimulation of a bond that usually feels good. These inherent obstacles are often outside their awareness and perhaps beyond their ability to change. The explanation for the inability to form appropriate attachments lies in the developmental framework; that is, it is often assumed that the critical period of attachment was missed and cannot easily be reestablished despite the constancy of the adopting parents because the critical period for attachment has passed.

Another potential complicating factor in a client's ability to form a therapeutic relationship is the impact of trauma on neurological development (Egeland, Yates, Appleyard, & van Dulmen, 2002). Many young clients have already experienced significant stress and trauma, often at the hands of those closest to them. Neurological changes as a result of trauma can negatively affect the attachment process.

In the case of clients who were adopted, this creates significant stress for the loving families who are attempting to provide for these challenging children. Sometimes recognizing the difficulty the children experience in close relationships can ease some of the parents' concerns, simply through the knowledge that it is not their fault. Of course, adoptive parents must still contend with the challenge of adjusting to a reality quite different from their dreams of parenthood. A supportive, psycho-educational approach may be helpful to parents at this time.

If these obstacles are encountered in therapy, seeking alternative motivators to help the client embrace the need for change may be helpful. The motivation may be to decrease negative interactions with parents. If so, that becomes the bond in the therapeutic work. If the young clients are not engaged, it is difficult to be effective. A more appropriate intervention might involve working with parents if your young clients are unwilling to engage at present. Clients cannot be forced to embrace a need for change.

Demonstrating the Difference in the Therapeutic Relationship: Managing Resistance

Although we may tell children and adolescents that communication in our sessions with them will be different, they become aware of those differences through our actions. As they observe these differences, ideally they will accept the implicit permission to talk about their sensitive issues in a more open and honest manner, or at least to commit to behavioral change. This shift is necessary to help them change. The support will help carry them through the difficult process of change and maintain the persistence necessary to remain optimistic and committed to the final outcome. Informing the children, adolescents, and parents of the various aspects of the change process, including possible setbacks, will enhance their ability to be successful.

Adolescents, in particular, may be suspicious of most adults in their lives, until given a reason to believe otherwise. For this reason, there is often an opportunity to behave differently with adolescents in the very first session. Many adolescents may come into counseling with a sullen or negative attitude. Even younger children would often rather be playing outside, watching TV, or playing a video game, or they may feel nervous about the session. Since this piece of information is fairly obvious, making it overt can have a positive impact on the session. You may say something like, "How did you feel about coming in today?" If there is little response, you can follow up with, "Well, it doesn't seem like you feel very happy about being here. I remember that you didn't feel very good about coming in even from the first time we met." The difference in this kind of direct statement to young clients is that you began talking about the proverbial "elephant in the living room" in the first meeting and continue that discussion when resistance resurfaces (Miller, 1993).

Continuing open discussions about resistance serves to set the norm that therapy is a place where people can be direct with one another and nothing bad happens. The change experienced by the client from that norm may be minor or major, but it is probably fairly big in terms of stretching family taboos. For that reason, talking directly may provoke anxiety, and your client may have ambivalent feelings about opening up because of the anxiety. These feelings could become overpowering and push the client back into the usual patterns for her family? For example, the client may become angry with you as a distraction from going deeper into her true feelings. A patient and supportive response is best in such cases. Responses of this type will facilitate positive rapport with your clients and help them move toward therapeutic work. Again, making their discomfort overt and directly addressing whether talking is against a family norm will facilitate therapeutic work and strengthen the therapeutic alliance. Clients will feel freer to explore feelings and thoughts that do not feel safe and to discuss their decisions and choices in a more productive way. Of course, talking—even directly—is not always the optimal intervention when working with children and adolescents.

Play to Your Client's/Family's Strengths

Even from the first session, an emphasis is placed on the client's and family's strengths. What is the client and family already doing well that can be adapted to help them be more successful in the therapeutic task at hand? For example, if you are attempting to help the child or adolescent deal with stress, what adaptive, physical strategies already exist in her repertoire? Does your client play soccer? Dance? Ride a bike? Perform gymnastics? Practice Tai Kwan Do? What about the parents? Do they walk in nice weather? Are family bike outings a regular activity? Incorporating a shared physical activity can help relieve stress for all family members and provide some positive bonding time. Just the simple act of engaging in a shared activity, one that is more physical than verbal, can increase the positive feelings among family members. The use of physical activity is discussed later in this chapter as an outlet for other emotional responses as well.

Existing Support Systems

So much variability exists between families in the depth of respective support systems. That variation is related to family factors, as discussed in Chapter 2, and to the individual community where the family resides. Additionally, cultural overlays interact with these individual and family factors.

Multicultural Issues

The type of support available to a family varies by ethnicity and cultural factors. For example, African American families generally emphasize a kinship network and church in terms of their social support. With increased mobility of families for economic survival, the support of extended family may be less available, particularly for Caucasian or recently immigrated families. It may require creative thinking and familiarity with the community to help these families become more grounded in social support systems. Schools can offer some support, depending on how active their parent association is. If this is not an option, community groups such as Parents Without Partners may offer support. Other types of support groups may focus on problems the family is facing (e.g., CHADD for families of children with attention deficit, NAMI for individuals and families with mental illness). Community libraries often have reading groups for young children and sometimes offer film or summer reading programs for adults and families. The more you can do to help clients and their families become connected and feel supported by the community, the more successful interventions will be with this family. For recently uprooted families, the support system you help them generate may become an integral component of a positive adjustment for all family members.

CHANGE: THE WORK OF THERAPY

Change is strengthened, and more likely to be maintained, when it occurs on emotional, psychological, and behavioral levels (Carey, 2001). Ideally, an approach involving several different techniques will intervene at an affective level, through interpersonal relationships; using sensations, behavior, cognition, and imagery; and through physical means, such as exercise and diet (Keat, 1996). Using a combination of drama, art, play, and humor can help you meet children where they are, engage them in the therapeutic process (Smith & Nylund, 1997), and respect their individual differences enough to further the work and strengthen the therapeutic alliance. Creative approaches to therapy increase children's level of comfort, giving them permission to explore sensitive or difficult issues for themselves (Hobday & Ollier, 1999).

Difficulty discussing problems or feelings for children and adolescents often has a developmental factor that makes even identifying problems or taking responsibility for feelings a challenge. Resolving this difficulty may require accessing emotion, affect, and thought through some other means than verbalizing (Wilson & Ryan, 2002). Dependent on the nature of the issues at hand (e.g., trauma that occurred at a preverbal stage, or the words to describe it were lost due to a dissociative reaction), nonverbal creative approaches may be necessary to begin reaching the affect and working through initial change. As therapy continues and the client can more readily identify the issues, combining creative approaches with more traditional perspectives will enhance the depth and success of the work.

Therapeutic Approaches

Working stages of therapy often require some degree of trial and error when adapting general techniques to specific clients. Although much of our discussion has focused on the interaction between children or adolescents and their families, it is important to begin exploring other techniques as well. The remainder of this chapter provides an overview of various techniques that may be used in combination.

Play Materials

When beginning therapists approach young children, they often think of using a play therapy approach, but their actual practice (due to limited training opportunities) is often more similar to using play materials than engaging in play therapy. The distinction is an important one to understand. Using play materials is often a good mechanism to engage children initially in the therapeutic setting. The counselor often directs or guides such interactions (e.g., draw a picture of your family) or uses materials to help the child or adolescent deal with nervous energy (e.g., koosh ball, play dough). Either of these techniques serves to help young clients feel less self-conscious and more comfortable in the therapeutic setting. They have something to occupy their hands and discharge any nervous energy that might otherwise distract them from being able to verbalize with the counselor. However, in contrast to play therapy, the emphasis continues to be on the verbal interactions, punctuated by drawing or other nonverbals that may become a part of the therapeutic interaction.

Some children may ask to bring in a friend or family member to play the therapeutic game. Generally, this is not a good idea as it changes the focus and dynamic of the interaction. The child may be given the impression that therapy is "just for fun." Although therapeutic interactions should feel positive for the child, that is not the primary goal.

CREATIVE THERAPIES

Play therapy is suggested by some as an intervention across ages, even into adolescence (Breen & Daigneault, 1998; Wilson & Ryan, 2002). The ability to employ play therapy with adolescents depends on their self-concept, level of flexibility or fluidity in their thinking and self-concept, and a decision whether this is an appropriate choice of intervention. Some adolescents continue to have difficulty with verbal expression, particularly about sensitive topics. If they are open to it, play therapy may be an appropriate intervention for these adolescents, particularly if a component of their presenting issue involves being "stuck" or fixated at a particular developmental level. If the adolescent's development has been uneven, the use of play therapy may reach that developmental component of the adolescent that is still functioning at a younger level.

If play therapy feels inappropriate or the adolescent is hesitant to participate in such techniques, then other creative therapies may be employed, such as drawing, poetry writing, journaling, or psychodrama. Use of such techniques helps to strengthen the child's or adolescent's ego, or internal core, allowing the client to move forward in the difficult process of accessing the affect and working through blocked feelings (Oaklander, 1997). The process of helping the child feel safe enough to continue working is an ongoing task and challenge.

Journaling/Narrative Techniques

Narrative therapies such as journaling provide interventions at both psychological and emotional levels. Approaching the journal as a more creative endeavor can enhance the process of change as well. Journaling is a technique that works to further the process and can be used outside of session as well to maintain changes. Many young clients are familiar with the general process through personal diaries or use of the general technique at school.

Schools and changes in teaching methods have exposed many children to the concept and activity of journaling. Journaling is a wonderful therapeutic technique, which has proven health and psychological/emotional benefits. It also has a great deal of inherent flexibility, which makes journaling a wonderfully broad therapeutic technique. We can ask clients to write specific letters, make lists, record behaviors, engage in a stream-of-consciousness entries, and review their decision-making process. This flexibility and its consistent results make journaling one of our more powerful therapeutic techniques. Variations can include self-affirmations, behavioral reminder lists, and thought substitutions.

When prescribing the use of a journal, one must caution the client not to use it as a diary to simply record daily events. This is particularly true for children who have maintained journals as part of their classroom obligations. They may need to relearn the use or orientation of the journal as a more therapeutic "assignment." Part of your role will be to help the client make the distinction between the use of a diary and the use of a journal, the latter being for self-expression and self-exploration at an emotional level. Another caution about the use of journals or therapeutic letters is the possibility that clients may become flooded with emotions as they explore these dormant and distant parts of themselves. If clients reach a point of emotional flooding or feeling overwhelmed by their feelings, they need to be instructed to cease the activity until the next session. For certain clients, the journal can open a well of emotions that may be too strong or overpowering to retain control. In those instances, they may become mired in a cycle of emotions from which they have no escape or defense. In a worst case scenario, these clients—generally those with fragile ego strength or those with a strong need for emotional support from others—may decompensate toward psychosis or suicidality. It is not necessary to share the worst case scenario with clients but encourage them to stop the journaling activity if they reach this point and resume it during the safety of the session. Your role is to help guide them through these strong emotions and tease out the current reactions from the overwhelming well of feelings that have been stuffed away for various reasons. In some cases the family doesn't allow expression of emotions; in others, abused children have learned to disown part of themselves in order to survive.

Therapeutic letters are a specific form of journaling designed to facilitate the expression of buried or repressed emotions. A therapeutic letter is directed to an individual, situation, emotion, or disorder from whom the client cannot expect to receive a productive response if confronted in reality or someone the client cannot confront due to death or separation. In addition to being used with individuals, the therapeutic letter can also be addressed to parts of oneself or specific disorders or illnesses (e.g., alcoholism or ADHD). The intent of the letter is to release the suppressed feelings and allow the client to recognize things that have been lost as a result of the experience or relationship with the target of the letter.

The following should be included in a therapeutic letter:

- *Expression of the usually mixed or ambivalent emotions.* The tone of the letter will likely be strong and may include foul language. You may need to give your clients permission to use strong language, not for effect but because of the strong emotional tone of such language, which allows for expression of taboo feelings and creates a release.
- *Description of the things the client has lost* as a result of the experience or relationship. This section may include such things as loss of trust in others and oneself, loss of innocence, questioning one's view of oneself and the world, or wondering if she will ever be happy.
- *Direct expression of what the client would like to see happen to the individual.* You may be appalled and disturbed by some of the client's strong feelings, and it is your duty to explore with the young client the difference between fantasy and reality. The client needs to clearly understand that none of these actions can happen in reality but represent her strong feelings toward the perpetrator or others in her life. With children and adolescents, the letter can be an initial springboard to productive discussions between parents and children when appropriate. When abuse is involved, it may be counter-therapeutic to foster such discussions. Children or adolescents may not benefit from such a confrontation until later in their lives. Once again, think in terms of a developmental context and what would be in the best interest of your client. Each family situation dictates a different response from the counselor—thus, the importance of good training, continuing education, and peer consultation and support.
- *Finally, a positive perspective on how they will move forward from here.* This will include not being controlled by a situation no longer present in their daily lives and may evolve into a list of goals to work toward following the release of these long-suppressed emotions. The letter may also be used at some point to begin a discussion with other individuals, which may or may not occur within the context of therapy, or may not occur at all beyond the initial therapeutic letter. In those cases where a positive confrontation is unlikely, use of Gestalt techniques, such as the empty chair or staging a play or telling a story, may offer productive alternatives for internal change.

Music in Therapy

Similar to journaling, the simple use of music can be an important part of a multiple modality approach to treatment. Music therapy has significant opportunity for maintaining changes by acting as an accessible cue after discharge from an inpatient program, once outpatient therapy has ended, or at the end of the school year. Music can provide another method of expression unrelated to language, that can help clients connect with their affect and emotions (Rolvsjord, 2001). In addition to self-expression through playing music, listening to music can provide emotional release or comfort.

When paired with a new behavioral response, music becomes a tool for change. Simply hearing the music from a particular therapeutic intervention can cue the new response, or at least the awareness of a reminder or choice to respond differently. Music used in therapy has been shown to increase the coping skills of children and adolescents, particularly with regard to anxiety and pain management. When used in conjunction with physical concerns, range of motion and language skills have also been shown to improve. Other benefits that can be transferred to any number of settings and are often used in schools include increasing social skills and improving relationships and self-expression (Daveson & Kennelly, 2000).

COGNITIVE-BEHAVIORAL THERAPY WORK IN SESSION

Cognitive-behavioral therapy is a technique used with children and adolescents as well as with adults. This approach works well with externalizing disorders, despite the broad range of different presentations for the behaviors associated with these disorders. In practice, this translates to an approach that may be described as trial and error. In essence, you are challenged to take the general techniques of cognitive-behavioral therapy and explore with each client and her family how best to tailor and implement this approach for her. An important aspect of the intervention is that of identifying specific triggers or situations that elicit the response. Given that many of your clients will not have well-developed self-monitoring skills, you will probably need to enlist the aid of parents, teachers, or school counselors, particularly if working in the private sector outside that setting.

FAMILY THERAPY

Family therapy can be an important part of a planned approach to treatment with children and adolescents. When approached with knowledge of individual differences and developmental stages, the approach of combining various interventions has been identified as an effective approach with aggression, attention deficit, anger, depression, anxiety, and chronic health conditions (Kendall, 1994). The potential gains of a family approach are similar to the advantage of using multiple forms of assessment when completing a psychological evaluation. Our assessment is enhanced by various perspectives provided by different instruments or by people from various settings who know or work with the client. Likewise, the interventions are strengthened by helping individuals explore and address issues from these multiple perspectives of different aspects of their lives.

A family approach is often used when working with children and adolescents. Indeed, it is usually the most effective treatment. Children and adolescents, in particular, cannot be treated in isolation. Our interventions are much more effective when adopting a systems approach that involves family members and sometimes school and community individuals who work with your client. When working with families and younger clients in families, it is often helpful to review the ground rules with the entire family prior to beginning family sessions. These ground rules include issues of confidentiality, "secrets" or managing contact outside the family session, expectations regarding further work on resolving the conflict that may occur inside sessions, and agreements about commitment to the process of change. In some families, it may be necessary to review ground rules in detail, particularly if aggression or extreme anger is part of the family fabric at the time of your interventions. The initial session in these high-risk cases should include issues of safety, contingency plans, or plans to use during crisis. Just by opening up clear discussion about the risky behaviors, the dynamics of the family can be changed in a positive way that provides insulation against potential violence or angry outbursts (McAdams & Foster, 2002).

The ability to provide family therapy and the manner in which that therapy is provided will vary based on your setting as much as on your theoretical orientation or approach to therapy. Different factors are strengthened or weakened on the basis of various settings (Boyd-Franklin & Bry, 2000). Traditionally, little family therapy was provided in the schools, but that is changing as the school is rapidly becoming one of the few commonly shared experiences for many people in this increasingly diverse nation (Carlson & Hickman, 1992). Schools in some communities are taking a more active role in providing support to marginalized families or those who have little sense of community or connection (Smith & Nylund, 1997). Henggeler (1999) has shown that a multisystemic approach involving family and community-based treatments are more effective clinically and economically than placements in working with more serious clinical problems. Increased accountability for families is achieved through the involvement of multiple agencies. The accountability translates to an increased level of support, enhancing the family's practical resources and sense of support, making the family system more resilient and able to respond to change and challenge.

Although family therapy in school and inpatient or day treatment settings may not resemble traditional family therapy in outpatient settings, interventions can still be provided with a family focus. Often, it is more effective and realistic to offer a family therapy group approach in institutional settings, such as schools, residential centers, or inpatient or day treatment programs. Offering family therapy as a group provides an immediate sense of support among parents who are struggling with similar practical and emotional challenges. For those parents who may not be able to bring themselves to discuss their family situation with anyone else, the parent group can provide a safe place to let down one's guard and accept feedback and support from others. In a school setting, the focus may be more directly related to academic functioning or behaviors that interfere with that functioning than the focus found in a treatment center, but surprisingly many of the topics may be quite similar (e.g., young adults making poor choices for themselves, experimenting with self-destructive substances and actions, or possessing poor self-monitoring skills).

In contrast to providing family therapy in a group setting, which is more similar to a psycho-educational support group, individual family therapy provided in an outpatient setting or in the home has a more intimate feeling and also offers more of a challenge to the therapist to maintain boundaries. Family dynamics are strong and can be so powerful that you may feel yourself being "sucked" into the family, serving a substitute role for another family member. This is more likely to occur early in your work with a family, as you're just beginning to understand the family's structure and the function of various members' roles within the family. Without the knowledge of how members interact and what their role is as you make your interventions, you can easily be recruited into a family role (Minuchen, Rossman, & Baker, 1978). This problem is so common that it is important for you to equip yourself with knowledge of your own potential weaknesses and vulnerabilities where you might get drawn into the fray of family dynamics. Your role will be diminished, and family members will lose direction as they continue their usual maladaptive patterns with you in tow. This is yet another reason why it is critical to engage in self-exploration of your own potential biases and feelings about children, adolescents, parenting, and families.

With good boundaries in place, you can insert yourself into the family, either in the home or office setting, and use your powers of observation to guide healthy interventions. Remember to focus interventions on "here and now" as much as possible in order to reduce the potential for conflict from unresolved issues within the family and to help the family embrace, practice, and learn new strategies of talking, behaving, and being with one another. Areas to focus on include helping the family be more flexible, less rigid, less authoritarian, and closer in terms of support and communication (Walsh, 1993).

Sometimes in working with families, you will become aware of family patterns that may make interventions more challenging. Whether you become aware of these patterns through your own observations or through the use of an intervention such as genograms (described later in this chapter), these patterns can impact your choice of interventions. If the family participates in a genogram or is aware of patterns on their own, such as a history of depression, you may be able to impact change at an intergenerational level by talking with the family about coping mechanisms for depression that are generally effective. The advantage of a family approach can be in the strength and support members can provide to each other in such situations (Kaslow & Racusin, 1994).

BRIEF THERAPY

Brief therapy is often described as more goal oriented and less focused on affect or etiology. Client relief of symptoms or behavioral change is generally the aim of brief approaches. For this reason, cognitive-behavioral approaches are often the treatment of choice. This presents some problems with younger clients, because of their ongoing intellectual development. We have noted repeatedly that traditional "talking therapies" are ill suited for children and adolescents. Often, a brief approach with very young clients will focus on parenting techniques and providing external structure for children until they are developmentally able to do so themselves.

Even with older children and adolescents, external structure is often the centerpiece of treatment because of the young clients' inability or unwillingness to engage in treatment themselves.

As noted, the working stages of therapy are usually the middle sessions, after initial goals have been agreed upon and a tentative course of therapy outlined. The length of therapy will determine your treatment approach to a certain extent. You may need to consider brief courses, such as solution-oriented brief therapy (Araoz & Carresse, 1996; Selekman, 1993) or Kreilkamp's (1989) intermittent brief therapy as possible approaches to time that may be limited by the family's resources, the family's schedule, school schedules, or managed care constraints. Aspects of brief therapy are covered in more detail later in this chapter.

A solution-oriented approach embraces an almost businesslike or coaching approach to therapy, beginning by identifying solutions to the presenting problems. Although present, empathic statements are not at the center of these interventions and are involved primarily in rapport building. Once behavioral change is achieved, or goals are met, therapy is terminated.

Kreilkamp's (1989) intermittent approach to brief therapy is practical for working with children and adolescents. He outlines a course of therapy that is sporadic or intermittent over time. The client comes in for an initial problem and that is resolved. At that point sessions stop, but may be easily restarted by the client when another problem arises. This approach is well suited for children and adolescents because it fits well within a developmental framework. It is common to work with a child or adolescent around a particular issue and to terminate therapy. Six months later, the client's family phones about concerns that may be related to the initial presenting problem or a different developmental issue. Some families find a sense of comfort in knowing initial contacts have already been established and can be easily reinitiated with a phone call.

GROUPS

Groups, even with diverse issues, have been shown to be helpful for intervention in schools, particularly with a solution-focused approach (LaFountain, Garner, & Boldosser, 1995). The assumptions underlying this approach are similar to the short term or brief therapy approach. A positive aspect of this approach is that it is more empowering for young clients, who may feel "safer" in a group setting. A similar solution may apply to all group members, and this approach still preserves their privacy. As such, the group approach can enhance young clients' participation. Groups lend themselves well to social skills training and have been used in schools for a broad range of interventions, such as managing anger, building self-esteem, coping with divorce, handling grief/loss, and even coping with the experience of having parents who are incarcerated.

In addition to basic social skills training that is often best conducted in groups in schools, *empathy training* can be another focus for helping these children "get outside themselves" to understand others and the impact of their actions on others.

Specific techniques that are suggested include writing to enhance self-reflection and participation in groups to help increase understanding of diverse experiences (Breggin, Breggin, & Bemak, 2002).

Play Therapy

Play therapy is primarily focused on nonverbal interactions and the therapist's attempts to interpret the child's fears, concerns, conflicts, and wishes from a more projective standpoint. For this reason, the novice counselor is cautioned against overinterpreting as a result of his or her own internal biases or any information that has come from other sources. For example, if a counselor is engaging a child in play therapy as the course of a custody evaluation, it is highly likely that the play themes will reflect a parent's attempt to bias the child, or her own reinterpretation of reality. A biased response is particularly likely if the client has met with other professionals prior to coming to see you. Current studies show the ease with which children's memory can be influenced (Alessi & Ballard, 2001).

It is often helpful to use games and toys in a more general way to facilitate discussion, even if play therapy is not the goal of the intervention. General games like checkers, Connect Four, dominoes, or Chinese checkers can be used as a general focus (Schaefer, 2000) that allows for some discharge of the nervous energy the child or adolescent is experiencing while talking about sensitive topics. Moderating the child's ability to play and continue to focus on therapeutic issues is part of your job as therapist. You may need to switch to another play vehicle if it begins to interfere with the work (Landreth, 2002). Using games and toys in this way, as you can see, is very different from a play therapy approach that encourages the child's freer exploration of the play area and its materials. This is part of the underlying rationale of allowing the play materials to become projectives for the child's inner conflict and concerns. Thus, as with any projective technique, caution needs to be taken in interpreting the themes of a child's play. Throwing dolls off the roof of the doll house may just be activity and testing the limits of a new situation. The superficially destructive act probably doesn't mean that the client wants to kill everyone in the family. For children of a young age, it is the process of play therapy, not the production of insight that provides relief and healing for them.

Children are kinesthetic learners. They learn by doing, more at certain developmental levels than others. Allowing them to move about the therapy room or engage in basketball, a walk, or dance in a residential center can all enhance the work of therapy, partially due to the positive effect on rapport and partially due to the increased level of comfort physical movement allows. The movement allows for release of nervous energy and facilitates expression through other means such as talking, writing, or drawing.

Active techniques are most beneficial with children. Involve them in drawing out their behaviors and solutions to problems. Role-plays work for children and adolescents when practicing new skills or using their strengths as coping skills. You can help the client identify resources in her world to use as supports. Give her permission to imagine herself as successful.

CHECKING COUNTERTRANSFERENCE

In working with children, adolescents, and families, many opportunities and pitfalls can affect the process of therapy, if you are unaware of your own perceptions and biases. Subtle indications of countertransference that may arise as you are implementing techniques include almost any kind of strong emotional feeling: a strong need to use one game or avoid drawing, feelings of sympathy or anger for the client, or identifying either the client or the parents as "the bad guys" somehow at fault for what's happening, for example. Feelings of this type are more likely related to your own feelings than they are triggered by the client's issues. If you do not recognize this, it will cause problems in your work with the family. The challenge of balancing in child-centered family therapy is only successful when you can remain balanced within yourself as you interact with the family. Your own sense of balance will provide a calming effect on the family, which is generally a good outcome as many of our families suffer from repeated chaos, a condition that interferes with their ability to be resilient (see Chapters 6 and 7). More information about countertransference and therapist reactions to clients is provided in Chapter 11 and in the workbook.

CHALLENGES IN THE WORKING PHASE

Psychopathology

Psychopathology presenting in childhood often continues into adulthood. For this reason much of our work with children and adolescents has a long-standing impact on their lives and, as such, has a broad ripple effect in the likelihood of success in transmitting effective coping skills.

Adaptive functioning, or the ability to use positive and productive coping skills, can serve as a buffer against stress and a tool to move beyond potential negative effects of depression, anxiety, and other psychological symptoms. Motivation for change is not always observed among children or adolescents because they are unaware of the cause-and-effect connection, or they may feel hopeless about things actually changing.

For those children and adolescents who engage in more externalizing and acting-out behaviors, there is a higher likelihood of trouble with the law during young adulthood and of dropping out of school. Some authors suggest using screening mechanisms to identify those youth who might be at risk for these later problems in order to provide a higher level of intervention or perhaps a more effective method of coping to avoid those eventualities (Stoeop, Weiss, McKnight, Beresford, & Coehen, 2002). For these clients, the opportunity to foster community contacts can provide a sense of connection and feeling grounded. Such a connection with just one adult may make a difference in their success.

Multiple Symptoms

Multiple symptoms also make work with clients more complex. Typical examples of those who experience multiple challenges include those with attention deficit disorder, Asperger's disorder, mild forms of autism, and other developmental disorders. Similar challenges are presented by multiple disorders that present simultaneously, a condition often termed *co-morbid*. Many co-morbid conditions include symptoms of aggression toward others or oneself, consistent with externalizing and internalizing behaviors. Examples include aggressive behavior that is often seen in oppositional defiant disorder or conduct disorder and that may be co-morbid with attention deficit disorder. Self-mutilation is often seen in depressive disorders and may occur alongside bipolar disorders as well (Frazier, Doyle, Chiu, & Coyle, 2002). The role of reinforcement in maintaining self-mutilating behaviors has been reviewed, noting a positive correlation (Marcus, Vollmer, Swanson, Roane, & Ringdahl, 2001).

Thus, for children with co-morbid conditions, those reinforcing factors need to be considered in your treatment. Either peer or parental influence can have a limiting or maintaining effect on self-injurious and aggressive behaviors; as such, those influences must be explored when developing the treatment plan and throughout treatment. Exposure to violence through the media and video games is another influencing factor in promoting and maintaining aggressive tendencies that may need to be limited as part of the treatment intervention (Bushman & Anderson, 2001). These issues will be further addressed in later chapters.

Parental Attachment

Another factor to be considered in the development of problematic behaviors and in the ability of the young client to change is the quality of the attachment between the child or adolescent and her parents. For families in which a healthy bond has been formed and for whom there has been no interruption of the parent-child relationship throughout critical attachment phases in infancy (usually between 18 and 24 months), the attachment provides both leverage and desire to work together as a family. The leverage is provided to the parents based on the child's desire to please, which has grown out of the foundation of a positive attachment between parent and child.

Unfortunately, this bond does not always form in the optimal way, if at all. For example, in reactive attachment disorder, often observed in children who experienced early trauma or placement with an adoptive family during the attachment phase, the bond may not have been formed with adoptive parents. It is becoming more clear that the attachment process is a critical developmental incident that has a certain time frame in which to occur; if that opportunity is missed, the child may endure the results throughout her life. Without the attachment, the child has no motivation to please the parent because there is no bond between them. It is almost as if each is operating as a separate entity within shared living space. For children with reactive attachment disorder, the actual experience of being close or emotionally intimate with others creates great inner distress and anxiety and often culminates in angry outbursts that are actually an unconscious attempt to reestablish the emotional distance that feels normal to these children.

Therapeutic interventions are difficult with children and adolescents who have not been able to form a strong emotional attachment with their parents. In these cases, our interventions must focus on external structure and consequences from a cognitive behavioral perspective to induce change within the adolescent. The work with the parents must focus on loss of their ideals regarding family and parenting and coming to terms that their reality is far different from what they had imagined the experience of being a parent would be.

TOYS AND TOOLS

The value in using toys, games, and creative techniques with children and adolescents is that these approaches often use learning styles that are more developmentally appropriate and less threatening than direct discussion (Luborsky, 2001). Sometimes, a child or even an adolescent is unable to directly talk about her experiences. Take the example of abuse. It is not uncommon for victims of abuse to recant their disclosure or deny their experience because the emotions associated with accepting the abuse as part of their own experience is overwhelming. Less direct methods of expression are more effective at those times. Specific approaches include play therapy, therapeutic games (Hall, Kaduson, & Schaefer, 2002), psychodrama, role-plays, therapeutic storytelling, affirmations, journaling, bibliotherapy, and biographies/hero emulation. Use the child's strengths as much as possible when individualizing or tailoring your interventions to your specific client.

"Comic Strip" Problem Solving

It is difficult for many children and young adolescents to engage in self-observation or monitoring. Therefore, it is unlikely that they will be able to sit on your couch and identify precedents and antecedents of their actions. However, one way to facilitate this type of self-observation is to use a "comic strip" or "film strip" technique. Have the client draw pictures about the event—usually a conflict, getting in trouble, or making a bad choice. Have her include her feelings, and any thoughts related to the choices she made. Even if she may be unaware of her feelings, they may be expressed through the drawings.

A modified cartoon approach that helps to break down the behavior and thought processes into manageable chunks can guide the process for younger children without overwhelming them. The process works with children through middle school or junior high, depending on developmental level, as well as with children and adolescents who struggle with attention deficit or those who have difficulty self-monitoring. The technique makes their experiences more concrete and easier to understand and can be used as a reminder after developing a plan. Through the use of this technique, you can help clients to identify and organize their behavior into manageable pieces that can be understood more easily.

In this technique, simply divide a piece of paper by drawing lines to form boxes. Number the sections in order, 1 to 6 with older children and 1 to 4 with younger children to keep the problem-solving approach consistent with the limitations of their developmental capacity. Have the client draw in the sequence of events, beginning with box 1, which should include the precipitating events or triggers for the client's reaction and continuing throughout the course of action in the remaining boxes. As the client draws the sequence, discuss thoughts and feelings matched to each action box.

Following the drawing and discussion, proceed to the intervention planning phase. At this phase, you and the client will produce a second sheet of boxes similar to the first, but in the intervention phase your goal is to replace the maladaptive response with more appropriate coping mechanisms. Thus, you may have a number of different action choices in your intervention. For example, if the child has become angry on the playground, possible interventions may include walking away from the target child, choosing another play activity, or eliciting a teacher's aid.

This scenario can also help you understand how the client processes information. As with most interventions, the possibility of a successful outcome is enhanced by increasing the client's participation in the planning and implementation phases. The greater ownership the client feels in the intervention, the more likely she is to implement the process. Another factor is the client's level of comfort in using the intervention. If the child thinks the suggestion is stupid or silly or makes absolutely no sense, then she will have little motivation for using the plan. Thus, the more actively engaged the child is in the planning process, the more you can help her use her enthusiasm to fuel the change process. Here again is a point where the strength of the therapeutic alliance comes into play. The stronger the alliance, the more likely the client is to try the intervention, because of the trust in the working relationship. The attention and work toward developing this strong alliance in the early phases of therapy will continue to have positive reverberations throughout this critical working phase and later in termination, to help the client maintain therapeutic gains.

Gingerbread Feelings

With younger children or older clients who have difficulty identifying feelings and emotional states, we can help them use their body to identify initial cues of an impending angry outburst or response. Drawing again provides a good introduction to explore these hidden feelings. Use a general body outline like a gingerbread man drawing to identify feelings within the client. By providing a stimulus that is impersonal and has plenty of room for internal drawing, the client can begin to explore and objectify internal states. We may need to provide prompts if the client is unable to think about types of images on her own. Part of this ability is closely related to being able to visualize and use imagery. By the working phase of therapy, you should have a good idea of your client's skills and ability to use these modalities.

Abstract Expression

Abstract drawings may also be used as stimuli in feeling identification and expression. For some clients, a greater distance between their feelings and themselves is necessary to move forward or make progress. For these types of clients, even identifying feelings as their own in a remotely direct process (e.g., the gingerbread approach), feels too frightening and may trigger defense mechanisms and resistance. For example, they may respond by becoming angry, deny any concerns, or say the activity is just stupid; they remain unaware of the purpose these defensive responses serve in maintaining a distance from their own feelings.

In these cases, you may use a more abstract drawing approach, such as asking them to create a generalized drawing about their feelings or a representation of how someone might feel with those types of emotions. Again, as in the other drawing approaches, the client may require a prompt to begin the process. For example, you may use a lightning bolt to express strong feelings, a black or red scribble across the page to denote anger or frustration, or blue teardrops to represent sadness. For some clients who may be more self-conscious about their drawing skills or feel constricted and inhibited, your prompts (by providing such general examples) can give them permission to explore these parts of themselves or to explore previously unknown styles of expression.

Body Work

Other mechanisms for anger management include identifying the place of anger or any other feeling within the client's identity, family expectations, or their own body. In some families, anger is an acceptable form of expression, whereas showing signs of vulnerability, such as crying or sadness, is unacceptable. In other words, what does anger mean for this client? Is it an attempt to cover up a deeper pain that she feels unsafe to express? Is the anger a sense of entitlement? Is anger the only emotional expression modeled in the home? If you can help clients understand the intertwined role between anger, sadness, and family expectations, then you have a good prognosis for a positive outcome with your clients.

Asking the client to talk about the physical experience of anger or sadness can provide a more kinesthetic approach that works well for many child and adolescent clients (Wilson & Ryan, 2002). It helps them identify and own the feelings and gives them a physical cue that might serve as an early self-monitoring mechanism to redirect the anger, for example. Bringing the family into such discussions as support may help in the maintenance of new behavioral responses.

TECHNIQUES

Expressive Techniques

Drawing techniques, such as comic strip problem solving, gingerbread feelings, and abstract expression to identify feelings, can move therapy forward. Asking clients to create posters or collages to identify aspects of themselves can help them express feelings. Drawing the family is a helpful projective technique and can be an icebreaker to help the child feel comfortable in early sessions. As a projective technique, family drawings can provide insight for the therapist into the child's inner world and understanding of family relationships. Typically, you can use the positioning and size of family members to extrapolate general information and talk in more detail using the drawing as a stimulus. Additionally, children who have been abused or are developmentally delayed may produce drawings that are incomplete or unusual (e.g., with missing or exaggerated body parts) or may represent an idealized family life, which bears little or no similarity to their real lives and families. As with the use of any projective technique, the counselor is cautioned against over-interpretation. Without advanced training, the optimal and most ethical use of drawings is to facilitate the therapeutic work through discussion, discovery, and implementation of interventions.

Genograms

Genograms offer a helpful alternative to other strategies used to explore family history with children because the genogram serves to objectify the information and the task, making the child or adolescent feel less the focus of the intervention. The activity also provides an opportunity for the child to explore her identity within the context of family members' lives, family history/legacy, family identities, careers, and possibly family secrets. Drawing the parents into the activity fleshes out the biographical information and may also provide some positive reinforcement for the client's identity and strengths.

A genogram (McGoldrick & Gerson, 1985) uses basic symbols such as circles and squares to represent male and female members of the family as in the accompanying example. Various lines are used to represent connection: straight for uninterrupted relationships, jagged for conflict, with a dash in the center for divorce, and an X through the symbol representing deceased family members. Basic information such as dates of birth and death, names, professions, and personal characteristics, such as artistic, grouchy, or fun-loving, may be added. See Figure 5.1.

Storytelling

Another interactive technique, which allows some distance for the young client from her own specific concerns is that of storytelling. This can take the form of mutual storytelling, as promoted by Gardner (2002), in which the therapist and client alternate in adding to a story. Even the old gossip and telephone games from around the campfire can be incorporated into play therapy activities. For example, a therapist and young client may bury toy figures in the sand and engage in a narrative about what is happening or how the figures "feel" during the play.

Bibliotherapy/Heroes

With those children for whom motivation and direct discussion are difficult, hero emulation can be a good tool. Directing them toward positive role models within

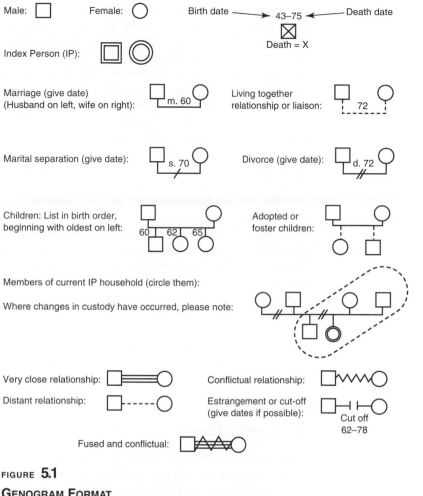

Reprinted by permission of Dr. Monica McGoldrick.

FIGURE 5.1

GENOGRAM FORMAT

Symbols to describe basic family membership and structure

their own lives or through the media may help them to become more grounded in themselves and within the therapy. It also helps keep the issues at a safer distance, working more effectively with those children for whom direct ownership of their decisions and actions is difficult and a constant impediment to positive change. Engaging the child or adolescent in tasks outlining the specific characteristics they admire about the hero can be a way to identify goals for changes within themselves.

Bibliotherapy works well with all ages, given the right resources. With younger children, using some of the therapeutic readers on anger management, sadness, and other topics can work well in session, as can posters representing feelings for identifying reactions to the world around them. For older children, adolescents, and adults, assigning certain chapters as homework between sessions, writing about it between sessions, and discussions at later sessions can be familiar formats to address difficult feelings and behaviors. This can also help to normalize typical reactions to usual and unusual life events.

School libraries or school counselors may be good resources for age-appropriate therapeutic books. Many titles are available on a variety of topics, including anger management, dealing with divorce, and making appropriate choices. For example, some professional organizations publish books that are directed toward children and teens, such as the American Psychological Association or the American Counseling Association. Private publishers also have books available that are directed toward this audience, such as Free Spirit Publishing, ChildWork/ChildPlay, or Courage to Change.

Autobiographical sources or essays to expose clients to the experiences of others and to present them with different ways to think, talk, and cope with life stressors or specific aspects of their presenting concerns can be a powerful and engaging approach. Many resources are available, including first-person essays from teens themselves, their parents, and the professionals with whom they work.

Reading, unfortunately, is not a way to reach everyone. Many youth today prefer to watch a video rather than read. Several sources are available to help screen video sources as well (e.g., *Video Hound* or *Rent Two Films and Call Me in the Morning*). Videos can offer an updated alternative to traditional bibliotherapy.

Therapeutic Games

Many positive therapeutic games are available. Use of games is often helpful to deepen the work at this phase. Children and preadolescents often reach an impasse in being able to express themselves. At those times, therapeutic games can help the child talk about scenarios describing school, friends, and family. The classic game is *The Talking, Feeling, and Doing Game* by Richard Gardner (1975). This is a wonderful tool for younger clients who may have difficulty with direct expression or in talking about their own experiences and choices. The format of this game and many others facilitates discussion by objectifying problems and moving emotionally away from the pain of the child's own experiences and feelings. By using the cards to solve problems, young clients are put in the role of helping out another by devising potential plans and solutions, which may also be applied to their own life situations. Children can move toward ownership of their problems and concerns at a more comfortable pace and in a manner similar to "saving face" from an Eastern perspective.

The game can also be used as part of the ongoing therapeutic assessment of children and adolescents, providing links to explore their responses to situations you may not have the opportunity to observe or have sources to provide the information.

Role-Plays and Psycho-Drama

Psycho-drama can involve the therapist and the child, a group of children, a family, or a child and puppets in acting out various life concerns and new ways of behaving. In the case of new behaviors, the interactions become more similar to role-plays than psycho-drama, but all continue to have that sense of drama in their presentation. These types of therapeutic interactions are merely a more stylized or directed form of the free play in play therapy. Because the client takes on the role more directly, psycho-drama and role-play are more appropriate for older children who have progressed to a developmental stage consistent with a more sophisticated understanding of life roles, ability to understand others' feelings and situations, and ability to observe (at least at a minimal level) the potential impact of their own actions.

Physical Exercise

Anger management control often involves an impulse control component. Prior to implementing any anger management techniques, one needs to assess the child or adolescent's ability to control her impulses. If the client has a tendency to act impulsively or is already somewhat out of control you need to be more conservative in selecting interventions. For such clients, solitary physical activities to divert angry energy may be an effective intervention. Many schools restrict recess time for young children with anger problems; however, this consequence often backfires, creating even more unfocused energy within the child that tends to erupt later. Schools may need to become more flexible and creative in accommodating children with a need for physical release. Therapeutic physical activities should be overseen by understanding adults who can provide a structure and continue to adapt activities as children's ability for self-control increases. It is important not to alienate these children from the school system, as this sets up a greater likelihood for disinterest and dropping out in junior high or high school. A nondestructive physical activity focuses on the anger, not on destructive acts. As noted with journaling and therapeutic letter writing, it is the therapist's responsibility to assess the likelihood that clients can use this technique without becoming negatively focused on destruction or violent actions toward the object of their anger.

The client can release by running and thinking about her anger toward the individual. As the child or adolescent becomes tired from the physical activity, she can also release the anger. If this client has difficulty letting go of these angry responses, then the use of imagery or other methods may be more appropriate for her.

Physical exercise also has proven benefits for depressive symptoms, which may or may not be expressed as anger for children and adolescents. It is more common to see irritability and anger in depressed youth, so if the client increases physical activity, lifting of other depressive symptoms may also be observed.

Identifying Triggers

Triggers are external events, people, thoughts, or feelings that precipitate certain behaviors. Individual triggers, or cues, are different for everyone. Identifying triggers is the initial step in a process that will ideally involve an internal process of self-monitoring by child and adolescent clients. Initially however, the process may only involve external observations as a backdrop for providing the intervention. A technique that can be used to prompt the younger child to begin to think about these triggers is that of the "comic strip" technique, described earlier in this chapter. Breaking the event down into its components provides information about specific triggers and a greater sense of mastery. A positive sense of self-efficacy is necessary to move forward in making change.

The comic strip technique also allows exploration of the child's cognitions and affect about the behavior or event. What was the client thinking or feeling just prior to her acting-out or externalizing behavior? Typical externalizing behaviors include yelling, punching, or running away; the complete list is as wide reaching as the individuals themselves (Durlak, Rubin, & Kahng, 2001). Exploration of the child's cognitions helps to tailor the interventions. If the child denies the behavior, you know you have a long way to go. However, if the child recognizes her part in the behavioral ballet, the interventions are likely to be more positive and can be constructively implemented. Of course, we need to remain cognizant of the child's developmental level and expect cooperation and complicity with treatment within that framework. As noted throughout the text, interventions at an inappropriate developmental level decrease our effectiveness as clinicians and increase frustration within the client and family system, possibly setting up or feeding into preexisting unrealistic expectations from parents. This dynamic may exacerbate parent/child relationships.

MULTIDISCIPLINARY APPROACHES

Medication

Children or adolescents may already be receiving medication when they come for psychological services, or that may be an issue that arises for consultation throughout the course of your work. Many people, parents and professionals alike, have ambivalent feelings about the use of medications with children, and it is vitally important to use caution with medications. However, some children do benefit from medication for extreme symptoms that may be out of the child or adolescent's control. Medications are commonly used for symptoms of ADHD, autistic features, depression, enuresis, Tourette's syndrome, and severe mental retardation with co-morbid behavior disorders (Vitiello, 2001).

Collaborative Treatment in Complex Cases

During the working stages of therapy, it may become obvious that a multidisciplinary approach may be necessary due to the complexity of co-morbid conditions. One of the more common collaborations involves prescribing medication. Whether a child or adolescent is on medication when they come to you, your sessions can provide a good source of feedback for the treating physician or psychiatrist. It is often a good idea to obtain permission to communicate, so that you can share pertinent observations. Such a collaborative approach not only improves client care, but also helps you feel more supported and less alone in treatment efforts. The latter can be an important factor for those who may be in a private practice setting.

Psychologists and counselors have a role in providing input into evaluation and decisions regarding appropriateness of medication consultation, providing effective adjunctive therapy, and assisting in compliance monitoring (Brown & Sammons, 2002). As with assessment for children and adolescents, it is important to involve multiple sources in obtaining feedback about medication effectiveness by involving parents and school and medical personnel (Achenbach, McConaughy & Howell, 1987). Always be aware of the balance that it is necessary to maintain between working with the child or adolescent client and parents (Brown & Sammons, 2002). Just as it is necessary to maintain a balance and parallel relationships in establishing rapport, it is critical to do so around medication management as well. Medication compliance can easily become a power struggle in families, setting the stage for therapeutic impasse or unproductive conflict. Adolescents and children often are unaware of the effects of medication (Brown & Sawyer, 1998; Zametkin & Yamada, 1999) and, as such, may be more reluctant to be compliant, particularly if family dynamics include conflict or oppositional behaviors already.

Mixed results have been seen in the use of medication to attempt to treat multiple symptoms (Michael & Crowley, 2002). However, for many child and adolescent clients, although the medications may not be effective on their own, they can provide a "window of opportunity" so that the adjunctive therapies may be more effective.

In addition to depression as a common co-morbid disorder, anxiety often coexists with depression. One fourth to one half of depressed youth have comorbid anxiety disorders, and 10 percent to 15 percent of anxious youth have depression (Axelson & Birmaher, 2001). In some instances, this co-morbidity is also associated with a higher level of suicidal ideation, particularly in generalized anxiety disorder (Masi, Mucci, Favilla, & Millepiedi, 2001). It's possible that the coexistence of generalized anxiety and depression makes hopelessness feel more severe, thus making suicide seem like a more viable option. For many children and adolescents with a predisposition toward anxiety, internalized negative self-perceptions combined with expectations for difficult life challenges contribute to the development of extreme hopeless feelings (Dadds & Barrett, 2001). The concordance between anxious and depressed youth is in the area of negative affect and may be related to a negative bias in information processing (Axelson & Birmaher, 2001). The negative perspective, in conjunction with passive or withdrawn responses to stress, often fosters a fear response in some children and adolescents, setting up a repetitive cycle that maintains the anxiety (Ollendick, Langley, Jones, & Kephart, 2001). Such findings are consistent with the relative success reported with cognitive behavioral strategies in the treatment of both depression and anxiety.

Factors in Effective Interventions

In a review of the literature, Morris and Nicholson (1993) identified therapist and client variables as well as additional factors that impact the therapeutic relationship and the process of therapy. Therapist characteristics included style, presence, proxemics (or how the therapist manages physical closeness), warmth, empathy, expertness/status, values, self-concept, nonverbal communication, and race, while client variables included expectations, imitation, and type of presenting problem. Other factors with potential impact on the relationship include management of confidentiality and working with certain populations such as gay, lesbian, and bisexual teens or mentally challenged youth (Morris & Nicholson, 1993).

Effective interventions include both individual and family therapies, with family techniques focusing on modifying family patterns of interaction, specifically improving communication and positive coping strategies, with the aim of decreasing anxiety. Individual interventions focus on cognitive behavioral strategies aimed at self-perceptions and developing skills in developing self-efficacy.

The working stage involves helping clients use the therapeutic relationship and trust developed through positive rapport to begin to identify, own, and work through positive solutions to their own issues and life problems. Parents may be an important part of this working-through process, or children and adolescents may require some continued distance until they trust that their parents can be supportive. This determination will depend on your assessment of the parental relationship as well as clients' perception of the relationship. Bring in the parents as appropriate; timing and titration are important in being successful. These are important aspects that are learned with experience, not necessarily through books.

Discussion Questions

1. Why is the therapeutic alliance important during the working stage of therapy? What factors enhance or detract from the effectiveness of the therapeutic relationship, including those that are specific to work with children and adolescents?
2. How do monitoring, balance, trust, and confidentiality relate during the working stages of therapy?
3. List and discuss factors that may affect "working through"?
4. Brief therapy techniques as applied to work with children and adolescents are unique in what ways?
5. Which techniques may be more effective with clients who are less verbal.
6. Describe three different cases when using a genogram would be the optimal intervention.

7. What cautions do you need to inform the client of with regard to the therapeutic letter technique?
8. What reactions might be indicative of a countertransference reaction for you as a therapist?
9. Why or why not would you use a therapeutic game in the first session?
10. For what situations or clients would a group intervention be appropriate?

Final Stages of Counseling

Introduction

The final stage of therapy is one of assimilation and separation, similar in some ways to the individuation/separation process of adolescence. The goal of counseling is to help the client become appropriately independent from the therapist. Children and adolescents will not become completely independent because of their age and developmental level. Young clients will continue to remain interdependent with their parents throughout their lives in one way or another. Hopefully, the process of treatment has enhanced the ability of all family members to maintain those relationships positively. The exception to such an outcome would include situations in which there has been some type of abuse within the family. In those cases, a greater level of independence may have been part of the therapeutic goal. These therapeutic challenges will be reviewed in Chapter 9.

The goal in the final phase of therapy is to assist the child and adolescent client in integrating therapeutic gains and working toward termination. Termination will involve helping the client view himself as more independent and capable and may include developing a maintenance plan. A maintenance plan can be similar to a therapeutic contract or a no-harm contract (Chapter 7) in its outline; however, the specific focus will include appropriate responses to various life situations. For example, the adolescent client with whom you've been working has struggled with depression. An appropriate maintenance plan could include the triggers or situations that might precipitate a depressive episode (e.g., failing a test, feeling rejected by peers, conflict with parents). The next phase of the plan would include responses that have been effective for the client during treatment (e.g., journaling, writing down thoughts as a precursor to talking with the person, getting some exercise).

Other factors that affect the termination process include differences in length of treatment and the reasons for termination. As discussed more fully in Chapter 12, external constraints such as managed care guidelines or the end of the school year are often part of the reason for termination. Each of these brings a different challenge to the termination, which will be considered in this chapter. An important component of ending any therapy involves helping the client transition to being able to use personal sources—initially in addition to your professional resources and eventually in place of the professional relationship. Children who feel they have few resources may actually view the termination of counseling as a negative outcome or punishment. Building informal support systems throughout the course of therapy helps the client and family maintain a healthy level of functioning after therapy ends.

THE FINAL PHASE OF THERAPY: RECOGNIZING WHEN THE WORK IS COMPLETE

Ideally, the termination of treatment is a decision made by all involved and is based on achieving therapeutic goals (Greenberg, 2002; Wachtel, 2002). Although the goals may have changed throughout the course of treatment, effectively managing the presenting concerns is generally considered as part of the reason for termination (Goldfried, 2002). With children and adolescents, and many adult clients as well, a more realistic approach is intermittent therapy (Greenberg, 2002; Kreilkamp, 1989). Such an approach is particularly well suited to children and adolescents because of the continual changes experienced as they grow and develop. It is much more realistic to assume (at least with parents, but this message can also be communicated directly with your older clients) that you continue to be available to them, despite termination. Some clients have a need to return, while others do not (Greenberg, 2002). The factors relating to recidivism (or returning to therapy) include the degree of support available to the client, degree of conflict within the family, personal resources and resiliency, and the initial presenting concern. The simple statement that you are available when they need you provides a measure of assurance and is essentially a norming mechanism for your clients, giving them permission to return, just as they would with their family physician. Such an intermittent approach provides a comforting continuity of care for clients and families.

FACTORS RELATED TO PREMATURE TERMINATION

Termination is the clinical description for the end of therapy. Although it is preferable to plan for termination, that is not always possible. Obstacles to continued therapy often include external constraints such as treatment setting, managed care guidelines, a family's decision, or the ending of the school year. Some clients may begin therapy and simply not return because they are not ready to begin therapeutic work at that time.

Many factors contribute to the timing of termination, particularly when working in a child-centered family approach. Termination becomes more complicated in this context, partially due to the increased number of people involved and partially related to specific issues about the client's family, including structure, belief systems, and expectations for the outcome of therapy. Parents may have unrealistic expectations about how therapy may change their child, and when those ideals are not achieved, they may decide to seek services elsewhere or simply terminate any type of treatment.

Family relationships also play a role in termination. *Family structure* refers to the degree of emotional distance or closeness in the family's relationships. In enmeshed or close family relationships, little separation or individuation among family roles exists. Role blurring, in which family members' roles are unclear because they are so close, may occur. Children may actually take on parental responsibilities in this type of family structure (Walsh, 1993). Families with poor role differentiation may become uncomfortable because of the distance inherent in the counseling process. The level of discomfort may become so great that termination is initiated as a result. Families with more emotional distance are less likely to experience discomfort as a result of separate sessions. However, if a family approach is required in an attempt to increase communication and closeness, family members may experience a similar discomfort, again resulting in termination.

Family beliefs can interfere with treatment in several ways. Family beliefs may include a view of the family as self-sufficient, including a distrust of strangers or formal helpers, or the family may have a taboo against openly discussing problems. If family members view themselves as self-sufficient, they are more likely to flee prematurely from therapy. The belief that they can manage their own problems is usually coupled with a taboo against talking about family issues. Both of these beliefs work against long-term participation in counseling. Difficulty trusting a formal helping network can arise from negative interactions with authorities or social service agencies (Walsh, 1993). Commitment to therapy for families with any of these types of beliefs will be less than that for a family that is able or willing to ask for help. For those families who eagerly accept assistance, termination may actually be more difficult, because they have become used to having the support available as if you were part of their extended family.

The family's expectations for treatment may be unrealistic as well. Idealized views of what therapy can accomplish are often associated with the belief that the child or adolescent is "the problem." The child or adolescent then becomes the identified client and a scapegoat in some ways for the family's woes (Bowen, 1972). Unfortunately, this pattern actually has the potential to become a self-perpetuating prophecy when unrealistic goals of therapy cannot be achieved, and the child or adolescent becomes the "failure" again.

The family factors described previously make premature termination much more likely and interfere with productive therapy in most cases.

RECURRENCE OF SYMPTOMS UPON TERMINATION

Although all clients and families vary in their readiness and ability to terminate successfully from therapy, the contrasts can be even more striking with children and adolescents. We are all aware of the tendency for clients to exhibit new symptoms or revisit old symptomatology near the termination of treatment. Motivation for the recurrence of symptoms is hypothesized to be related to recapitulation of earlier losses and separations (Donoghue, 1994). Essentially, the client reverts to old behavior patterns when the strong feeling and anxiety about termination surface.

Client awareness of this recurrent behavior in children and adolescents is usually more limited than it is in adults, dependent on the respective developmental level at the time of termination. Even if clients are provided with information about how it may feel toward the end of therapy, it will probably be difficult for a child or adolescent to distinguish between anxiety over the change (i.e., termination) and old feelings arising from another source. Bembry and Ericson (1999) suggest that termination becomes a more difficult process for adolescents who have experienced other losses in their lives. Ending the therapeutic relationship recapitulates emotions around previous losses and makes the transition more challenging. Managing emotions with a concrete termination plan that outlines coping strategies for use when the client feels stressed or down is probably the most practical approach with this age group. The plan can also function as a transitional object (Winnicott, 1993) for the therapeutic relationship. In some settings, such as a school, continued informal contact may be possible. The level at which such contact would be therapeutic needs to be determined in terms of each client's level of functioning. The level of developmental functioning for most of our young clients makes review and working through feelings related to other losses unproductive and confusing in many cases.

Your role as therapist requires that you determine whether the symptoms are simply recurrent in response to termination or if the symptoms are recurring in response to other internal or external stimuli. The process of differential diagnosis, reviewed in Chapter 3, may be helpful to you in teasing out these behaviors. Obviously, if you determine the symptoms are separate from the termination process, those plans may need to be modified. Making such a decision in cooperation with parents is optimal. The appropriate decision is critical in terms of its potential to shape the child or adolescent's behavior. If the client becomes aware of an apparent connection between increased symptoms and continuation of therapy, the behavior may continue as a result.

REVIEWING THERAPEUTIC GAINS

Dependent on the client's developmental level, talking about gains and reviewing possible options when feeling stressed or down can be sufficient for termination. With younger children, it is often more effective to involve parents in the termination process with the goal of reinforcing the gains. The collaborative approach to termination helps children understand they will continue to be supported and feel safety of the structure from their parents monitoring the gains made in therapy. For children at an in-between stage, simply writing down coping skills they can use on their own as a reminder helps empower clients.

With children, you must also exercise your knowledge of the vast developmental differences that exist even within the normal range, in making an assessment of whether behavioral changes at the time of termination are within the normal range or consistent with a need for continued treatment.

The success of rapport building will also impact termination. If the young client has not fully committed to therapy, you may need to introduce the concept of termination to parents. If that is the case, termination may be reached sooner rather than later because of the client's refusal to work in therapy. If this is your assessment, you need to convey that to the parents and explore available options. It is unethical to continue treatment when progress is unlikely.

BALANCING BETWEEN CHILDREN, ADOLESCENTS, AND PARENTS

Maintaining the balance between children and parents is the challenge of working in a child-centered family approach. Therapists perpetually balance their efforts between their young clients and their parents, working hard to keep both sides engaged. Once either parents or clients become less invested in therapy, termination becomes more likely. Expectation for a specific outcome is strongly associated with parents' investment in therapy. Parents' agenda and commitment may ebb and flow, depending on their own expectations of success, the level of involvement they feel, and financial limitations in certain settings. Specific factors associated with low parental expectations for therapy include (Nock & Kazdin, 2001):

- economic disadvantages
- status as an ethnic minority
- severity of the child or adolescent's presenting problems (particularly for oppositional, aggressive, antisocial, or running away behaviors and truancy)
- the client's age (often more invested with younger children)
- level of parental stress or depression

A strong correlation also appears to exist between parental expectation for positive outcome and parents' level of participation in treatment. Parents are more likely to participate if they have a high expectation for a positive outcome, and their involvement is probably a strong factor in a more positive outcome. Thus, it appears that the expectancies set up a self-fulfilling prophecy of sorts in that lowered expectations precede intermittent participation. When viewed in this way, it is not surprising that a negative outcome is often preceded by sporadic participation and skepticism about the value of the therapeutic process.

ASPECTS OF TERMINATION ACROSS SETTING

Although some aspects of termination may vary with setting, the basic aspects are relatively similar. In private practice, community agency or hospital settings, the termination may be more traditional in that further work is unlikely. However, it is becoming more common, particularly in working with children, that counseling does not terminate in the traditional sense but rather becomes more sporadic or intermittent. Working from this type of model is more similar to that of the school counselor who can assume future contact with clients due to the nature of the setting. In the school setting, continued contact is assumed until the termination of the formal relationship when the student graduates to the next level, leaves for the summer, or moves out of the district. In private practice, those artificial boundaries do not exist. Therefore, for professionals in a private practice or outpatient agency setting, therapeutic relationships may continue for years, mirroring the ethical and legal obligations in our work with children and adolescents.

Brief Episodic Therapy

For those clients with whom you have an ongoing professional relationship, the initial work of rapport building continues to have a positive ripple effect. Clients and families may return after years when they meet another developmental challenge. This is a satisfying part of professional life, and it also serves to reinforce the impact of your work with clients. When clients return after an absence, you have the rare opportunity to see outcome and follow-up in action. How did your interventions work? This is a wonderfully unique aspect of working with children and adolescents—being able to see significant changes in clients as they grow and develop, perhaps in part because of your work.

A client's return demonstrates that rapport was well established. It can be exhilarating and a little chilling to see the impact of your relationship with clients in such a way. It reinforces the need to be cognizant of the power of the therapeutic relationship. Your therapeutic work may have ended, but as in an ideal termination, the client and his family continue to carry your work with them and may return for further assistance when the relationship has been solid and positive. This communicates that you're doing something right.

A successful and productive termination is part of fostering that "legacy," if we may wax so poetic about the artistic and soulful side of our work. When planning for termination, your professional setting will guide some clinical decisions throughout the process. If you are in an inpatient setting, planning for discharge typically begins as soon as the client enters the hospital. In some ways, this has become even more true with the influence of managed care in shortening hospital stays. A hospital's role has become one of rapid stabilization and release. In this context, a crucial aspect of your termination planning is the aftercare process— helping the client in referral to an outpatient therapist, who may be part of your facility or an independent practitioner in the community. Timing is crucial in setting up the aftercare and, depending on the client's mental status, usually is best arranged within a week of discharge. If you are working in an inpatient setting, make every attempt to contact the community provider before the client's discharge. Such action is a professional courtesy and a positive relationship builder for your connections in the community. And the advance information will certainly help the community professional's work with the client.

Managed Care

The influence of managed care on therapy is usually in shortening the length of stay. However, the staff of the managed care organization can be helpful in terms of identifying those who may be approved providers to continue to work with this family. In some instances, clients may have already established a therapeutic relationship with a provider to whom they can return. Having the option to return to continue working with someone the client already knows is positive as long as the client was comfortable with that professional relationship and/or there are no other constraints on that decision (e.g., insurance complications, therapist's agreement that he and the client are well suited to continue working together). Continuity of care in returning to an already established professional relationship can facilitate therapeutic work.

School

In the school setting, similar planning may begin occurring in the spring to plan for continued counseling throughout the summer months, if needed, and identify resources for interim counseling. If the school counselor has been working with someone in the community throughout the year, then the transition may be more seamless than if the referral process begins from scratch. Even in those schools where crisis counselors or contract counselors are available through various grants and publicly funded programs, it may be necessary to find a new counselor with the ending of the school year.

REFERRAL

The referral process is a specific type of termination that involves balancing an ending and a beginning. Most referrals are made more successful by viewing them as a transition and helping the client identify specific issues for continued work with the new therapist. The specific steps of the referral process are outlined in Chapter 11. If possible, a face-to-face meeting can help allay anxiety and ultimately reduce the likelihood of premature termination. Discussion about the transfer should include the typical points covered in termination and may also review emotional aspects of the termination unique to a referral, including anxiety about the new therapy and sadness over the loss of the current therapist. Typical reasons for transfer include therapeutic impasse, need for a different area of expertise, changes mandated by managed care, or a family move.

TERMINATION PLANNING

Termination planning begins by informing the client of the anticipated plans. Even for brief breaks in therapy (e.g., summer vacations, conferences), the client may experience feelings similar to abandonment that termination may trigger. Whether for short breaks or termination, preparation for a break in the therapeutic relationship can follow a similar format, as outlined in the following list. The critical factors include the client's plan regarding coping skills and the prior development of a community support network for the client.

TERMINATION PROCESS

1. Discuss the termination with your client well in advance.
2. Share with the client your feelings about working with him. Hopefully they were truly positive, but if this feels disingenuous to say, find some strengths or personality characteristics that you can honestly highlight toward the end of therapy. Highlighting the client's work in therapy can also be part of this initial discussion. The discussion can begin in the second-to-last session or as part of the final session. Based on the level of rapport established and the length of time you and the client have been working together, the client might not return for the final session. This happens more frequently with clients in relatively brief therapeutic relationships. It is not uncommon for longer-term clients to suggest continuing the relationship outside of therapy now that "it's over." You will want to avoid developing such relationships on the basis of your ethical code. Responding to pressure from a client about extending the relationship maintains a dual relationship. Despite termination of therapy, the power is unequal, making the client vulnerable. Beginning and ending the final session with positive information sets a productive tone for the client's departure.
3. Ask the client what he has gained from the therapeutic process. Engage in this discussion by expanding on those gains as appropriate. Allow the client to go first in listing therapeutic gains. This way, he is not influenced by your perceptions of the therapeutic work before he has had a chance to own and describe it.
4. Follow up with your perception of the client's strengths and how you have seen those used positively in therapy. Reflect on your perception of the working relationship with the client.
5. Review with the client those coping skills that have worked well for the client. Again, give the client the opportunity to discuss these gains first, then provide your insights and suggestions. Provide the client with materials to write down reminders if he would like to do so.
6. Depending on the client's level of integration with the new skills and perspectives, together you may want to develop a written plan about how to address certain situations, similar to a no-harm contract. You might even produce something together that outlines specific responses for certain triggers. The plan can become a reminder regarding specific behaviors and coping skills and also of the therapeutic relationship. If the client is still operating at a fairly concrete level, or if the termination is imposed by outside constraints (e.g., the ending of the school year or early release from a hospital program), then this document becomes even more important in helping the client to be successful. The document may serve as a transitional

object for the client and help him carry with him the positive aspects and strength of the therapeutic alliance. If the time in therapy has been brief prior to termination, the working alliance is probably less well developed, and the tool becomes more of a lifesaver to help the client move toward a healthier place. Interim work with another professional to help the client by providing external structure, if termination occurred early, may be necessary. If managed care is an issue, informal support such as the school counselor or a pastor may be a necessary support.

7. Identify a list of potential resources and actions beyond the coping skills for the client's use. Remember to invite him to return if that is appropriate. If that is not an option due to external or setting constraints, then help identify new resources at the college counseling center, for example, or through family members and community agencies. This list is similar to the section of a no-harm contract that identifies options and resources for the client when suicidal feelings are experienced between sessions. A similar format can be used with clients who are terminating. Having a concrete resource like the list can provide a tool for the client to enhance the likelihood of success after termination. The list becomes even more critical following premature termination and, as such, may be an important tool to develop early in your sessions so that the client has the list available if the family decides to terminate without notice.

8. Remember to maintain appropriate boundaries with the client. Many clients will attempt to continue the relationship on a more informal level to keep you in their lives (e.g., inviting you to school functions, sporting events, or out for a soda). It is best to reiterate that no matter how much you enjoyed working with them that you probably won't be able to attend these events.

PREMATURE TERMINATION

What happens if your clients don't come back? This is also known as *premature termination,* which can occur for several reasons, usually related to family dynamics, parental perceptions, specific problems being addressed, and even the age of your client. Bailey and Hamilton (1987) found varying levels of perceived effectiveness of therapy, given the age of clients. Although outcome studies with children and adolescents are relatively rare, this study followed up with families 6 to 12 months following termination. Treatment interventions for the children included "clear rules, rewarding acceptable behavior, and using time-out," while interventions with adolescents included "communication, negotiating, and contracting skills." Significantly more parents of children described a successful outcome than did parents of adolescents. Significant differences were seen, as would be expected, for premature termination, which often occurs more frequently with adolescent populations. Parents have less control over adolescent compliance, and more negative patterns may have built up within the family prior to seeking treatment for the families of adolescents. Even the developmentally appropriate task of helping their adolescent children begin to separate is challenging for many families, depending on the birth order (e.g., is this the last child in the home?), "goodness of fit" between the parents and adolescents' temperaments, and preexisting patterns of communication and conflict.

Behavioral problems are common presenting concerns among children, and level of severity for those problems has been identified as a factor in early termination (Derisleyl & Reynolds, 2000), which relates to unrealistic parental expectations. Although a strong therapeutic alliance can serve as a buffer against symptom severity, it is often not a strong enough factor to prevent early termination. The stress of specific problems can be a termination factor, but the family's resiliency is affected by other issues as well. These factors include:

- family characteristics, including socioeconomic status and parents' childhood experiences and how they relate to their own parenting practices
- parental characteristics (their own reaction to stressful life events)
- child characteristics and severity of behavioral problems such as level of oppositional, aggressive, or antisocial behavior, intellectual functioning, and peer relationships (Kazdin & Mazurick, 1994)

Since more people are involved in the therapeutic process for children and adolescents, the reasons for premature termination may be complex, but the client's willingness to participate and general compliance with tasks throughout various aspects of their lives can be a factor. Some of these potential factors relate to the level of commitment from the early stages of therapy and the apparent reasons for seeking therapy. One factor is whether parents have erroneously identified the child or adolescent as a sort of scapegoat when the entire family system is a more salient issue. Of course, parental influence can be a strong factor as well. Parents face competing demands. If they are more preoccupied with survival needs, as indicated in Maslow's hierarchy, they may have less energy available to devote to structuring and guiding the lives of their children, including participation in therapy. Hutchinson (1990) found that termination of counseling for some children is actually experienced more as punishment, due to the lack of emotional support available in troubled home environments. The chaos inherent in some families often leads to premature termination due to problems with transportation, multiple stressors competing for parental attention, or lack of commitment to the process due to attention to survival needs.

Another factor arising out of the family system is discomfort with the level of pain experienced as a result of therapy. Many families hide the pain and cover up with acting-out behaviors and avoidance that is taken away through the process of therapy. "Secrets" present in the family system that may be exposed through therapy are yet another factor; the family reacts by withdrawing, or manipulation may be used to sabotage therapy by one of the members (Weeks, 1989). A primary area identified as a potential contributor to premature termination by the therapist is difficulty maintaining balance within the family system (e.g., too close an alignment with client or parents).

Client Reactions

Client reactions to our interventions are another significant area affecting termination. Obviously, if clients interpret our interventions as ineffective, they will be more likely to terminate, unless they are getting some emotional needs met from the simple act of meeting for sessions. If you determine this is the possible secondary gain a client is obtaining from sessions when little progress is being made, it is important that you assist the client in increasing his level of social support outside of therapy and help him become more embedded within the community. Perhaps the client is actually a more appropriate candidate for group therapy, where he can focus on interpersonal relationships, social skills, and social anxiety—factors that may be interfering with his ability to make connections outside therapy.

As noted in Chapter 3, informing clients that it is your responsibility to share with them your perceptions of therapeutic impasse and discuss options, you need to let them know when therapy feels ineffective, just as you have asked them to inform you. Clients may experience a negative emotional or affective response to a good intervention. In other words, when you are on target with an intervention, certain clients will feel uncomfortable with their emotional responses. This is similar to the issue identified earlier as too much "pain" driving clients from treatment. McCullough, Winston, Farber, and Porter (1991) found that clients who experienced an affective response as opposed to a defensive response following therapist intervention were more likely to identify improvement as a result of therapy and less likely to terminate prematurely.

Therapist Reactions

Many therapists have reactions to client's premature termination, particularly early in their training and professional careers. Although it is important to review the case on your own, with colleagues, or in consultation with your supervisor so that you may identify any potential areas for your improvement, the likely reason for premature termination is usually within the dynamics of the family. Regardless, as a professional, you must come to terms with the residual feelings that may be experienced after early termination. Your reactions will be affected by the specific dynamics of the family. Were you more invested in the child or adolescent client, or the parents? In other words, who were you identifying as the "client," or did you like one better than the other? Did you find yourself overidentifying with the adolescent client? If so, that alignment may have interfered, creating some countertransference of which you were unaware. Did you identify too closely with the parents, possibly driving the adolescent away because therapeutic interactions had simply become too similar to those with other adults in the adolescent's life? Exploring the answers to these questions here and in the workbook can strengthen your understanding and effectiveness of your own work and help prevent premature termination in the future.

Length of Treatment

Another factor in premature termination may be in the simple matter of definition of length of treatment. Petarik and Finney-Owen (1987) found differences between client and therapist definitions in terms of expected length of treatment. Thus, premature termination, as defined by the therapist, may be a result of that definition. It is important to give clients some idea of relative length of treatment at the outset. If nothing else, provide them with an interim time frame for reassessment. The author usually suggests informal reassessment after three or four sessions. After that length of time, it is possible for the family and therapist to have some idea of the potential prognosis and ability of the client to be effective in therapy.

In addition, therapists in the Petarik and Finney-Owen (1987) study underestimated the impact of the client's dislike of therapy or the therapist in early termination. This is another important aspect of work with all clients, but particularly with children and adolescents. If they don't like us—if they think we smell funny or look weird, or just don't get it—they will not work in therapy. You may want to include this as a potential reaction in the summary of your early appraisal. If clients or their parents are not comfortable in treatment, then the work will be difficult, if not impossible. Be emphatic that you want clients to let you know if it feels like something is not working. You can make adjustments in the therapeutic process to a large degree; that flexibility is part of the inherent process of meeting clients where they are. As such, you not only need to give your clients permission to speak about what's inside, you need to enlist their aid openly to participate in doing so. This is another aspect of the therapeutic relationship that differs from other relationships clients have outside therapy. This openness creates a positive effect.

Cultural Factors

Cultural factors may contribute to a negative therapeutic interaction that can lead to premature termination. Misinterpretation often occurs in cross-cultural counseling (see Chapter 11). For those without training, awareness, or sensitivity to potential cultural differences, the lack of knowledge may lead to misdiagnosis or misinterpretation (Westrich, 1994). Art may provide a way to help bridge the language or communication gap when cultural differences are present. In addition, the therapist and client need to complete significant exploration into potential contributing factors to head off premature termination.

Community Support

For clients with few external or community supports, helping to identify and possibly develop these resources should be an integral component of your interventions early in therapy. These clients may be at greater risk for premature termination, partially due to the parents' focus on "survival issues" for the family.

However, it is even more critical for these young clients to have adequate support systems or at least a few individuals available at school or through a community program to shore up their resources to enhance the likelihood of a successful transition and outcome.

Some schools and counselors offer programs designed to involve families in their students' school life, while other communities offer positive programs, often through the YMCA or a community recreation center. The possibility of getting students involved in volunteering, even at fairly young ages, can be another option to increase a positive sense of community resources. Many high schools require students to volunteer for community service projects as part of their curriculum or college preparatory programs. Even for those adolescents in the juvenile justice system, the requirement of community service can often be an initial bridge to become involved in more prosocial activities or to find a mentor, if approached positively.

CONSOLIDATING GAINS

Consolidating gains in the final stages of therapy is an essential part of helping the child or adolescent client take ownership of the progress made in therapy. Reviewing coping skills and strategies to implement the skills helps the client be more successful in using them following termination. Role-play toward the termination phase may be helpful in reinforcing positive, healthy responses.

A parallel process is undertaken with the parents, reviewing their changes in parenting skills and family management learned in treatment. The process of reviewing gains and helping the clients and parents experience therapy as more of an equal relationship with the therapist is an important component of the successful termination. It is necessary to help clients make this shift to increase their successful transition from the regular support of therapy to managing and making healthy decisions on their own (Wetchler & Ofte-Atha, 1993). Essentially, we are empowering our clients throughout the process of therapy and continuing to do so at termination. Many parents also experience a sense of loss at termination because of the support they have received in the child-centered family approach. Termination efforts need to be sensitive to the parents' responses as well as those of children, helping them see themselves as effective parents and individuals.

ETHICAL CONSIDERATIONS

It is important to remember that your professional obligations continue with the client despite termination. Avoiding dual relationships, bartering relationships, or collaborative ventures continues to be the standard for the professional relationship. Most professional organizations provide minimum time limits before a change in the relationship is considered acceptable. When working with children and adolescents, it is likely that the family will return for services within those time limits. It is best to avoid dual relationships, even if it is tempting to help out a needy, young client by providing opportunities for lawn mowing or running errands.

DISCUSSION QUESTIONS

1. What factors might make termination difficult for the client?
2. What factors might complicate termination for the therapist?
3. How can young clients and parents be involved in the termination process?
4. What strategies help the client transfer skills from therapy after termination?
5. Discuss differences in the termination process across various treatment settings.
6. What cultural factors need to be considered upon termination?

SPECIFIC PROBLEMS AND DISORDERS

This part is designed to help readers recognize and differentiate between commonly seen disorders and to understand the experience from the perspectives of young clients and their families. A further goal of these chapters is to explore how to identify and implement interventions most likely to benefit these clients and their families.

A common feature of many presenting problems is that of mood disorders, either as a primary or secondary concern. Chapter 7 will review diagnostic and treatment considerations for depression, anxiety, and obsessive-compulsive disorders. Sample interview questions and a no-harm contract will provide specific tools that can be applied immediately.

Behavioral problems are frequently seen as the initial manifestation of psychological and emotional disturbances in children and adolescents. Consistent with developmental levels, behavior often provides the only release available to young clients. Chapter 8 will review unique and common characteristics of several disorders, including Attention Deficit, Conduct, and Oppositional Defiant Disorders. Effective treatment approaches, including family factors, will be included.

Although behavioral presentations may be similar for developmental and externalizing disorders, the ability to differentiate between these disorders is essential for effective treatment. Chapter 9 will review unique aspects of developmental disorders, such as Asperger's and autism, in addition to specific factors associated with eating disorders.

Children and adolescents respond to life challenges in ways that are as unique as each individual. However, similar challenges are possible in the lives of many of our clients. Helping them recognize the aspects of their own response that are normal can be empowering for young clients. Special issues of sexuality, social skills, and bullying will be reviewed in Chapter 10.

MOOD DISORDERS

INTRODUCTION

Mood is something we expect to be variable. It is not considered a trait, even when a "mood" becomes less transient, such as in chronic depression or dysthymia. Mood disorders comprise a large percentage of most clinicians' caseloads, either as the primary presenting problem or as part of a more complex, multisymptom presentation. Thus, learning how to identify and manage such disorders is a primary concern in training. Cognitive-behavioral approaches are the most common interventions, but medication may also be required. For more resistant depression and anxiety, a combination of medication and therapy achieve the most effective results, though compliance can be a problem (Keller, Hirschfeld, Demyttaraere, & Baldwin, 2002) and results with children and adolescents are sometimes mixed (Michael & Crowley, 2002).

For many with mood disorders, the tendency is to turn inward or away from interaction with others and the world. For this simple reason, the term *internalizing disorders* is also used to describe disorders in which the tendency is to turn symptoms onto themselves as opposed to acting out against others. The description of turning inward does not completely fit for young clients; there is often a certain level of acting out regardless of the specific disorder with children and adolescents because of the interaction between developmental levels and style of self-expression.

This chapter will discuss depression, bipolar disorder, anxiety, obsessive compulsive disorder, and suicide. Family factors and treatment approaches will be included as well.

DEPRESSION

Description

Recognition of depressive symptoms, such as sadness, negativity, and depression in children and adolescents has increased in recent years (Seligman, Reivich, Jaycox, & Gillham, 1995). As our understanding of depression has broadened, others suggest that the prevalence rates may actually be increasing (Lewinsohn, Rohde, Seeley, & Fisher, 1993) rather than just a broadening knowledge base affecting our perspective. It is now recognized that young people experience depression (Reich et al., 1987); according to one report, as many as 9 percent of the population have experienced at least one episode of depression by age 14 (Lewinsohn et al., 1993).

Although some symptoms presenting in childhood and adolescence are similar to those for adults (e.g, lack of motivation, low energy), it is understood that a broader range of symptoms may be observed in this population (e.g., aggression, irritability, or somatic complaints). The specific presentation of depression in children and adolescents can vary with age. Despite the difficulty reported in attempting to diagnose young children, Ialongo, Edelsohn, and Kellam (2001) found that self-reports of children as young as 5 or 6 were accurate in the prediction of later depressive symptoms. Therefore, inquiring about mood may be helpful in diagnosis and in encouraging parents to "listen" to emotional concerns, even for very young children. Certainly, there exists general agreement that children are accurate self-reporters by middle to late elementary age (Weisz, Weiss, Wasserman, & Rintoul, 1987).

In its earliest presentation, below age 3, depressive symptoms are more consistent with failure to thrive, which may be a more familiar syndrome to some. This presentation involves a low energy level, lack of interaction with others and the environment, little emotional expression with the possible exception of tantrums, and possible feeding or eating problems.

For children between the ages of 3 and 5, strong fears and frequent accidents may be observed. Being overly apologetic or intensely angry about mistakes or failure to complete age-appropriate tasks are also seen. According to one study, percentage of time spent in play was significantly less for depressed children as compared to other children of the same age, and the quality of the play was more disjointed (Mol Lous, De Wit, De Bruyn, Riksen-Walraven, & Rost, 2000).

Children in early grades (ages 6 to 8) may begin to complain of aches or pains without apparent cause. Some estimate the prevalence of physical symptoms at more than 50 percent beginning at this age and continuing throughout adolescence (Williamson et al., 2000). Aggressive behavior may also begin to manifest at this time. Clinging behavior may recur, along with avoidance of new situations or challenges.

Presentation between the ages of 9 and 12 may include more morbid thinking, excessive worries, or sleep problems. Negative self-image and self-blame also affect a large percentage (more than 60 percent) of depressed preteens, and these symptoms may continue throughout adolescence (Williamson et al., 2000). Adolescents often present with more anger and irritability than sadness, accompanied by uncommunicativeness and hypersensitivity to criticism. Although rebelliousness toward parents and a tendency to "shut them out" is normal in adolescence, those behaviors become more extreme and more constant in depressed youths. A common observation of depressed adolescents is a change in peer groups and an accompanying change in behavior (e.g., toward delinquent acting out).

The Harvard Mental Health Letter (2002) estimates that at least 50 percent of depressed children and adolescents have at least one other coexisting condition. The most common coexisting conditions include anxiety disorder, conduct disorder, eating disorder, or substance abuse.

With depressed children, fear and anxiety are often components of the depression, perhaps precipitated by a family move or a downward turn in peer relationships. Depressive symptoms often manifest as irritability in children and adolescents, and typical symptoms of excessive sleep and decreased motivation may also be observed. Fear or anxiety can precipitate depressive symptoms that may reflect a feeling of powerlessness in the face of overwhelming stressors. A critical component of treatment is helping clients identify their own goals and dreams. Part of this process will likely include identifying obstacles as well and helping them feel empowered.

INTERVIEW QUESTIONS FOR PARENTS IN SCREENING FOR DEPRESSION

- What changes have you observed in appetite, sleep patterns, and relationships with friends and family?
- What areas of life does the child find satisfying? Has this changed?
- What is the family history with regard to depression, anxiety, or substance abuse?
- Has the child or adolescent been more irritable lately?
- What about risk-taking behavior? Does this seem related to self-destructive or suicidal ideation or intent for this child or adolescent?
- Is it difficult for the child to engage in tasks that used to be easy?

EXCERPT FROM CLIENT INTERVIEW

THERAPIST: *What kinds of things make you feel good about yourself?*
CLIENT: *Nothing.*
THERAPIST: *Do you ever feel so sad that you feel like hurting yourself?*
CLIENT: *I never would.*

(Note that at this point, you may want to follow up with the no-harm contract covered later in this chapter, particularly if the client is new and you're not sure about her level of safety.)

Diagnosis and Treatment

Diagnostic criteria are the same as for adults outlined in the DSM. The most effective results combine medication and therapy (Keller et al., 2002) when medication is needed, although there are some mixed results (Michael & Crowley, 2002).

Family therapy or a child-centered family approach is often the first course of action for children and adolescents. If ineffective, then medication may be necessary. A genetic predisposition toward depression is often present in those for whom medication is eventually prescribed.

Seligman and colleagues (1995, p. 238) suggest a positive psychology approach in their clinic, in which they encourage "children to think about their thinking." Such a self-reflective approach builds on the developing self-observation skills of children and adolescents to help them focus on positive self-talk and problem-solving skills. The approach allows children and adolescents to understand that other options are available to them, helping to work against feelings of hopelessness so often associated with depression (Abela, 2001).

Although still undergoing scrutiny, SSRIs (e.g., Prozac, Zoloft, or Paxil) are commonly used with children and adolescents without many side effects; however, a cautionary approach is always recommended when considering medication for children.

Impact of Depressive Symptoms on Social Interactions

Developing social skills and relationships are such an important part of life for children and adolescents that it is important to review the potential impact on that aspect of life for those with depressive symptoms. Recurrent negative thoughts and perceptions may influence children to attend selectively to stimuli and aspects of social interactions that foster maladaptive social skills and tend to perpetuate depressive symptoms (Rudolph & Clark, 2001). A negative view of self and others and skewed information processing about social situations (Armsden & Greenberg, 1987; Kaslow, Rehm, & Siegel, 1984; Quiggle, Garber, Panak, & Dodge, 1992; Rudolph, Hammen, & Burge, 1997; Shirk, Van Horn, & Leber, 1997) have been associated with depressive symptoms (Shirk, Boergers, Eason, & Van Horn, 1998), and have been identified as potential precipitants to depression (Cummings & Cicchetti, 1990; Kaslow, Rehm, & Siegel, 1984; Rudolph, Hammen, & Burge, 1997; Shirk et al., 1997, 1998).

Interpersonal theories of depression highlight the role of attachment and social skills in disrupting relationships and maintaining maladaptive patterns of interaction in those who suffer from depression (Barnett & Gotlib, 1988; Coyne, 1976; Lewinsohn, 1974), with the interpersonal aspect possibly contributing to maintenance of depressive symptoms as well. For children, this often becomes even more challenging due to the difficulty in mastering appropriate social skills, when starting from a deficit, and lacking the skills or knowledge necessary to change. Increased depressive symptoms may also impede the process from a motivational standpoint. Similar to adults with depression, children and adolescents may simply lack the energy or feel disinterested.

The associations between depression and poor social skills are well documented (Gotlib & Hammen, 1992; Hammen & Rudolph, 1996; Weisz, Rudolph, Granger, & Sweeney, 1992). Specific problems in terms of social skills include poor problem solving, tendencies to become isolated or withdrawn, irritability, inability to emphasize or accurately read social cues, and difficulty maintaining friendships (Altmann & Gotlib, 1988; Baker, Milich, & Manolis, 1996; Cole, 1990; Connolly, Geller, Marton, & Kutcher, 1992; Goodyer, Wright, & Altham, 1990; Kennedy, Spence, & Hensley, 1989; Patterson & Stoolmiller, 1991; Quiggle et al., 1992; Rudolph et al., 1994). Children internalize the comments of those around them, a process that appears to be exacerbated with symptoms of depression (Cole, 1991; Cole, Martin, & Powers, 1997; Cole & Turner, 1993), as compared with nondepressed children (Weisz et al., 1992), making negative comments even more powerful for children with depression.

Depression, Social Skills, and Self-Esteem

Negative self-concepts and negative views of those around them are consistently seen in children who are depressed (Gencoz, Voelz, Gencoz, Pettit, & Joiner, 2001), with or without accompanying aggression (Rudolph & Clark, 2001). Depression appears to be the mediating factor in negative self-perception, regardless of other strengths that may be observed in the child or adolescent (Abela & Veronneau-McIrdle, 2002; Gencoz et al., 2001). However, those with aggression as a primary concern display an aggrandized self-concept and are more often indifferent to the experiences of others. Children with a primary presenting concern of depression tend to display prosocial behaviors with peers—a positive behavior that is not always met with positive results due to the interaction with the child's negative self-concept. The negative self-concept can work against the positive aspects of the prosocial behavior, with self-questioning sometimes leading to peer rejection (Rudolph & Clark, 2001).

Poor self-esteem is also seen in children or adolescents with a prior diagnosis of ADHD. It is hypothesized that the difficulties and challenges accompanying the presentation of ADHD (e.g., problems with peers, difficulty organizing, challenges in completing reading or math) often precede the presentation of depressive symptoms, and certainly build on an already fragile self-concept (Treuting & Hinshaw, 2001). As with any co-morbid condition, these challenges require a more complex treatment approach, incorporating attention not only to behavioral management of attention deficit symptoms, but also incorporation of interventions aimed at accompanying symptoms of depression. More details specific to intervention for ADHD are addressed in Chapter 8.

Family Factors

As with most of our discussions about etiology of symptoms and disorders, it is imperative to review family factors, particularly with our population of children and adolescents. A common question in the literature is the impact of parental behaviors, including mental illness, on the experience within the family for children and adolescents, specifically with regard to the development of psychopathology and length of treatment (Kaminski & Garber, 2002). Lieb (2002) found that major depression in parents increases the overall likelihood of depressive symptoms and other emotional problems in their children. Nomura, Wickramaratne, Warner,

Mufson, & Weissman (2002) found similar support for identifying parental depression as a significant risk factor for the development of depression and anxiety in their children, while marital conflict was associated with substance abuse in adolescents. The results of this longitudinal study found support for continued symptomatology into adulthood (Nomura et al., 2002).

Davis, Sheeber, Hops, & Tildesley (2000) found that both male and female adolescents were more likely to develop depressive symptomatology when living with parents displaying similar symptoms, particularly within the context of marital conflict. Others have identified these factors as important in the development of symptoms and in their maintenance (Kaslow, Deering, & Racusin, 1994). Other studies have reported similar findings of a relationship between marital conflict and adjustment problems in adolescents (Beardslee, Versage, & Gladstone, 1998; Keller et al., 1986), and a link between parental and adolescent depression (Fendrich, Warner, & Weissman, 1990; Keller et al., 1986).

Beyond the impact on children and adolescents who present for treatment (Barrera & Garrison-Jones, 1992; Fendrich, et al., 1990; Stark, Humphrey, Crook, & Lewis, 1990), an effect from parental symptoms has been noted in community samples as well. Parental depression also has been identified as a factor in the development of depressive symptoms in their children. The symptoms are present in the children and adolescents, but not treated (Cole & McPherson, 1993; Hops, Lewinsohn, Andrews, & Roberts, 1990).

Much of the recent emphasis on family factors in the presentation of depressive symptoms has been directed toward the quality of the marital relationship, suggesting that staying together for the sake of the children may not shield them from the negative impact of depressive symptoms (Cummings & Davies, 1994). Perhaps in those marriages, avoiding a negative impact on the children or adolescents becomes a question of what type of environment will be healthier over time, because the avoidance of depressive symptoms may not be possible. Part of this work has also focused on interactional patterns among family members, teasing out the part that children and adults contribute (Fincham, Grych, & Osborne, 1994; Sheeber, Hops, Alpert, Davis, & Andrews, 1997; Slesnick & Waldron, 1997). Parental distress often serves to blur appropriate boundaries, by drawing the child in as a caretaker of the parent (Davies & Cummings, 1994; O'Brien, Margolin, John, & Krueger, 1995), setting the stage for potential problems later in the child's development, such as not responding to parental authority, acting out as a pseudo-adult or substitute partner, or focusing on the parent's problems instead of the child's own developmental tasks (Conger, Patterson, & Ge, 1995; Emery & O'Leary, 1984), and may lead to self-blame, learned helplessness, or hopelessness (Nolen-Hoeksema, Girgus, & Seligman, 1986).

Another important factor to consider is the interaction between the stage of development for the family and that of the child or adolescent at the time marital conflict occurs. A greater likelihood that adolescents will become involved in marital conflict (Cummings, Ballard, & El-Sheikh, 1991), coupled with the increase in depressive symptomatology that often occurs in adolescence (Lewinsohn, Hops, Roberts, Seeley, & Andrews, 1993), makes the development of conflict during that phase of the adolescent's life potentially volatile in terms of emotional consequences. In fact, the influence of the family has been found to be more salient in the development of depressive symptoms in adolescents than peers (Barrera & Garrison-Jones, 1992; McFarlane, Bellissimo, Norman, & Lange, 1994).

Parental Impairment

As noted in our discussion of family factors, being part of a family has the potential to impact mental health for children and adolescents in that environment. Sometimes, being part of a family means living with parents who may be impaired. Typical challenges beyond those noted previously include a parent's substance abuse, mental illness, stress with jobs or relationships, or suicide. A number of factors converge to affect the ability of the child or adolescent to cope with these family situations. These include the family's resiliency, the child's resiliency, the child's age at the time of the incident, frequency (is it a one-time incident or recurrent pattern?), and general issues of self-esteem and psychological well-being for the child or adolescent.

Loss of a parent or family member to death is a traumatic event, and circumstances surrounding the death can make adjustment to the loss more difficult (e.g., sudden, unexpected death such as a fatal accident or rapid onset disease). The death in such situations is inconsistent with beliefs and expectations. In the death of a child, there are clear adjustment challenges for a number of reasons, but particularly around the expectation that children outlive their parents. Whenever a life event occurs that is inconsistent with our expectations, the adjustment process is made more difficult.

These assumptions about difficult transition have been held about suicidal deaths as well. However, actual findings have been ambivalent. Some individuals experience a preoccupation with the lost family member as well as with suicide in general (Ness & Pfeffer, 1990), while others report no differences in their own thinking about suicidality, a decrease in emotional distress (McIntosh & Kelly, 1992; Reed, 1993; Reed & Greenwald, 1991), and a relief that the family member is no longer suffering (Cleiran, Diedstra, Kerlkhof, & Wal, 1994). A recent study of children's reactions to parental suicide found that these children experience more anxiety, anger, and shame around the death when compared to children who lost a parent to death from another cause (Cerel, Fristad, Weller, & Weller, 1999). Increased acting out and a greater number of psychiatric symptoms were observed for approximately two years following the death in the group who lost a parent to suicide.

Results from other studies imply that life with parents who eventually commit suicide may have been difficult even before the loss. For example, almost all individuals (85 percent to 98 percent) who commit suicide have struggled with depression, substance abuse, or some type of mental illness symptoms (Cerel et al., 2000; Rich, Fowler, Fogarty, & Young, 1988; Shepherd and Barraclough, 1976). Substance abuse appears to be a significant risk factor for successful suicide completion when coupled with an affective disorder (Rich et al., 1988).

Family life may continue to be challenging for some children and adolescents, due to an increased likelihood that the surviving parent may also develop psychiatric symptoms. Pfeffer, Martins, Mann, & Sunkenberg (1997) found that

50 percent of surviving parents reported significant levels of depression. Adjustment post-suicide appeared to be difficult for children and adolescents in Shepherd and Barraclough's (1976) study as well and was exacerbated by poor parental functioning or multiple school changes five to seven years following the suicide.

Evidence of other chronic stressors, including medical problems, financial problems, and legal issues, also exist in families where a parent commits suicide (Cerel et al., 2000; Rich et al., 1988). Adults who committed suicide were reported by Rich, Warstadt, Nemiroff, and Fowler (1991) to have experienced an average of two stressful life events in the year prior to the suicide. Stressors involving interpersonal conflict, separation, or rejection were more often identified as precipitants to suicide for adults committing suicide in middle age (Rich et al., 1991).

A family may feel even more isolated following suicide than from a loss due to other types of death because of a lack of social support (Alexander, 1991). Community members often are uncertain how to respond and as a result may withdraw from the family when more support, particularly from outside the family for children and adolescents, may be needed (Calhoun & Allen, 1991). In those cases, if the parent is unable to foster community involvement for the child or adolescent, that can be an important role for the therapist. Brainstorm with the client about sources of support at school or church or in other community groups. Anxiety may be a barrier to involvement in some of these social activities, however. Depression and anxiety are often experienced as co-morbid disorders in children.

ANXIETY

Managing anxiety is a much more common concern for children and adolescents now than 20 years ago. Extenuating circumstances of a more uncertain time in our own country can exacerbate the already increasing anxious responses of our youth. Feeling unsafe enough to be away from family members to go about daily activities of attending school is a huge complication that requires a combined response of support, firm limits, and clear expectations.

Family participation becomes even more crucial when dealing with generalized anxiety or separation anxiety. Part of the challenge in addressing fears and worries is the potential reality of the client's concerns. Limiting exposure to newscasts or realistic disaster movies is an important step the family can take to reduce anxiety. Focusing on normal family routines and increasing a sense of connectedness and normalcy are important. Family support of the child, while important and necessary, needs to be maintained in the context of normal family roles and limits. In other words, don't allow the child's anxiety to manipulate and control the family or you as the therapist working within that system. Balancing in this way—being supportive while providing firm, consistent limits—is difficult for some families and may require a more active role on your part.

Work with the child is usually more successful when using a combination of verbal and creative techniques as reviewed in Chapter 5, depending on developmental level and verbal skills. Short-term medication may be a helpful adjunct if some symptoms of anxiety appear beyond the child's control (e.g., frequent upset stomachs or other physical complaints that interfere with functioning). The primary message to children of any age with separation anxiety disorder or any form of anxiety is that they will continue attending school. Other factors of daily living may be negotiable to help manage anxiety, but school attendance is not. Some parents suggest home schooling in the face of severe separation anxiety. While their feelings of frustration and helplessness are understandable, allowing the child to stay home is not in the child's best interests. If the family had already decided to home-school before the presentation of the anxiety disorder, the decision may be based on other merits that will be advantageous to the child.

Description

Anxiety disorders are being more frequently observed in the population of children and adolescents (Anderson, Williams, McGee, & Silva, 1987; Bird, Camino, & Rubio-Stipec, 1988; Costello, 1989; Kashani & Orvashel, 1990; McGee et al., 1990), often observed in conjunction with other traits and behaviors, including shyness, lack of self-confidence, hyperactivity, or social withdrawal (Quay & La-Greca, 1986). In a longitudinal study following young girls who were identified as having traits of shyness, later developed symptoms of anxiety (Caspi, Henry, McGee, Moffitt, & Silva, 1995). A tendency to exhibit fear or withdrawal in new situations was found to be associated with an increased likelihood of developing anxiety disorders (Biederman, Rosenbaum, & Bolduc-Murphy, 1993; Kagan, Reznick, & Snidman, 1988).

Ialongo, Edelsohn, Werthamer-Larsson, Crockett, and Kellam (1994) identified an association between anxiety symptoms and difficulty with reading and math in first graders who did not meet the criteria for a diagnosis of an anxiety disorder. Thus, for some children, skill deficits may precipitate symptoms of anxiety. The longitudinal work of Ialongo and colleagues (1995) following these first graders to fifth grade revealed continued anxiety, and presence of anxiety was also predictive of achievement scores in later grades. Those children who self-reported anxiety in first grade were significantly more likely to be in the lowest third of achievement scores in fifth grade. Could treatment of anxiety symptoms in some cases be as concrete as remediation for math and reading skills?

Prevalence rates for anxiety in a general patient population between the ages of 7 and 11 were 8.9 percent (Costello, 1989), while rates from a clinic population of adolescents were 8.7 percent (Kashani & Orvaschel, 1988). Separation anxiety disorder rates in a community sample ranged from 2.9 percent to 4.6 percent (Bowen, Offord, & Boyle, 1987; Costello, 1989). Prevalence rates for social phobia are at about 1 percent in children ranging from 8 to 17 years old in studies completed in New Zealand and the United States (Anderson et al., 1987; Kashani & Orvaschel, 1990; McGee et al., 1990).

Approximately one third of children and adolescents have symptoms consistent with at least two anxiety disorders (Kashani & Orvaschel, 1990; Strauss & Last, 1993). It is estimated that between 28 percent (Strauss, Last, Hersen, & Kazdin, 1988a) and 69 percent (Kashani & Orvaschel, 1988) experience anxiety and depression as co-morbid. Young clients who experience this co-morbid presentation of anxiety and major depression are usually older at the time treatment is sought and often experience more severe anxiety than those without the accompanying depression (Bernstein, 1991; Strauss et al., 1988a). There appear to be associations between anxiety and ADHD (Anderson et al., 1987; Biederman, Faraone, Keenan, Steingard, & Tsuang, 1991; Bird, Camino, & Rubio-Stipec, 1988; Last et al., 1987b; Strauss, Lease, Last, & Francis, 1988b), OCD, and PTSD (Bernstein & Borchardt, 1991). These conditions are covered in separate sections. Between 15 percent and 24 percent of children presenting with an anxiety disorder also display symptoms consistent with ADHD (Last et al., 1987b).

Family History

Family history is a factor in the presentation of anxiety disorders. A genetic component increases the likelihood of the presentation in children of adults with anxiety disorder (Turner, Beidel, & Costello, 1987; Weissman, Leckman, Merikangas, Gammon, & Prusoff, 1984); in addition, there is the aspect of modeling or learned behavior for the child who lives with an anxious parent. Studies have reviewed family patterns in the children of parents with agoraphobia or obsessive-compulsive disorder, finding significantly higher rates of anxiety in the children (Turner, Beidel, & Costello, 1987). In a study comparing family histories of normal children with those diagnosed with anxiety or ADHD, the families of the children with anxiety also had the highest rates of anxiety (Last, Hersen, Kazdin, Orvaschel, & Perrin, 1991). Keller and colleagues (1992) studied children whose parents were diagnosed with a mood disorder and identified anxiety disorders in 14 percent of the children. Although these studies did not explore the possibility of environmental factors, that is a strong possibility in the maintenance of anxious behaviors in these youth.

Attachment styles have been identified as another potential factor in the development of anxiety disorders. Specifically, an insecure attachment between mother and child has been associated with development of anxiety disorders (Warren, Huston, Egeland, & Sroufe, 1997). It is important to include parents in the treatment process to explore the possibility for intervention at a systemic level to effect greater change. Parents can learn to encourage children's excitement as opposed to nervous anticipation, to encourage participation instead of withdrawal, to encourage appropriate independence rather than intrude into the child's life, and to support participation despite anxious feelings, thus fostering the development of positive self-efficacy (Lieberman & Zeanah, 1995).

Prognosis

The outcome for anxiety disorders appears variable (Bernstein, 1990). Keller and colleagues (1992) described the course as "chronic" with few remissions, over a course of 4 to 8 years. In a clinic study, Last, Perrin, Hersen, and Kazdin (1996) found the highest remission rate (96 percent) for separation anxiety disorder and the lowest remission rate for panic disorder (70 percent). Those who did recover from anxiety symptoms did so within the first year following diagnosis. The earlier the age at onset, the longer the course of treatment. On follow-up at 3 or 4 years, one third of the population had developed new psychiatric disorders, while one half met the criteria for an additional anxiety disorder (Last et al., 1996). Many authors note that the definition of *recovery* is also important. For example, even with return to school for a child with separation anxiety disorder, what is the quality of time at school? Is it riddled with anxiety? Follow-up findings were consistent with continued problems, such as socially and emotionally constricted lives, despite a return to school (Berg & Jackson, 1985; Coolidge, Brodie, & Feeney, 1964; Hersoy, 1985). Therefore, continued treatment to assist with overall adjustment may be warranted. Considering the prevalence of anxiety disorders, such services may be best provided at the school in the form of social skills and self-esteem groups.

Associations between childhood anxiety disorders and adult psychiatric disorders are not clear. Retrospective studies have been completed that show some associations between adult agoraphobia and childhood separation anxiety disorder (Berg, Marks, McGuire, & Lipsedge, 1974), while Moreau and Follett (1993) suggest separation anxiety may precede depressive disorder and adult anxiety disorders.

REVIEW OF SPECIFIC ANXIETY DISORDERS

Features of commonly seen disorders are outlined in this section: separation anxiety disorder, generalized anxiety disorder, social phobia, and panic disorder.

Separation Anxiety Disorder

Separation anxiety disorder is characterized by extreme anxiety around separation from attachment figures. Although normal at younger ages (e.g., stranger anxiety around the age of 2), one of the hallmarks of separation anxiety disorder is its later presentation. The other clearly identifying symptom is extreme reaction upon separation from caretakers, approaching panic in some children (Gittelman-Klein, 1988). Age at onset is estimated at around 7 years, but families may not seek treatment until age 10 (Last, Perrin, Hersen, & Kazdin, 1992), presenting relatively equally among genders. Lower socioeconomic status has been identified as a potential risk for separation anxiety disorder (Last et al., 1992; Velez, Johnson, & Cohen, 1989).

In many cases no specific precipitator can be linked to the onset of separation anxiety disorder, but it is common to find a history of mild anxiety or social phobia in the families of children who present with this disorder. Even, if a precipitant is identified, making that link known to the child—in other words, helping them feel safe about their fear—is often insufficient to ameliorate the symptoms. Many fears presented with separation anxiety disorder are diffuse and may relate to any number of tragedies that may befall the caretakers or the child. The diffuse nature of the anxiety creates problems in helping the child develop a sense of safety after it has been disrupted. Common precipitants include tragedies seen on the news, such as auto accidents, bombings, or tornadoes. Because separation anxiety presents in older children, they have some awareness of the likelihood that such events might occur and are out of the control of their parents. This baseline level of rational thought works against helping them manage a sense of safety.

Generally, more symptoms are observed in younger children with separation anxiety disorder than in older children who present with the disorder (Francis, Last, & Strauss, 1987). At ages 5 to 8, worries focus on harm to parents or caretakers and school refusal. However, in slightly older children (ages 9 to 12), extreme distress upon separation is observed, while in adolescents, physical complaints and school refusal are more frequent (Last, Francis, Hersen, Kazdin, & Strauss, 1987a). School refusal is the most common symptom observed across all age groups.

Generalized Anxiety Disorder

Generalized anxiety disorder is characterized by worry and anxiety that is more free-floating. The excessive worry becomes attached to various events or people throughout the day. At times, it may be experienced as pervasive, yet without description, so that it almost becomes a state of being for the child or adolescent. Generalized anxiety disorder can become an immobilizing force in the client's life. If the anxiety becomes overwhelming, the child or adolescent may entertain suicidal thoughts as a mechanism to stop the constant worry. Excessive worry often seems to focus on fears of harm to self or important figures in the child's life (Achenbach, Conners, Quay, Verhulst, & Howell, 1989; Bell-Dolan, Last, & Strauss, 1990).

Using the older classification of "overanxious disorder," Werry (1991) noted that the presentation of this disorder is approximately equal across gender until adolescence, when the disorder is seen more often in girls. The disorder tends to be more prevalent in Caucasian children from middle- and upper-class families (Last et al., 1987b).

Generalized anxiety disorder may include physical symptoms such as agitation, fatigue, preoccupation with the objects of worry making concentration difficult, irritability, or sleep problems (American Psychiatric Association, 1994). Older children and adolescents seem to experience more symptoms than younger children (McGee et al., 1990; Strauss et al., 1988b), perhaps because of heightened intellectual capacity and cognitive development. The nature of the symptoms tends to focus on future-oriented worry (Strauss et al., 1988b) and fear of catastrophes, which serves to keep the fears present in the adolescent's mind. The constant state of anxiety may be held in the body as well as the mind, creating muscle tension and contributing to heightened vigilance or fatigue. Developing coping strategies, including muscle relaxation and some sense of control, can be a helpful intervention for some.

Social Phobia

Social phobia is characterized by persistent fear of social situations or performance anxiety in certain cases (DSM-IV). The phobia usually is associated with novel situations, new people, or unfamiliar circumstances. An extreme form of social phobia seen in children and adolescents, particularly young children, is selective mutism (Black & Uhde, 1995). For example, the child may elect to talk at home, but not at the new school setting. This is perplexing for those around the child in familiar surroundings, until the anxiety component is identified. The extreme degree of anxiety and uncertainty about how to behave or how others will react in social situations, creates a measure of immobilization with social phobia, similar to that mentioned for other anxiety disorders. Social skills training, role-playing, and building a social support network at school can be helpful interventions.

Social phobia appears to be more prevalent in girls than in boys, presenting more often in Caucasian children from middle- and upper-class families (Francis, Last, & Strauss, 1992).

Panic Disorder

Panic disorder in children and adolescents is characterized by extreme anxiety and is often manifest in physical symptoms, such as heart palpitations, sweating, racing thoughts, and agitation. The onset is spontaneous and unexpected, often having a frightening effect on the client and those around her. The precipitant may not be clear during the initial presentations.

EXCERPT FROM A SAMPLE INTERVIEW SCREENING
FOR ANXIETY WITH A YOUNGER CLIENT

THERAPIST: *What makes you feel happy?*
CLIENT: *Being at home with Mom and Dad.*
THERAPIST: *What else makes you feel happy?*
CLIENT: *I don't like to do much else.*
THERAPIST: *What do you think about when you're not home with Mom and Dad?*
CLIENT: *I think about being home a lot.*
THERAPIST: *What other things do you think about a lot?*
CLIENT: *I think about getting sick or Mom and Dad getting sick. Sometimes I think about people getting hurt.*
THERAPIST: *How do you feel when you think about these things?*
CLIENT: *Afraid*
THERAPIST: *What other things are scary?*
CLIENT: *Sometimes I have scary dreams.*
THERAPIST: *About what?*
CLIENT: *Getting hurt.*

SAMPLE INTERVIEW QUESTIONS IN SCREENING FOR OBSESSIVE COMPULSIVE SYMPTOMS

THERAPIST: *What kinds of things do you think about a lot?*
CLIENT: *I count stuff, and sometimes I think about what I have to do at school.*
THERAPIST: *When you are thinking about school, what do you do about it?*
CLIENT: *I think about it at bed, and sometimes I have to get up and make sure my homework's in my bag.*

THERAPIST: *What happens if you don't get up and check?*
CLIENT: *I can't go to sleep if I don't check. I just keep thinking about it.*
THERAPIST: *What other routines do you have?*
CLIENT: *I count stuff—before I go to bed, I count my stuffed animals. I count how many times I brush my teeth.*
THERAPIST: *What happens if you stay at a friend's house?*
CLIENT: *I try not to do it there.*

Part of your evaluation needs to determine the level of control the child or adolescent seems to feel about the behaviors. If the child doesn't seem to be able to control the behaviors or thoughts in any disorder with a repetitive component, a medication consult may be warranted. Fluvoxamine has been shown to enhance the efficacy of treatment in conjunction with therapy (Neziroglu, Yaryara-Tobias, Walz, & McKay, 2000).

TREATMENT OF ANXIETY DISORDERS

Obviously, the central feature binding each of these separate presentations is anxiety, albeit in a slightly different format for each. In cases of co-morbidity, the clinical picture becomes more complex, requiring that treatment efforts be tailored not only to the symptoms of anxiety, but also to include symptoms for the co-existing conditions. Typical treatment approaches include cognitive-behavioral (Albano & Kendall, 2002) and family therapies (Ginsberg & Schlossberg, 2002). Successful treatment for separation anxiety includes helping the child separate from the primary caretaker. A variety of supportive techniques may be combined with the rapid return to school to help support the child in being able to stay at school for longer and longer periods of time. It is important to balance being supportive without reinforcing the child's preferred tendency to remain at home or with the caregiver. Involving the child's school and parents is critical for the successful implementation of these behavioral approaches (Mansdorf & Lukens, 1987). Kearney and Silverman (1990) reported full attendance for six of seven children treated with cognitive-behavioral approaches.

Kendall (1994) also found positive results using cognitive-behavioral therapy for children with separation anxiety disorder, generalized anxiety disorder, and co-morbid depressive symptoms. Cognitive interventions included listing anxious thoughts and feelings, learning to recognize physical indicators of anxiety, and implementing a plan when these situations arose. Behavioral interventions included relaxation, exposure, role-playing, and rewards. Positive results were maintained at one year follow-up.

Another factor to consider in the treatment process is the developmental level of the children with whom you are working. Participants in Kendall's (1994) study were between the ages of 9 and 13. Clearly, most children at that age have the cognitive skills necessary to engage in this type of therapy. For younger children or for those who are developmentally younger, pushing them to use coping skills beyond their capacity will only serve to frustrate clients and their parents, exacerbating symptoms instead of improving them. Similarly, use of psychodynamic techniques that explore fears and anxieties work well with older children whose cognitive capacity has developed to that level; however, they are ineffective, and potentially frustrating, for younger children (Bernstein et al., 1997). Use of the psychodynamic approach is helpful when the focus helps anxious children develop a sense of competence, particularly around themes of separation, independence, and self-esteem (Bernstein et al., 1997).

A goal of involving the family in therapy is to interrupt the cycle that is maintaining the behavior (McDermott, Werry, Petti, Combrinck-Graham, & Char, 1989). Dysfunctional family patterns foster and maintain insecurity (King & Noshpitz, 1991). Those patterns should be the target of interventions.

Medication may be considered as an adjunct to therapy in certain cases, to treat co-morbid conditions or excessive anxiety that is interfering with daily functioning. The goal of therapy, regardless of whether medication is involved, is to promote a sense of mastery and competence (Bernstein et al., 1997). The new behavioral pattern needs to be strong enough to resist extinction, even without medication, for a successful outcome.

COGNITIVE THERAPIES AND POST-TRAUMATIC STRESS DISORDER (PTSD)

Cohen, Mannarino, Berliner, and Deblingter (2000) identify four major components of cognitive behavioral therapy when working with trauma. These include exposure, cognitive processing/reframing, stress management, and parental treatment. Although research generally supports symptom reduction in clients who participated in these studies, the specific contribution of each of the four components has not been as fully explained in the literature.

Part of the problem in identifying the efficacy of a specific treatment factor lies in the large variations usually observed in the population of children and adolescents. Not only are developmental differences widely varied, but family structure is as well. For example, using cognitive behavioral interventions with PTSD, one must be aware of developmental differences in various types of self-monitoring and control, including ability to monitor level of arousal, ability to engage in cause-and-effect reasoning, level of expressive language and understanding, and ability to process social information (Vernberg & Johnston, 2001). Examples of techniques that can be modified for working with various ages include coping skills training, cognitive restructuring (e.g., dealing with irrational beliefs that may have arisen out of the trauma), education, and information giving. Although some clinicians may emphasize exposure to trauma-related stimuli, this approach should be avoided unless you are working with a client who possesses very positive ego strength and a strong, supportive family.

BIPOLAR DISORDER

Diagnostic Features

Bipolar disorder in children and adolescents has received increasing attention in the literature and practice over the past decade, with estimates indicating approximately 20 percent of all individuals with bipolar disorder experience their first episode between the ages of 15 and 19; however, disagreement regarding actual prevalence persists (Carlson, 1990). The age of early onset is often identified at 18, while others place it at age 13 (McClellan et al., 1997). Despite the increased emphasis on these problems for teens and families, some confusion about the differences between presentation for children and adolescents as compared to adults remains an issue (Carlson, Fennig, & Bromet, 1994). Clarifying these distinctions is helpful for appropriate diagnosis and effective intervention.

Although the diagnostic criteria for bipolar disorder in adolescents is the same as for adults (DSM-IV), many of the characteristics of bipolar disorder in children and adolescents differ from the classic "cycling" observed in later presentations (Wozniak, Biederman, & Kiely, 1995). The initial episode for adolescents may be either manic or depressive and often presents for less than the one-week duration criteria required for diagnosis (Akiskal, 1995; APA, 1994; Carlson & Kashani, 1988; Lewinsohn, 1995). Rapid cycling is much more likely to be observed in children and adolescents (Geller et al., 1995; McClellan et al., 1997). Presentation is roughly equal across gender (Costello, 1989).

For 20 percent to 30 percent of adolescents who experience a major depressive episode, mania may later develop (Geller, Fox, & Clark, 1994; Rao, Ryan, & Birmaher, 1995; Strober & Carlson, 1982). Risk factors associated with eventual presentation of mania include: (a) rapid onset depression with psychomotor retardation and psychotic features in some; (b) family history of bipolar disorder; and (c) presentation of mania after treatment with antidepressants (Strober & Carlson, 1982). Hyperactivity is also an associated feature for those who develop mania following a depressive episode (Carlson, 1990; McClellan et al., 1993; Venkataraman, Naylor, & King, 1992; Werry et al., 1991).

An atypical presentation of mania is often observed in children and adolescents, another factor contributing to the difficulty of making a clear diagnosis (Bowring & Kovacs, 1992). Irritability, rapid mood changes, agitation, and rapid thoughts are frequently seen in adolescents, but not with the same persistence as observed in adults (McClellan et al., 1997). Because of societal and developmental constraints, typical manic behaviors may not be observed in adolescents. It is critical not to confuse the symptoms that can be consistent with mania in this age group (e.g., reckless behavior, grandiosity) with normal developmental challenges or more common childhood disorders, such as braggadocio, poor judgment, or imaginary play (McClellan, Werry, & Ham, 1993). More complex presentations of mania in adolescents can include: (a) psychotic symptoms such as hallucinations, paranoia, or thought disturbances; (b) mixed features of mania and depression; and (c) behavioral deterioration (Akiskal, 1995; Goodwin & Jamison, 1990).

Differential Diagnosis

Overlapping symptoms and mixed presentations often create diagnostic confusion when comparing bipolar disorder with other disorders, creating the need for caution on the part of the clinician when making a diagnosis. Symptoms of bipolar disorder can be similar to ADHD or conduct disorder (Weller, Weller, & Fristad, 1995), agitated depression (Swann, Secunda, & Katz, 1993), post-traumatic stress disorder (Borchardt & Bernstein, 1995), borderline personality disorder (Akiskal, 1981; Kutcher, Marton, & Korenblum, 1990; Garnet, Levy, Mattanah, Edell, & McGlashan, 1994), or other disruptive behaviors (Carlson, 1990; Gittelman, Mannuzza, Shenker, & Bonagure, 1985; Wozniak et al., 1997).

Attention deficit and conduct disorders have both been described as having a more consistent presentation, with an earlier onset (approximately age 7) as compared to bipolar disorder (onset at age 12 to 13) and a greater variability in symptom expression (McClellan et al., 1997). It is critical for the clinician to remain cognizant of the influence of cultural factors in diagnosis. As discussed in Chapter 6, differences in symptom presentation across various ethnic groups can lead to misdiagnosis. The current version of the DSM-IV-TR (2000) is a good resource to consult for cultural aspects of each disorder when specific questions arise.

Family Factors

Regardless of theoretical orientation, most work with children and adolescents is embedded within a family context. Methods that have met with success include a psycho-educational approach, focusing on providing information about the disorder, improving communication, and working on problem-solving skills within the family (Clarkin, Carpenter, Hull, Wilner, & Glick, 1998; Glick et al., 1985; Simoneau, Miklowitz, Richards, Saleem, & George, 1999). Challenges to the success of family approaches have included characteristics of the families themselves, primarily families with emotional distance or poor attachment (Strachan, Feingold, Goldstein, & Miklowitz 1989). The presentation of the disorder may be influenced through interaction with family members also diagnosed with bipolar disorder, and treatment is often exacerbated by such interactions (Rice, Reich, & Andreasen, 1987; Strober, 1992b). Treatment efforts are also challenged by co-morbid conditions frequently seen, such as ADHD, conduct disorder, or a high rate of substance abuse (Borchardt & Bernstein, 1995; Carlson, 1990; Kovacs & Pollock, 1995; West, McElroy, Strakowski, Keck, & McConville, 1995). Generally, a tendency to be less responsive to treatment has been observed in adolescents with bipolar disorder (McGlashon, 1988, Strober et al., 1995) as well as an increased risk for completed suicides (Brent, Perper, & Goldstein, 1988; Brent, Perper, & Moritz, 1993; Brent et al., 1994; Welner, Welner, & Fishman, 1979).

Earlier onset of bipolar disorder in children has been associated with family history of bipolar disorder (Strober, 1992b; Todd, Neuman, Geller, Fox, & Hickok, 1993; Todd, Reich, & Reich, 1994). Rea, Goldstein, Miklowitz, and Weisman (2000) found the affective interactional style of family members involved in treatment could represent an obstacle to effective treatment, suggesting that learning more about family members prior to treatment may help the therapist to tailor treatment to potential problems that may arise during family therapy.

Medication

Pharmacological treatments have been identified as a necessary component in the treatment of early onset bipolar disorder (McClellan et al., 1997), despite the paucity of literature in the area (Alessi, Naylor, Ghaziuddin, & Zubieta, 1994; Kafantaris, 1995; Strober, 1992a; Viesselman, Yaylayan, Weller, & Weller, 1993). Lithium treatments have been reviewed in adolescents, finding a relapse rate of approximately 38 percent for those compliant with their medication (Strober, Morrell, Lampert, & Burroughs, 1990). The same study suggested that a period of 18 months is required for the treatment to be effective. Medication use in children and adolescents is complicated by developmental factors, and as always, caution is required in any plan involving medication interventions.

SUICIDE

Although suicide in children and adolescents is something we often don't like to think of as possible, the trend has been increasing in frequency over the past two decades. Whether it is an artifact of reporting and increased awareness about childhood and adolescent depression or a real increase may be open to debate, but the increased openness about suicide in this population gives us the opportunity to be more proactive in our efforts to prevent suicide and provide support.

Our understanding of reckless behavior, impulsivity, and depression in a developmental context allows us to recognize now that behaviors that simply seemed reckless could be suicidal gestures, particularly in younger children. So the question becomes how to evaluate a true risk of suicide from an impulsive gesture? This becomes a question of developmental level, self-awareness, and ability to self-monitor. Many children and adolescents feel "down" or stuck without a positive plan of action because their problem-solving skills (related to cognitive, physical, and emotional developmental levels) are still evolving. What factors push that "stuck" feeling to the next level of pursuing suicide as a viable option?

We can review a variety of factors that help in assessing the degree and likelihood of acting on a suicidal gesture (Wise & Spengler, 1997; Pfeffer, 1986).

Evaluating Suicidal Risk

History of Prior Attempts   Any prior history makes the threat more real. In exploring the prior history, look at specific factors surrounding previous attempts. What was the level of awareness? In other words, did this appear to be a deliberate attempt at self-harm? Was the history a suicidal gesture, or was it more consistent with self-mutilation? Self-mutilation serves many purposes other than suicide.

These behaviors are often associated with borderline features or as attention-seeking measures, but also serve the purpose of anxiety relief, self-punishment, and grounding. Learning more about the experience of self-mutilation and the prior means used in suicide gestures can assist with evaluation of motivation and repetition of previous behaviors. Even with children and adolescents, exploring the affective experience of these previous behaviors can be helpful. Depending on the developmental level of the young client, she may be able to recognize the same feeling in a current suicide gesture as in a previous one. This can be an important evaluation tool in teasing out motivation. The importance of identifying motivation lies in tailoring the intervention. For example, if the adolescent is angry and wants a reaction from others, that can guide the intervention toward more productive behaviors and away from suicidal gestures or self-mutilation.

Exposure to People in Family or Community Who Have Committed Suicide   The effect of cluster suicides (Shaffer, 1988; Wilkie, Macdonald, & Highdahl, 1998) has long been documented and discussed in professional circles. Part of this thinking is consistent with the old notion that suicide should not be discussed directly. However, the risk in cluster suicides or in knowing someone who has committed suicide is that the personal knowledge or relationship makes the choice of suicide seem more viable. It is almost a modeling factor, particularly with younger children. If Uncle Frank committed suicide, then it must be OK. Obviously, family rules and norms around the knowledge of suicide and feelings about suicide will be factors in whether the behavior can be accepted as viable or a legitimate option.

Degree of Pain   The degree of emotional or psychological pain is the most common stressor in pushing people to consider suicide. For children, feeling abandoned or alone is often a factor in increasing the degree of pain. For adolescents, it is often the occurrence of simultaneous multiple stressors (e.g., final exams, breakup with significant other, fight with parents) that increases the pain to such a degree that the apparent avoidance afforded from suicide becomes inviting. You may often hear such things as "I didn't know what else to do," epitomizing the lack of problem solving (Spence, Sheffield, & Donovan, 2003).

Ego Strength   Feeling defeated decreases one's problem-solving ability. Ego strength refers to the ability to withstand stress, patricularly internal conflict. At times, the counselor must adopt the role of guide or positive sense of self when the client's ego strength is not at a level where she can effectively provide this function for herself. The role of the therapist may essentially feel like being a crutch or a stronger extension of the client, in providing a positive strength and motivation to proceed.

Depth of Coping Skills/Lack of Rigidity in Thought Patterns/Impulsivity (Ability to Stop and Think)   Many of the factors discussed in this section, when combined, serve to narrow the apparent options available to the client. As those options are narrowed, the individual is essentially coping at a more primitive, or possibly a "fight or flight" (Garmezy, 1991), "all or nothing," or "black and white" level. These types of coping responses or styles of attribution are more rigid and less mentally healthy. A more flexible style of thought or problem solving provides additional choices and expands the options available to the client during this time of crisis. The therapist adopts the role of collaborative problem solver with regard to this temporary deficit during the time of crisis.

Sense of Purpose in Life   Oftentimes, suicidal feelings are precipitated by a loss of direction or a setback that feels like an insurmountable obstacle to the client. This could be an obstacle in any area of the client's life: school; job; romantic relationship; loss of friendship, family member, or pet; or failure to achieve an important life goal. If the client has wrapped herself up in the goal and then perceives a significant obstacle, the sense of failure may feel overwhelming and immobilizing, making it impossible for the client to move toward a productive use of her usual coping skills. The danger in the client's response to these events lies in her interpretation of them. If the client makes an attribution that they are at the root of the problem, the suicidal risk can become greater, because options seem more limited.

Recent Life Events/Stressors   These life events and stressors, such as hospitalization, can be similar to the obstacles experienced in taking away one's sense of purpose. If the client can attribute the stressors to the situation rather than her character, a more positive coping strategy is likely. The client is more likely to believe that a mistake or fluke can happen to anyone when she does not attribute the cause to herself.

Feeling of Connection With Others   The client's support system available from her social network and her living arrangements will be dependent on the client's history of prior mental illness or suicide attempts. Many times, a history of serious mental illness can exhaust the resources generally available to the client. If that is the case, the client's living arrangements need to be reviewed even more closely. If the client lives alone, the information available about means to complete a suicide attempt may be less accurate. The client may withhold information about means. Prior knowledge about suicide attempts can be helpful in determining the client's tendency to withhold such information or to be forthcoming about available means in her home. If you are uncertain or unable to determine the client's level of honesty about available means, it may be better to err on the side of caution in protecting your client. More considerations about determining possible effects of those strategies for protection are addressed under the section on hospitalization.

Other Factors   Other factors to include in an assessment of suicide risk include:
- substance abuse
- medical history
- hopelessness
- depression, anger, and other intense feelings (Explore the affect driving the suicide.)
- gender and age issues
- specific plan
- intent
- means

THE ENTIRE CLIENT: ADDITIONAL CONSIDERATIONS

1. Screen for suicidality and past attempts in the initial session, and following changes in depressive symptoms and/or challenging life events.
2. Assist the client in controlling her environment to make means unavailable. You may need to enlist family members or others within the client's support system. Be sure to obtain appropriate releases in developing such a plan.
3. Identify and enhance client strengths within herself and her support system.
4. Reinforce her positive connections with life and reasons for living, no matter how small (e.g., caring for the cat, desire not to disappoint parents).
5. Fully explore the client's thoughts and feelings about acting on her suicidal ideation and any fantasies she may have about others' reactions to her death.
6. Be clear and direct in communication regarding suicide and plan or intent.
7. Incorporate client strengths and determination to survive in development of no-harm contract.
8. Consider the potential impact of hospitalization or other potential interventions. Review the interaction between client trust and safety. Will hospitalization erode the therapeutic relationship to an ineffective level? Or is the likelihood of suicide so great that hospitalization is required to ensure the client's safety?
9. Remain aware of your own potential countertransference reaction with the client. Do not overreact or underreact to the suicidal risk. Have you also struggled with this client? Has the client almost exhausted your therapeutic reservoir, placing you in the same burned-out position as many within the client's informal support system? Or do you find yourself overidentifying with the client, becoming too protective and in doing so, possibly crossing therapeutic boundaries?
10. Be emotionally present for the client, communicating your genuine interest and caring for the client. The lack of caring from others is often a part of the emotional distress and isolation a client feels when suicide appears to be a more viable option for her. Your caring presence can convey a tangible reason for her to refute her suicidal plans or intent. At least one other person cares about her, thinks she has value, and is interested in her.

Planning Ahead: Avoiding Risk

No-Harm Contract   At times, it may become necessary to use a *no-harm contract* with children and adolescents. When working with this population, the parents are your best ally, and you may be their primary support system in a time of crisis. The no-harm contract is dated and lays out a statement of intent not to harm oneself, generally specified within a certain time frame (e.g., until the next face-to-face session or phone call). In certain cases, it may be helpful to outline specific resources, including phone numbers or e-mail addresses, that can be used when overwhelming feelings are experienced between sessions.

No-Harm Contract (Sample)

I, _____, agree not to harm myself (between today and
my next appointment/contact with my therapist, Dr. Pledge).
If I have thoughts of hurting myself, I will:

_____

People I can call when I'm feeling this way:

_____

_____

_____

_____   _____
Client Signature   Therapist Signature

_____   _____
Date   Date

_____

Social Supports   Develop a social support system for use at times of stress and
other times as well. This network may include people already in the client's life,
perhaps one or more of those persons included in the no-harm contract, at least as
a starting place. Remember, the client's problem-solving ability is limited at the
time of making the suicidal statement or gesture. Having at least one name on the
list (which may be yours) is necessary to help the client feel connected and less isolated. Social isolation often fuels feelings of worthlessness, lack of purpose in life,
or feeling that the client has no place in society. Physically making a list provides a
tool the client can use upon leaving your office. It can also serve as a transitional
object, representing you as a positive influence in the client's life. The value of a
transitional object for those clients with poor ego strength is well documented in
the psychodynamic literature.

Indirect Attempts   Risky behavior often observed in children and adolescents
may be a suicide attempt. As noted in the earlier statistics, suicide among children
and adolescents is a growing problem. Historically, risky behavior and suicide attempts in these age groups were not recognized as serious attempts, and it is unclear how many clients were lost as a result. Parents may also tend to minimize
reckless or hopeless behavior as "just a phase." Your role as a clinician is to balance
the likelihood of a real attempt without frightening the family into immobilization
or panic. Employ parents as part of the active support system to ensure the client's
safety. Review important factors such as available means, supervision, and safety
(or crisis) plan to follow if the client takes action toward suicide. Parents can be the
most important part of the treatment team when it comes to providing supervision
for child and adolescent clients in between therapy sessions.

Supporting Clients' Strengths   Identify and focus on things your clients look forward to and that help focus on their strengths:

- emphasizing the sense of purpose in their life and/or work
- feeling connected to at least one other person
- connecting with their motivation for living

DISCUSSION QUESTIONS

1. Review family and risk factors associated with each of the disorders in this chapter.
2. What is the purpose of the no-harm contract?
3. How does parental impairment affect the mental health of children and adolescents?
4. Explore your own feelings about working with a client who is suicidal.

EXTERNALIZING DISORDERS

INTRODUCTION

This chapter focuses on what are commonly referred to as *externalizing disorders,* because those who experience these disorders display a tendency to express symptoms outwardly against the environment or others. For children and adolescents, some variability of presentation will be observed, but this commonly accepted frame is used to organize our discussion. The review includes general aggressive behaviors, attention deficit, oppositional defiant and conduct disorders, borderline and antisocial features, and substance abuse. Acting out is a common thread in these disorders, a behavior that can extend to aggression at times.

AGGRESSION

The roots of aggression are varied, and much controversy exists as to the true etiology of aggressive behavior—whether it is modeled or has more of a genetic base. One might ask why etiology matters; the answer is that the origin of this disorder relates directly to the clinician's hypothesis of the problem, an initial factor in identifying an appropriate intervention. Some models identify early socialization experiences as a factor in the development of aggressive behavior, theorizing that early negative experiences are generalized to other relationships in an almost defensive, or at least a learned, manner (Dodge, 1993; Lochman & Dodge, 1998; Rogosch, Cicchetti, & Aber, 1995). Recent research provides support for both skill-deficit and cognitive-distortion models (Rudolph & Clark, 2001).

Cognitive models explaining aggressive behavior point to individual differences in processing information as a factor in maintaining these patterns of behavior (Crick & Dodge, 1994; Dodge, 1993). If, as these authors suggest, a deficit exists in the individual's knowledge base or problem-solving ability, then our interventions must target a skill-building or educational approach. Appropriate interventions may include targeting irrational beliefs, walking through children's and adolescents' perceptions of social situations to identify encoding problems, misunderstandings about others' intent or reactions, or simple lack of knowledge about appropriate social skills or responses to others.

Inaccurate self-perceptions are commonly associated with aggressive behavior in children and adolescents (Rudolph & Clark, 2001), which seems to be a central component of the behavior's maintenance. An apparently inflated self-concept in relation to others is reported in aggressive children, in contrast to a deflated self-concept in children with depression (Boivin, Poulin, & Vitaro, 1994; Hughes, Cavell, & Grossman, 1997; Hymel, Bowler, & Woody, 1993; Patterson, Kupersmidt, & Griesler, 1990). This phenomenon is consistent with the recent emphasis on bullying behavior, in which aggression serves a purpose for the individual by increasing his unrealistic sense of self as he puts others down. Self-estimates of rejection by peers is often underestimated (or ignored) by aggressive and bullying children or adolescents (Lochman, 1987; Lochman & Dodge, 1998). These findings are consistent with what many have observed during interactions with aggressive children and adolescents—that is, a generally negative attitude toward self, others, and life, particularly with regard to tasks that are difficult or challenging. For these children and adolescents, the negativity often covers up deficits of which they may be unaware or choose to be unaware. Specific problem areas associated with aggression in the literature include increased inappropriate social responses such as coercion or lack of cooperation, and a lack of more positive social skills, such as assertiveness, turn-taking, or support (Bierman, Smoot, & Aumiller, 1993; Crick & Dodge, 1994; Dodge, Pettit, McClaskey, & Brown, 1986; Garber, Quiggle, Panak, & Dodge, 1991; Quiggle, Garber, Panak, & Dodge, 1992). These behaviors often begin a cycle of repeated peer rejection or at a minimum, a lack of acceptance by peers (Boivin & Hymel, 1997; Little & Garber, 1995). All these behaviors make social relationships more difficult for children or adolescents with aggressive behavior (Rudolph & Clark, 2001), an isolating effect similar to that discussed with other disorders.

ANTISOCIAL BEHAVIOR

Statistics show a steady increase in the number of juveniles being held in detention centers, training schools, incarcerated in recent years (Puritz & Shang, 1998), as well as increases in school suspensions and expulsions (Ingersoll & LeBoeuf, 1997). Some authorities describe these behaviors as antisocial, indicating that a chronic pattern of antisocial behavior is often associated with diagnoses of oppositional defiant or conduct disorder (Horne & Sayger, 1990; Kazdin, 1987). The prevalence of conduct disorder is estimated between 2 percent and 9 percent of the children in the United States; it has been found to be relatively stable across the life span (Miller, 2001), and is labeled antisocial behavior in adults. In addition to other behaviors associated with the disorder, animal cruelty is receiving new attention as an important prognostic marker, thought to exist in 25 percent of children with conduct disorder. It is often one of the earliest symptoms observed (Miller, 2001).

Oppositional or defiant behaviors can also be consistent with bullying, physical assault, or robbery that are reported by approximately 12 percent of secondary school students (Nolin, Davies, & Chandler, 1995). Increased attention to verbal, social, and emotional aspects of abuse is highlighting different forms of bullying across genders, fostering the likelihood of change with this recognition (Crick, Casas, & Mosher, 1997; Hazler, 1996; Morita, Soeda, Soeda, & Taki, 1999; Rigby & Slee, 1999b). Bullying has been defined as "repeated, unprovoked, harmful actions by one child or children against another." Examples of bullying are wide ranging and include physical, verbal, and emotional intimidation, as discussed in Chapter 10. Examples of physical bullying include hitting, kicking, pushing, and grabbing or taking objects from another, all of which are fairly standard, almost stereotypical bullying behaviors.

More subtle forms include psychological or emotional taunts, including name calling, threatening, making faces, or ostracizing (Olweus, 1991). A recently identified characteristic of bullies that may actually serve to perpetuate the bullying is the more aggressive response seen after being faced with threatening behavior by another and the surge of power accompanied by an apparent sense of justification in choice of bullying behaviors (Bullock, 2002). Deficits in empathy and problem-solving skills, coupled with modeling of physicality to solve problems in some families, have been associated with children and adolescents who bully (Loeber & Dishion, 1984; Vladimir & Brubach, 2000).

Incidents of being bullied are reported by 25 percent to 50 percent of children (Bullock, 2002). Boys are usually bullied by other boys, while 60 percent of girls report being bullied by boys as well. Although girls are reported to bully others, it seems that they are less willing to acknowledge their behavior (Roland, 1989). Gender differences are noted over time, with the incidence of bullying by girls decreasing with age, while it remains fairly constant for boys (Sharp & Smith, 1991).

Although bullying is not always at the same level as some of the other antisocial behaviors listed previously, recent research has offered models (Loeber & Stouthamer-Loeber, 1998), frameworks (Hazler & Carney, 2000) for understanding possible "pathways" or progressions of behavior, or scales to identify children or adolescents who may be at risk (Rigby, Cox, & Black, 1997). Elliott (2000) identifies two broad categories of destructive interpersonal violence: affective and predatory. As the labels might imply, the orientation can be directed toward others (predatory) or more diffuse (affective). Predatory violence is described as "cold, callous, and casual" by Elliott (2000, p. 15), and can be planned or impulsive.

Elliott (2000) characterizes affective aggression by the apparent diminished control seen in such disorders as intermittent explosive disorder, episodic rage, or other organic pathologies. One of the primary distinctions between acting out against others, including animals (Miller, 2001) or acting out against property may be present in the early choices these youth make. The model, or the Cooperativeness Scale, can provide a quick screening and a way to think about appropriate interventions immediately and in the context of the potential prognosis. Not surprisingly, those students who score lower on the Cooperativeness Scale were more likely to engage in bullying behavior or to be the victims of bullying (Rigby, et al., 1997). Of concern is the apparent pattern of bullying behaviors that can continue over the life span, when early onset is observed (Batsche & Knoff, 1994; Baumeister, 2001; Olweus, 1991), similar to early animal abuse.

Intervention is necessary at the individual and systems level for this rampant concern. Bullock (2002) suggests schools can be an important part of the intervention, providing support at three levels: (1) schoolwide, (2) in classrooms, and (3) with individuals. Adding families into these interventions makes them more effective. Bullock (2002) suggests developing a schoolwide plan that includes students and teachers, identifying appropriate and unacceptable behaviors and outlining specific consequences for bullying behaviors. She also recommends schoolwide mentoring programs to support those who are being bullied. Teachers need to be included when making such major cultural change within the school.

ATTENTION DEFICIT HYPERACTIVITY DISORDER

Many people have strong affective reactions to externalizing disorders, of which attention deficit hyperactivity disorder (ADHD) has some components. For example, do you feel kids with ADHD are just bad kids whose parents can't control them? What other assumptions have you heard about ADHD? Can you understand their life experiences well enough to help them?

Early treatment for attention deficit disorder is encouraged to avoid possible negative effects resulting from consequences of inattention and impulsivity, as well as later presentation of depressive symptoms that is sometimes experienced. Although prevalence studies report that boys outnumber girls in the presentation of attention deficit disorder, recent studies suggest that ratio is changing. A review of data from the U.S. National Ambulatory Medical Care Survey indicated three times the number of ADHD diagnoses for girls in 1991–1992 and in 1997–1998. Although the diagnosis for boys increased during the same time, it was twice the previous number (Robison, Skaer, Sclar, & Galin, 2002). Based on these figures, it appears that not only is the incidence of ADHD increasing among girls, but the quality of the experience is changing for girls as well, which leads to the question, Are there different ways to treat boys and girls with attention deficit disorder? The common diagnosis for girls had been attention deficit without hyperactivity, which would lead to an affirmative response in that treatment would differ. However, if the presentation for girls is indeed moving closer to that historically associated with boys, then the interventions may be more similar. With attention deficit without hyperactivity, impulsivity is still observed as are mild externalizing behaviors, usually related to lack of personal responsibility for behaviors and choices (Gershon, 2002).

The growing number of girls diagnosed with ADHD is identified as a potential trend for health and school officials in terms of meeting the needs of this growing population, who can be disruptive and require resources to be diverted from other students, depending on the severity of the diagnosis. However, the increase in diagnosis may not reflect accurate diagnoses or may be confounded by other areas. In many instances, inattention is the primary diagnostic factor, but it is well known that poor concentration and inattention can result from emotional concerns as well, such as depression, anxiety, stress, medical issues (e.g., asthma or allergies), preoccupation with family changes, or simply personal temperament (Cushman & Johnson, 2001).

Attention deficit is routinely identified around age 7 when children begin a more formal educational process, but some are diagnosed as they begin preschool. Although medication is often suggested as part of an intervention, the opportunity to learn self-monitoring skills in therapy is also necessary.

ADHD often makes academic tasks challenging. For therapists, it may be difficult to maintain the attention of children with ADHD throughout the session. Therapists may find themselves feeling taxed in the same way as adults are outside the therapeutic setting in working with these clients. Boys used to dealing actively with their issues and concerns will probably engage in the same active coping strategies as they do outside the session. The well-practiced responses used to avoid discomfort in dealing with internal and external challenges often become obstacles to change. The client's lack of self-awareness can compound challenges in therapy.

EXCERPT FROM SAMPLE INTERVIEW FOR ADHD

THERAPIST: *What are some things you like about school?*
CLIENT: *Recess and lunch. (Girls will usually identify friends.)*
THERAPIST: *What are some things you don't like about school?*
CLIENT: *The work.*
THERAPIST: *Sometimes the work can be hard. What is it about the work that you don't like?*
CLIENT: *Sometimes it's kind of hard—mostly I just don't like it.*

The interview with parents should focus on these issues.

- Medical history—frequent ear infections, insertion of eustachian tubes, and enuresis are frequently associated with attention deficit disorder.
- Focusing abilities at home and school—many parents refute the diagnosis by talking about how their children are able to focus on video games, television, or other activities they enjoy. That is typical for children with attention deficit disorder. It is difficult for children with ADHD to persist, a skill required when the work is boring or not of interest to the child.
- Organizational skills—"lost" assignments and persistent difficulty in bringing home materials needed for homework are common challenges for children with ADHD.
- Problems following a sequence of directions or in following through on long-standing routines.
- Some difficulty noted with transitions.
- Risk behaviors—is there some evidence of thrill seeking?
- Effect of consequences—for children with ADHD, consequences may have a variable effect or no effect at all. Some days, a consequence may appear to be having the desired effect, but that response may disappear the next day.

A distinction can be made between what the child can do and what the child doesn't want to do. The latter is willful behavior and should be addressed with consequences, while the former indicates a need for teaching, guidance, and structure. Some clients with ADHD have a need for additional excitement and thrill seeking. Fire setting may be one example of such a need, which is closer to the conduct disorder end of the attention deficit continuum.

Description

The overall prevalence rate for ADHD in the general population, including adults and children, is estimated at 3 percent to 5 percent. Of children and adolescents presenting to a clinic for services, up to one half are diagnosed with ADHD, and 15 percent to 20 percent struggle with some type of symptoms throughout their lives (Pary et al., 2002). The disorder is four to six times more common in boys than girls. Boys are more likely to act out behaviorally, while girls more often present with inattention. Approximately half of children diagnosed with ADHD also meet the criteria for oppositional defiant disorder, or some kind of conduct disorder (Pary et al., 2002).

Specific functional deficits are observed in memory, organizational skills, ability to anticipate consequences of behavior, and difficulty with transitions. Problems are also frequently observed with social relationships, self-monitoring, and learning disorders, particularly in reading and math. Impulsivity often makes normal classroom behavior difficult for those with attention deficit disorder.

Successful treatment outcomes are observed with the use of stimulant medications. Parents and teachers are often closely involved in attempts to increase the client's likelihood for success by structuring the environment. The child may develop some compensatory mechanisms himself over time.

Accompanying depressive symptoms often develop as the client experiences frustration over academic tasks and encounters difficulty making friends or following the rules at school. Antidepressants may be prescribed for the depressive symptoms but have not shown any consistent impact on the attention deficit symptoms.

Recent studies have confirmed a link between alcohol use and smoking in parents with presentation of ADHD, substantiating anecdotal reports (Tercyak, Lerman, & Audrain, 2002). Parents report feeling challenged by children with ADHD (Harrison & Sofronoff, 2002), perhaps contributing to an ongoing interactive cycle between presentation of symptoms and parental frustration.

Conduct Disorder

Conduct disorder may be treated with a variety of techniques. Your choice of technique depends on your specific assessment of the severity of the problem and the client's individual strengths and obstacles. Think of conduct disorder as existing near the end of a continuum, an extreme manifestation of attention deficit disorder. Understand that clients with conduct disorder may also have problems focusing their attention, following through with multiple directions, organizing themselves, projecting the consequences of their actions, or feeling empathy. Awareness of these limitations can help in tailoring interventions to your client. Do not further confuse or frustrate the client by attempting to focus on tasks that work against the client's natural tendencies rather than building on them. Having the client participate in developing an external form of structure and monitoring will increase his sense of ownership and likelihood to follow through. Two specific approaches that have been found helpful with conduct disorders include cognitive problem solving and family therapy (Nathan & Gorman, 2002).

Additionally, similar to the discussions of social skills deficits for children with autistic features, some children and adolescents with conduct disorder tend to misinterpret social cues and have difficulty understanding the feelings and reactions of others as a consequence of their own actions. In addition to the basic social skills training that is often best conducted in groups in schools, to facilitate an increased understanding of the impact of their actions, empathy training can be another focus for helping these children "get outside themselves" to understand others and the interactions of their own actions on others' feelings. Specific techniques that are suggested include writing to enhance self-reflection and participation in groups to help increase understanding of diverse experiences (Breggin, Breggin, & Bemak, 2002).

OPPOSITIONAL DEFIANT DISORDER

Oppositional defiant disorder (ODD) is characterized by a persistent pattern of negative behaviors, most often directed toward authority figures. These negative behaviors include defiance, disobedience, and hostility (American Psychological Association, 1994). Recent studies highlight the potential social problems often experienced by children with ODD, ADHD, conduct disorder, or any combination of these disorders. These complications in social skills appear to arise out of deficits in those same areas. Children, primarily boys between ages 7 and 12, often display fewer verbal problem-solving skills and more often engage in physical or aggressive solutions (Matthys, Cuperus, & Van Engeland, 1999).

Early onset of ODD during the preschool years appears to be associated with a more chronic presentation, with symptom duration from ages 2 (Speltz, McClellan, DeKlyen, & Jones, 1999) to 7 (Campbell, 1995) for clients from clinic samples. Community samples reported similar stability of symptoms with early onset (Achenbach, Howell, McConaughy, & Stanger, 1995a, 1995b; Pianta & Caldwell, 1990; Pianta and Castaldi, 1989; Richman, Stevenson, & Graham, 1982; and Verhulst and Van der Ende, 1992).

One fourth of boys with ODD were found to develop symptoms of conduct disorder over a 3-year period, while half maintained a diagnosis of ODD without developing symptoms of conduct disorder and 25 percent showed a remission of ODD symptoms during that same period (Lahey, Loeber, Quay, Frick, & Grimm, 1992). By comparison, Biederman, Faraone, Milberger, and Curtis (1996) found that 32 percent of their sample from a clinic of children with ADHD and ODD symptoms also displayed conduct disorder symptoms. These findings show a clear relationship between symptoms for these three disorders, but no clear etiology or progression of symptoms has been demonstrated to date.

CONTRIBUTING FACTORS

Attention deficit and oppositional defiant disorders often coexist, and some describe an interactive relationship, suggesting that facets of one disorder may fuel the other (Burns & Walsh, 2002). Attention deficit is the most commonly co-occurring disorder with behavior problems, and many suggest that the impulsivity and hyperactivity associated with attention deficit problems may facilitate the development of behavior or conduct problems (Lahey, McBurnett, & Loeber, 2000; Loeber, Green, Lahey, Frick, & McBurnett, 2000; McMahon & Estes, 1997).

A link between ODD and conduct disorder has been investigated in several studies (Biederman, Faraone, Milberger, & Curtis, 1996; Frick, Lahey, Loeber, Stouthamer-Loeber, Christ, & Hanson, 1992; Lahey et al., 1992; Loeber, Lahey, & Thomas, 1991; Loeber, Green, Keenan, & Lahey, 1995), without clear results. Results suggest that although ODD appears to precede the development of conduct disorder, the majority of children with ODD do not develop symptoms of conduct disorder.

FAMILY FACTORS

Hyperactivity and impulsivity are also identified as risk factors in parent/child relationships. These factors often make parenting such children more frustrating and may create more conflict in the parent-child relationship. Some authors identify hyperactivity and impulsivity as key factors in the development of ODD (Dishion & Patterson, 1999; McMahon & Estes, 1997). Risk factors associated with development of conduct disorder, following initial presentation of ODD, include lower socioeconomic status, parent's antisocial personality disorder, and poor parenting skills (Faraone, Biederman, Keenan, & Tsuang, 1991; Frick, Lahey, & Loeber, 1992; Lahey et al., 1992; and Schacher & Wachsmuth, 1990).

TREATMENT OF EXTERNALIZING DISORDERS

For children with a combined presentation of ADHD and ODD symptoms, a multimodal treatment approach was found to be more effective than a single treatment method of medication alone (Swanson et al., 2001).

SUBSTANCE ABUSE

Substance abuse is a problem coexisting with many of the externalizing disorders, partially as a self-medication behavior (a way to avoid the discomfort created by situations and consequences of behavior) and partially related to the impulsivity so commonly experienced with these disorders. Unfortunately, substance abuse produces many negative effects of its own, often exacerbating what may be an already shaky existence and self-esteem.

Description

Substance abuse is becoming an issue for children and adolescents at increasingly younger ages, making treatment difficult because of the relative lack of self-monitoring and understanding about the potential consequences of their actions. Using alcohol and other drugs can harm them physically, and the resulting damage can affect motivation and make it difficult to complete tasks. (Tripathi, Lal, & Kumar, 2001). In addition, parents may not be thinking about drug use as a possible factor, given their children's young age, allowing the use to continue and possibly entrenching its use as a coping mechanism. Family relationships have been shown to have a positive influence on child and adolescent decisions about drug use. A close, supportive relationship between the parent and child is associated with less drug use in adolescence (Brook, Whiteman, & Finch, 1993). These findings are consistent with other work about the continuing influence of parents on their children throughout adolescence.

The influence of parents on children can also have a negative effect. Negative behaviors, such as aggression, antisocial acts, and drug use, are observed in children and adolescents whose parents engage in deviant behavior, in families where greater conflict exists between parents and children, and in those families with less emotional warmth and closeness (Kazdin, 1987; Stein, Newcomb, & Bentler, 1993). Adolescent personality characteristics, such as defiance, impulsivity, and psychopathology have also been associated with drug use (Brook, Whiteman, Finch, & Cohen, 1998).

Adolescents often use drugs and alcohol, and sometimes sexual acting out, as ways of self-medicating. Even self-mutilation can become a distraction from the pressures adolescents may be feeling. Eating disorders can be a way to try to regain control of the environment. What's being described are the secondary gains of these maladaptive behaviors. At first glance from a rational perspective, these behaviors are merely self-destructive, but there is more going on with these situations than just acting out. Part of the role of therapy in the lives of children and teens who are using these measures to distract themselves from emotional pain is to identify what the behaviors are covering up or diverting attention away from for the client. Your clients and their parents may not be aware of what the focus of distraction actually is, but if they become psychologically minded and invested in the process, these secondary gains can usually be identified. For those clients who are not psychologically minded and only marginally invested in the process, reduction of negative, external consequences will probably provide the motivation. Tailor your interventions to meet your clients where they are. With these two types of clients, two different approaches will be used. With the former, a combination of insight-oriented and cognitive-behavioral approaches will be effective. With the latter, the primary focus will be cognitive-behavioral.

Peer Influence

Peer influence can be a factor in child and adolescent substance use and other acting-out behaviors. For those children and adolescents who feel estranged from their families, the peer group and any activities that might help them fit in become much more inviting. The peer group becomes more powerful and influential for those who do not feel grounded in their family relationships. This can become a repetitive cycle for those who may be estranged from their families as part of the foster care system. Another group that may have difficulty connecting with family members are those who have been unable to form adequate attachments to their parental figures, such as those diagnosed with reactive attachment disorder. A driving force behind acting out behavior for these children and adolescents is a desire to be connected. For those who have been able to form an attachment but now have more emotional distance, the acting out behaviors become their ticket to entry into certain peer groups. For those without the history of positive attachments, the acting out becomes the way for them to receive attention in a way that feels comfortable; negative attention is more comfortable for these young people than the warmth of intimacy or a close emotional bond. The anxiety experienced when parents try to get close is often so great that it actually pushes them further away. This reaction is often observed in anecdotal reports of parents who describe an outburst of negative behavior or acting out following being praised for a period of good behavior or a specific positive act. These types of interactions between parents and children create frustration and a negative spiral that is difficult to rebuild. Depending on the severity of the attachment disorder, outside placement may need to be sought because the emotional distance inherent in that setting feels ultimately more comfortable to the client.

For children and young adolescents attempting to join a group to compensate for the lack of support from their family, the task of gaining acceptance may more difficult than one would initially assume. Peer group status is an important factor for this younger age group in terms of their ability to be accepted by others (Leasel & Axelrod, 2001). Popularity by association and perceived status are factors that will allow some to be accepted by the group more easily than others. The more times an adolescent is rejected by a group or several groups, the more likely is that individual to seek out the support of more marginal groups and more likely to use drugs or alcohol to gain acceptance within the group.

SHARED CHARACTERISTICS OF EXTERNALIZING DISORDERS

The externalizing disorders share many common characteristics in terms of diagnosis, co-morbidity, and treatment. Risk factors often arise out of the client's own impulsivity and lack of attention to social and environmental cues. Many function better with a relatively high level of structure, due to the difficulties encountered with transition and change. Chronic problems in maintaining peer relationships can leave individuals somewhat socially isolated.

DISCUSSION QUESTIONS

1. What common features exist among the externalizing disorders?
2. Do common risk factors exist?
3. What is the preferred course of treatment for each of the disorders outlined in the chapter?
4. Is there a progressive nature of symptoms among the externalizing disorders?
5. How do family factors affect presentation of externalizing disorders?

Developmental Disorders

Introduction

The mood and externalizing disorders reviewed in Chapters 7 and 8 are often observed as co-morbid conditions with other presentations. The possibility of combinations of different problems or disorders, embedded within the context of normal or abnormal development, can present quite a challenge. This chapter reviews developmental disorders, including Asperger's, autism, borderline features (referred to by some as *multiple complex developmental disorder),* and eating disorders.

Asperger's Disorder/Autism

Children and adolescents with Asperger's tend to have difficulty sustaining attention and persisting on academic tasks. However, one of the hallmarks is the consistent difficulty recognizing social cues and engaging in appropriate social interactions. Restricted and repetitive patterns of activity, interests, and routine are also key features (American Psychiatric Association, 2000). Some problems with anger regulation when routines are disrupted are also noted.

Asperger's syndrome or disorder is within the general classification of pervasive developmental disorders. In a recent study after a two-year follow-up, young children (under age 6) with Asperger's displayed stronger social skills and less autistic symptoms (Szatmari, Brywon, & Streiner, 2001). Children diagnosed with autism who had developed verbal skills during the two years were similar to those diagnosed with Asperger's at the beginning of the study. Researchers are looking at the possible overlapping trajectory in the development of Asperger's and autism. This clustering of similar disorders has been labeled *autism spectrum disorders,* referring to those disorders that share similar symptoms of repetitive behavioral patterns and difficulty with social interactions (Lorimer, Simpson, Myles, & Ganz, 2002). Preliminary indications may provide directions for future research and treatment, based on these commonalities.

This has been the case in other disorders with some overlap in symptomatology, such as ADHD and Tourette's syndrome (Tsai, 1992).

Awareness about autistic features and the benefit of earlier diagnosis is on the rise. However, differences in individual presentations of the disorder as a result of the complex interaction of developmental patterns and symptom presentation make clear identification of the disorder difficult (Coucouvanis, 1997). As a result, general guidelines regarding potential markers of the disorder that parents might observe have been offered to aid in early diagnosis (Filipek, Accardo, & Baranek, 1999). General categories include communication, social concerns, socialization, and behavior. A few examples of communication concerns might be a child not responding to her name, variable language use, delayed language, or not waving good-bye. Examples of social concerns include lack of social smiling, poor eye contact, unusual independence, or appearing to be in her own world. Socialization examples are lack of interest in other children, in reciprocal play, or in imitation games such as pat-a-cake. Behavioral examples include having tantrums, unusual attachment to toys, perseverating on certain things, displaying excessive sensitivity to textures or sounds, or engaging in odd movement patterns. (Filipek, Accardo, & Baranek, 1999).

Murray (1996) identifies four symptoms that are almost always present in children with autism: social isolation, cognitive deficits, language deficits, and ritualized motor activity. Difficulties with social relationships are a hallmark of autistic disorders, continuing throughout the life span (Murray, 1996). Recognizing appropriate social cues and understanding emotion are two significant challenges for individuals with autistic features. Autistic individuals are often more comfortable with objects than with people, and some develop almost obsessive attachments with certain types of objects (e.g., vacuum cleaners). Tantrums or extreme emotional responses are often observed without any clearly identifiable stimulus.

Cognitive deficits may include some level of mental retardation or learning disorder for many with autism (Yirmiya & Sigman, 1991), but not with Asperger's (*DSM-IV*). Ability to focus attention on central features is often impaired, as is the ability to imagine how others perceive the world or themselves (Murray, 1996). Language problems are another hallmark of autistic disorders (Fein, Pennington, Markowitz, Braverman, & Waterhouse, 1986; Frith, 1989; Goodman, 1989). Although individual presentations vary, many autistic children do not speak, may echo others, or use language components incorrectly (Murray, 1996). Finally, repetitive movements that appear to be without any goal are also strongly associated with autistic features. These may include aimless twirling, hand waving, or body rocking. A strong necessity to maintain consistency in routine and environment are also observed in autistic individuals. Success of treatment depends on severity of symptoms, in conjunction with early intervention.

Early intervention can provide the opportunity to implement behavioral strategies prior to any emotional consequences (e.g., depression, angry attitude) that often develop in response to negative social interactions with peers and adults in the undiagnosed child's environment. An example of such an early preventive procedure is the "social story" tested for use in the home by Lorimer and colleagues

(2002). Historically, interventions have focused on improving positive social inter-actions, decreasing negative symptoms or problem behaviors, and building skills (Dunlap & Koegel, 1999). Other important interventions include developing em-pathy to improve social interactions, improving self-monitoring skills, and being taught basic information about social rules (Dunlap & Koegel, 1999; Hadwin, Baron-Cohen, Howlin, & Hill, 1997; Ozonoff & Miller, 1995).

In 1998, an estimated 5,000 children with autistic features were "main-streamed" into regular classrooms in schools throughout the country ("Giant Steps for Autistic Kids," 1998). The challenges inherent in managing extraneous stimuli and social interactions in that setting can be overwhelming for some children, pre-cipitating the use of maladaptive coping skills that create additional problems and a somewhat circuitous cycle that may be hard to reverse. Difficulty speaking and interacting appropriately with others are typical characteristics of the disorder; they make successful functioning in the public school system problematic. Addi-tional characteristics include extreme sensitivity to clothing, background noise, or even certain food textures. These stimuli often overwhelm the senses of the child with autism. Individualized intervention is an important part of the intervention. Giant Steps is a program in Montreal that works with autistic children with the goal of integrating them into the public school system. They estimate such inte-gration can take from three months to two years, depending on individual differ-ences. A "shadow," as Giant Steps aides are called, accompanies the child to public school after leaving the controlled preschool environment ("Giant Steps for Autis-tic Kids," 1998).

Therapeutic Interventions

Interventions for individuals with autism or Asperger's are similar to those for all children in terms of being more effective when administered at the time of the be-havior (Dunlap & Koegel, 1999; Hauck, Fein, Waterhouse, & Feinstein, 1995; McGee, Krantz, & McClannahan, 1984; Pierce & Schreibman, 1997; Sugai et al., 2000). Children respond positively to a "teachable moment" that arises when a new response can be taught at the time the more automatic or impulsive response gen-erally manifests. The ability to learn a new behavioral response is enhanced be-cause the child's understanding of the specific situation becomes linked to the new response that is taught at the time the behavior occurs. For children and adoles-cents with autistic spectrum disorders, those teachable moments often focus on empathic skills, or helping the individuals understand or "guess" what others might be thinking. This other-oriented thinking is quite foreign to children and adoles-cents who have difficulty getting outside themselves to make sense of their envi-ronment and develop appropriate solutions and actions (Hadwin et al., 1997). A relatively new intervention that addresses these empathic issues is the "social story" developed by Gray (1995).

Traditional treatment efforts have adopted a multidisciplinary approach, in-cluding professionals from special education, various developmental therapies (e.g., speech-language, occupational therapy), and behavioral management (Hurth, Shaw, & Izeman, 1999; New York State Department of Health, 1999).

Social Story   The *social story* incorporates traditional behavioral aspects of rehearsal and sometimes includes pictures or videotapes to improve learning and retention (Hagiwara & Myles, 1999; Swaggart et al., 1995). Such a multimodal approach enhances learning for almost any type of child, regardless of special disorders. A typical social story includes four different types of sentences designed to increase the individual's understanding of a social situation and to be able to identify a good behavioral choice for herself: (1) descriptive, (2) directive, (3) perspective, and (4) control (Gray, 1996). Descriptive sentences lay the groundwork by defining a specific social situation and describing how people generally behave in these situations. The descriptive portion provides a template for the child or adolescent with an autistic spectrum disorder, a road map, if you will, that provides a starting place. Internal confusion is often the initial response to social situations, followed by behavioral choices that often don't fit the current situation. Directive sentences provide instruction regarding appropriate responses to the situation outlined by the descriptive sentences. The next phase is the perspective sentence, which provides insight into what others might be thinking or feeling in reaction to the prescribed situation. Finally, the control statement addresses relevant cues developed by the individual using the social story to aid in future retrieval (Gray, 1996). The content of stories is tailored to the individual on such topics as talking with adults or talking with friends.

A preliminary study regarding the use of social stories to reduce pretantrum behaviors reported positive results regarding the approach's effectiveness (Lorimer et al., 2002). The social story appears to be a proscribed method to provide specific information about expectations for the individual, and regarding others, in various social situations. Transitions and novel situations have historically been identified as problematic for children with autistic spectrum disorder and ADHD. The success of the technique makes intuitive sense when understood in the context of specific information about such situations. A common intervention with the population has been to prepare them for transitions by telling them in advance (e.g., we'll be leaving for school in ten minutes or after you tie your shoes). The social story expands the basic technique, making it even more applicable with the specific information provided, and helps manage anxiety around the unknown or unexpected.

Play Therapy for Autistic Children   A multimodal approach combining music, language, and play has produced positive outcomes for children in their transition to specialized or mainstream classrooms since its introduction in the early 1980s ("Giant Steps for Autistic Kids," 1998). The program, Giant Steps, was developed in Canada by music therapist Darlene Berringer to form a positive relationship with public school systems in shoring up the skills of this socially challenged population. The curriculum focus is on helping students develop coping skills to extraneous stimuli, particularly sound. The program appears to use components of desensitization, for once the children become acclimated to a certain level of sound stimuli, while using their newly developed coping skills, additional sounds are added incrementally. Although the director of the program does not describe it as such, it appears that her method is somewhat consistent with *auditory* *integration,* an approach that has not received broad professional support (American Academy of Pediatrics, 1998). The goal of auditory integration is to decrease the sensitivity to sound by systematic exposure to music, but it is accomplished through headphones (Levy & Hyman, 2002), an apparent difference from the Giant Steps approach. The length of time for integration into the public school system ranges from three months to two years. Most children begin in preschool or kindergarten, achieving integration during the early elementary years. Despite the program's long-standing history and apparent success, critics cite the lack of formal evaluation or follow-up regarding the continued performance of its students as a concern. Perhaps this is a research project in the making for an interested student.

Using Technology   Because of the primary difficulty with social relationships and distracting stimuli from interpersonal interactions, computers and video games are often a comfortable haven for autistic children. Silver and Oakes (2001) have built on this strength for autistic children in the development of a computer program designed to improve their social and communication skills. The program uses randomly selected photographs of different facial expressions and then guides the client through a series of questions and answers about the emotions being exhibited. Results show significant improvement in emotional recognition after eight 30-minute sessions with the computer program. Children and adolescents can also work with the program independently, increasing their sense of confidence and self-efficacy through use of the program. A positive transfer of learning has been noted by the children and adolescents who have used the program, but follow-up studies are needed to confirm those anecdotal reports (Silver & Oakes, 2001). Carter (2001) found generalization of language-based interventions only to the home environment in her study of a separate population of school-age children.

Individual Characteristics   Individual characteristics are also part of the interaction that determines acceptance by the peer group. A general factor is the child's need for affiliation. The two terms used to describe this factor are idiocentric and allocentric (Dayan, Doyle, & Markiewicz, 2001). *Idiocentric* individuals generally have less of a need for affiliation and are more focused on their own goals and desires, while those with *allocentric* tendencies have a higher need for affiliation and may focus more on characteristics that will help them be more accepted by the group, such as cooperation and negotiation. Being able to get those needs met helps foster a more positive sense of self-efficacy and self-esteem (Dayan, Doyle, & Markiewicz, 2001). Conversely, a high need for affiliation may force some children and adolescents to succumb to what they perceive as external pressure to "fit in." They may be willing to sacrifice themselves, their personal control, and their decision making to the group because of the need to feel accepted. Parents often do not understand this almost pathological need to be accepted. What may be happening at one level for these young people is that they feel as if they have a "hole" they are trying to fill, by following the decisions of others who are providing an escape as well.

For children with limited, delayed, or impaired social skills, acceptance by peers is often even more challenging than for other children and adolescents.

Autism is being recognized as more of a continuum-based disorder than was originally thought, similar to attention deficit disorder. Therefore, for an increasing number of children and adolescents in the school system, autism is recognized as having some impact on their experience, most notably in the social arena. Studies also support the concerns about social skills deficits in that those with autism or autistic features are often less able to appropriately interpret social cues, especially in verbal interactions (Loveland, Pearson, Tunali-Kotoski, Ortegon, & Gibbs, 2001). Autism or autistic features tend to interfere with the individual's ability to appropriately apply social norms or interpret social interactions accurately.

An inability to interpret and respond accurately to social interactions can lead to conflict with peers and adults. Conflict is certainly not specific to children with challenges such as autism or attention deficit disorder, and developmental considerations are a part of managing conflict as well. Younger children more often attempt to influence others through coercion than through disengagement (Laursen, Finkelstein, & Townsend, 2001). However, disengagement is often the action that adults provide to children to resolve peer conflict. This presents a misunderstanding on the part of adults with regard to the ability of children and adolescents to act beyond their developmental ability. Such misunderstandings can create additional conflict between children and parents or other adults around them. Negotiation becomes more common in relationships between children and adolescents as they get older and are better able to exercise their intellectual skills.

Although autism presents specific challenges to children and adolescents in navigating the public school system, new approaches and understanding of the disorder have all but eliminated a life of unproductive isolation that might have once been their fate. A number of personal accounts or memoirs are available that speak to this new understanding of autistic features and managing the challenges inherent in the disorder.

BORDERLINE PERSONALITY DISORDER IN CHILDREN

Borderline personality disorder is well documented in adults, and professionals working with children and adolescents are observing similar symptoms in clients with whom they work as well. Towbin, Dykens, Pearson, and Cohen (1993, pp. 779–780) describe a "chronic syndrome of disturbances in affect modulation, social relatedness, and thinking." Theirs is one of the early works to identify these concerns and to test the hypothesis that this syndrome might be considered a developmental disorder; some prefer to classify it as an unspecified pervasive developmental disorder (Burd, Fisher, & Kerbeshian, 1987; Dahl, Cohen, & Provence, 1986). Advantages to conceptualization as a developmental disorder include the disparity between the child/adolescent presentation and that of adults (Towbin et al., 1993). Others have described the syndrome as a combination of externalizing and internalizing symptoms and cognitive deficits (Bemporad, Smith, & Hanson, 1987; Kernberg, 1997; Robson, 1983).

Although aspects of the presentation in children and adolescents are difficult, that is one of few similarities with the adult presentation. A problem in diagnosis is the lack of a consistent or well-defined presentation as the child grows and matures. Features of the syndrome include increased anxiety, difficulty with relationships, problems modulating affective responses, and instances of apparent thought disorder. Manifestation of these symptoms may be sporadic and can mimic other disorders, making diagnosis difficult. Finally, these features are not atypical in a clinical or hospital setting for the age group (Towbin et al., 1993). Mania has also been observed in young children (ages 2 to 7) as a co-morbid condition with pervasive developmental disorder in 21 percent of the sample (Wozniak et al., 1997). This rate is consistent with that observed in children under age 12, who presented with mania without pervasive developmental disorder (Wozniak, Biederman, & Kiely, 1995; Wozniak et al., 1997).

Historically, the clinical presentation described has been labeled *childhood schizophrenia,* but the term is ambiguous without clear diagnostic criteria and lack of continuity with regard to symptoms from childhood to adulthood. Another clear concern about the label is its volatility, consistent with general concerns about diagnosing children and adolescents. A diagnosis of schizophrenia can be quite a burden to carry throughout one's life, particularly if it has been used as a catchall phrase to describe a cluster of difficult symptoms that may actually be more consistent with developmental differences than psychopathology. As clinicians, we are doing harm if a diagnosis is provided that is inaccurate or incomplete.

The diagnostic label *borderline syndrome of childhood* fails to provide an accurate course of the disorder in the same way as does childhood schizophrenia. There is a lack of continuity in symptoms from childhood to adulthood, a similarity to other disorders involving poor object relations (e.g., autism, chronic post-traumatic stress disorder, reactive attachment disorder), diffuseness of other symptoms within the cluster, and the child or adolescent's continuing developmental process (Towbin et al., 1993). Lofgren, Bemporad, King, Lindem, and O'Driscoll (1991) note that it is unlikely for children experiencing this syndrome to continue the same patterns into adulthood. Rutter (1985) likewise notes that labeling a child as having a personality disorder is inconsistent with the ongoing process of development in which the child's personality is being formed. Personality formation is not a static process but rather continues over time, despite any interruptions or impairments experienced along the way that may affect cognitive abilities, affect regulation, or social relationships (Towbin et al., 1993).

Multiple Complex Developmental Disorder

Despite these concerns, the term *multiple complex developmental disorder* (MCDD) has been adopted to describe this diffuse presentation (Cohen, Paul, & Volkmar, 1987; Towbin et al., 1993; Lincoln, Bloom, Katz, & Boksenbaym, 1998). The key factors associated with MCDD include: (1) difficulty regulating affect and anxiety, as evidenced by generalized anxiety, irritability, unusual fears, episodes of panic, or rapid mood changes without apparent external stimulation; (2) social skills impairment, as evidenced by disinterest, detachment, avoidance, or inability to maintain peer relationships; and (3) cognitive impairments, evidenced by bizarre ideation, repetition of nonsense syllables, magical thinking or thinking inconsistent with development level. Many of these symptoms may sound similar to other developmental disorders, such as autism or Asperger's, and there is some crossover in presentation. This presents evidence of the need for gathering information from a variety of sources in making the diagnosis. In addition, the therapist must observe the child over time while making appropriate behavioral interventions to build skill levels.

Varying levels of severity are observed in these children, as with most disorders. Depending on individual presentation, the level of cognitive impairment may be a factor in the ability of the child or adolescent to participate in basic skill building. Gold, Carpenter, Randolph, Goldberg, and Weinberger (1997) identified a problem in working memory for children with this syndrome, while Seguin, Pihl, Harden, Tremblay, and Boulerice (1995) suggested a possible association between executive function deficits and aggression. Paris, Zelkowitz, Guzder, Joseph, and Feldman (1999) note the difficulty in completing tasks, higher levels of error, and failure to learn from mistakes for the 7- to 12-year-olds in their study. They suggest that the neurological underpinnings of the disorder in children is similar to that of borderline personality in adults (van Reekum, Links, & Mitton, 1996). Despite disagreement on the etiology, the key in treatment for this and many childhood disorders is to design interventions to optimize development within the constraints of presenting symptoms (Towbin et al., 1993). For example, preparing children for transitions is a simple intervention that can teach a skill about managing the anxiety they might normally experience as a result of such changes.

Risk Factors

It is well known that many mental illnesses or episodes of disorders may be precipitated by psychosocial stressors. Several studies have also found a link between family functioning and the presentation of borderline or MCDD symptoms in children, including trauma, neglect, or abandonment (Bemporad, Smith, & Hanson, 1982; Kestenbaum, 1983), abuse (Goldman, D'Angelo, DeMaso, & Mezzacappa, 1992), or the presence of severe pathology in the parent, such as chronic depression, substance abuse, or antisocial personality features (Goldman, D'Angelo, & DeMaso, 1993). Guzder, Paris, Zelkowitz, and Feldman (1999) found a strong link between a history of sexual abuse in their sample of children ranging in age from 7 to 12 years and the presentation of borderline or MCDD symptoms. Thirty-four percent of the sample had been sexually abused, information which was supported by reports from other agencies or adults involved in the children's lives at the time of the study (Guzder et al., 1999). Evidence from this study provides further support for a link between abuse and symptoms that are consistent with pathology, when the symptoms may have actually developed as a maladaptive response in reaction to trauma. Even the incidence of abuse in the population being studied could be related to family factors of being neglected or not closely supervised, placing them at greater risk for trauma as well as psychological symptoms (Fergusson, Lynskey, & Horwood, 1996; Nash, Hulsely, Sexton, Harralson, & Lambert, 1993).

Eating Disorders

Work with eating disorders in children and adolescents will inevitably involve a family approach. With early intervention, family involvement can be critical in preventing a disordered eating pattern from becoming an eating disorder. Important components of family treatment include reducing blame within the family system, increasing acceptance of family members, and improving problem solving within the family system (Lask & Bryant-Waugh, 2000). The latter may include a focus on communication, and the implementation may be strengthened by role-plays, including some role reversal during which parents may gain a greater understanding of what it feels like to be their daughter. The experiential understanding of their daughter's plight may be more powerful than any other intervention in helping them take responsibility for their own behaviors and expectations and begin to turn around patterns of behavior in the family to promote healthier interactions and, by extension, healthier eating patterns.

Another important component of intervention at the individual level is the use of cognitive behavioral techniques to address the issues of disordered body image and irrational thought patterns. An approach that involves behavior modification, cognitive therapy, and family systems is, as with other multimodal approaches, a more effective intervention (Robin, Bedway, Siegel, & Gilroy, 1996). Medication needs to be considered as part of a multimodal approach as well. In addition, thought patterns often have a compulsive component as well, making it difficult for young clients to redirect thoughts toward other activities or use of new coping skills. Exploration of the degree of control clients have over these thoughts may be a key factor in determining the appropriateness of a medication consult to help with the repetitive thoughts.

Description

Eating disorders have become a much more common concern in recent years. In a national survey of students in grades 5 through 12 (Neumark-Sztainer & Hannan, 2000), 24 percent of the students described themselves as overweight, while almost half (45 percent) of the girls and 20 percent of boys reported they had been on a diet at some point. Disordered eating patterns were reported in 13 percent of the girls and 7 percent of the boys participating in the survey. Only 24 percent of the girls and 5 percent of boys had discussions about disordered eating patterns with health care professionals. As these figures suggest, disordered eating patterns and eating disorders are often not directly addressed by children, adolescents, or even health care providers. Because of the secrecy often surrounding eating patterns, it becomes even more important for clinicians to be aware of risk factors, symptoms, and stressors.

Issues of body image and weight are prevalent among today's youth. Although more of an issue for girls and young women, concern over body image also affects some boys, particularly those who might be involved in sports such as wrestling that emphasize size. Satisfaction with body size appears to be related at least partially to socioeconomic status. Neither girls nor boys of lower socioeconomic status felt badly about themselves if they were overweight, but girls in middle and upper class families were much more preoccupied with weight and much less satisfied with their appearance (O'Dea & Caputi, 2001).

REVIEW OF ANOREXIA AND BULIMIA

Although the diagnosis of eating disorders is becoming more specific (e.g., binge-eating disorder), two primary presentations continue to be those of anorexia and bulimia. The discussion focuses on identification and treatment of those two primary disorders.

Anorexia Nervosa

Description   Anorexia nervosa combines obsessive thoughts and negative thoughts (usually anxiety or anger) about food, eating, and body image with compulsive behaviors around eating and exercise. At its most extreme, the individual is near starvation. Depending on the age at which adolescents begin starving themselves, there can be long-standing effects on physical, social, and emotional development (Lock, 2001). In addition to the symptoms of anorexia nervosa, it is relatively common to observe co-morbidity with other disorders, such as depression, anxiety disorders, and obsessive compulsive disorder (Thornton & Russell, 1997). The highest incidence of anorexia is reported in adolescents (White, 2000). Prevalence rates nearing 50 percent in young women are reported by some sources (Lock, 2001). Although prevalence rates are not available for young men, anorexia is becoming more common in that population as well.

Onset   Although onset is generally identified at around age 17 (Lock, 2001), preadolescents are often presenting with early symptoms of the disorder as well. Weight concerns in elementary school, peers' attention placed on weight and eating, and the level of identification with certain media presentations in magazines, television, and movies have been identified as early onset symptoms (Taylor et al., 1998). Historically, it has been suggested that the roots of this disorder are found in family dynamics around control as one approaches adolescence and often feels out of control (Bruch, 1973). An alternative perspective suggests that the attempts to reduce food consumption are actually an attempt to revert to a less complicated time in the adolescent's life (Crisp, 1997).

Unfortunately, certain risk factors are inherent in Western culture, such as the impact of advertising campaigns and the media, the emphasis on dieting and weight, teasing by peers, initial separation from parents, or discomfort in discussing certain issues with parents (Lock, 2001). Family history of an eating disorder in a parent, grandparent, or close family relative is often reported in those who develop an eating disorder, with some studies focusing on the interactional style of these adults as being more intrusive or controlling (Agras, Hammer, & McNichols, 1999;

Stein, Wooley, Cooper, & Fairburn, 1994). Some mothers promote mother-daughter dieting as if it is a positive bonding experience, when the opposite has been found to be true (Streigel-Moore & Kearney-Cooke, 1994). Hill and Pallin (1998) note that even without a specific focus directed toward the adolescent eating patterns, if parents engage in their own dietary restraint, the children are aware and likely to be influenced, while others (Smolak, Levine, & Schermen, 1999) note that verbal statements from parents are much more powerful. Negative attention from male parental figures about girls' physical appearance may have an even greater influence than any from maternal figures (Schwartz, Phares, Tantleff-Dunn, & Thompson, 1999). Parental attitudes have been identified throughout the literature as having a significant impact on an individual's dissatisfaction with her body (White, 2000).

Part of increased parental concern may be related to increasing cultural attention on obesity as well. Obesity is becoming more prevalent in Western culture, creating another subpopulation for whom weight loss and exercise become constant concerns. The emphasis on dieting and weight reduction place these youth at risk for the development of an eating disorder, most likely anorexia because of the similar dynamics between that disorder and dieting (Hill, 1993). Because of these cultural influences, focusing on weight or diet is a concern for many in the U.S. population, with as many as 70 percent of adolescent girls estimated to be focused on dieting or weight issues (Lock, 2001). These findings were consistent with the results of a large national study completed by Felts, Parrillo, Chenier, and Dunn (1996), in which weight and dieting attitudes of more than 10,000 high school students were surveyed. Felts and colleagues (1996) found that 75 percent of the sample were trying to lose weight, and 25 percent perceived themselves as overweight. Girls as young as 8 were found to be aware of dieting or actually engaged in a diet (Hill & Pallin, 1998; Morena & Thelan, 1995).

Dieting or "dietary restraint" has been associated with the sense of control that some young women experience at a time in their lives when control and autonomy are important developmental issues (Streigel-Moore, Silberstein, & Rodin, 1986). The association between dietary restriction and control initiates a pattern that becomes repeated due to the satisfaction inherent in striving toward developmental milestones, setting the stage for the starvation behaviors consistent with anorexia nervosa.

Diagnosis   Undue attention on appearance may push some adolescents to experiment with food restriction or exercise programs as part of normal development. As such, the attention may also serve as a trigger for a true eating disorder. Because of this factor, it becomes even more critical to differentiate between disordered eating and an eating disorder. The diagnostic criteria for anorexia nervosa include both medical and psychological components because of the interaction with food intake. The medical component defines a threshold at 85 percent of expected body weight as one criteria for an eating disorder (DSM-IV). In other words, if the individual's weight drops below 85 percent of what is expected as an ideal weight for their height and weight, the criteria are met. The psychological criteria include intense anxiety or fear about gaining weight and a distortion of body image (i.e., thinking they look "fat" or larger than they are).

Treatment   Anorexia nervosa is one of a few psychiatric disorders where medical hospitalization may be required. In severe cases, the starvation may become so extreme that the client's life is threatened. Although a physician is probably involved by the time the disorder reaches that stage, it may be necessary to talk with the client and parents about the necessity of medical treatment if the client's physical health status warrants that. Even if hospitalization is never required, an important component of treatment will include psycho-education about the physical effects of the disorder. Potential health complications include changes in production of the growth hormone, problems in hypothalamus functioning, bone marrow abnormalities, structural changes within the brain, cardiac dysfunction, gastrointestinal difficulties, and pubertal delay or interruption for males and females (Lock, 2001). Risk of death as a complication of anorexia nervosa is estimated between 6 and 15 percent (Lock, 2001); half of those attributed to suicide. For these reasons, it is important for therapists to work collaboratively with physicians for those clients who are at greater risk for health complications.

Family and Individual Approaches   Outpatient treatment approaches have included nutritional advice; individual, family, or group therapies; and cognitive-behavioral approaches. Lock (2001) reports that the Maudsley method developed by Dare and Eisler in London has been more effective than individual therapy for adolescents, with positive results maintained five years post-treatment; however, Robin, Siegel, Moye, Gilroy, Dennis, and Sikand (1999) found similar effectiveness in their study comparing behavioral family systems therapy and ego-oriented individual therapy. And LeGrange, Eisler, Dare, and Russell (1992) compared conjoint and separated family therapy, finding comparably positive results regardless of the specific type of family intervention. Conjoint family therapy was defined as traditional family sessions with all members present in the same room, and separated family therapy involved the parents in a separate session and the adolescent in an individual session (LeGrange et al., 1992). Longer treatment for individual approaches was the primary difference noted in the comparison by Robin and colleagues (1999) of individual and family therapies, while the results of LeGrange and colleagues (1992) suggest that it is not necessary for all family members to be present for each intervention for the treatment to be effective, although family involvement is important.

In opposition to the usual treatment focus on conflicts and anxieties that perpetuate the disorder without involving the family, the Maudsley approach includes the family as an empowered part of the treatment team. Family members are encouraged to participate in family meals and given a major role in helping make their child better. Critical components of the Maudsley approach include: emphasis on balanced food intake becoming more regular over time, identifying and modifying irrational thought patterns, supporting family interactions, gradually returning control over eating to the adolescent, and fostering adolescent individuation and the parents' separate functioning as a couple (Dare & Eisler, 1997; Dare & Scmukler, 1991). Aspects of the Maudsley approach echo Minuchin's process of empowering families in their own treatment and that of the Milan system's perspective in family members supporting one another (Lock, 2001).

A similar approach to family intervention produced lasting results in the treatment of anorexia nervosa (Robin, Siegel, Bedway, & Gilroy, 1996; Robin, Siegel, Koepke, Moye, & Tics, 1994). Robin and colleagues (1994, 1996) first defined the adolescent as unable to care for self, followed by parents being coached to work as a team in managing the adolescent's eating, branching out to address maladaptive thoughts and family functioning. When the target weight is reached, the adolescent resumes more control over eating and therapy focuses on problem solving, communication, and adolescent individuation. To achieve successful treatment, combining elements of the Maudsley approach with those of Robin and colleagues will produce positive results that can be maintained over time, an important issue considering the recurrent cognitions regarding eating and body image.

The Maudsley approach has been reported as less effective for young adults (18 or older), those also beset with other chronic illnesses, or those who binge and purge; it is designed for those individuals who are seriously ill (Lock, 2001) and, as such, may have exhausted other treatment options. Individual family dynamics also need to be reviewed. Those families with negative interactions may actually exacerbate symptoms with more intense contact. Individual therapy has been identified as more effective for clients with late onset (around age 18) anorexia nervosa (Robin et al., 1999; Russell, Szmulder, Dare, & Eisler, 1987).

Important components of individual therapy sessions include emphasis on ego strength, coping skills, healthy independent functioning, interpersonal skills, and the relationship of theses factors to eating, weight expectations, and body image (Robin et al., 1999). Specific therapeutic interventions used by Robin et al. (1999) emphasized: (1) the therapist focuses on helping the adolescent; (2) the therapist respects the adolescent's autonomy and need to separate from her family; (3) the therapist would not pressure the adolescent to gain weight or change attitudes about food; (4) the therapist would help the adolescent identify healthy choices available to her; and (5) the therapist would help the adolescent develop coping skills that would not require deprivation or self-starvation.

Bulimia and Binge Eating

Description   Bulimia and binge eating disorder share the behavior of binge eating, although bulimia also includes purging as an attempt to remove calories from the body following the episode of bingeing. People who binge often have preferred foods for bingeing, such as carbohydrates and sweets. Cereal, cookies, and ice cream are common bingeing foods. If the bulimia has become relatively chronic, the individual may have developed a preference for "foods that come up easily." When living in a group situation where privacy is limited, regurgitation may be hidden in more private living areas. There is usually shame associated with the bingeing and purging behaviors, affecting the individual's desire to keep the disorder a secret.

It is estimated that 3 percent of women and 0.3 percent of men suffer from bulimia or binge eating disorder. Binge eating in milder forms is estimated in two thirds of college women at least once a year. More than 15 percent of college-aged women have deliberately purged by vomiting or using laxatives following an episode of binge eating.

Binge eating is often associated with other psychiatric disorders, such as anorexia nervosa, borderline personality disorder, alcoholism, and perhaps most frequently, depression (APA Work Group on Eating Disorders, 2000). Although not a co-morbid condition, a history of sexual abuse has been associated with bulimia (Kenardy & Ball, 1998; Perkins & Luster, 1999; Wonderlich, Brewerton, Jocic, Dansk, & Abbott, 1997). More than half of individuals with an eating disorder have a history of depression, and approximately 40 percent of those with severe bulimia have a history of anorexia. These findings are also consistent with Stein and Hedger's (1997) findings in their study of seventh, eighth, and ninth grade girls about their self-perceptions regarding weight. Increased dieting and depression were related to higher weights, particularly among girls who defined themselves as fat. These coexisting conditions place certain adolescents at greater risk for the development of an eating disorder (White, 2000).

Onset   The onset for bulimia and binge eating disorder is typically in adolescence, similar to anorexia. A positive family history for eating disorders is associated with the presentation of bulimia and binge eating disorder. A genetic predisposition has been found in twin studies (Harvard Mental Health Letter, 2002), as has the tendency for these disorders to be found in clients who may be overweight themselves or whose parents are overweight. Other contributing factors include cultural attitudes about food, beauty, and health; peer pressures; sexual anxieties; family conflict; parenting factors; or child abuse (Harvard Mental Health Letter, 2002). "Dietary restraint" has been associated with bulimia as well as anorexia (White, 2000). Polivy and Herman (1993) explored the link between binge eating and dietary restraint and proposed that the deprivation of certain foods leads to a binge, through both psychological and physiological means. Dieting may precipitate a number of the brain chemistry changes associated with eating disorders (Lauer, Gorzewski, Gerlinghoff, Backmund, & Zihl, 1999; Roser, Bubl, Buergin, Seelig, Radue, & Rost, 1999; Smith, Fairburn, & Cowen, 1999).

Diagnosis   Bulimia is defined by the American Psychiatric Association Work Group on Eating Disorders (2000) as two or more episodes of binge eating (i.e., consuming a large quantity of food in two hours or less) at least twice weekly for three months, followed by purging (i.e., vomiting, using laxatives, or diuretics). Fasting episodes and intense exercise are often part of the disorder, as is the likelihood that the individual experiences shame around the eating disorder and attempts to engage in the behaviors in private.

Binge eating disorder is being considered for inclusion as a psychiatric diagnosis. The tentative definition by the APA work group (2000) includes bingeing without purging, specifically characterized by serious distress over the behaviors that would include three of the following at least two days weekly over a period of six months: rapid eating, eating until uncomfortably full, eating when not hungry, eating in secret, or feeling disgusted or full after eating.

Treatment and Prevention   Cognitive-behavioral therapy conducted over 12 to 20 weekly sessions has received the most attention from researchers. The goal of cognitive-behavioral therapy is to help clients examine their eating and exercise habits and substitute more positive ways of coping with feelings and situations that may trigger an episode of bingeing or purging. Other facets of cognitive-behavioral therapy include attention toward modifying self-destructive beliefs and distorted thinking (usually around weight or body image) and adjusting the value placed on physical appearance. Psycho-educational efforts focused on nutritional counseling and the negative physiological impact of purging are often included as part of the intervention. Recent studies show that cognitive-behavioral treatment is more effective than supportive or supportive-expressive therapies (Harvard Mental Health Letter, 2002).

Group therapy has been shown to be moderately effective for the treatment of bulimia, but no research is reported on the effectiveness of family therapy with bulimia (Harvard Mental Health Letter, 2002).

Treatment efforts have also included prescription of selective serotonin reuptake inhibitors (e.g., Prozac or Zoloft), but reports vary regarding the effectiveness of medication with bulimia (Harvard Mental Health Letter, 2002).

Prevention efforts have been sparsely researched, although results indicate little effect from education alone (White, 2000), and some efforts have actually increased participants' tendency toward dietary restraint (Carter, Stewart, Dunn & Fairburn, 1997). With a population of young women, more positive results were observed when participants used a computer software program targeting dieting, body dissatisfaction, and negative body image (Winzelberg, Taylor, Sharpe, Eldredge, Dev, & Constantinou, 1998), implying a more private, individual process might facilitate positive change. Similarly, participation in a class on body image (Springer, Winzelberg, Perkins, & Taylor, 1999) did appear to improve attitudes and reduce behavioral risk factors, based on pre- and post-test results. Springer et al. (1999) noted a conscious decision to omit information on weight and nutrition, which may have helped by not "teaching dieting." The most powerful aspect of prevention seems to be healthy self-confidence, particularly in elementary and middle school girls (Taylor et al., 1998). Self-confidence appeared to modulate the risk factors and prevent the development of further eating disorder symptoms.

Identification of risk factors may be part of a primary prevention program. The McKnight Risk Factor Survey (IV) is recommended for elementary, middle school, and high school students (Shisslak et al., 1999) due to its comprehensive nature. The instrument not only identifies those students at risk, but also highlights protective factors that could be an important component of intervention programs. The use of such an instrument could also be part of awareness efforts (e.g., Eating Disorders Awareness Week) and efforts to involve parents (White, 2000). As noted, parental participation appears to be a powerful component of treatment, and as such, it could be extrapolated that their participation in prevention is equally important for lasting change. The content of curriculum for parents would include information about negative impact of parental comments and observations, positive communication strategies, self-awareness regarding their own body image and food issues, and building on protective factors (White, 2000).

Helping these children and adolescents develop a more positive body image can take time. Exploration of their heroes and idols is an important component of treatment in that it can provide you with information about their perceptions of people they would like to emulate. Discussion of family ideals, goals, and expectations can also provide additional information about the client's self-image. Even reviewing interactions between parents and the client can provide insight into the messages the client may have internalized. Help the client tease out which are her own messages (maybe very few in reality) and which are those of someone else that have been "implanted" within her mind. After identifying the source and theme of the internal messages, determine their relative impact on the client at present. The more strongly embedded messages have been more internalized by the client and will be more difficult to confront. For those clients, their self-image may be so negative that consideration of suicide may become more viable.

DISCUSSION QUESTIONS

1. Identify distinguishing features of Asperger's Disorder.
2. What types of treatment have shown potential for treatment of Asperger's?
3. What are the key features of each of the major eating disorders?
4. What role do family interactions usually play in eating disorders?
5. What are the key features of multiple complex developmental disorder?

Normal Challenges and Psychosocial Issues

Introduction

Various life challenges and events present themselves to children and adolescents throughout life. For some children and teens, these transitions appear to be normal—that is, the adjustment process appears relatively smooth and without problem. However, for others, any one of these life events could be enough to create adjustment problems in many areas of their lives. Regardless of the etiology for such responses, whether it be a heightened sensitivity or temperamental difference, the task as a therapist is to respond with empathy and understanding. The topics included in this chapter include current research on sexual identity formation, complications in dating, bullying, and the experience of being gifted. Also addressed is the importance of various support systems in the adjustment process.

Psychosocial Stress Factors

Psychosocial stress factors is the term used to describe various life challenges that clients or their families may be facing. These stress factors can serve as precipitants for behavioral, psychological, or emotional reactions. For example, being exposed to a fire is an event that may occur for people in many walks of life. How would a child likely respond to such a stressor, particularly if it was his home? How can a therapist assist a child in reestablishing a sense of safety and security following such trauma? Longitudinal studies indicate that children whose family has lost a home to fire have fairly consistent responses regardless of whether they were present at the time of the fire. Typical concerns include a paradoxical response of worry and frustration with other family members (Greenberg & Keane, 2001). An overview of typical challenges and responses to various life stressors is the focus for this chapter. The more knowledge available to you as the counselor, the better equipped you are to develop an effective and appropriate plan of intervention. Let us first consider school, a common experience for almost all youth and an environment that can provide positive and negative events.

SCHOOL EXPERIENCES

Gay and Lesbian Youth

School has not always felt like a safe place to gay and lesbian youth, and it continues to feel and be unsafe, according to a Human Rights Watch recent report (2001 p. 12). Based on interviews with adolescents, parents, and school personnel in seven states, the report notes that "bullying and violence against gay students is often ignored." Gay and lesbian students described spending a significant amount of time and energy to keep themselves safe to and from school and from bullying while at school.

At some schools and in certain communities, support groups have been created for gay and lesbian students (Gerstel, Feraios, & Herdt, 1989; Treadway & Yoakham, 1992). GLSEN, the National Gay, Lesbian and Straight Education Network, is one example of a nationally based group supporting formation of local support groups. GLSEN is a good source of information and questionnaires that can be used by faculty to assess the climate toward homosexuality at schools. However, the impact of belonging to such groups has not received much attention. Despite the fact that it is becoming more common for gay and lesbian youth to "come out" during high school (Rofes, 1989), the process remains difficult. Theoretically, the support of others might make the process feel less threatening.

Bullies

Although bullies have been a problem for decades, the issue seems much more prevalent for kids today than for previous generations. Issues around feeling bullied and marginalized are now identified as potential factors in many incidents of school violence that have occurred in recent years. In a sample of students at a large middle school, Espelage, Bosworth, and Simon (2000) found that less than 20 percent of students reported no incidents of bullying behaviors in the previous month. That's a fairly small percentage of the population that is not troubled by some type of intimidation at school. The results of continued exposure to intimidation can lead to feelings of learned helplessness (Seligman, 1975), a negative self-image, and possibly depressive symptoms as well.

Coming into contact with some type of bullying behavior is clearly becoming more the norm than not. And the unfortunate aspect reported by many students of all ages is that school personnel simply do not respond to concerns. Many schools appear to have adopted a laissez-faire attitude in which students are expected to manage conflict for themselves, even adopting peer conflict mediation programs. Some of the peer mediation programs offer a wonderful alternative to "telling the teacher," but from anecdotal reports and horrifying outcomes of school violence, it appears that these efforts are inadequate. Anecdotal reports are mounting evidence of the negative effect of peer interactions so severe that some children—with the support of their parents who have also felt unsupported by school personnel—have chosen to transfer schools or resort to home schooling to preserve their mental health and well-being.

Seeking mental health services as a result of teasing and bullying is becoming more common as well. However, even with therapy, the scars travel with the student to the new situation, perhaps bearing the seeds of a victim's presentation. As such, the legacy of feeling unsupported by authority figures can carry a far-reaching negative effect.

We need to look at the child in the larger systems context for both the target and the bully. Recent reviews of this social problem indicate that the bully's actions are partially related to his or her own level of self-esteem and self-image. The bully attacks others in an attempt to make himself or herself feel more powerful, more popular, and better liked by peers. Unfortunately, these "positive" outcomes are often at the expense of the bully's classmates. An important part of the intervention process with bullies is not only to empower the victims, but for the adults in the school and community to take an active role in preventing the negative interactions. The issue of modeling is also being reviewed with regard to the bully's behavior. Some studies show increased association between exposure to violence and violence acted upon others (Loeber & Stouthamer-Loeber, 1998). The exposure can be through the media or in the personal lives of the children and adolescents.

Bullying behavior is being conceptualized as more of a continuum on which certain adolescents exhibit a range of negative coping and control mechanisms. It is not clear what impact modeling has in bullying behavior, but Espelage, Bosworth, and Simon (2000) note some associations between family characteristics and bullying behavior. The use of physical disciplinary measures was significantly associated with bullying behaviors. One might draw the conclusion from this finding that those who feel bullied at home are learning to bully others. Spending time with adults who promote nonviolence and provide strategies for conflict resolution without resorting to physical means had a positive influence in reduction of bullying behaviors. Finally, the study found that those youth who spent more time with peers and less with adults were more likely to engage in bullying behaviors. The negative peer influence could include any number of antisocial activities, such as vandalism, fighting, and stealing. Influencing bullying behavior may be best done in a setting where the counselor is well aware of the peer group norms and relationships with one another, such as the school. The counselor may be able to have a positive impact in reducing the community's climate of accepting bullying by changing that norm within the school setting. Involvement in groups that provide specific tools and coping skills can help turn these behaviors around. A parallel group for parents may add just the right dimension for more permanent change. Some schools are also putting on a play, entitled "Bang-Bang You're Dead" (Mastrosimone, 1999) to increase awareness of the impact of bullying and begin to change the school climate.

Other studies provide further support for links between exposure to violence and aggressive behaviors, as well as more frequent symptoms of post-traumatic stress disorder and depression (Cauffman, Feldman, Waterman, & Steiner, 1998; Giaconia, et al, 1995; Steiner, Garcia, & Matthews, 1997). Flannery, Singer, and Wester (2001) found that violent male adolescents who had attacked someone with a weapon were more likely to exhibit significant levels of anger, dissociation, and post-traumatic stress when compared to similar males who had not engaged in violent behavior. Violent females exhibited a broader range of symptoms, including a higher level of suicidal ideation. Interestingly, males in this study reported being victimized by others more frequently than females. Thus, the presentation of violent behavior could be seen as justified by the youth themselves, almost in a self-defensive fashion. This is an important area of awareness on the part of professionals working toward identification of potential harm to self or others, an area that is difficult to predict. The role of the school in promoting a positive community is becoming more apparent in its importance for change.

Social Skills

Social skills are often identified as a deficit for many bullies, children and adolescents with anger problems, and even gifted children. For many of our clients, much of what they display in session begins at home. Do people talk there? Is there an inherent respect in communication or an underlying sense of defensiveness or brittleness, as if the style of communication is not genuine? Do unspoken messages interfere with open communication? As you interact with clients, you will gain a sense of their communication style and how this affects their view of themselves and others. This information can be used in interventions involving self-esteem and social skills.

Although social skills can be practiced through role-play in individual sessions, the optimal intervention is group. Groups can be provided in an outpatient setting, such as private practice or agency, but are more commonly seen as part of inpatient or residential treatment programs and schools. The difficult aspect of group treatment in these settings is the discontinuity due to discharge from the program or the end of the school year. It can often be hard to find ongoing support in the community to help maintain changes. As such, social skills may become easily lost as the client reverts to old styles of actions and decision making, which may involve bullying others. Schools may have a role in helping some students maintain more prosocial styles of interaction.

Anger

Anger management is becoming a much more common problem for many clients, regardless of age. When working with children and adolescents about anger, an initial challenge is to determine if the anger is viewed as a problem for the child or adolescent or if it is only the adults around the child who view the anger as problematic. As you get involved in the family system, you will begin to form your own opinion about how problematic the anger is. Your opinion will provide important feedback to the client and his parents and may become a catalyst for change, whether at the level of the client (internally), with the parents and the larger family system (around parenting techniques and expectations), or a combination of the two.

As noted in previous discussions about problem identification and the dynamics surrounding the young client's presentation into therapy, the identified client may not view the concern as a problem. Many times the only problem the child or adolescent identifies is the reaction of those around him. If he were not caught or if his teachers and parents wouldn't "overreact," there wouldn't be a problem. Through the process of normal development and defense mechanisms, as young people are still growing, changing, and forming their identities, their awareness and ability to identify and observe their choices and behavior objectively may be limited. It is normal for their perspective to be skewed in such a way, but that is part of the process and challenge of therapy—to help them identify, acknowledge, and change problematic behaviors without jeopardizing their normal developmental process. As such, we have to look for ways to help them begin to identify their responses to situations and life events in healthier and more appropriate ways.

Review of the family system is important for aspects of modeling as well. Just as with social skills, angry responses are often learned. Interventions may require a family approach to elicit true change. If angry responses are present in the parents as well, an assessment of the potential for abuse or violence also needs to be made, and appropriate action taken as necessary.

Gifted Children

Gifted children and adolescents often present a challenge to those around them because of the relatively uneven development across social and emotional realms when compared to intellectual development. Common problem areas include peer relationships, motivational problems, and fitting in at school and home (Neihart & Reis, 2002). These problems may be compounded by a perception that being different is somehow wrong or the fault of the gifted child (Robinson, 1996). This perception can have a detrimental effect on self-esteem, adding another area for treatment.

Because of their intellectual giftedness, many such children and adolescents present challenges to the authority of teachers and parents, often creating additional problems. By seeing themselves as different from others, they often develop a perspective that they do not need to follow the rules. Working with gifted children around these attitudes can be challenging. Some similarities exist when working with children with attention deficit as well, so you may be able to use similar techniques or protocols around this aspect of feeling outside of the rules or norms.

Helping the client understand that despite his perceptions and desires, he is still viewed as a child in certain settings may lead toward his acceptance of limitations. Additional concrete measures, such as avoidance of negative consequences, may provide further motivation for change. It is often a difficult balance to achieve when trying to maintain a positive self-image for the client while helping him adjust that image slightly in what he may experience as a "downward" fashion. Many children and adolescents view themselves as equals, not just gifted clients, as a result of societal attitudes and changes in child-rearing practices. This shift presents a challenge for professionals and parents who are attempting to help guide these precocious young people. Respect for their individuality is a key aspect of the therapeutic foundation and may give you the leverage needed to help them develop enough flexibility, understanding, and maturity to accept limitations that present themselves. Helping clients negotiate these boundaries can provide them with tools for managing frustration throughout their lives.

An internal challenge for many gifted students, partially related to their self-perception of themselves as perfect and apart from others, is the frustration they experience when they, or their performance, are not perfect. This strain can lead to negative self-perceptions and negative interactions with others, due to their inability to manage the feelings of frustration, combined with their own expectations of perfectionism. Helping gifted children understand that being gifted doesn't mean being perfect all the time is a challenge in treatment. However, as in work with all children and adolescents, focusing on their individual strengths, juxtaposed against what may be developing areas, is one possible approach to foster their self-acceptance.

DATING

Dating is a specific form of social relationship, an early experiment with intimacy for most teens. What types of relationship patterns have been learned for this young person? Is dating a form of salvation for them in terms of escaping from a difficult home situation? Are they running toward a relationship too quickly as if they are trying to push forth an identity only formed in their minds? Most young people at this age are still trying to figure out who they are; they really have no strong sense of identity at this point. That can make some young people vulnerable to potential abuse in these early intimate relationships.

Dating is part of the experimentation by which adolescents engage in the process of forming their own identity and finding out who they are. Stretching beyond their previous boundaries is like trying on a new identity. This is how they learn who they are. These attempts may or may not become part of the client's adult personality. Part of your role as a counselor may be to help them identify what kinds of relationships are healthy for them and which might be destructive. They may already be enmeshed in an unhealthy relationship when they come for services.

A relationship becomes potentially destructive when the adolescent loses sight of what may already be blurred or indistinct boundaries between himself and others. Many adolescents erroneously try to complete themselves through relationships with others rather than developing themselves. Healthy adolescents are able to balance a relationship with their own needs, but for those who are struggling with internal conflict, personal identity, or emotional problems at home, the relationship may represent a haven, a way to feel better about themselves, or simple distraction. Danger lies in the situation where an adolescent begins to lose sight of himself as a result of the dating relationship, setting up a potential risk to be abused or manipulated. Helping the client develop at least one or two outside interests may be as far as the intervention can go initially. Many of these young people have isolated themselves from others in focusing on the relationship, setting the stage for manipulation and potential abuse. Exploring the adolescent's thoughts and desires about the relationship can help identify a potential path for intervention and certainly provides insight into the degree of enmeshment in the dating relationship.

The level of violence in dating relationships among teens is a concern. Granted, adolescents are learning how to behave in intimate relationships, a part of normal development. However, the types of behaviors that are being displayed in those relationships are often not consistent with caring relationships. James, West, Deters, and Armijo (2000) found that teens reported psychological, emotional, and physical abuse in these close relationships. Typical behaviors by partners included damaging possessions, threatening behavior, insulting remarks in front of others, being scratched, shoved, or having their arms twisted and fingers bent. Interestingly, other studies (Gaertner & Foshee, 1999; Spencer & Bryant, 2000) found a greater incidence of dating violence in rural areas as compared to suburban and urban areas. A gender difference found by Spencer and Bryant (2000) is that more males reported being slapped, hit, or kicked. The tendency toward violence appeared to have an inverse relationship with the level of commitment in the relationship (Gaertner & Foshee, 1999).

Although less attention has been devoted to violence in same sex relationships, Freedner, Freed, Yang, and Austin (2002) have conducted preliminary research in the area. Dating violence was reported across gay, lesbian, and bisexual relationships. Bisexual males were at greatest risk for any type of abuse, while bisexual females reported a greater incidence of sexual abuse. Concerns about threats of violence were greatest for lesbians, while being "outed" was a greater concern for bisexuals. Overall, the authors recommend that community education efforts about dating violence include a focus for gay, lesbian, and bisexual relationships as well.

Educational efforts introduced as teens begin dating in early to mid-adolescence have been effective in reducing physical and emotional abuse in those relationships, as well as diminishing the effect of emotional distress after the negative interactions. (Wolfe et al., 2003), across cultural groups. However, such efforts may be working against community influence in many cases. Malik, Sorenson, and Aneshensel (1997) found strong correlations between community violence and dating violence among adolescents. Community education efforts and involvement of parents may be necessary in order to effect change when attempting to reduce violence among teens in dating relationships.

Dating for younger children may have other meanings and challenges. An early push toward dating in younger children may signify areas for concern. Such behavior is consistent with low self-esteem—looking for ways to feel better about himself through relationships with others. If the dating has sexualized components, there may be a history of abuse, or the child may be responding to media and peer influence. The problems in exploring the sexual aspects of the relationship are the client's potential defensiveness and his level of skewed thinking about the meaning of the sexuality. Typical responses from clients may indicate that they see nothing wrong in their decisions to be sexually active. Intervention can be more difficult in these cases because there may already be a degree of dissociation around their actions. Sometimes intervening against the defensiveness can provide a more positive prognosis, because the defensiveness may be part of an internal conflict with their own behavior. Exploring the meaning of the sexuality for clients can help expose any pressure they may be feeling to engage in the behavior to maintain the relationship or to "plug holes" in their own psyche. These "meanings" will guide your interventions by helping you understand clients' worldviews and their view of themselves. What are they trying to obtain through their behavior? Usually, they are unaware of what their behavior represents.

Dating provides additional information about a client's boundaries. A tendency to become lost in the relationship may signify a history of problematic boundaries and difficulty separating oneself from others. Explore family history to determine the existence of any such patterns. Focusing on these therapeutic tasks can increase the client's awareness of choice points and allow him the option of making healthier choices. Again, dating is normal, but at a later age, particularly when coupled with these components.

EATING DISORDERS

Work with eating disorders in children and adolescents will inevitably involve a family approach and can often have a social component in group work as well. A group format can have a positive impact in terms of modeling appropriate behaviors, in addition to feeling supported. Parents can also be involved in parallel group treatment to encourage their critical involvement. Important components of family treatment include reducing blame within the family system, increasing acceptance of family members, and improving problem-solving within the family system (Lask & Bryant-Waugh, 2000). The latter may include a focus on communication, and the implementation may be strengthened by role-plays, including some role reversal during which parents may gain a greater understanding of what it feels like to be their son. The experiential understanding of their son's plight may be more powerful than any other intervention in helping them take responsibility for their own behaviors and expectations, and begin to turn around patterns of behavior in the family to promote healthier interactions and by extension, healthier eating patterns. Another important component of intervention at the individual level is the use of cognitive behavioral techniques to address the issues of disordered body image and irrational thought patterns. An approach that involves behavior modification, cognitive therapy, and family systems is, as with other multiple modality approaches, a more effective intervention (Robin, Bedway, Siegel, & Gilroy, 1996). These effects can be magnified through group efforts (Harvard Mental Health Newsletter, 2002).

As noted in many of these discussions, the role of the school may provide the one common experience for many youth. As such, it has become an increasingly important component of the community support system for children and adolescents. Helping children and adolescents reach out within their community to form a healthy support system can be an important tool to work on as part of a total intervention focus, and in planning toward termination.

DISCUSSION QUESTIONS

1. How can schools serve as a support system for gay and lesbian students? Are there any dangers in such an approach?
2. What types of techniques might be appropriate for clients who have difficulty verbalizing and expressing emotions? What limitations are there to these techniques?
3. How are family dynamics, bullying, and anger related?
4. Describe the role of community or adult support for children and teens?
5. What are some potential concerns in dating relationships?

PROFESSIONAL ISSUES

The intent of this section is to provide practical information to explore the process of therapy in the context of one's own biases, professional ethics, and the experience encountered in different professional settings.

The interplay of bias and ethics can provide the basis for a sound clinical practice or introduce poor judgment, ineffective, and possibly harmful interventions. The key to effective practice is self awareness, also a key in understanding cultural differences. Chapter 11 will review concepts related to bias in clinical practice, including multicultural issues and general concepts of ethical professional behavior.

Each treatment setting offers a different set of challenges, and may require a slightly different skill set or professional orientation. Learning about typical approaches required in various settings can foster professional development and career decisions on the basis of personal strengths and professional skills. Chapter 12 will review various treatment settings and typical approaches associated with each of those settings (e.g., school counselor, private practice, residential or inpatient centers).

THERAPEUTIC RELATIONSHIP: BIAS AND ETHICS

INTRODUCTION

Throughout the text to this point, the analogy has been made of the therapist's person as a tool for therapy. Effectively wielding this tool requires self-awareness regarding biases, in addition to training about developmental levels and family process. In this chapter we explore potential factors that might affect our work despite our best efforts, potential problem areas, and ethical functioning. Although not meant to frighten you, this chapter may expose you to potential outcomes you may not have considered. Highlighting multicultural differences that can influence outcome will help increase your self-awareness and heighten your sensitivity. The workbook exercises accompanying this chapter are designed to help you understand more fully the importance of self-knowledge and awareness, in a way that is unique to our profession.

MULTICULTURAL ISSUES IN COUNSELING

Multicultural issues have been incorporated into many of the discussions of various aspects of working with children, adolescents, and families. The focus in this chapter is on the impact of cultural differences in our work with clients. Lefley (2002) highlights the importance of multicultural awareness in providing effective interventions, suggesting that a multicultural approach should include awareness of your own value system and potential biases, and how these personal issues may affect your professional interactions.

Cultural differences in parenting and disciplinary styles have been identified as a factor in the development of conduct disorders, for Caucasian and African American children (McLoyd, 1998; Simons et al., 2002). Harsh, inconsistent parenting, coupled with uninvolved parenting has been associated with symptoms of conduct disorder among African American children (Dodge, Pettit, & Bates, 1994; McLoyd, 1990; McLoyd, Jayaratne, Ceballo, & Borquez, 1994; Simons et al., 2002;

and Brody et al., 2003). Older siblings who engage in violent or delinquent behavior have also been cited as a factor in the development of conduct problems in their younger siblings (Bank, Patterson, & Reid, 1996; Garcia, Shaw, Winslow, & Yaggi, 2000), as have environmental factors, such as living in an economically depressed or disadvantaged community (Brody et al., 2001; Brooks-Gunn, Duncan, & Aber, 1997). Environmental factors in communities across the United States, such as socioeconomic status and level of violence, seem to affect children of various ethnic groups in a similar fashion (Brody et al., 2001; Simons et al., 1996). However, strong academic performance of the older siblings has been associated with a better outcome for younger siblings (Brody et al., 2003). Educational efforts introduced as teens begin dating in early to mid-adolescence have been effective in reducing physical and emotional abuse in those relationships, as well as diminishing the effect of emotional distress after the negative interactions (Wolfe et al., 2003), across cultural groups.

Cultural differences that encourage the participation of extended family in caretaking of children also seems to provide a positive buffering effect, referred to as *collective socialization processes* (Brody et al., 2001). Neighborhoods with such active involvement by adults show less violence (Sampson, Raudenbush, & Earls, 1997), greater prosocial competence (Elliott et al., 1996), and less affiliation among peers engaging in problematic behaviors (Brody et al., 2001), across racial boundaries. Structuring parental involvement is an option when the community is positively involved.

Parent training of preschool children to reduce conduct problems in this young age group found positive results across ethnic groups (Gross, Fogg, & Tucker 1995; Tucker, Gross, Fogg, Delaney, & Lapporte, 1998; Gross et al., 2003). Consistent results were shown in response to decreasing the parents' use of coercive discipline (e.g., yelling, hitting, or verbally aggressive behaviors), while increasing their use of positive, supportive parenting practices (e.g., encouragement and praise). Another school-based intervention program for older children aimed at treating internalizing and externalizing problems found positive results, but no differences across ethnic groups for African American or Caucasian students (Weiss, Harris, Catron, & Han, 2003). Ethnic differences have been noted, however, in style of communication when comparing African American and Caucasian families on the variable of expressed emotion (EE). Wuerker, Haas, and Bellack (1999) found African American families more likely to assert control toward other members, and less likely to respond submissively. Obviously, these differences in family communication style need to be considered when working throughout therapy, but particularly when identifying target problems and goals.

In making diagnosis, as noted throughout the text, care and attention needs to be taken with regard to classification by Western standards, particularly as cross-cultural adoptions are increasing, and families continue to immigrate to the United States from cultures throughout the globe. As noted throughout our discussions of cultural factors, differences can be variable. These differences may be attributable to factors in the acculturation process as noted in Chapter 2. For example, Weisz, Weiss, Suwanlert and Chaiyasit (2003) found differences in identified syndromes of psychopathology when comparing children of the United States and Thailand. Strong agreement across the two cultures was found for only a few syndromes, such as somatic complaints. Ratings of severity differed in most other areas, including aggressive and sexual behaviors. This is in contrast to previous studies comparing more similar cultures such as Holland and the United States, in which the identified problems matched more closely (Achenbach, Verhulst, Baron, & Althauls, 1987; de Groot, Koot, & Verhulst, 1994; and Verhulst, Achenbach, Althaus, & Akkerhuis, 1988).

The findings of Weisz et al. (2003) suggest caution in applying Western standards of psychopathology unilaterally to dissimilar cultures, particularly if the individuals have not been assimilated into the majority culture. One must remember that the classification of problem behavior is embedded within the respective culture. For example, somatic problems are likely to be interpreted as a concern across cultures, consistent with the comparison even across dissimilar cultures (Weisz et al., 2003). Parents have a universal concern about their children's well-being, concerns that usually arise at the level of good physical health. This may provide an explanation for the concurrence among cultures for these types of symptoms.

In contrast, norms for aggressive behavior differ across cultures, similar to the disparate ratings identifying aggressive and destructive behavior as a more serious problem by Thai than U.S. parents. Weisz et al. (2003) found that Thai parents rated aggressive behaviors as the primary concern for boys and hyperactive behavior as their major issue with girls, while U.S. parents identified withdrawn and somatic behaviors as their primary concerns for both boys and girls.

Therapists also need to exercise caution in assuming that clients and families will hold the same biases about the value of "talk" therapy. Just because a client or family is in your office doesn't imply that all members are equally supportive of the process. Awareness of general cultural differences may enhance your effectiveness in establishing rapport. McGoldrick (2002) has summarized different cultural responses to therapy as an intervention. She notes that African American clients may be reluctant to participate in therapy because of assumptions about counseling being an extension of "white" institutions toward which they may feel distrust. Conversely, talking and analyzing personal experience is highly valued and accepted within Jewish culture. English heritage seems to foster a pragmatic approach to therapy, with family members often inquiring "what difference will it make?" This approach is often adopted by adolescents as well. The tendency in Asian cultures is often to avoid talking directly about problems, and the perception of the therapist as an authority figure can make it less likely for these clients to feel comfortable in being candid. Irish, Norwegian, and Sioux Indians share an aversion to talking, however for differing reasons. Irish clients may feel embarrassed to talk about what they perceive as mistakes or failures, while Norwegians may not feel comfortable talking negatively about family members. For Sioux Indians, family roles might prohibit talking to or about certain family members as well. Although these guidelines are general, we need to be cautious not to perpetuate stereotypes by assuming that each of these orientations applies to all members of their respective cultures. In doing so, we would be doing harm. The guidelines should serve to increase awareness of possible explanations for resistance or unusual responses in therapy. These differences extend to individual responses to various life events as well, including death, coping, seeking help, and the identification of problem behavior.

Adding to the challenge of working with culturally diverse clients, is the difficulty often experienced in identifying treatment goals. As noted in Chapter 2, adults usually initiate services. The young client may not agree on the need for services, because they do not wish to be reminded of problematic behaviors, or simply do not identify problems because of developmental differences between adults, adolescents, and children. These factors present the initial challenge in treatment that may reverberate throughout the course of your sessions, or result in early termination if perceptions vastly differ among the therapist, parents, and young clients.

Agreement on the target problem is a challenge when working with children and adolescents (Hawley & Weisz, 2003; Yeh & Weisz, 2001). Although parents and therapists agreed in their identification of the most common concern—disobedience at school or home, clients between the ages of 7 and 17 identified schoolwork as the most pressing problem. Despite these differences, therapists managed to balance concerns from both parents and young clients in successful treatment, with over half of therapists in the study identifying a blend of goals combining concerns of parents and children. However, over 60% of therapists failed to identify target problems that families had presented as a concern. As the authors note, this presents a serious dilemma not only for practical interventions, but also as a possibility for early termination as discussed in Chapter 6. Recent results indicate that nearly a third of parents seeking treatment at a community mental health center terminated due to lack of agreement about goals (Garcia & Weisz, 2002). Beyond parental dissatisfaction is the challenge of engaging young clients in therapy without the complication of disagreement over goals (Shirk & Saiz, 1992; Sommers-Flanagan & Sommers-Flanagan, 1995).

Differences in therapist level of training was associated with the degree of agreement or disagreement about problems. Unlicensed trainees were more likely to agree with young clients in the identification of the target problem (Hawley & Weisz, 2003). The combination of relative inexperience and lack of attention to parents' or young clients' perceived goals certainly sets the stage for ineffective treatment. Necessary components of trust and collaboration in the working alliance are likely to be absent, negatively affecting treatment process and outcome (Horvath & Luborsky, 1993; Liddle, 1995). Interestingly, ethnic differences were not identified among the Caucasians, African Americans, Hispanics, Asian Americans, or those of mixed heritage who participated in the study as clients.

Constantine and Arorash (2001) found that African American and Hispanic clients reported higher expectations of therapists' multicultural competency than Asian, Caucasian, or biracial clients. Again, we are reminded of individual differences within each of these cultural groups in order to avoid perpetuating new stereotypes (Alessandria, 2002). Allowing the client to take the lead in exploring cultural issues has also been identified as a positive factor in those who describe therapy as successful (Pope-Davis et al., 2002).

Counselor training has been identified in other studies as a factor in perceived competence. Clients have identified concerns about counselor empathy and conceptualization skills, and those with less training in multicultural issues were perceived as less competent (Constantine, 2001; Fuertes & Brobst, 2002), and the perceived level of confidence impacted the perception of competency. Increased multicultural competency may relate to the experiential nature of many courses in this area (Pressly, Parker, & Jennie, 2001), pushing therapists to address their own biases, stereotypes, and assumptions.

THERAPIST BIASES

As therapists, we are not without biases. We grew up in families and neighborhoods teaming with biases and prejudices, just as our clients did. Although our training increases our potential awareness of the impact of our own experiences on our work, it does not guarantee it. It's what we choose to do about those biases that makes a difference in our ethical (or unethical) decisions. Ignorance—or lack of awareness—is no defense for behavior that may be harmful to a client. At the very least, awareness of individual biases is necessary for productive work with clients. Ideally, a therapist will have participated in personal counseling to address these issues. The goal is to be aware of biases before sitting down with clients, while there is still an opportunity to effect change before harm is done.

An additional point that has been made about personal work or counseling is that trainees generally report the experience has a positive impact on their increased understanding of the client's role. These trainees have the opportunity to experience the power differential in the relationship, to understand firsthand the change process, to know how difficult it can be to ask for help, and then to participate in the hard work of therapy. Therapists who have engaged in their own counseling are well aware of these important nuances and what they are asking of their clients. Ultimately, they are also more aware of the potential gains from therapy. As we explore what impact biases can have on therapeutic work, we will refer to the literature on work with gay and lesbian clients to illustrate potential concerns.

Impact of Stereotypes in Therapy

What effect can a stereotype have on our ability to be effective as therapists? Isn't being aware of potential biases enough? Barrett and McWhirter (2002) reviewed these questions in their work on possible biases around the issue of sexual orientation of clients. Casas, Brady, and Ponterotto (1983) found that stereotypes held by therapists interfered with their ability to accurately process information about their clients who were gay or lesbian. Extending from the literature on information processing, the finding of Casas, Brady, and Ponterotto implies that the emotional response of the therapist prevents accurate understanding of the client. The emotional response apparently serves as a filter, blocking unbiased information from the therapist's awareness. This is a frightening finding, particularly with regard to the therapist's lack of awareness about his or her own biases and the potential impact on therapy. Obviously, this is an area that conflicts with the premise of ethical practice, even if the therapist is unaware of personal biases. Without personal awareness of the precipitating factor, the therapist must look to other potential cues to identify client concerns. For example, the therapist (or her colleagues) may notice that clients are not returning for services. There are many "no-shows," or failure to keep outpatient appointments. Such a situation may force the therapist to find out what's wrong, why clients are not returning. A much more positive approach would be taking a proactive stance earlier in one's career to become aware of potential ethical pitfalls. Then the likelihood of damage to your clients or potential for litigation could be avoided, or at least reduced. Take advantage of opportunities to explore potential biases long before you may be confronted with them in session. The need for such exploration does not end with formal training. It continues throughout one's professional life. Just as our clients are faced with challenges and life changes, so are we. Any of these life events may affect our professional ability; therefore, a continual sensitivity to potential biases is necessary.

Interestingly, Casas, Brady, and Ponterotto (1983) found that therapists tended to retain more information about specific clients when that information was consistent with the therapists' existing stereotypes. This is reminiscent of attributional or confirmatory bias, which should be familiar to those who have taken graduate courses. Such a bias promotes a selective sifting through available information to glean those aspects consistent with already held beliefs. Applying these concepts to sexual orientation, Garfinkel and Morin (1978) found that therapists in their work described heterosexual clients as "more psychologically healthy" than their lesbian and gay clients. This is another frightening finding, because it speaks to the heart of the power that is inherent in the therapeutic relationship, specifically with regard to diagnostic issues. It is easily conceived that a diagnosis could be made on the basis of therapist biases that might carry the client throughout life and could affect decisions about health care coverage, study abroad, college admission, or job placement. Garfinkel and Morin (1978) and more recent research from Friedman and Lilling (1996) also found that male therapists were consistently more negative in their judgments regarding emotional well-being for gay and lesbian clients, as compared to female therapists.

The fact that these biases seem to be persistent in our profession is of great concern. The level of care for gay and lesbian clients is reduced when therapists provide biased, inadequate, or inappropriate treatment for this population due to the influence of their own personal biases (Carney, Werth, & Emanuelson, 1994; Herek, 1998). Although that is clearly a concern for a large portion or our clients, an additional concern is raised regarding the training process for our profession. What does it say about our profession when issues about bias and prejudice are routinely discussed with little apparent effect? These findings hold a message for training programs—and for each of us as individual professionals, regardless of where we find ourselves in our professional development. The responsibility rests with each of us to complete our own personal work to address these potential biases.

Others have suggested that heterosexual therapists are more uncomfortable working with homosexual clients of their own gender than the opposite gender (Gelso, Fassinger, Gomez, & Latts, 1995; Gentry, 1986). Once again, this raises significant concerns for the therapist's ability to work well, given such a level of discomfort, particularly if the therapist is not allowing herself to be aware of the root of the feelings. There is a much higher risk of negatively impacting therapy or acting unethically in situations when the therapist experiences a vague discomfort or irritation, but does not explore a possible connection with client issues (e.g., missing appointments, arriving late, being preoccupied during session, continually rescheduling). The bottom line is that we must be honest with ourselves.

Gelso and colleagues (1995) found that female therapists experienced more of a block when attempting to recall specific information about lesbian clients, as compared to male therapists working with lesbian clients. Similar findings have been reported for male clients (Hayes & Gelso, 1993). However, contradictory findings exist as well. Liddle (1995) found that female therapists in an analog study expressed greater respect for lesbian clients than for heterosexual clients. In comparing the findings of these two studies, it is important to consider potential differences between the therapists in the studies, to note the impact of an analog study versus self-reports from actual experiences, and to ponder the potential impact of biases that may influence participants to attempt to "look good" or give politically correct answers.

Awareness and Referral

On a positive note regarding self-awareness for therapists, Crawford, Hemfleet, Ribordy, Ho, and Vickers (1991) found that counselors with a higher level of homophobia (e.g., a noticeable emotional response to thoughts of working with a homosexual client) did not accept such clients into treatment. This is positive in that it demonstrates the appropriate behavior of referring to others if your own biases are so strong they may interfere with therapy. It is best for clients to begin work with someone with whom they will be able to continue. To ensure continuity of care, each therapist must be aware of his or her own biases.

Unfortunately, these findings also support the likelihood that gay or lesbian clients will encounter hostile or unsupportive therapists in seeking services (Garnets, Hancock, Cochran, Goodchilds, & Peplau, 1991), as may other types of clients against whom therapists may hold biases. Each of us must take responsibility for ourselves. As these studies illustrate, if you don't attend to these biases, they don't just lie dormant. They are triggered by your interactions with clients, and that's when you risk losing conscious control of yourself and your practice. *Countertransference reaction* is the term to describe these reactions, when something from our own subconscious or unconscious (outside our conscious awareness) begins to affect interactions in the present. That is a not a reaction you want.

COUNTERTRANSFERENCE REACTIONS

What are countertransference reactions—some Freudian, analytical concept, right? The concept certainly has its roots in psychoanalysis. As the results of all the studies cited as examples in this chapter show, the phenomenon is occurring. Those biases, stereotypes, and prejudices that are barely out of reach of your conscious awareness tend to create problems for you in session. The potential becomes even greater when you are working with children and adolescents, due to strongly held, sometimes idealized or polarized notions about family.

Because of the volatility of family issues for ourselves as well as our clients, therapists need to be aware of potential countertransference reactions, particularly with children and adolescents. Potential issues cluster around:

- our own feelings and experiences about parenting, both from being children and being parents (or not)
- over- or under-identification with child and adolescent clients
- feelings of sympathy toward abused clients
- rigid expectations for behavior of children or adolescents
- failure to apply appropriate developmental standards
- inappropriate boundaries with clients (e.g., feelings of sexual attraction, spending excessive time with child or adolescent clients outside of session, displacing or discounting effectiveness of child's parents)
- frequent thoughts about the client outside of sessions
- attempts to solve clients' problems, provide advice, or "parent" them
- excessive physical touch or hugging

This list can serve as a reminder or guideline to "check yourself" from time to time. A good rule of thumb is if something's feeling weird, it probably is. Trust your feelings just as you encourage your clients to trust their feelings. In addition to this general guideline, specific experiences in the therapist's personal life may affect reactions to certain types of clients or certain issues in therapy. If some of these life events have occurred to you, it would probably be a wise idea to do a little personal work around these issues and explore your feelings as openly as you can. If you find yourself at an impasse, you may want to consider referring clients who come to you for services with issues closely related to your own.

IMPACT OF THERAPIST'S PERSONAL HISTORY ON THERAPY

History of Abuse in Therapist

It is common to discuss individual motivations for seeking out the field of counseling, social work, or psychology during graduate training, but this type of discussion diminishes in frequency later in one's professional career. However, the impact of those initial reasons can often resonate throughout one's work with clients, particularly if there is a history of trauma or abuse in the therapist's personal background. A survey completed by Pope and Feldman-Summers (1992) found that 69.9 percent of female respondents and 32.8 percent of the male respondents had a history of physical or sexual abuse. Of those, one-third reported abuse during their childhood or adolescence. Survey respondents were clinical and counseling psychologists. How does such personal history affect practice, and what implications does it have for other types of life experiences in the therapist?

Depending on the therapist's awareness and personal work around issues of abuse, we know that countertransference is a likely outcome. Possible responses might be to discount the client's reaction to her own abuse or to overcompensate in identifying or sympathizing with the client. Despite the prevalence of people who were abused, most survey respondents (Pope & Feldman-Summers, 1992) felt their graduate training left them ill-prepared to manage the complexities of the client's abuse or trauma issues while balancing their own potential countertransference issues. This gap in graduate training can set the stage for unethical, substandard, or harmful treatment. Although specific ideas for improving graduate training have been suggested (Borys & Pope, 1989), personal therapy may be the most viable option for therapists to address these issues at present.

Further complicating factors exist for a therapist who works with children and adolescents who have been abused when the therapist has a similar history. These include the risk of triggering unresolved issues, triggering flashbacks, overidentifying with the client, or even experiencing erotic feelings (Pope, Tabachnick, & Keith-Spiegel, 1986). Therapists with a personal history of abuse sometimes experience fear or anxiety when clients relate instances of their own sexual or physical abuse. In a study conducted by Pope and Feldman-Summers (1992), the median age during abuse was 7, with a range from age 1 to 16 years old. Even though our examples focus on issues of abuse, anecdotal evidence is consistent with generalization of such responses to other traumatic life events as well.

Of concern with regard to practice, are the findings that more than 40 percent of the sample (Feldman-Summers & Pope, 1994) reported a period of time during which they were unable to remember some or all of their own abuse experiences. Being unaware of their own experiences creates a situation in therapy where the therapists' strong affective response could be misinterpreted as a reaction to clients, although the clients are merely serving as a mirror for the therapists' experiences. "Forgetting" is a common reaction to abuse and was found to be consistent across gender and age in the study (Feldman-Summers & Pope, 1992).

Fortunately, only 3 percent of the sample reported memories of their own abuse being triggered by work with abused children, adolescents, or families, while 25 percent to 50 percent reported their own therapy alone or as a factor associated with their recollection (Feldman-Summers & Pope, 1992). The fact that therapists were seeking their own therapy is positive generally, in terms of the decreased likelihood that working with abused children and adolescents may trigger flashbacks or memories in session. Of course, individual differences regarding personal experiences of physical or sexual abuse affect therapists' memories. It is often more likely that individuals will "forget" their own experience of abuse when it is more severe (Briere & Conte, 1993; Herman & Schatzow, 1987).

As the studies show, it is critical for therapists to address issues from their personal histories. It may be easy for therapists who have not been abused to eschew these findings, but that is an irresponsible response. Biases and personal feelings about any number of issues can affect therapy. The need remains for all therapists to explore these personal issues, whether through their own therapy or other means.

Therapist's Own Therapy

The value for therapists of seeking one's own therapy has been recognized for many years (Freud, 1963; Fromm-Reichman, 1949; Guntrip, 1975). Typical benefits include increased empathy and understanding of the experience of the therapeutic process for clients, as well as working through personal issues that might contribute to a therapeutic impasse if left unresolved. A survey completed by Pope and Tabachnick (1994) provides interesting insight into the experience of therapy by therapists. Eighty-four percent of the sample of 800 psychologists had participated in therapy. Of those participating, 22 percent described therapy as "harmful," 61 percent reported clinical depression, and 29 percent reported suicidal ideation. Twenty-six percent described being "cradled," or held closely like an infant, by the therapist, 20 percent withheld information from their therapist, and 10 percent reported a breach of confidentiality. Although these statistics illuminate the range of experiences in therapy, they also highlight relatively high rates of negative experiences in that setting. It is unclear from the study, but an assumption can be made that the respondents remained committed to their chosen field despite their personal experiences. Enhancing the therapist's level of skill was identified as the third most beneficial aspect of being in therapy (Pope & Tabachnick, 1994). Perhaps some participants were able to use their negative therapeutic experiences as a learning opportunity to guide their own approach and increase their awareness of potential reactions to clients for which they could prepare.

Managing Therapist Feelings Toward Clients

Although we will always have reactions toward our clients, certain clients will trigger stronger emotional reactions within us than others. The possibility for many more "layers" of countertransference reactions is greatly multiplied when working with children, adolescents, and families. We are all aware of the power of families, whether the context is professional or personal. Systems and family theories suggest that we carry our families with us long after our physical separation from them or after losing them to death. How are we to manage these myriad responses within ourselves and prevent them from affecting our clinical work? Honesty about the feelings, personal work, and perseverance are suggested now, just as Winnicott (1949) urged many years ago. In order for us to function effectively, we must acknowledge our feelings and reactions toward clients, which may include bits of our own biases and prejudices or even thoughts we find consciously disturbing, such as sexual attraction toward clients.

Sexual Intimacy With Clients

Bajt and Pope (1989) reported on the prevalence of sexual intimacy in therapeutic relationships with children and adolescents. Eighty-one instances of sexual intimacy between therapists and minor clients were reported by the 90 respondents to the survey. Fifty-six percent of those instances involved female clients, while

44 percent involved male clients. Female clients were between the ages of 3 and 17, while males were between the ages of 7 and 17. The mean age for females was 13.7 and 12.5 for males.

This area has not been addressed adequately in the literature. It is of particular concern for those working with sexually abused clients who may attempt to act out their admiration or positive feelings for the therapist through sexual intimacy. It is not uncommon for severely abused children or adolescents to attempt to "connect" with their therapists using the way they have learned to display affection. Many abused children and adolescents erroneously believe that sexual intimacy is part of a close relationship and may attempt to convey their positive feelings toward the therapist through this learned behavior. Responding to these interactions and managing them therapeutically can be a major challenge. For some therapists, no amount of training can prepare one for the feeling of "being propositioned" by these young, vulnerable clients. The first order response is to remain calm, supportive, and centered. Any shock, personal revulsion, or titillation needs to remain internal during the session, including any potential ripple effects that may affect the session without your conscious awareness. This view reiterates that of Langs (1982) who identified "unrecognized countertransference" as the most significant factor in therapeutic failure.

The ill effects of being unaware of transference and countertransference have even made their way into the legal arena, as support for a malpractice suit. Support for malpractice is usually predicated on the professional failure to meet a particular standard of care. In the case of Zipkin v. Freeman (1968), the judge stated in his ruling that the psychiatrist "mishandled the transference phenomenon which is a reaction psychiatrists anticipate and which must be handled properly." The judge went on to state that "the court indicated that even less extreme expressions of the therapist's attraction to the patient (e.g., swimming, dancing) may constitute malpractice."

General studies involving therapist attraction to clients (i.e., without separating out attraction on the basis of client's age) have reported that attraction is quite common. Pope, Keith-Spiegel, and Tabachnick (1986) reported 87 percent of 575 survey respondents had experienced a sense of attraction to their clients (95 percent of male therapists and 76 percent of female clients). Although only a small percentage of professionals acted on the attraction (9.4 percent of male therapists and 2.5 percent of female therapists), feelings of guilt, anxiety, or confusion did result from simply having a sense of attraction toward a client. Half the respondents did not seek any type of guidance or training about the feelings, and of those who did, only 9 percent described the consultation as effective. Despite these results, it is imperative that therapists seek consultation and professional support from colleagues around these issues.

During our professional training, we routinely obtain supervision as we develop our skills, but it is unlikely that those training experiences will provide exposure and skill development in all areas. Because of the nature of our profession and the fact that our bodies and minds are our vehicles for treatment, ongoing attention to professional issues and potential interaction with personal biases is critical for successful, ethical, and effective work.

TOUCH IN THERAPY

Touch in therapy with children and adolescents is a major grappling point for many therapists. For those working with clients with a history of sexual abuse, almost all forms of touch are discouraged. For those who have been abused, touch may have become sexualized and thus can be misinterpreted, particularly with adolescents. For others who have been sexually or physically abused, touch may invoke fear, again working against your ability to establish a therapeutic rapport. Many clients may seek out a hug from the therapist (Pope & Tabachnick, 1993). It would be non-therapeutic, and perhaps detrimental to the therapeutic relationship, to refuse the hug. However, therapists need to remain aware of their intuitive responses in responding to clients' requests for hugs. If the request or the actual hug feels intrusive, it probably is a good idea to monitor the client's reaction to the hug for secondary gain, and consider consultation or supervision around managing the physical touch in session.

THERAPEUTIC IMPASSE

What about those clients who tend to stick in your mind? You find yourself repeatedly returning to client concerns, issues from the session, or other factors surrounding the case. These are certainly "warning signs" that should give you pause for more consideration. It is important to determine the "sticking point" if you are to be effective in your work with such a client. Is there an impending court case involving the client or your work with the client? Preoccupation with a legal matter is not unusual, particularly if going to court is an unusual occurrence for you. Do you notice that you are overidentifying with this client—feeling sympathetic, wanting to do things for the client beyond your normal therapeutic relationship (e.g., going to dance concerts, baseball games, interfering between the adolescent and her parents)?

In considering an impasse, it is often necessary to revisit personal biases to determine if some of your own issues are impeding therapeutic progress or to explore potential gaps in your professional knowledge to increase your skill level. There are several strategies for addressing these potential concerns even if they are outside your conscious awareness. Pope, Sonne, and Holroyd (1993) suggest the following: (a) consult colleagues, (b) review the clinical literature, (c) introspect, (d) seek supervision, or (e) consider personal therapy.

Consultation and supervision do not stop when your internship is over. One of the unique aspects of our profession is that of using ourselves as the instrument of intervention with our clients. In other words, our own feelings, perceptions, body of expert knowledge, and focus of attention need to be "tuned in" to the client. A colleague or more experienced professional can often provide a different perspective to fill in gaps, or give just the right feedback to signal a shift in our own perceptions that may have been blocking the therapeutic process. Consultation or supervision provides enough distance to allow a more objective perspective to emerge. Researching the clinical literature can also perform a similar function in providing a slightly different perspective, a new hypothesis, or even a novel approach to the therapeutic impasse.

Beginning the personal exploration at an individual level through journaling is often a convenient and comfortable process to begin the introspection process. This may be your first choice when you feel too confused to put the impasse into words, when the issues resonate with some of your personal issues too closely (although that can be a reason to seek consultation or supervision), or you are temporarily in a situation where consultation or supervision is not available.

The common mechanisms in all of these approaches are gaining objectivity through emotional distancing and facilitating a shift within yourself about this client. The shift is similar to what you help your clients work toward in therapy. Maintaining the same perspective is not productive for the client or therapist. In some ways, the impasse can push you toward changes within yourself as a therapist, which is an exciting by-product of the profession—the continual need to grow and develop personally and professionally.

A final consideration during a therapeutic impasse is the issue of referral. The impasse may be signaling the end of productive therapy for you and this client, or it may reflect the need for a hiatus in your work to allow the client to work in another modality. Perhaps the impasse signals a need for more intensive treatment, such as a day treatment program or perhaps a different modality, such as group to help the client practice certain social skills and gain feedback from peers.

Another reason for referral is lack of knowledge or expertise in a certain area. None of us is an expert in everything. By being honest with yourself about these potential deficits, you can help your client move forward. It is always possible to work together again after the focus on areas outside your expertise if appropriate. Being aware of practice areas outside your expertise and choosing not to practice in them is a strength and clearly a sound ethical approach to practice.

ETHICS

As mental health professionals, we are bound by ethical principles and standards of practice. These principles are generally formulated by professional organizations (American Psychological Association, 2002; National Association of Social Workers, 1999; American Psychiatric Association, 1999; American Association for Marriage and Family Therapy, 2001; American Counseling Association, 1995), and despite basic differences in the orientation or focus of these groups, the principles share many commonalities. Even though many ethical issues have been addressed already in this chapter, the remainder will focus on special ethical challenges.

Special Ethical Situations

AIDS and HIV Infection   AIDS or HIV infection continues to paralyze many people in terms of appropriate responses to people who are suffering. Boccellari and Dilley (1989) have noted how difficult it can be for therapists to acknowledge their own ambivalent or negative feelings toward their clients with AIDS. However, that denial can lead to negative therapeutic outcomes for these clients when therapists are unaware of their true feelings (Reiser & Levenson, 1984). Counseling individuals with AIDS requires grief work and sometimes a duty to warn, if the client has knowingly engaged in unprotected sex with others. Ideally, the client has contacted these individuals who have been placed at risk, but legal standards are increasingly making the determination that therapists have a duty to protect in such cases. Consult your ethical guidelines and local authorities regarding the laws in your jurisdiction. Of course, it is necessary to document any efforts to warn that you have taken.

DOCUMENT SECURITY   Documentation from a duty to warn action would be included as part of a client's record. In the security of a major hospital setting, management and protection of documentation requires an entire department, commonly called the Medical Records Department. In other settings, responsibility for the sanctity of records often falls to the clinicians themselves. Additional problems are now being raised around the security of electronic records.

What are the basic requirements for preserving confidentiality of client records? Records must be physically secured, and policies and procedures must be developed and maintained to manage confidential information within the office (e.g., support staff, phone calls, mail, computer screens, other reports and messages on desktops). You must know whether and how it is permissible to share confidential information with other professionals within and outside of your office, with family, or in other requests (e.g., courts, schools, physicians). Other issues involve informed consent and releases, working with mandated clients, breach of confidentiality (e.g., mandated reporting, health/HIV issues, substance abuse, etc.), professional liability, and ethical standards vs. legal standards of care.

ELECTRONIC RECORDS   Pope (2001) suggests maintaining a separate, stand-alone computer without any external connections specifically for confidential records as a certain method to protect against computer corruption or unintentional file transfer through hacking or intrusive viruses. He reports that college counseling centers or similar clinics face a challenge due to the networking of their computers, a problem that has been resolved by prohibiting use of Microsoft Outlook or other e-mail and file transfer programs to protect security in some of those settings. It is important for management and administrative staff to be aware of potential security weaknesses of computer networks and the possible impact of online connections on confidential records, but they cannot shoulder the entire responsibility.

Therapeutic Boundaries and Sexual Contact With Clients   One of the most flagrant and most discussed ethical boundary violations is that of sexual interactions with a client. However, little work has focused on managing those aspects in working with children and adolescents. Examination of boundary violations in therapeutic relationships is usually discussed in the literature through review of ethics cases, malpractice proceedings, and licensing boards (Pope, Tabachnick, & Keith-Spiegel, 1986).

Harm from sexual contact between therapists and clients is well documented throughout the literature. Many clients experience an extreme feeling of violation and damage in their ability to trust. Some may even experience a psychotic break requiring hospitalization. These types of results speak directly to the vulnerability of our clients in therapy, a condition that becomes even more magnified when our population is that of children and adolescents. The normal power differential inherent in the therapeutic relationship is skewed even further because of the societal differences between children or adolescents and adults, making them more vulnerable to boundary violations.

A recent survey completed by Pope and Vetter (1991) reported findings of 958 clients who had been involved in a sexual relationship with a therapist. Approximately 48 of the clients in this sample were minors at the time of sexual contact with the therapist. A third of the sample had a history of some type of sexual abuse. Not surprisingly, 90 percent of the sample were reported to have been harmed by a sexual relationship with the therapist that occurred during the course of therapy. Of those clients who engaged in sex with the therapist following the termination of therapy, 80 percent reported being harmed by the interactions. Hospitalization and suicide attempts were reported in 11 percent and 14 percent of the sample, respectively, while 1 percent completed a suicide attempt. Only 17 percent of those who identified themselves as having been harmed by the sexual interactions recovered fully.

Many ethical guidelines suggest a minimum wait of one to two years after the formal termination of therapy before pursuing any type of relationship with a client. However, others suggest that it is never appropriate to engage in any type of relationship with clients, certainly not sexual, regardless of the length of time since cessation of therapy (American Psychological Association Ethical Principles, 2003 p. 1605). The more cautious approach is recommended. The ethical principles of the American Psychological Association further state that the burden of demonstrating lack of exploitation rests with the psychologist, which would represent quite a large task.

Seeking supervision or consultation when the therapist becomes aware of feelings of attraction toward a client is a positive strategy in therapeutic, ethical, and legal terms. Pope, Tabachnick, and Keith-Speigel (1987) found that those respondents who felt more "uncomfortable, anxious, or guilty" were also more likely to seek supervision or consultation. This group comprised 70 percent of the sample. It is a professional strength to seek out consultation or supervision when you become aware of therapeutic challenges, whether they are in the area of boundary violations or some other issue. A comprehensive approach to supervision during graduate training, which includes managing sexual feelings, increases the likelihood that therapists will seek out supervision when they are independently functioning professionals (Pope, Tabachnick, & Keith-Speigel, 1987).

Dual Relationships   A dual relationship is defined as having two different roles in your relationship with a client. For example, a dual relationship in graduate school would consist of obtaining personal therapy from your advisor, or the classic romantic relationship between a student and a professor. Examples of dual relationships with child and adolescent clients include being a coach and therapist to the child, or being the adolescent's therapist and hiring him to mow your lawn. Any of these relationships create ethical problems because of the opportunity to influence or coerce the client, even unintentionally. The client is placed in a situation of potential harm because of the power differential inherent in the therapeutic relationship.

Dual relationships are much more common in rural communities and small towns where there are simply fewer people. However, they also exist in graduate programs, when professionals have civic or leisure roles within a community or just run into clients around town. Kitchener (1988) provides a helpful frame in the context of role theory. Each of us attaches certain expectations and obligations to the various social roles in our society and daily lives. Conflict arises when those expectations and obligations present us with incompatible demands between these roles. In other words, as a therapist, your role to help the client is clear. Your volunteer position as choir director is a completely different role for you. No problem presents itself until your client also joins your choir. At that point, an emotional response often results from the discomfort of conflicting roles. The discomfort may make the social interactions uncomfortable, unhealthy, or even destructive.

For these reasons, dual relationships are unhealthy in our profession, but there may be certain situations where the role conflict is unavoidable (Adleman & Barrett, 1990; Haas & Malouf, 1989; Keith-Spiegel & Koocher, 1985). Graduate school offers a good example in that students often interact with faculty in many different roles. Small communities offer another common example of multiple roles in social interactions. In those instances, it is the responsibility of the therapist to consider potential implications of the dual relationship and to structure interactions to protect or serve the client's best interests as much as possible.

Borys and Pope (1989) completed a national survey of more than 2,000 psychologists, psychiatrists, and social workers on the topic of dual relationships. Findings reflected no significant differences in respondent beliefs about sexual contact with clients before or after termination, nonsexual dual roles, social involvement, or financial involvement with clients. Professionals responding to the survey reported a cautious approach to dual relationships. Such an approach represents good professional decision making and appropriate responsibility to client well-being.

In some situations, such as the rural community or small town, it is much more difficult to avoid a dual relationship with your clients. Some school counselors may also be responsible for teaching or coaching or hold some type of public office. Managing these types of dual relationships requires care, attention to detail, and thoughtfulness. Ongoing consultation or supervision may be helpful to maintain appropriate boundaries in such a situation. As the professional in the relationship, you must consider the potential impact on the client of any such relationships. Consultation can be quite important in providing different perspectives about the potential impact on the well-being of the client. For example, you may be raising money for a charity. At first glance, there is nothing wrong in asking for contributions to a well-known charity. It's for a good cause, right? Perhaps. But what if your clients feel obligated to contribute because they want to please you, don't want to anger you, or think that contributing will somehow make them closer to you? Any of these situations have undertones of transference; the client may be motivated to participate because of the unequal nature of the relationship. That makes it unethical because asking for a donation may take advantage of the client at an unconscious level, regardless of how good the charitable cause may be.

Bartering is another example of a dual relationship. Perhaps you decide to provide therapy to a new foreign exchange student from Bosnia in exchange for yard work. This clearly constitutes a dual relationship despite its "mutual benefits." Consider, however, that employing the student through a bartering arrangement puts you in the more powerful position twice over—as therapist and as employer. The constraints felt by a student, particularly one from another culture, will influence any therapeutic relationship, and it is most likely that the influence will not be in a positive or healthy direction.

When dual relationships cannot be avoided, you need to discuss the situation and appropriate expectations with your client. Explain that even though you are her tennis coach and her therapist, you will still be working together as a team. Expand on your usual discussions regarding confidentiality, meeting outside of session, and the necessity for the client to be extremely open without concern for hurting your feelings. In fact, you might need to express an expectation for the client to collaborate by speaking up about the weird feelings she may experience at practice or in session. Keeping a journal may help the client acknowledge these feelings. An extremely open therapeutic relationship and your modeling of appropriate behaviors for the client are paramount to your success in situations when dual relationships cannot be avoided.

Ethical Decision Making

Ethical decision-making models have been presented in the professional literature for the past couple of decades, starting with general models addressing moral behavior (Rest, 1984) or providing dimensions of ethical theory and codes in the context of professional identity, social, and legal issues (Woody, 1991). Other models, developed around the same time, elaborated on these standards by providing specific questions to help practitioners explore particular ethical dilemmas (Haas & Malouf, 1989; Handelsman & Martin, 1992). These step-by-step approaches focus on exploration of the pertinent professional, legal, and societal factors involved in the situation and what might be the costs or benefits of deviating from accepted standards. Finally, the latter approaches evaluate the ethics of the suggested solution prior to implementation. Such attention to detail in determining potential consequences of professional action provides a mechanism for clinicians to review decision making alone or through consultation with others.

Kitchener's (1988) decision-making approach offers three factors to consider in assessing potential harm from a dual relationship:

- The more divergent the expectations are that are associated with the respective roles, the greater is the potential for harm.
- The more similar the obligations are that are associated with the respective roles, the more difficult it becomes to be objective, and the likelihood of divided loyalties or polarity increases.
- The greater the difference in terms of power and status between roles, the more likely it becomes that some kind of exploitation will occur.

The value in Kitchener's (1988) guidelines is the clear structure for determining potential harm. By using the client's well-being as the foundation for your decision making, you are choosing the ethical "high road" and grounding your decisions well away from myopic or self-serving actions that could harm you as well as the client.

Gottlieb (1993) also outlines a three-step model for ethical decision making, identifying the significant components as

- the balance of power within the relationship
- the length of the relationship
- the outcome of the professional relationship (a clear ending point vs. an intermittent, continuing relationship)

In analyzing an ethical dilemma, Gottlieb (1993) suggests that each dimension be evaluated in terms of the degree to which it is present in the relationship. For example, at one extreme, you may observe a significant difference between the apparent power between yourself and the client in a therapeutic relationship that has been ongoing for a few years and will likely continue intermittently. These factors, according to Gottlieb's model, describe a situation where harm to the client is likely to occur.

AREAS OF PRACTICE/EXPERTISE

Continuing education is an important part of ethical practice and is routinely required by most licensure and certification boards across the country. Even if you continue learning, though, some areas of practice may not be clear strengths for you. Ethically, you should not work with clients in areas where you question your own skill base. Possible remedies to the situation include pursuing a course of education and training for yourself or referring the client.

Working with other professionals to provide similar services to the same client is not ethical, but if you coordinate the treatment and ensure that you are each working on separate issues, this kind of collaboration can be successful. It is usually most effective when conducted in an interdisciplinary style, as the various disciplines help clarify appropriate professional boundaries (e.g., psychiatrists working with medication and psychologists providing therapy). For example, school counselors can work with children on social skills, behavioral issues in the classroom, or study skills at the same time the family is working with a therapist in private practice as long as the therapist is focusing on different issues.

COUNTERTRANSFERENCE REACTIONS LEADING TO REFERRAL OR OBTAINING SUPERVISION

Seeking supervision or consultation or making a referral are among your best options if you feel you are experiencing a countertransference reaction with a young client. With new clients, consider whether any issues in the presenting concerns list (e.g, intake form, referral information) produce a specific reaction in you. For example, when you read that you're going to be working with a 14-year-old boy who has acted out sexually with a neighbor girl, do you get a knot in your stomach? Do you immediately feel sympathetic toward the girl and revulsion toward the boy? Do you recall an experience of your own, or a close friend or family member's, that makes you identify too closely with the client or the girl? Any of these reactions may be an initial clue that you might need to think about referring this client to another professional.

Don't let professional pride get in your way when you have an inkling that you may need to consider referral. Consult with a peer or supervisor even before that first meeting with the client, if possible. Ethically and professionally, it takes courage and a sense of your strengths and areas to stretch to ask for assistance or be willing to expose what you might consider your weaknesses to a colleague or supervisor.

For an ongoing client, what types of uncomfortable or unusual feelings or reactions have you noticed in working with this client? If you were to learn about the sexual acting out described previously after you had been working with the boy and his family around the primary issue of impulsivity and poor decision making, how would you feel about this shift? You need to be cautious about your reaction when you first learn about sexual behavior (as discussed in Chapters 3 and 4). Remember that an important part of your role is to introduce a stable, calming influence into the family system. Managing your personal reactions is another part of your own awareness about biases and hidden feelings. In other words, a typical reaction you might have in normal conversation might be similar to the questions posed when exploring your reaction to a new client (e.g., revulsion, disgust, anger). If the reaction is strong, you may need to obtain supervision or consultation to continue working with this client and family. If your feelings are overwhelming, you will probably need to pursue referral, as feelings of this intensity will certainly interfere with therapy. Such strong feelings will impede your ability to be supportive and nonjudgmental of your client. Referral may be the best and most ethical option.

PROCEDURE FOR REFERRAL

1. Consider potential sources for referral in your area. If you are working in a school, an agency, or even private practice, you may have colleagues who specialize in certain areas to whom you can make a referral. This process is often easier than making a referral into the community. Arranging a meeting

between a new therapist and an existing client helps with the transfer or referral process. This may also be a necessary part of termination (see Chapter 4).

2. Talking with a client about a referral is usually a simpler process with a new client than with an existing client. In both cases, it is best to focus on the client's best interests when discussing a referral. Explain to the client and parents that, in your opinion, the referral source will be better able to meet their needs and work more effectively toward resolution.

3. Although referral is optimal, it is possible to work with a client and family on a new area if you obtain adequate professional support for yourself. If after obtaining consultation or supervision, you determine that you will be able to work effectively with the client, be certain to make arrangements for continued consultation or supervision, particularly during the early phases of the transition in working with an ongoing client or when getting started with a new client.

ETHICAL ISSUES IN WORKING WITH FAMILIES

In most cases, the child or adolescent in a family will be the identified client, but other family members (e.g., siblings or parents) may also require treatment. This presents a dilemma to the therapist. Although it may make intuitive sense to work with the entire family, that is not the best situation, ethically speaking. Families may wish to have you work with them all "because you know everything" about the family dynamics. Although this may feel like a logical, even flattering, approach, it creates blurred boundaries and may complicate treatment. Even working within a child-centered family approach can present challenges with adolescents, who may become suspicious that you are siding with the parents or sharing confidential information with a parent. The best approach is to help the family find another competent therapist who will be a good fit for them. You can have the family sign releases to share information to facilitate sharing your perception with the new professional, thus easing the transition for the family. A similar approach (of sharing information) can be helpful when you are making a referral for other reasons as well.

STRUGGLING WITH MANDATED REPORTING

Although mandated reporting when working with children and adolescents primarily involves reporting suspected abuse or neglect, it can also involve the "duty to warn," which results from the Tarasoff decision, a court case in California (Tarasoff v. Regents of University of California, 551 P2d 334, 431 (Cal 1976)). If you receive information from a client that she intends to harm someone else, the Tarasoff decision states that you must inform that person. It might also be a good idea to inform law enforcement to ensure everyone's safety.

Mandatory reporting should have been addressed in the initial discussion of confidentiality with your client. However, if the need for reporting occurs, you need to be prepared for a change in the existing therapeutic relationship. Some families drop out of treatment, an unfortunate outcome considering they are attempting to get help. A negative response from a client or family following mandatory reporting is not uncommon.

However, mandatory reporting is a professional obligation, an area which it is usually better to err on the side of caution. Making a report creates some potential for change in the family system. Although the prospect of change can be frightening for adolescents about whom you're reporting, they may also experience a sense of relief and empowerment knowing that they are not alone in their situation.

Most reports are made independently by the therapist to the state Child Protective Services hotline. However, in school districts, some principals prefer to be involved in the process and will actually make the call after being informed of the situation. A report is warranted whenever you believe a child is being neglected or abused physically, emotionally, or sexually. If you have questions about whether the information you have constitutes abuse, call the hotline and ask for input. Most states have a toll-free number listed in the local phone directory, or you can always obtain information by calling local child protective service agencies.

A release of information is not required for making a mandatory report. It is one of those situations where confidentiality may be breached and this exception should be included in your initial confidentiality discussion with clients and families.

CONCLUSION

Therapists do well to follow the seven general principles, sifted from the large group of behaviors surveyed by Pope, Tabachnick, and Keith-Spiegel (1987):

- Do no harm.
- Practice in your areas of competence.
- Engage in no exploitive behaviors.
- Treat clients with the basic respect that all deserve.
- Protect confidentiality.
- Act only after obtaining informed consent.
- Practice with principles of social equity and justice.

DISCUSSION QUESTIONS

1. Discuss potential harm from dual relationships.
2. Review factors important to the process of ethical decision making.
3. How can a therapist's own experience affect therapy with certain groups of clients?
4. What factors can increase the therapist's awareness of possible countertransference issues?
5. What is the purpose of mandatory reporting? Who must report?

PROFESSIONAL ISSUES ACROSS TREATMENT SETTINGS

INTRODUCTION

This chapter addresses a number of professional issues for the therapist, including self-care, potential biases with certain populations, ethical issues, and factors to consider in your decision about what type of treatment setting is best suited to your work style. Many factors affect our style of practice, from theory to the constraints of the setting in which you are working. This chapter discusses the impact of external constraints on the choice of modality and treatment planning, and the constants or standards of practice that exist across all settings (e.g., informed consent and confidentiality). The varied responses of children at different ages to various modalities and approaches is reviewed. For example, varying responses to group and individual therapies at different ages and in varied treatment settings are addressed. In addition, the setting or location where therapy is provided can also have significant impact.

The information in this section can also be applied in determining what treatment setting might provide the best fit for your skills as well as for the needs of your clients and their families. By being aware of the limits and strengths of various settings, you can determine the appropriate level of intensity to meet your client's presenting concerns and the family's needs for additional support in treatment.

TREATMENT SETTING FACTORS TO CONSIDER

As you read this section, you will notice a progressive nature to the level of intensity in services and the level of restriction in treatment. The intensity of treatment corresponds to the level of severity for the client's presenting concerns. More severe symptoms and presentations often require more intensive interventions to produce change.

Level of Restriction

Most professionals, clients, and families prefer the least restrictive environment that provides the fewest limitations on daily activities. Less restriction has benefits and challenges. The benefits include continuing with a relatively normal routine, with the usual support system in place. These same factors can also present a challenge in certain cases. Behavioral change is difficult when the usual cues remain the same. In such circumstances, the rate of change may be slower, but the new behavior may be stronger when confronted with the same behavioral cues. At times a level of restriction is needed for effective treatment, as in substance abuse treatment. Generally, however, the maintenance of normal routines enhances a feeling of well-being and positive self-efficacy. Maintaining consistent support also enhances the maintenance of any change.

Need for Structure

With certain presenting problems, a greater need for external structure exists, such as with suicidal gestures or a psychotic break. In these circumstances, a more restrictive environment provides consistent monitoring, no access to means to harm oneself, and intensive therapeutic interventions.

Need for Long-Term Remediation and Structure

Cases of severe, chronic behavioral concerns (e.g., conduct disorder), nonresponsiveness to other interventions (e.g., reactive attachment disorder), or psychotic presentations may require long-term care, such as residential or group treatment centers.

SCHOOL COUNSELING

School counseling provides one of the more accessible and seamless approaches to counseling, in that the services are available throughout the school year to students and their parents. The school counselor is a phone call away from parents and a short walk down the hall from regular classes. Although the role of the school counselor has changed dramatically over the last 10 to 20 years, the familiarity of the role for previous generations can help diminish some of the stigma associated with counseling in other settings and make accessing support less of an obstacle. For some individuals, the school counselor may be the only accessible contact for mental health services. Lack of resources, suspiciousness of professionals or mental health approaches, or preoccupation with family survival issues may prevent some families from accessing any other sources of support. Some families may not be supportive of their child receiving services regardless of available resources, but the child or adolescent at least has the opportunity through the school counseling service.

The scope of counseling that can be provided within the school setting is necessarily limited. Although most schools are seeing their roles change in terms of becoming more involved with families and community, the counselor in this setting still is often unable to provide the depth of services that a counselor in a mental health center or other community agency may offer. This poses a problem for the school counselor who is now faced with more challenging concerns and for families who may not be seeking services elsewhere. Many schools are able to supplement their counseling services with additional personnel from grants, such as social workers or crisis counselors, helping to broaden the base of services available. It is important to remember, though, that the role of the school counselor is to provide services that enhance students' academic performance. In light of that mission and schools' limited resources, counselors may not be able to provide the primary level of support some students or families may be seeking.

The bulk of counseling services provided by the school counselor includes individual and group counseling either within the format of classroom guidance or therapeutic, semi-structured groups, in addition to traditional "guidance" and career activities. As outlined in many school districts, specific expectations are in place with regard to the amount of time a school counselor is to devote to certain types of activities, these percentages change from elementary to middle to junior high to high school settings.

Competing demands exist for counselors in some school districts. Counselors are also given lunchroom duty and bus duty, and they may offer release time to classroom teachers. These administrative tasks can often confound the effectiveness of the school counselor due to the dual roles created. Administrative responsibilities of the school counselor can make it more difficult to establish rapport. This presents a challenge with regard to dual relationships that does not exist in other settings. The most challenging dual relationship for school counselors often arises out of the juxtaposition of authoritarian and counseling roles when asked to perform administrative tasks (e.g., filling in for the principal).

These dual roles for school counselors in some districts can make it more difficult to be effective in the traditional counseling session. However, some school counselors remark favorably about the impact of having additional information available about students' performance, peer groups at school, and other "current events" within the school milieu that are known to the counselor simply as a result of being part of that community. Having information available from multiple sources does enhance our ability to be effective, but a note of caution is warranted about using that information as heavy-handed leverage in school counseling sessions. It is necessary for the school counselor to keep separate the various roles in his relationships with students. Keeping dual relationships to a minimum is in the best interest of students.

Attempts to strongly persuade or coerce students on the basis of "inside" information is unethical. However, counselors can use that information productively by being honest about knowing it. You may not be able to reveal the specific source of the information, but you can let the student know you are aware of it and attempt to use the information productively in session. Examples include knowing the student received a detention, was sent to the office, or had a scuffle in the cafeteria.

That information is available to you because you are at the same school. In other types of therapy settings, the information might be withheld from the counselor. In the school setting, you can let students know what you know, push their resistance, and perhaps make more use of the limited time you have available in the session.

If you have not already done so, confronting the student with your information may provide a cue to review the limits of confidentiality. Given the "drop-in" nature of school counseling, you may not have discussed confidentiality yet. Being at a school, information can be shared on a "need-to-know-basis" with administrators or teachers. However, it is important to remain cognizant of the phrase *need to know*. The role of everyone at a school, including the school counselor, is to enhance students' ability to succeed in school. Ask yourself when you are thinking about sharing something about a student whether disclosing that sensitive information will enhance their academic performance. If you are unable to determine how it will help the student, there is no reason to share the information.

In certain cases, student success can be enhanced by sharing pertinent information with other school professionals. As a school counselor, your time may be limited, but you may be able to depend on others for support. For example, in schools fortunate enough to have this position, the home-school communicator can help families feel more comfortable with the school and more trusting of efforts to help their children succeed. The role of the home-school communicator has been helpful in many schools to provide a connection to school beyond that provided by the school counselor, helping families feel more connected to the school and helping children feel more supported in educational efforts. This is particularly helpful in families who have become distrustful of the system or in those who do not value education. The services of the home-school communicator bridge a gap between the traditional school counselor and in-home services and may provide one of few interventions that some families are willing to accept. Sharing information with home-school communicators can help them be more effective in their interventions.

Principals at most schools are certainly in the administrative chain of command, but that doesn't mean every detail of student counseling sessions must be shared with them. Each school and district have different procedures and regulations. As a school counselor, you may need to take an advocacy role at times regarding the confidentiality of your records. Applying the need-to-know rule with other administrative staff is certainly appropriate and well within your role as a counselor. In the area of mandatory reporting of possible abuse or neglect, most schools have a policy that the principal be informed prior to the call being made or at least after the call has been made. Such a policy does not interfere with the confidentiality of your records, particularly if the principal will be the likely source of contact if authorities come to the school to conduct a portion of their investigation with the child or adolescent. At another level, consulting with a professional who is also a mandatory reporter may help you work through any questions or anxiety experienced as a result of making the call. Feeling uncomfortable making a call as a mandatory reporter is a common experience, particularly early in your career.

When working with other agencies or mental health personnel outside the school system, a release of information is needed to communicate about students and to plan or coordinate services. Most school offices or the outside professional's office will have releases available. The release of information form indicates the name of the student, provides a place for a parent/client signature and a witness, and lists a beginning and ending date for the release and the scope and purpose of the release (e.g., to coordinate treatment or treatment planning, to assist in provision or services or diagnosis, to communicate about medications or treatments to be administered at the school). The form should also list the name of the agency to release the information, the name of the agency to receive the information, and whether the release is bidirectional or unidirectional (i.e., are agencies sharing information, or is one agency simply providing information to a second group?)

Family counseling within the school system is usually not provided in the traditional sense, but brief interventions of one to two sessions may help move the process along in terms of academic performance and college planning. It is important to note that some schools are moving toward more family support in this regard. Community services may be overbooked and thus unavailable to families, or agencies may not have the trust of families. The school becomes a hub for reaching these families. The fact that families will receive some services is positive, but school personnel may end up overwhelmed by the broad range of responsibilities.

Additionally, schools are being asked to provide more and more support to families and children simply because they are one of the few places in our society where children share a common experience. Examples of this type of intervention include responses to community crises and emergencies, such as counseling offered to students after their peers die in an auto accident. As such, many social service and community agencies are attempting to use this environment for providing needed interventions, including sex education, school safety, and values education. DARE is an example of promoting prosocial values on drug abuse prevention.

It is sometimes necessary to provide counseling services in settings other than the school, such as inpatient psychiatric programs, residential treatment facilities, or correctional programs. In this setting, the counselor may adopt more of a case manager role in terms of acting as a liaison between various disciplines and staff members.

AGENCY SETTINGS

In a community mental health setting, a counselor is most likely exposed to a broader variety of problems that can be appropriately addressed in his professional setting, as compared to the school counselor. In this setting, the therapist has a greater latitude for involving the family and working with other agencies, including the school and any counselors focusing on enhancing the client's ability to learn. The modality within an agency more often involves a family approach, although it is likely child-focused. Parent groups are also often provided in an inpatient or day treatment setting.

The approach to treatment in some agency, inpatient, and day treatment settings may be interdisciplinary, with different professionals on the treatment team. The team may include counselors, social workers, psychologists, nurses, occupational therapists, speech language pathologists, and psychiatrists.

When working as part of a team, it is important not to mirror the family's dysfunctional dynamics. Team members can be easily split by families, causing confusion and competing goals in therapy. A team split by family dynamics may mirror the negative interactions of the family and possibly replicate some of the negative behaviors or immobilization the family experiences. Although these feelings and perceptions may work to inform the therapy, it is best to maintain a professional awareness and avoid such entrapments, when possible. One way of doing so is to keep in mind the boundaries and roles for each treatment discipline, so as not to overlap or confuse treatment. Remain aware of your own responses to a family in these circumstances. If you often find yourself thinking about a particular family or acting as a strong advocate for them in team meetings, you may want to review your own potential countertransference.

Multidisciplinary treatment provides an ideal approach in some ways due to the comprehensive intervention for a child and his family. Obviously, this treatment approach is limited for many clients but offers an intervention appropriate for more serious problems.

INPATIENT OR DAY TREATMENT PROGRAMS

An extension of the multidisciplinary approach is found in an inpatient or day treatment setting. That setting offers the least amount of concern about external influences or challenges to treatment compliance, because the agency has a higher level of control over the client's environment, daily regime, and contact with others outside the treatment team. This can be a plus when attempting to stabilize an individual, but it provides a limited picture of the client's interactions with others in less structured settings. Thus, this modality is best suited when the aim is stabilization, perhaps after a suicide attempt.

In a day treatment or inpatient setting, the counselor needs to be aware of the potential for a skewed perspective of the individual's true level of functioning. Use of a systems or team approach that involves as many significant adults from all aspects of a child's life is preferred. The client may be able to present as more or less healthy than he truly is due to the limited number of stressors to which he is being exposed on a daily basis. Additionally, some adolescents and younger children may attempt to manipulate the system by "faking good" to achieve an early release. In these situations, the symptoms recur fairly quickly following discharge. A team approach is often used in such a setting, so counselors may be working with professionals from other disciplines and, as in the case with the school counselor, may be required to set boundaries on their professional role and involvement. Usually, an after-care plan helps delineate specific areas of responsibility.

A community-based systems approach offers several advantages:

1. The child experiences, at a very real level, the manifestation of the community's interest in his success.
2. The communication and active interdisciplinary involvement creates a safety net and the structure that children with multiple challenges require.

3. Caregivers feel less overwhelmed in providing treatment because they are no longer the sole provider, but part of a team. Parents also benefit from this web of caregivers.
4. Children and adolescents learn to ask for assistance in a positive way and also recognize they can't get away with as much as they might like to think they can, due to the external structure provided by this network of professionals.

PRIVATE PRACTICE

Private practice offers considerable flexibility to the professional in this setting but has other limitations. It is necessary to pursue licensure and obtain professional liability coverage for independent practice. There is limited interaction with other professionals and significant constraints on practice from managed care companies, which often require periodic updates on treatment to obtain approval for additional treatment sessions. These demands are time consuming and encroach upon the confidentiality of the therapeutic relationship. Thus, it is critical for the private practitioner to inform the client of these issues when discussing the limitations of confidentiality. Information about managed care is included as part of forms covering informed consent and limits to confidentiality. It is important for clients to understand that information must be shared with their insurance or managed care company in order to receive approval for services. Many clients are aware of this before coming in as plans may require an initial phone call for authorization before beginning treatment. Many private practitioners inform clients about the possible need to call prior to the first appointment. Treatment planning may involve the managed care personnel in addition to the client and family.

HOME-BASED SERVICES

An alternative approach sometimes encountered in private practice or when working with an agency is that of providing services in the home. Some advantages of in-home treatment include the opportunity to observe family interactions in a more natural setting. This basis is similar to Piaget's naturalistic approach, which can often provide a more realistic and honest appraisal of family life and relationships.

Another advantage to in-home care is similar to the rationale behind behavioral interventions with children. It is always best to intervene at the time of the misbehavior in order to help the child understand the situation, thoughts, and feelings associated with the specific behavior. The immediacy of the intervention enhances the child's learning. Similarly, parents can learn from interventions and observations shared at the time of the interaction. Perhaps parents have been unaware of how their interactions (e.g., tone of voice) are perceived by their child or adolescent, until someone outside the family provides feedback.

For certain types of behaviors, specifically externalizing disorders, positive results have been observed from in-home treatment, but it was noted that the child's level of compliance was a significant factor in positive outcome as well (Lay, Blanz, & Schmidt, 2001).

RESIDENTIAL TREATMENT FACILITY

At the other end of the spectrum from receiving treatment in the home or "least restrictive environment"—a basic tenet of community mental health policy—we find residential or group treatment centers. These treatment centers serve a role in providing intensive on-site services for children and adolescents who have exhausted other resources. The exhaustion of resources may include community treatment providers as well as a family's ability to provide care. Some children and adolescents who come into residential care may simply be placed there temporarily because of the need for more intensive services, or the need may be more permanent, such as the loss of parents or parental figures to care for them in combination with the need for psychiatric or behavioral care (Levine, 2000).

Treatment outcome for residential centers is as varied as the reasons for seeking such intensive services. As with most treatment, individual characteristics appear to be as much a factor in treatment outcome, as are the treatment methods (Larzelere, et al, 2001; Llyons, Terry, Martinovich, Peterson, & Bouska, 2001). Additionally, each treatment center is unique, making comparisons difficult. Another complicating factor in making comparisons between effectiveness of various programs is the failure to complete treatment. Estimates are that up to half of children admitted to residential centers may be discharged early, paradoxically due to problematic behavior (Sunseri, 2001). However, comparison between in-home treatment and residential centers shows a slightly more favorable outcome for home treatment (Mattejat, Hirt, Wilken, Schmidt, & Remschmidt, 2001).

ISSUES TO CONSIDER IN YOUR DECISION-MAKING PROCESS

As can be seen in this discussion of treatment settings, these external factors affect your effectiveness and scope of practice. For beginning level counselors and therapists, these constraints may be important factors in career decision making. As a professional, do you envision yourself administering and interpreting tests alone, as part of a team, or rarely? Do you see yourself working independently with children, adolescents, and families in a model similar to that of traditional private practice, or are you more comfortable working closely with other colleagues to share some of the emotional burden and/or work collaboratively in providing a comprehensive treatment approach at one facility? Granted, the continuity of care is positive, but how comfortable do you find yourself in thinking about these settings? Your preferences and needs for certain types of treatment settings may vary over time throughout your own professional development.

ASPECTS OF PROFESSIONAL DEVELOPMENT

As you continue your professional growth and development, your confidence will increase as you become more proficient in your skills and critical thinking abilities. Throughout this progression, you will also become progressively more comfortable with your identity as a professional. You may notice a slight shift toward thinking of the contributions you might make to your profession rather than solely focusing on what things you need in training.

Personal and Professional Growth

It is important to understand the necessity of personal and professional growth in our profession, similar to the unique self-awareness necessary to provide effective therapy. Exercises in the workbook address professional development throughout. I hope you are finding them helpful. The process of professional development includes skill and knowledge acquisition and the ability to own the identity of a professional, to begin trusting oneself to make decisions on the basis of training experiences and professional knowledge. The spontaneity required during the session is daunting for many beginning level professionals. A major challenge for students is learning to trust that they will be able to respond appropriately in session when the time comes. Part of this self-trust is built on the basis of good supervision and clinical experience. The remaining portion is built on your self-acceptance and ability to appropriately own the professional skills required to meet the challenges. Hopefully, you are developing the necessary skills to enjoy the spontaneity and challenges that make our profession unique.

Clinical Supervision

Clinical supervision is an essential component of any professional's training experience. Supervision is akin to the old apprentice model of master craftsmen and the residency model of medical training. The purpose of such intensive training and supervision is to develop a view of oneself as an independent professional, to trust one's own skills in that regard, and to learn to practice spontaneously in terms of responding to a myriad unpredictable and unexpected clinical concerns. Some compare the supervision relationship to that established in therapy with the child client and his family (Balsam, 2001). The process of mutual respect moves the therapy and supervision forward. Support is needed for the family and the developing therapist when self-doubt and questioning arises. Asking for help when in training and in practice is ethically sound professional behavior. The process of supervision helps integrate theory and practice, while highlighting any initial areas of personal discomfort. The integration process helps the professional in training to conceptualize salient issues about the client and move forward with appropriate treatment interventions.

Professional Development and the Change Process

As professionals, we continue to grow and develop throughout our careers just as we progress through the phases of human development. Factors specific to our professional growth and development include moving from a novice to an expert level of functioning. The literature and our personal experience tell us that a shift occurs as we become increasingly more confident and comfortable with our level of clinical skills and our professional intuition. Part of becoming a good therapist is honing our powers of observation. We become attuned to the subtle nuances in voice and body language and to the more obvious discrepancies between what our clients said in a previous session and what they have shared today or to the differences between verbal and body language.

Another skill that will develop over time is the ability to recall, analyze, and integrate all the details of ongoing therapy. To some extent, this skill entails taking extensive notes, but most of the detail lies in our own memories. One of my professors in a psychoanalytic seminar shared the analogy of therapy as a memory track being revisited with each subsequent session (personal communication, Michael Patton, 1992). I often remember that description as I sit with clients in session and tidbits of helpful information—in far greater detail than I have included in any clinical documentation—flood back into the session. This skill allows me to be a good therapist. This ability to weave the sessions together as though they were continuous interactions and to form separate threads of discourse for each topic until their relationships are revealed is the essence of therapy that allows our clients to move forward. The complexity of this therapeutic skill is apparent and develops over time.

Staying Focused and Ethical

For the beginning level therapist, it is difficult even to know what to say next to a client, let alone juggling several different topics at different emotional and psychological levels simultaneously. However this skill does develop. This is the benefit of practicum and direct experience in providing counseling: No experience can simulate the process of ongoing counseling.

As counseling professionals, we also need to explore the possibility of our own therapy—preferably in both individual and group settings—to better understand the experience of being a client and to be aware of our own biases. We should not ask our clients what we may not have been asking of ourselves. This speaks to the heart of the exercises in the companion workbook that explore potential biases so that we may be more fully present in our therapy sessions. Knowing how to use supervision and peer consultation is an important skill to improve our work with clients continually beyond formal training. Keeping in mind the challenge of working cleanly on client's issues, and not our own, can feel overwhelming for beginning level clients, but it is possible to maintain a neutral stance.

Ethical issues in working with children and adolescents may be even more challenging than those that arise while working with other populations. A recent survey suggests that ambiguities in practice and in determining ethical practice may be complicated by the various developmental levels of our clients (Mannheim et al., 2002). At one level, this can be seen as a very real issue for clinicians, just as it is for parents. Appropriate expectations of what our child and adolescent clients may be able to understand and act upon are an important part of ethical practice. If we are pushing our clients beyond their developmental level in the same ways as others in their lives may be doing, this could be considered unethical practice.

In addition, working with children, adolescents, and families provides many varied opportunities for countertransference reactions. Workbook exercises are designed to assist you in sorting out your own feelings, thoughts, and experiences about all these phases of life. Each of us has varied reactions to our experience, and we may not be aware of all of those reactions. Unfortunately, those issues can make it hard for us to engage in ethical practice.

In order to be effective and ethical, we must know in our hearts (professionally) that something is amiss. We must be able to recognize these small voices of dissent within ourselves. Professional experience will lead us to be aware that some of our own personal issues may be reaching out to this particular client at this particular point in time as countertransference, our personal reaction to a client's issues.

Once you've recognized and named a problem, now what? Good question. What comes next is a personal course of therapy, journaling, peer supervision, or any other number of mechanisms to help you focus on your reaction to the client. If, even after these interventions, you are unable to focus in a healthy manner on the client, then you may need to consider referral to another professional for this client. During that period of referral, further individual work is required on your part to tease out the internal obstacles of working with this issue. Personal therapy has long been recommended, and professionals generally report positively regarding their own experiences (Grimmer & Tribe, 2001).

Specific experiences identified as helpful included the opportunity to observe a therapist in practice and obtain support, personal growth and insight from the therapeutic process itself. Clinical supervision is an important aspect of training that builds the professional's ability to make accurate diagnoses (Brammer, 2002). The reflective practice fostered by supervision and enhanced by personal therapy is consistent with positive professional development practices in other fields as well (Osterman & Kottkamp, 1993). Being able to explore alternative perspectives has also been recognized as an important factor in professional training, an experience that is available through supervision and personal therapy, in addition to the multiple perspectives available in group supervision (Eriksen & McAuliffe, 2001).

Flow: Trusting Yourself

Normal professional development moves from a level of anxiety to confidence, from a knowledge base of a novice to that of an expert, toward being able to respond spontaneously to various therapeutic challenges. Progressing to a more comfortable and confident professional stance allows you to achieve a level of flow within the therapeutic process. *Flow* (Csikszentmihalyi, 1991) is defined as that process of getting lost in the moment, of being so engaged in the process, creative or otherwise, that you may lose track of time. Your focus becomes so targeted that you may experience a feeling of being "really on." Flow in therapy is achieved when both the counselor and client are fully engaged in the session and work of therapy.

Sapienza and Bugental (2000) follow a similar perspective in their comments on self-care, suggesting that therapy is similar to communing with our own life force. Their perspective is reminiscent of the view that psychotherapy is an artistic endeavor. I have to agree with certain elements of both these perspectives. In those sessions when a true connection has been made, therapy flows. I can feel the connection between myself and my clients, and it is not one that requires touch of any kind. It feels almost electrical in its energy.

In contrast, Sapienza and Bugental (2000) describe a situation where the therapist may feel out of sorts, chaotic, distracted, and make the connection between these situations and burnout. Their logic does make sense. If one is feeling distracted, it takes additional energy to focus in session and to stay on track with the client. Potentially more destructive is the possibility that as a therapist, you may be unaware of your lack of focus and continue to practice mindlessly. This presents a dangerous and unethical situation.

Sapienza and Bugental (2000) remind us of the basic tenets of a humanistic approach: None of us knows more about our client's life than the client. This offers the core of basic respect we must display toward our clients. It is a privilege to be able to work so intimately with other human beings in this way. They trust our expertise and our approach so much that they will share intimate details of their lives with us that they may not have shared with anyone else. Maintaining our awareness about the magnitude of our role in our young clients' lives can keep us focused and ethical in our interactions with them.

Healthy Boundaries

Many in the helping professions err on feeling overly responsible for others. We cannot change our clients. We can facilitate change with them, if they allow us. Consider this old joke: How many counselors does it take to change a light bulb? Only one, but the light bulb has to want to change. Corny, yes, but also true. Our clients can change, but we are not responsible for that process within them. Adopting this perspective frees us to be present with the client, as Sapienza and Bugental (2000) suggest. This perspective relieves us of the pressure of doing the work for the clients; it prevents burnout and allows us to mirror and reflect to our clients, facilitating their individual work.

A more complex balance must be achieved in order to achieve this "flow" when working with children, adolescents, and families. A central challenge in working as a child/adolescent therapist lies in the ability to flexibly and successfully negotiate between various aspects of yourself and in monitoring the individual client, his family system, and the interactions with school and other community groups, including peers and possibly authorities or other professionals.

Because of this complexity, attention to and awareness of personal boundaries are necessary for you to be effective in working with children, adolescents, and their families. The age-old adage of engaging in your own personal therapy is an important component of training that is likely to contribute to positive ethical functioning as an independent professional. By learning how to recognize your own boundaries, limitations, and/or biases, you can be a more effective clinician. The workbook provides opportunities to explore these personal issues so that they don't become an obstacle to your own ability to use your internal tools to the best advantage of your work and your clients.

Internal Flexibility

This internal work allows you to move more fluidly between being able to relate to and identify with your child and adolescent clients while drawing on the adult side of your training and expertise simultaneously. This challenge can separate more successful clinicians from those for whom establishing rapport is more difficult. Part of this balancing act also involves being able to identify and relate just as well with parents while maintaining a positive, working relationship with young clients. It is a definite challenge for many clinicians to be able to shelf those personal biases about parenting and what it means to be a child within a family when engaging in a child-centered family approach.

Smile. Engage. Be a "kid" psychologist in a grown-up professional body. Being able to transition between your adult and child-like or adolescent selves is a skill that will serve you well as a therapist of young clients. That fluidity within yourself will allow you to connect with children, adolescents, and parents in a way that is more powerful and authentic than acting as most adults in young clients' lives interact with them. Being able to move back and forth without getting stuck in your own biases and beliefs is part of the ethical challenge as well.

FINAL ETHICAL NOTES

In counseling children and adolescents, the systems approach often requires collaboration with a multidisciplinary team that may include physicians, school counselors, social service staff, teachers, and parental figures. It may be necessary to talk with other community members who are involved with the adolescent or child client and have information to share, such as a scout leader or coach. This perspective can be challenging in terms of the pragmatics of time, scheduling, joint meetings, and the management of the various roles in terms of providing the optimal coordination of care.

In smaller communities, you may have dual relationships with clients or their families. Take all precautions to keep these to a minimum. Balancing ethical boundaries and confidentiality issues between needs of parents and children or adolescents can be difficult when working with this population, but this balancing act will become more comfortable throughout your professional development.

Balancing personal and professional lives is important for you as well. Part of your self-care plan should include time for yourself for rejuvenation. Just as we "prescribe" some fun, positive activities for our clients, we need to give ourselves permission to engage in them, too. Such boundaries and separation allow us to be more effective in both personal and professional areas of our lives.

Firm boundaries are also important in the area of dual relationships to keep professional relationships separate from personal relationships. It is unethical to have a dual relationship with a client. The most glaring example is that of a sexual relationship, which is prohibited under most professional organizations' ethical guidelines. However, it also refers to other more casual forms of interaction. Examples of situations to avoid include joining a book club where a client is a member or bartering with a client for services (he mows your yard, and you provide therapy). Because of the power differential inherent in a therapeutic relationship, you are essentially taking advantage of your client if you engage in these other types of relationships. Additionally, these types of relationships interfere with the work you are trying to facilitate for the client. Clients may seek out other types of relationships with you due to their transference issues, idolizing you in the same way a young child idolizes a parent. When working with children and adolescents, it's important to remain even more clear about appropriate boundaries, but you need to do so in a way that does not feel hurtful or rejecting toward the client. If you find yourself in a situation that feels uncomfortable, as always, consult your colleagues or a supervisor.

Issues reviewed in this text should provide some insight into the challenges of various types of work as well as the rewards. In conjunction with the exercises in the workbook, you should have identified a good combination of your strengths and areas that may feel like too much of a stretch. Use that information to develop your own professional development and self-care plan as you move on in the next phase of professional development.

Privileged Work

As we work with clients, we must keep in mind what a privilege it is to work with our clients. They allow us entry into their intimate, emotional worlds. When we notice ourselves becoming jaded (e.g., by poking fun at clients, by becoming exasperated with them, by being late for appointments or missing them altogether), these are potential indicators of burnout. These behaviors send the clear message that we need to focus a little attention on self-care or possibly that some of the client's issues or life situations have touched us a little too close to home. In either of these cases, we need to seek supervision or consultation from a colleague to work through our reactions to this particular client.

Countertransference as Self-Knowledge

Although we have discussed the phenomenon of countertransference throughout the text, we have not made the connection between self-awareness and countertransference. Essentially, we are talking about our reactions to clients, and as we know, with children and adolescents, these responses are generally more varied than when working with adults. Due to the range of client experiences, our own expectations about childhood and parenthood, and our own experiences with these life events and phases, specific exploration is needed to enhance our therapeutic effectiveness and our ethical behavior in providing counseling to these minors and their families.

Countertransference Reactions

One of the factors to consider when working with special populations such as abused clients, physically violent clients, clients with physical limitations, clients with sexual orientation that differ from you is your own reaction. As therapists and counselors, we are often asked to work with issues that may be hard to talk about in normal conversation. In fact, that is a large part of our skill base as therapists—being able to talk about difficult things. Our learning how to talk about these difficult things is enhanced by our analysis of what's difficult for each of us as individuals. By figuring out what's hard to talk about and why, we can facilitate our effectiveness with clients. This is related to the long-held perspective that psychologists, counselors, and analysts need to participate in personal therapy to explore biases, work through unresolved issues, or learn how to deal with issues that may be sensitive for us when similar perspectives may surface later in work with clients.

What I have just described is essentially countertransference. Your personal reactions to clients occur whether you are aware of them or not. A crucial emphasis in this chapter is on those sensitive areas to help you begin your self-exploration process to increase your awareness of personal biases. Potential indicators of countertransference include negative feelings toward the client; feelings of boredom or sleepiness in session; strong feelings of any type toward the client; sympathy, extreme admiration, or dislike for the client; or overidentification with the client. Note that when working with children and adolescents in a family approach, countertransference may occur with the client as well as the parents.

The workbook provides a mechanism and promotes self-exploration by helping you identify your own potential countertransference issues that may impede therapeutic work with clients. For example, if you have a bias against single mothers or teenagers becoming pregnant, you must be aware of these feelings in order to work well with clients who may be faced with these issues. Granted, none of us would wish for a teenager to become pregnant, but it is often our feeling about abortion or adoption that may create problems for us in providing counseling for others. If you feel so strongly that you are unable to set those feelings aside and work with the client's feelings, then you need to seriously consider referral to another professional.

Problems arise when you are unaware of your own strong feelings. The workbook exercises are designed to help you stretch enough to explore and be aware of those biases. If you are unaware of those feelings, then you may behave in ways that feel judgmental and nontherapeutic toward clients. Your actions that arise out of being unaware may be perceived by clients as negative, unsupportive, or judgmental. This may lead to further resistance and the client becoming unco-operative or dropping out of therapy. These are real dangers and obstacles to ef-fective therapy. Your level of self-awareness can make you a more effective clinician. Working with people in challenging situations can bring out biases of which you were completely unaware. Being unaware of biases is the danger—for yourself and your clients.

Just as increased self-awareness allows clients the ability to make informed choices in their lives, your own awareness informs your practice and ensures ethi-cal interactions. The challenge of maintaining your own awareness is an ongoing part of professional practice. Remaining open to the possibility that some of your own issues may be triggered by clients will strengthen your professional skills and your effectiveness as a therapist. I hope that you find joy in this challenge as you work with young clients and their families.

DISCUSSION QUESTIONS

1. Take a case example and determine the most appropriate treatment fit, based on discussions of restriction, severity, and other key issues.
2. What do you find exciting or daunting about the various treatment settings discussed in this chapter?
3. What major challenges are facing you in your current stage of professional development?
4. To what are you most looking forward in your own practice?
5. What behavioral cues might be a countertransference warning for you?

References

Abela, J. R. Z. (2001). The hopelessness theory of depression: A test of the diasthesis-stress and causal-mediation components in third and seventh grade children. *Journal of Abnormal Child Psychology, 29*(3), 241–254.

Abela, J. R. Z., & Veronneau-McIrdle, M. H. (2002). The relationship between self-complexity and depressive symptoms in third and seventh grade children. *Journal of Abnormal Child Psychology, 30*(2), 155–167.

Achenbach, T. M. (1991). *Manual for the child behavioral checklist/4-18 and 1991 profile.* Burlington, VT: University of Vermont, Department of Psychiatry.

Achenbach, T. M., Conners, C. K., Quay, H. C., Verhulst, F. C., & Howell, C. T. (1989). Replication of empirically derived syndromes as a basis for taxonomy of child/adolescent psychopathology. *Journal of Abnormal Child Psychology, 17,* 299–323.

Achenbach, T. M., Howell, C. T., McConaughy, S. H., & Stanger, C. (1995a). Six-year predictors of problems in a national sample of children and youth, I: Cross-informant syndromes. *Journal of the American Academy of Child and Adolescent Psychiatry, 34,* 336–337.

Achenbach, T. M., Howell, C. T., McConaughy, S. H., & Stanger, C. (1995b). Six-year predictors of problems in a national sample of children and youth, II: Signs of disturbance. *Journal of the American Academy of Child and Adolescent Psychiatry, 34,* 488–498.

Achenbach, T. M., McConaughy, S. H., & Howell, C. T. (1987). Child/adolescent behavioral and emotional problems: Implications of cross-informant correlations for situational specificity. *Psychological Bulletin, 101,* 213–232.

Achenbach, T. M., Verhulst, F. C., Baron, G. D., & Althaus, M. (1987). A comparison of syndromes derived from the Child Behavior Checklist for American and Dutch boys ages 6–11 and 12–16. *Journal of Child Psychology and Psychiatry, 28,* 437–453.

Adleman, J., & Barrett, S. E. (1990). Overlapping relationships: Importance of the feminist ethical perspective. In H. Lerman & N. Porter (Eds.), *Feminist ethics in psychotherapy.* New York: Springer Publishing Company.

Adler, A. (1982). The fundamental views of individual psychology. *Individual psychology: Journal of Adlerian theory, research and practice, 38,* 3–6.

Agras, S., Hammer, L., & McNichols, E. (1999). A prospective study of the influences of eating disordered mothers on their children. *International Journal of Eating Disorders, 25,* 253–262.

Ainsworth, M. D., Blehar, M. C., Waters, E., & Walls, S. (1978). *Patterns of attachment.* Hillsdale, NJ: Erlbaum.

Akande, A., Akande, B. E., & Odewale, F. (1994). Putting the self back in the child: An African perspective. *Early Child Development and Care, 103,* 103–115.

Akiskal, H. S. (1981). Subaffective disorders: dysthymic, cyclothymic and bipolar II disorders in the "borderline realm." *Psychiatric Clinics of North America, 4,* 25–46.

Akiskal, H. S. (1995). Developmental pathways to bipolarity: Are juvenile-onset depressions pre-bipolar? *Journal of the American Academy of Child and Adolescent Psychiatry, 34,* 754–763.

Albano, A. M., & Kendall, P. C. (2002). Cognitive behavioral therapy for children and adolescents with anxiety disorders: Clinical research advances. *International Review of Psychiatry, 4*(2), 129–134.

Alessandria, K. P. (2002). Acknowledging white ethnic groups in multicultural counseling. *Family Journal: Counseling and Therapy for Couples and Families, 10*(1), 57–60.

Alessi, H. D., & Ballard, M. B. (2001). Memory development in children: Implications for children as witnesses in situations of possible abuse. *Journal of Counseling and Development, 79*(4), 398–405.

Alessi, N., Naylor, M. W., Ghaziuddin, M., & Zubieta, J. K. (1994). Update on lithium carbonate therapy in children and adolescents. *Journal of the American Academy of Child and Adolescent Psychiatry, 33,* 291–304.

Alexander, V. (1991). Grief after suicide: Giving voice to the loss. *Journal of Geriatric Psychiatry, 24,* 277–291.

Allan, J., & Berry, P. (1987). Sandplay. *Elementary School Guidance and Counseling, 21*(4), 300–306.

Alsaker, F. D. (1992). Pubertal timing, overweight, and psychological adjustment. *Journal of Early Adolescence, 12*(4), 396–419.

Altmann, E. O., & Gotlib, I. H. (1988). The social behavior of depressed children: An observational study. *Journal of Abnormal Child Psychology, 16,* 29–44.

American Academy of Pediatrics (1998). Position paper: Auditory integration training and facilitated communication for autism (RE9752). *Pediatrics, 102,* 431–433.

American Association for Marriage and Family Therapy (AAMFT) (2001). *AAMFT Code of Ethics. American Association of Marriage and Family Therapy:* Alexandria, VA.

American Counseling Association.

American Psychiatric Association (2000). Diagnostic and Statistical Manual-IV-TR. Washington, DC: American Psychiatric Association

American Psychiatric Association, (1994). *Diagnostic and statistical manual of mental disorders,* 4th edition (DSM-IV). Washington, DC: American Psychiatric Association.

American Psychiatric Association Work Group on Eating Disorders (2000). Practice guidelines for the treatment of patients with eating disorders (revision). Supplement to the *American Journal of Psychiatry, 157*(1).

American Psychological Association (2002). Ethical principles of psychologists. *American Psychologist, 57,* 1060–1073.

American Psychological Association (1981). Ethical principles of psychologists. *American Psychologist, 36,* 633–638.

Anderson, J. C., Williams, S., McGee, R., & Silva, P. A. (1987). DSM-III disorders in preadolescent children: Prevalence in a large sample from the general population. *Archives of General Psychiatry, 44,* 69–76.

Andreozzi, L. L. (1996). *Child-centered family therapy.* Cambridge, MA: Wiley.

Aponte, H. J., & Winter, J. E. (2000). The person and practice of the therapist: Treatment and training. In M. Baldwin (Ed.), *The use of self in therapy* (2nd ed, pp. 127–165). Binghamton, NY: Haworth.

Araoz, D. L., & Carrese, M. A. (1996). *Solution-oriented brief therapy for adjustment disorder.* Philadelphia, PA: Brunner-Routledge.

Armsden, G. C., & Greenberg, M. T. (1987). The inventory of parent and peer attachment: Individual differences and their relationship to psychological well-being in adolescence. *Journal of Youth and Adolescence, 16,* 427–454.

Aras, S., Hammer, L., & McNichols, E. (1999). A prospective study of the influences of eating disordered mothers on their children. *International Journal of Eating Disorders, 25,* 253–262.

Arrington, E. W. (1987). Managing children's conflict: A challenge for the school counselor, *School Counselor, 32*(3), 188–194.

Askildsen, E. C., Watten, R. G., & Faleide, A. O. (1993). Are parents of asthmatic children different from other parents? Some follow-up results from the Norwegian PRAD project. *Psychotherapeutic Psychosomatics, 60,* 91–99.

Axelson, D. A., & Birmaher, B. (2001). Relations between anxiety and depressive disorders in childhood and adolescence. *Depression and Anxiety, 14*(2), 67–78.

Bailey, M. J., & Hamilton, T. (1987). Comparison of outcomes of behavioral therapy given families with children and families with adolescents. *Psychological Reports, 60*(1), 159–162.

Bajt, T. R., & Pope, K. S. (1989). Therapist-patient sexual intimacy involving children and adolescents. *American Psychologist, 44*(2), 455–468.

Baker, M., Milich, R., & Manolis, M. B. (1996). Peer interactions of dysphoric adolescents. *Journal of Abnormal Child Psychology, 24,* 241–255.

Bale, R. (1993). Family treatment in short-term detoxification. In T. J. O'Farrell (Ed.), *Treating alcohol problems: Marital and family interventions.* (pp. 117–144). New York: Guilford Press.

Balsam, R. M. (Ed.). (2001). *Psychodynamic psychotherapy: The supervisory process.* Madison, CT: International Universities Press.

Bank, L., Patterson, G. R., & Reid, J. B. (1996). Negative sibling interaction patterns as predictors of later adjustment problems in adolescent and young adult males. In Brody, G. H. (Ed.), *Sibling relationships: Their causes and consequences* (pp. 197–229). Norwood, NJ: Ablex.

Barber, B. K. (Ed.). (2002). *Intrusive parenting: How psychological control affects children and adolescents.* Washington, DC: American Psychological Association.

Barkely, B. H., & Mosher, E. S. (1994). Sexuality and Hispanic culture: Counseling with children and their parents. *Journal of Sex Education and Therapy, 21*(4), pp. 255–267.

Barnett, P. A., & Gottlieb, L. H. (1988). Psychosocial functioning and depression: Distinguishing among antecedents, concomitants, and consequences. *Psychological Bulletin, 104,* 97–126.

Barrera, M., Jr.; & Garrison-Jones, C. (1992). Family and peer social support as specific correlates of adolescent depressive symptoms. *Journal of Abnormal Child Psychology, 20,* 1–16.

Barrett, K. A., & McWhirter, B. T. (2002). Counselor trainees' perceptions of clients based on client sexual orientation. *Counselor Education and Supervision,* Vol. 41, No. 3, pp. 219–233.

Bartlett, E. E. (1996). *The Hatherleigh guide to child and adolescent therapy,* Vol. 5. New York: Hatherleigh Press.

Bartz, K., W., & Levine, E. S. (1978). Childrearing in black parents: A description and comparison to Anglo and Chicano parents. *Journal of Marriage and the Family, 40,* 709–719.

Bateson, M. C. (1990). *Composing a life.* New York: Penguin.

Batsche, G. M., & Knoff, H. M. (1994). Bullies and their victims: Understanding a pervasive problem in the schools. *School Psychology, 23,* 165–174.

Baumeister, R. (2001). Violent pride: Do people turn violent because of self-hate, or self-love? *Scientific American, 284,* 96–101.

Baumrind, D. (1991). The influence of parenting style on adolescent competence and substance use. *Journal of Early Adolescence,* 11(1), 56–95.

Beardslee, W. R., Versage, E. M., & Gladstone, T. R. (1998). Children of affectively ill parents: A review of the past 10 years. *Journal of the American Academy of Child and Adolescent Psychiatry, 37,* 1134–1141.

Bebbington, P., & Kuipers, L. (1994). The predictive utility of expressed emotion in schizophrenia: An aggregate analysis. *Psychological Medicine, 24,* 707–718.

Beck, A. (2003). *Beck depression inventory.* San Antonio: Psychological Corporation.

Bell, T. L. (1992). Dysfunctional parenting styles. *Addiction and Recovery,* 12(1), 12–15.

Bell-Dolan, D. J., Last, C. G., & Strauss, C. C. (1990). Symptoms of anxiety disorders in normal children. *Journal of the American Academy of Child and Adolescent Psychiatry, 29,* 759–765.

Bembry, J. X., & Ericson, C. (1999). Therapeutic termination with the early adolescent who has experienced multiple losses. *Child and Adolescent Social Work Journal,* 16(3), 177–189.

Bemporad, J. R., Smith, H. F., & Hanson, G. (1987). The borderline child. In J. Noshpitz (Ed.), *Basic handbook of child psychiatry* (Vol. 5, pp. 305–311). New York: Basic.

Benne, L. L. (1991). The human-animal bond and the elementary school counselor. *School Counselor,* 38(5), 362–371.

Bennett-Levy, J., Turner, F., Beaty, T., Smith, M., Paterson, B., & Farmer, S. (2001). The value of self: Practice of cognitive therapy techniques and self reflection in training of cognitive therapists. *Behavioural and Cognitive Psychotherapy,* 29(2), 203–220.

Ben-Sira, Z. (1997). *Immigration, stress, and readjustment.* Westport, CT: Prager.

Berendt, T. J. (1998). Exploring the effects of friendship quality on social development. In W. M. Bukowski & A. F. Newcomb (Eds.), *The company they keep: Friendship in childhood and adolescence. Cambridge studies in social and emotional development.* New York: Cambridge University Press.

Berendt, T. J. (2002). Friendship quality and social development. *Current Directions in Psychological Science,* 11(1), 7–10.

Berg, I., & Jackson, A. (1985). Teenage school refusers grow up: A follow-up study of 168 subjects, ten years on average after inpatient treatment. *British Journal of Psychiatry, 147,* 366–370.

Berg, I., Marks, I., McGuire, R., & Lipsedge, M. (1974). School phobia and agoraphobia. *Psychological Medicine, 4,* 428–434.

Bermudez, J. M. (1997). Experiential tasks and therapist bias awareness. *Contemporary Family Therapy,* 19,(2), 253–267.

Berns, I. (2001). Social reality and a child's wish for psychotherapy. *International Journal of Communicative Psychoanalysis and Psychotherapy,* 16,(1–2), 3–10.

Bernstein, G. A. (1990). Anxiety disorders. In B. D. Garfinkel, G. A. Carlson, & E. B. Weller (Eds.), *Psychiatric disorders in children and adolescents* (pp. 64–83). Philadelphia: Saunders.

Bernstein, G. A. (1991). Comorbidity and severity of anxiety and depressive disorders in a clinic sample. *Journal of the American Academy of Child and Adolescent Psychiatry, 30,* 43–50.

Bernstein, G. A., & Borchardt, C. M. (1991). Anxiety disorders of childhood and adolescence: A critical review. *Journal of the American Academy of Child and Adolescent Psychiatry, 30,* pp. 519–532.

Bernstein, G. A., Shaw, K., Dunne, J. E., Ayres, W., Arnold, V., Bendek, E., Benson, R. S., Bernet, W., Bryant, E., Gross, R. L., Jaffe, S., King, R., Kinlan, J., Leonard, H., Licamele, W., McClellan, J., & Zametkin, A. (1997). Practice parameters for the assessment and treatment of children and adolescents with anxiety disorders. *Journal of the American Academy of Child and Adolescent Psychiatry, 36*(10), 69S–85S.

Biederman, J., Faraone, S. V., Keenan, K., Steingard, R., & Tsuang, M. T. (1991). Familial association between attention deficit disorder and anxiety disorders. *American Journal of Psychiatry, 148,* 251–256.

Biederman, J., Faraone, S. V., Kiely, K. (1996). Comorbidity in outcome of attention-deficit/hyperactivity disorder. In Hechtman, L. T. (Ed.), *Do they grow out of it? Long-term outcomes of childhood disorders.* Arlington, VA: American Psychiatric Press.

Biederman, J., Rosenbaum, J. F., & Bolduc-Murphy, E. A. (1993). A 3-year follow-up of children with and without behavioral inhibition. *Journal of the American Academy of Child and Adolescent Psychiatry, 32,* 814–821.

Biederman, J., Faraone, S. V., Keenan, K., & Tsuang, M. T. (1991). Evidence of familial association between attention deficit disorder and major affective disorders. *Archives of General Psychiatry, 48,* 633–642.

Biederman, J., Faraone, S., Milberger, S., & Curtis, S. (1996). Predictors of persistence and remission of ADHD into adolescence: Results from a four-year prospective follow-up study. *Journal of the American Academy of Child and Adolescent Psychiatry, 35,* 343–351.

Bierman, K. L., Smoot, D. L., & Aumiller, K. (1993). Characteristics of aggressive-rejected, aggressive (nonrejected), and rejected (nonaggressive) boys. *Child Development, 64,* 139–151.

Bigler, S. R., & Liben, L. S. (1993). A cognitive-developmental approach to racial stereotyping and reconstructive memory in Euro-American children. *Child Development, 64,* 1507–1518.

Bijur, P. E., Kurzon, M., Hamelsky, V., & Power, C. (1991). Parent-adolescent conflict and adolescent injuries. *Journal of Developmental and Behavioral Pediatrics, 12*(2), 92–97.

Bird, H. R., Camino, G., & Rubio-Stipec, M. (1988). Estimates of the prevalence of childhood maladjustment in a community survey in Puerto Rico. *Archives of General Psychiatry, 45,* 1120–1126.

Black, B., & Uhde, T. W. (1995). Psychiatric characteristics of children with selective mutism: A pilot study. *Journal of the American Academy of Child and Adolescent Psychiatry, 34,* 847–856.

Boccellari, A., & Dilley, J. W. (1989). Caring for patients with AIDS dementia. In J. W. Dilley, C. Pies, & M. Helquist (Eds.), *Face to face: A guide to AIDS counseling* (pp. 186–197). San Francisco: AIDS Health Project, University of California–San Francisco.

Boivin, M., & Hymel, S. (1997). Peer experiences and social self-perceptions: A sequential model. *Developmental Psychology, 33,* pp. 135–145.

Boivin, M., Poulin, F., & Vitaro, F. (1994). Depressed mood and peer rejection in children. *Development and Psychopathology, 6,* 483–498.

Borchardt, C. M., & Bernstein, G. A. (1995). Comorbid disorders in hospitalized bipolar adolescents compared with unipolar depressed adolescents. *Child Psychiatry Human Development, 26,* 11–18.

Borg, M. G. (1998). The emotional reactions of school bullies and their victims. *Educational Psychology, 18,* 433–444.

Borgers, S. B., & Tyndall, L. W. (1982). Setting expectations for groups. *Journal for Specialists in Group Work, 7,*(2) 109–111.

Borys, D. S., & Pope, K. S. (1989). Dual relationships between therapist and client: A national study of psychologists, psychiatrists, and social workers. *Professional Psychology: Research and Practice, 20,* 283–293.

Bosma, H. A., & Gerrits, R. S. (1985). Contemporary approaches to the study of families with adolescents. *Journal of Early Adolescence, 5*(1), 69–80.

Bovair, K., & McLaughlin, C. (Eds.). (1994). *Counseling in schools.* London: David Fulton.

Bowen, R. C., Offord, D. R., & Boyle, M. H. (1990). The prevalence of overanxious disorder and separation anxiety disorder: Results from the Ontario Child Health Study. *Journal of the American Academy of Child and Adolescent Psychiatry, 29,* 753–758.

Bowen, M. (1972). Family therapy and family group therapy. In H. I. Kaplin & B. J. Sadock, (Eds.), *Group treatment of mental illness.* Nortvale, NJ: Jason Aronson Publishing.

Bowlby, J. (1969). *Attachment and loss* (Vol. 1). New York: Basic.

Bowling, S. W., Kearney, L. K., Lumadue, C. A., & St. Germain, N. R. (2002). Considering justice: An exploratory study of family therapy with adolescents. *Journal of Marital and Family Therapy, 28*(2), 213–223.

Bowman, R. P. (1987). Approaches for counseling children through music. *Elementary School Guidance and Counseling, 21*(4) 284–291.

Bowring, M. A., & Kovacs, M. (1992). Difficulties in diagnosing manic disorders in children and adolescents. *Journal of the American Academy of Child and Adolescent Psychiatry, 31,* 611–614.

Boy, A. V., & Pine, G. J. (1995). *Child-centered counseling and psychotherapy.* Springfield, IL: Charles C. Thomas.

Boyd, C. J. (1989). Mothers and daughters: A discussion of theory and research. *Journal of Marriage and the Family, 51*(2), 291–301.

Boyd-Franklin, N. (1989). *Black families and therapy.* New York: Guilford Press.

Boyd-Franklin, N., & Bry, B. H. (2000). *Reaching out in family therapy: Home-based, school, and community interventions.* New York: Guilford Press.

Bradley, C. R. (1998). Child rearing in African American families: A study of the disciplinary practices of African American parents. *Journal of Multicultural Counseling and Development, 26,* 273–281.

Brafman, A. H. (2001). *Untying the knot: Working with children and parents.* London: Karnac.

Brammer, R. (2002). Effects of experience and training on diagnostic accuracy. *Psychological Assessment, 14*(1), 110–113.

Breen, D. T., & Daigneault, S. D. (1998). The use of play therapy with adolescents in high school. *International Journal of Play Therapy, 71*(1), 25–47.

Breggin, P. R., Breggin, G., & Bemak, F. (Eds.). (2002). *Dimensions of empathic therapy.* New York: Springer.

Brent, D. A., Perper, J. A., Moritz, G., Baugher, M., Schweers, J., & Roth, C. (1994). Suicide in affectively ill adolescents: A case-control study. *Journal of Affective Disorders, 31,* 193–202.

Brent, D. A., Perper, J. A., & Moritz, G. (1993). Psychiatric risk factors for adolescent suicide: A case-controlled study. *Journal of the American Academy of Child and Adolescent Psychiatry, 32,* 521–529.

Brent, D. A., Perper, J. A., & Goldstein, C. E. (1988). Risk factors for adolescent suicide: A comparison of adolescent suicide victims with suicidal inpatients. *Archives of General Psychiatry, 45,* 581–588.

Briere, J., & Conte, J. (1993). Self-reported amnesia for abuse in adults molested as children. *Journal of Traumatic Stress, 6,* 21–31.

Brody, G. H., Ge, S., Conger, R., Gibbons, F. X., Murry, V. M., Gerrard, M., & Simons, R. L. (2001). The influence of neighborhood disadvantage, collective socialization, and parenting on African American children's affiliation with deviant peers. *Child Development, 72,* 1231–1246.

Brody, G. H., Ge, X., Kim, S. Y., Murry, V. M., Simons, R. L., Gibbons, F. X., Gerrard, M., and Conger, R. D. (2003). Neighborhood disadvantage moderates association of parenting and older sibling problem attitudes and behavior with conduct disorders in African American children. *Journal of Consulting and Clinical Psychology, 71,* 211–222.

Brook, J. S., Whiteman, M., & Finch, S. (1993). The role of mutual attachment in adolescent drug use: A longitudinal study. *Journal of the American Academy of Child and Adolescent Psychiatry, 32,* 982–989.

Brook, J. S., Whiteman, M., Finch, S., & Cohen, P. (1998). Mutual attachment, personality, and drug use: Pathways from childhood to young adulthood. *Genetic Society General Psychology Monogram, 124,* 492–510.

Brooks-Gunn, J., Duncan, G. J., & Aber, J. L. (Eds.). (1997). *Neighborhood poverty: Context and consequences for development.* New York: Lexington Books.

Brooks-Gunn, J., Duncan, G. J., Klebanon, P. K., & Sealand, N. (1993). Do neighborhoods influence child and adolescent behavior? *American Journal of Sociology, 99,* 335–395.

Brown, D. T., & Prout, H. T. (Eds.). (1999). *Counseling and psychotherapy with children and adolescents: Theory and practice for school and clinic settings* (2nd ed.). Brandon, VT: Clinical Psychology Publishing.

Brown, R. T., & Sammons, M. T. (2002). Pediatric psychopharmacology: A review of new developments and recent research. *Professional Psychology: Research and Practice, 33,* 135–147.

Brown, R. T., & Sawyer, M. G. (1998). *Medications for school-age children: Effects on learning and behavior.* New York: Guilford Press.

Bruch, H. (1973). *Eating disorders: Obesity, anorexia nervosa, and the person within.* New York: Basic.

Buehler, C., & Gerard, J. M. (2002). Marital conflict, ineffective parenting and adolescents' maladjustment. *Journal of Marriage and the Family, 64*(1), 78–92.

Bullock, J. R. (2002). Bullying among children. *Childhood Education, 73,* 130–134.

Burd, L., Fisher, W., & Kerbeshian, J. (1987). A prevalence study of pervasive developmental disorders in North Dakota. *Journal of the American Academy of Child and Adolescent Psychiatry, 26,* 700–703.

Burns, G. L., & Walsh, J. A. (2002). The influence of ADHD-hyperactivity/impulsivity symptoms on the development of oppositional defiant disorder symptoms in a 2-year longitudinal study. *Journal of Abnormal Child Psychology, 30*(3), 245–257.

Bushman, B. J., & Anderson, C. A. (2001). Media violence and the American public. *American Psychologist, 56*(6/7), 477–489.

Butcher, E., & Scofield, M. E. (1984). The use of a standardized simulation and process tracing for studying clinical problem-solving competence. *Counselor Education and Supervision, 24,* 70–84.

Cadwalladei, T. W., & Cairns, R. B. (2002). Developmental influences and gang awareness among African-American inner city youth. *Social Development, 11*(2), 245–265.

Cairns, R. B., & Cairns, B. D. (1994). *Lifelines and risks: Pathways of youth in our time.* New York: Cambridge University Press.

Calhoun, L. G., & Allen, B. G. (1991). Social reactions to the survivor of a suicide in the family: A review of the literature. *Omega, 23,* 95–107.

Campbell, C. A. (1993). Play, the fabric of elementary school counseling programs. *Elementary School Guidance & Counseling, 28*(1), 10–16.

Campbell, T. L., (2000). Physical Illness: Challenges to families. In P. C. McKenry & S. J. Price (Eds). *Families* and *Change.* (pp. 154–182). Thousand Oaks, CA: Sage Publications.

Canale, J. R., & Beckely, S. R. (1999). Promoting altruism in troubled youth: Considerations and suggestions. *North American Journal of Psychology, 1*(1), 95–102.

Cantrell, R. G. (1986). Adjustment to divorce: Three components to assist children. *Elementary School Guidance & Counseling, 20*(3), 163–173.

Carey, T. A. (2001). Investigating the role of redirecting awareness in the change process: A case study involving the method of levels. *International Journal of Reality Therapy, 20*(2), 26–30.

Carlson, C. I., & Hickman, J. (1992). Family consultation in the schools in special services. *Special Services in the Schools, 6*(3–4), 83–112.

Carlson, G. A. (1990). Child and adolescent mania: Diagnostic considerations. *Journal of Child Psychological Psychiatry, 31,* 331–342.

Carlson, G. A., Fennig, S., & Bromet, E. J. (1994). The confusion between bipolar disorder and schizophrenia in youth: Where does it stand in the 1990s? *American Academy of Child and Adolescent Psychiatry, 33,* 453–460.

Carlson, G. A., & Kashani, J. H. (1988). Phenomenology of major depression from childhood through adulthood: Analysis of three studies. *American Journal of Psychiatry, 145,* 1222–1225.

Carlson, J. (1982). The multimodal effect of physical exercise. *Elementary School Guidance & Counseling, 16*(4), 304–309.

Carney, J., Werth, J. L., & Emanuelson, G. (1994). The relationship between attitudes toward persons who are gay and persons with AIDS, and HIV and AIDS knowledge. *Journal of Counseling and Development, 72,* 646–650.

Carney, J. V. (2000). Bullied to death: perceptions of peer abuse and suicidal behavior during adolescence. *School Psychology International, 21,* 44–54.

Carter, C. M. (2001). Using choice with game play to increase language skills and interactive behaviors in children with autism. *Journal of Positive Behavior Intervention, 3*(13), 131–151.

Carter, J. C., Stewart, D. A., Dunn, V. J., & Fairbrun, C. G. (1997). Primary prevention of eating disorders: Might it do more harm than good? *International Journal of Eating Disorders, 22,* 167–172.

Casas, J. M., Brady, S., & Ponterotto, J. G. (1983). Sexual preference biases in counseling: An information processing approach. *Journal of Counseling Psychology, 30,* 139–145.

Casat, C. D., & Pearson, D. A. (2001). The mental status exam in child and adolescent evaluation. In H. B. Vance & A. Pumariega (Eds.), *Clinical assessment of child and adolescent behavior* (pp. 86–97). New York: Wiley & Sons.

Casimir, G. J., & Morrison, B. J. (1993). Rethinking work with "multicultural populations." *Community Mental Health Journal, 29,* 547–559.

Caspi, A., Henry, B., McGee, R. O., Moffitt, T. E., & Silva, P. A. (1995). Temperamental origins of child and adolescent behavior problems: From age three to age fifteen. *Child Development, 66,* 55–68.

Cauffman, E., Feldman, S. S., Waterman, J., & Steiner, H. (1998). Posttraumatic stress disorder among female juvenile offenders. *Journal of the American Academy of Child and Adolescent Psychiatry, 37,* 1209–1216.

Cerel, J., Fristad, M. A., Weller, E. B., Weller, R. A. (1999). Suicide-bereaved children and adolescents: A controlled longitudinal examination. *Journal of the American Academy of Child and Adolescent Psychiatry, 38,* 672–679.

Cheer, S. M., & Figgitt, D. P. (2002). Spotlight on fluvoxamine in anxiety disorders in children and adolescents. *CNS Drugs, 16*(2), 139–144.

Chi, T. C., & Hinshaw, S. P. (2002). Mother-child relationships of children with ADHD: The role of maternal depressive symptoms and depression-related distortions. *Journal of Abnormal Child Psychology, 30*(4), 387–401.

Chun, K. M., & Akutsu, P. D. (2003). Acculturation among ethnic minority families. In K. M. Chun & P. B. Organista (Eds.), *Acculturation: Advances in theory, measurement, and applied theory* (pp. 95–119). Washington, DC: American Psychological Association.

Clance, P. R., & Petras, V. J. (1998). Therapists' recall of their decision-making processes regarding the use of touch in ongoing psychotherapy. In E. W. L. Smith & P. R. Clance (Eds.), *Touch in psychotherapy: Theory, research and practice* (pp. 92–108). New York: Guilford Press.

Clarkin, J. F., Carpenter, D., Hull, J., Wilner, P., & Glick, I. (1998). Effects of psychoeducational intervention for married patients and their spouses. *Psychiatric Services, 49,* 531–533.

Cleiren, M., Diekstra, R. F., Kerkhof, A. J., & van der Wal, J. (1994). Mode of death and kinship in death and bereavement: Focusing on "who" rather than "how." *Crisis: Journal of Crisis Intervention and Suicide, 15,* 22–36.

Close, H. T. (1998). *Metaphor in psychotherapy: Clinical application of stories and allegories.* Atascadero, CA: Impact Publishers.

Cohen, D. J., Paul, R., & Volkmar, F. (1987). Issues in the classification of pervasive developmental disorders and associated conditions. In D. J. Cohen & A. M. Donnelean (Eds.), *Handbook of autism and pervasive developmental disorders* (pp. 20–39). New York: Wiley.

Cohen, J. A., Mannarino, A. P., Berliner, L., & Deblinger, E. (2000). Trauma-focused cognitive behavioral therapy of children and adolescents: an empirical update. *Journal of Interpersonal Violence, 15*(11), 1220–1223.

Cohen, R. I., & Harnick, A. H. (1980). The susceptibility of child witnesses to suggestion. *Law and Human Behavior, 4,* 201–210.

Cole, D. A. (1990). Relation of social and academic competence to depressive symptoms in childhood. *Journal of Abnormal Psychology, 99,* 422–429.

Cole, D. A. (1991). Preliminary support for a competency-based model of depression in children. *Journal of Abnormal Psychology, 100,* 181–190.

Cole, D. A., Martin, J. M., & Powers, B. (1997). A competency-based model of child depression: A longitudinal study of peer, parent, teacher, and self-evaluations. *Journal of Abnormal Psychology, 38,* 505–514.

Cole, D. A., & McPherson, A. E. (1993). Relation of family subsystems to adolescent depression: Implementing a new family assessment strategy. *Journal of Family Psychology, 7*(1), 119–133.

Cole, D. A., Tram, J. M., Martin, J. M., Hoffman, K. B., Ruiz, M. D., Jacquez, F. M., & Maschman, T. L. (2002). Individual differences in the emergence of depressive symptoms in children and adolescents: A longitudinal investigation of parent and child reports. *Journal of Abnormal Psychology, 11*(1), 156–165.

Cole, D. A., & Turner, J. E., Jr. (1993). Models of cognitive mediation and moderation in child depression. *Journal of Abnormal Psychology, 102,* 271–281.

Conger, K. J., & Conger, R. D. (1994). Differential parenting and change in sibling differences in delinquency. *Journal of Family Psychology, 8*(3), 287–302.

Conger, R. D., Patterson, G. R., & Ge, X. (1995). It takes two to replicate. A mediational model for the impact of parents' stress on adolescent adjustment. *Child Development, 66,* 80–97.

Conners, C. K. (1997). Conners Rating Scale–Revised. North Tonawanda, NY: Multi-Health Systems.

Conolly, J., Geller, S., Marton, P., & Kutcher, S. (1992). Peer responses to social interaction with depressed adolescents. *Journal of Clinical Child Psychology, 21,* 365–370.

Constantine, L. (1986). *Family paradigms.* New York: Guilford Press.

Constantine, M. G. (2001). Multicultural training, theoretical orientation, empathy, and multicultural case conceptualization ability in counselors. *Journal of Mental Health Counseling, 23*(4), 357–372.

Constantine, M. G., & Arorash, T. J. (2001). Universal-diverse orientation and general expectations about counseling: Their relation to college students' multicultural counseling expectations. *Journal of College Student Development, 42,* 535–544.

Coolidge, J. C., Brodie, R. D., & Feeney, B. (1964). A ten-year follow-up study of sixty-six school-phobic children. *American Journal of Orthopsychiatry, 34,* 675–684.

Cornille, T. A., & Brotherton, W. D. (1993). Applying the developmental family model to issues of migrating families. *Marriage and Family Review, 19*(3–4), 325–340.

Costello, E. (1989). Child psychiatric disorders and their correlates: A primary care pediatric sample. *Journal of the American Academy of Child and Adolescent Psychiatry, 28,* 851–855.

Cottone, R. R., & Claus, R. E. (2000). Ethical decision-making models: A review of the literature. *Journal of Counseling and Development, 78,* 275–283.

Coucouvanis, J. (1997). Behavioral intervention for children with autism. *Journal of Child and Adolescent Psychiatric Nursing, 10*(1), 37–47.

Cowen, P., & Hetherington, M. (1991). *Family transitions.* Hillsdale, NJ: Erlbaum.

Coyne, J. C. (1976). Depression and the response of others. *Journal of Abnormal Psychology, 85,* 186–193.

Coyne, J. C., & Anderson, B. A. (1989). The "psychosomatic family," II: Recalling a defective model and looking ahead. *Journal of Marital and Family Therapy, 15,* 39–148.

Crawford, L., Hemfleet, G., Ribordy, S. C., Ho, F. C., & Vickers, V. L. (1991). Stigmatization of AIDS patients by mental health professionals. *Professional Psychology: Research & Practice, 22,* 357–361.

Crawford, L. A., & Novak, K. B. (2002). Parental and peer influences on adolescent drinking: The relative impact of attachment and opportunity. *Journal of Child and Adolescent Substance Abuse, 12*(1), 1–26.

Crespi, T. D. (1994). Residential settings provide diverse challenges for school counselors. *School Counselor, 41*(3), 226–229.

Crespi, T. D., & Generali, M. M. (1995). Constructivist developmental theory and therapy: Implications for counseling adolescents. *Adolescence, 30* (119), 753–762.

Crick, N. R., Casas, J. F., & Mosher, M. (1997). Relational and overt aggression in preschool. *Developmental Psychology, 33,* 579–588.

Crick, N. R., & Dodge, K. A. (1994). A review and reformulation of social information-processing mechanisms in children's social adjustment. *Psychological Bulletin, 115,* 74–101.

Crisp, A. H. (1997). Anorexia nervosa as a flight from growth: Assessment and treatment based on the model. In D. M. Garner & P. E. Garfinkel (Eds.), *Handbook of treatment for eating disorders* (2nd ed., pp. 248–277). New York: Guilford Press.

Crompton, M. (1992). *Children and counseling.* London: Edward Arnold.

Crosbie-Burnett, M., & Newcomer, L. L. (1990). Group counseling children of divorce: The effects of a multimodal intervention. *Journal of Divorce, 13*(3), pp. 69–78.

Crouter, A. C., & Bumpus, M. F. (2001). Linking parents' work stress to children's and adolescents' psychological adjustment. *Current Directions in Psychological Science, 10*(5), 156–159.

Csikszentmihalyi, M. (1991) *Flow: The psychology of optimal experience.* New York: HarperCollins.

Cummings, E. M., Ballard, M., & El-Sheikh, M. (1991). Responses of children and adolescents to interadult anger as a function of gender, age, and model of expression. *Merrill-Palmer Quarterly, 37*, 543–560.

Cummings, E. M., & Cicchetti, D. (1990). Toward a transactional model of relations between attachment and depression. In M. Greenberg, D. Cicchetti, & E. M. Cummings (Eds.), *Attachment in the preschool years: Theory, research and intervention* (pp. 339–372). Chicago: University of Chicago Press.

Cummings, E. M., & Davies, P. (1994). *Children and marital conflict: The impact of family dispute and resolution.* New York: Guilford Press.

Cummings, N. A., & Wiggings, J. G. (2001). A collaborative primary care/behavioral health model for the use of psychotropic medication with children and adolescents: The report of a national retrospective study. *Issues in Interdisciplinary Care, 3*(2), pp. 121–128.

Cushman, T. P., & Johnson, T. B. (2001). Understanding "inattention" in children and adolescents. *Ethical Human Sciences & Services, 3*(2), 107–125.

Dadds, M. R., & Barrett, P. M. (2001). Psychological management of anxiety disorders in childhood. *Journal of Child Psychology and Psychiatry and Allied Disciplines, 42*(8), 999–1011.

Dahl, E. K., Cohen, D. J., & Provence, S. (1986). Clinical and multivariate approaches to the nosology of pervasive developmental disorders. *Journal of the American Academy of Child Psychiatry, 25*(2), 170–180.

Dare, C., & Eisler, E. (1997). Family therapy for anorexia nervosa. In D. G. Garner & P. E. Garfinkel (Eds.), *Handbook of treatment for eating disorders* (2nd ed., pp. 307–324). New York: Guilford Press.

Dare, C., & Scmukler, G. (1991). The family therapy of short history early onset anorexia nervosa. In D. B. Woodside & L. Shekter-Wolfson (Eds.), *Family approaches to eating disorders* (pp. 25–47). Washington, DC: American Psychiatric Press.

Darvishpour, M. (2002). Immigrant women challenge the role of men: How the changing power relationship within Iranian families in Sweden intensifies family conflict after immigration. *Journal of Comparative Family Studies, 33*(2), 271–302.

Daveson, B. A., & Kennelly, J. (2000). Music therapy in palliative care for hospitalized children and adolescents. *Journal of Palliative Care, 16*(1), 35–38.

Davies, E. M., & Cummings, E. M. (1994). Marital conflict and child adjustment: An emotional security hypotheses. *Psychological Bulletin, 116*, 387–411.

Davis, B., Hops, H., Alpert, A., & Sheeber, L. (1998). Child responses to parent conflict and their effect on adjustment: A study of triadic relations. *Journal of Family Psychology, 12*, 163–177.

Davis, B., Sheeber, L., Hops, H., & Tildesley, E. (2000). Adolescent responses to depressive parental behaviors in problem-solving interactions: Implications for depressive symptoms. *Journal of Abnormal Child Psychology, 28*(5), 451–468.

Davis, L., & Siegel, L. J. (2000). Posttraumatic stress disorder in children and adolescents: A review and analysis. *Clinical Child and Family Psychology Review, 3*(3), 135–154.

Dayan, J., Doyle, A-B., & Markiewicz, D. (2001). Social support networks and self-esteem of idocentric and allocentric children and adolescents. *Journal of Social and Personal Relationships, 18*(6), 767–784.

Deater-Deckard, K., Dodge, K. A., Bates, J. E., & Petitt, G. S. (1996). Physical discipline among African American and European American mothers: Links to children's externalizing behaviors. *Child Development, 32,* 1065–1072.

De-Bellis, M. D. (2002). Developmental traumatology: A contributory mechanism for alcohol and substance abuse disorders. *Psychoneuroendocrinology, 27*(1–2), 155–170.

De Groot, A., Koot, H. M., & Verhulst, F. C. (1994). Cross-cultural generalizability of the Child Behavior Checklist cross-informant syndromes. *Psychological Assessment, 6,* 225–230.

Derisleyl, J., & Reynolds, S. (2000). The transtheoretical stages of change as a predictor of premature termination, attendance, and alliance in psychotherapy. *British Journal of Clinical Psychology, 39*(4), 371–382.

Devine, P. G., & Elliot, A. J. (1995). Are racial stereotypes really fading? The Princeton trilogy revisited. *Personality and Social Psychology Bulletin, 21,* 1139–1150.

Dietrich, K. N., Ris, M. D., Succop, P. A, Berger, O. G., & Bornschein, R. I. (2001). Early exposure to lead and juvenile delinquency. *Neurotoxicology and Teratology, 23*(6), 511–518.

Dishion, T. J., & Patterson, G. R. (1999). Model building in developmental psychopathology: A pragmatic approach to understanding and intervention. *Journal of Clinical Child Psychology, 28,* 502–512.

Dodge, K. A. (1993). Social-cognitive mechanisms in the development of conduct disorder and depression. *Annual Review of Psychology, 44,* 559–584.

Dodge, K. A., Pettit. G. S., & Bates, J. E. (1994). Socialization mediators of the relation between socioeconomic status and child conduct problems. *Child Development, 65,* 649–655.

Dodge, K. A., Pettit, G. S., McClaskey, C. L., & Brown, M. M. (1986). Social competence in children. *Monographs of the Society for Research in Child Development, 51,* 1–85.

Doherty, W. J., & Allen, W. (1994). Family functioning and parental smoking as predictors of adolescent cigarette use: A six-year prospective study. *Journal of Family Psychology, 8*(3), 347–353.

Donoghue, K. (1994). The impact of the termination of brief psychotherapy, and its implications for counseling practice. *Counseling Psychology Review, 9,* 9–12.

Dornbusch, S. M., Ritter, P. L., Liederman, P. H., Roberts, D. F., & Fraleigh, M. (1987). The relation of parenting style to adolescent school performance. *Child Development, 58,* 1244–1257.

Dunlap, G., & Koegel, R. L. (1999). Welcoming editorial. *Journal of Positive Behavioral Intervention, 1,* 2–3.

Dunn, J., O'Connor, T., & Levy, I. (2002). Out of the picture: A study of family drawings by children from step-, single-parent, and non-step families. *Journal of Clinical Child and Adolescent Psychology, 31*(4), 505–512.

Durlak, J. A., Rubin, L., & Kahng, R. D. (2001). Cognitive behavioral therapy for children and adolescents with externalizing problems. *Journal of Cognitive Psychotherapy, 15*(3), 38–194.

Egeland, B., Yates, T., Appleyard, K., & van Dulmen, M. (2002). The long-term consequences of maltreatment in the early years: A developmental pathway model to antisocial behavior. *Children's Services, Social Policy, Research, & Practice, 5*(4), 249–260.

Elkind, D. (1991). Development in early childhood. *Elementary School Guidance & Counseling, 26*(1), 12–21.

Elliot, D. S., Hamburg, B., & Williams, K. R. (1998). Violence in American schools: An overview. In D. S. Elliot, B. Hamburg, & K. R. Williams (Eds.), *Violence in American Schools.* New York: Cambridge University Press.

Elliott, D, S , Wilson, W. J., Huizinga, D., Sampson, R. J., Elliott, A., & Rankin, B. (1996). The effects of neighborhood disadvantage on adolescent development. *Journal of Crime and Delinquency, 33,* 389–426.

Elliott, F. A. (2000). A neurological perspective of violent behavior. In D. H. Fishbein, (Ed.), *The science, treatment, and prevention of antisocial behaviors: Application to the criminal justice system.* Kingston, NJ: Civic Research Institute.

Emery, R. E., & O'Leary, K. D. (1984). Marital discord and child behavior problems in a nonclinic sample. *Journal of Abnormal Child Psychology, 12,* 411–420.

Emmanuel, R., Colloms, A., Mendelsohn, A., & Muller, H. (1990). Psychotherapy with hospitalized children with leukemia: Is it possible? *Journal of Child Psychotherapy, 16*(2), 21–37.

Engel, G. L. (1962). *Psychological development in health and disease.* Philadelphia: Saunders.

Enright, J. (1975). One step forward: Situational techniques for altering motivation for therapy. *Psychotherapy: Theory, Research and Practice, 12*(4), 344–347.

Eriksen, K., & McAuliffe, G. (Eds.). (2001). *Teaching counselors and therapists: Constructivist and developmental course design.* Westport, CT: Bergin & Garvey.

Erikson, E. (1980). *Identity and the life cycle.* New York: Norton.

Erikson, E. H. (1963). *Childhood and society* (2nd ed.). New York: Norton.

Erikson, E. H. (1966). Eight ages of man. *International Journal of Psychiatry,* Vol. 2(3), pp. 281–300.

Escovar, P. L., & Lazarus, P. J. (1982). Cross-cultural child-rearing practices: Implications for school psychology. *School Psychology International, 3,* 143–148.

Espelage, D. L., Bosworth, K., & Simon, T. R. (2000). Examining the social context of bullying behavior in early adolescence. *Journal of Counseling and Development, 78,* 326–333.

Essau, C. A., & Petermann, F. (Eds.) (1999). *Depressive disorders in children and adolescence: Epidemiology, risk factors, and treatment.* Northvale, NJ: Jason Aronson.

Evans, R. C. (1988). In C. J. Kestenbaum & D. T. Williams (Eds.), *Handbook of assessment of children and adolescents* (Vols. 1 & 2, pp. 1066–1083). New York: New York University Press.

Ezpeleta, L., Keeler, G., Alantin, E., Costello, E. J., & Angold, A. (2001). Epidemiology of psychiatric disability in childhood and adolescence. *Journal of Child Psychology and Psychiatry and Allied Disciplines, 42*(7), 901–914.

Fagan, J. (1998). Correlates of low-income African American and Puerto Rican fathers' involvement with their children. *Journal of Black Psychology, 24,* 351–367.

Falicov, C. J. (1995). Training to think culturally: A multidimensional comparative framework. *Family Process, 34,* pp. 373–388.

Falicov, C. J. (1983). *Cultural perspectives in family therapy.* Rockville, MD: Aspen Publications.

Faraone, S. V., Biederman, J., Kennan, K., & Tsuang, M. T. (1991). Separation of DSM-III attention deficit disorder and conduct disorder: Evidence from a family-genetic study of American child psychiatric patients. *Psychological Medicine, 21,* 109–121.

Farmer, E. M. Z., Burns, B. J., Chapman, M. V., Phillips, S. D., Angold, A., & Costello, E. J. (2001). Use of mental health services by youth in contact with social services. *Social Service Review, 75*(4), 605–627.

Fein, D., Pennington, B., Markowitz, P., Braverman, M., & Waterhouse, L. (1986). Toward a neuropsychological model of infantile autism: Are the social deficits primary? *Journal of American Academy of Child Psychiatry, 25,* 198–212.

Feldman, T. (2002). Technical considerations when handling questions in the initial phase of psychotherapy. *Journal of Contemporary Psychotherapy, 32*(2–3), 213–227.

Feldman-Summers, S., & Pope, K. S. (1994). The experience of "forgetting" childhood abuse: A national survey of psychologists. *Journal of Consulting and Clinical Psychology, 62,* 636–639.

Felts, W. M., Parillo, A. V., Chenier, T., & Dunn, E. (1996). Adolescents' perceptions of relative weight and self-reported weight loss activities: Analysis of YRBS national data. *Journal of Adolescent Health, 18,* 20–26.

Fendrich, M., Warner, V., & Weissman, M. M. (1990). Family risk factors, parental depression, and psychopathology in offspring. *Developmental Psychology, 26,* 40–50.

Fergusson, D. M., Lynskey, M. T., & Horwood, L. J. (1996). Childhood sexual abuse and psychiatric disorder in young adulthood: Prevalence of sexual abuse and factors associated with sexual abuse. *Journal of the American Academy of Child and Adolescent Psychiatry, 35,* 1355–1364.

Filipek, P. A., Accardo, P. J., & Baranek, G. T. (1999). The screening and diagnosis of autistic spectrum disorders. *Journal of Autism and Developmental Disorders, 29,* 439–484.

Fincham, F., Grych, J., & Osborne, L. (1994). Does marital conflict cause child maladjustment? Directions and challenge for longitudinal research. *Journal of Family Psychology, 8,* 128–140.

Fine, M. A., Voydanoff, P., & Donnelly, B. W. (1993). Relations between parental control and warmth and child well-being in stepfamilies. *Journal of Family Psychology, 7*(2), 222–232.

Fisher, T. A., Matthews, L. G., Robinson Kurpius, S. E., & Burke, K. L. (2001). Effects of client race-ethnicity on perception of counselor trainees: Study 1 and Study 2. *Education and Supervision, 41*(1), 3–12.

Flannery, D. J., Singer, M. I., & Wester, K. (2001). Violence exposure, psychological trauma, and suicide risk in a community sample of dangerously violent adolescents. *Journal of the American Academy of Child and Adolescent Psychiatry, 40*(4), 435–442.

Flynn, C. P. (2000). Why family professionals can no longer ignore violence toward animals. *Family Relations: Interdisciplinary Journal of Applied Family Studies, 49*(1), 87–95.

Forehand, R., & Nousiainen, S. (1993). Maternal and paternal parenting: Critical dimensions in adolescent functioning. *Journal of Family Psychology, 7,* 213–221.

Foreman, J., & Bernet, W. (2000). A misunderstanding regarding duty to report suspected abuse. *Child Maltreatment, 5*(2), 190–196.

Francis, G., Last, C. G., & Strauss, C. C. (1987). Expression of separation anxiety disorder: The roles of age and gender. *Child Psychiatry and Human Development, 18,* 82–89.

Francis, G., Last, C. G., & Strauss, C. C. (1992). Avoidant disorder and social phobia in children and adolescents. *Journal of the American Academy of Child and Adolescent Psychiatry, 31,* 1086–1089.

Frankenberg, W. K., Camp, B. W., & Van Natta, P. A. (1971). The Denver developmental screening test. *Validity of child development, 42,* 475–485.

Frazier, J. A., Doyle, R., Chiu, S., & Coyle, J. T. (2002). Treating a child with Asperger's disorder and co-morbid bipolar disorder. *American Journal of Psychiatry, 159*(1), 13–21.

Freedner, N., Freed, L. Y., Yang, Y. W., & Austin, S. B. (2002). Dating violence among gay, lesbian, and bisexual adolescents: Results from a community survey. *Journal of Adolescent Health, 31,* 469–474.

Freud, S. (1963). Analysis terminable and interminable. In P. Rieff (Ed.), *Sigmund Freud: Therapy and technique* (pp. 233–271). New York: Collier. (Original work published 1937).

Frick, P. J., Lahey, B. B., & Loeber, R. (1992). Familial risk factors to oppositional defiant disorder and conduct disorder: Parental psychopathology and maternal parenting. *Journal of Consulting and Clinical Psychology, 60,* 49–55.

Frick, P. J., Lahey, B. B., Loeber, R., & Stouthamer-Loeber, M. (1991). Oppositional defiant disorder and conduct disorder in boys: Patterns of behavioral covariation. *Journal of Clinical Child Psychology, 20,* 202–208.

Frick, P. J., Lahey, B. B., Loeber, R., & Stouthamer-Loeber, M. (1992). Familial risk factors to oppositional defiant disorder and conduct disorder: Parental psychopathology and maternal parenting. *Journal of Consulting and Clinical Psychology, 60,* 49–55.

Friedlander, M. L., & Heatherington, L. (1989). Analyzing relational control in family therapy interviews. *Journal of Counseling Psychology, 36,* 139–148.

Friedlander, M. L., Larney, L. C., Skau, M., Hotaling, M., Cutting, M. L., & Schwam, M. (2000). Bicultural identification: Experience of internationally adopted children and their parents. *Journal of Counseling Psychology, 47*(2), 187–198.

Friedman, R. C., &: Lilling, A. A. (1996). An empirical study of the beliefs of psychoanalysts about scientific and clinical dimensions of male homosexuality. *Journal of Homosexuality, 32,* 79–89.

Frisk, M. A. (1999). Complex background in children and adolescents with psychiatric disorders: Developmental delay, dyslexia, heredity, slow cognitive processing and adverse social factors in a multifactorial entirety. *European Child and Adolescent Psychiatry, 8*(3), 225–236.

Fristad, M. A., Glickman, A. R., Verducci, J. S., Tteare, M., Weller, E. B., & Weller, R. A. (1998). Study V: Children's interviews for psychiatric syndromes (ChIPS): Psychometrics in two community samples. *Journal of Child and Adolescent Psychopharmacology, 8*(4), 237–245.

Frith, V. (1989). A new look at language and communication in autism. *British Journal of Disorders of Communication, 24,* 123–150.

Fuligni, A. J., Yip, T., & Tseng, V. (2002). The impact of family obligation on the daily activities and psychological well-being of Chinese American adolescents. *Child Development, 73*(1), 302–315.

Fromm-Reichman, F. (1950). *Principles of intensive psychotherapy.* Chicago: University of Chicago Press.

Fromm-Reichmann, F. (1949). Notes on the personal and professional requirements of a psychotherapist. *Psychiatry: Journal for the Study of Interpersonal Processes, 12,* 361–378.

Fuertes, J. N., & Brobst, K. (2002). Clients' ratings of counselor multicultural competency. *Cultural Diversity and Ethnic Minority Psychology, 8,* 214–223.

Gaertner, L., & Foshee, V. (1999). Commitment and the perpetration of relationship violence. *Personal Relationships, 6,* 227–239.

Gamst, G., Dana, R. H., Der-Karabetian, A., & Kramer, T. (2001). Asian American mental health clients: Effects of ethnic match and age on global assessment and visitation. *Journal of Mental Health Counseling, 23*(1), 57–68.

Garb, H. N., Wood, J. M., Lilienfeld, S. O., & Nezworski, M. J. (2002). Effective use of projective techniques in clinical practice: Let data help with selection and interpretation. *Professional Psychology: Research and Practice, 33*(5), 454–463.

Garber, J., Quiggle, N. L., Panak, W., & Dodge, K. A. (1991). Aggression and depression in children: Comorbidity, specificity, and cognitive processing. In D. Cicchetti & S. Toth (Eds.), *Internalizing and externalizing expressions of dysfunction* (pp. 225–264). Hillsdale, NJ: Erlbaum.

Garcia, J. A., & Weisz, J. R. (2002). When youth mental health care stops: Therapeutic relationship and other reasons for ending youth outpatient treatment. *Journal of Consulting and Clinical Psychology, 70,* 439–443.

Garcia, M. M., Shaw, D. S., Winslow, E. B., & Yaggi, K. E. (2000). Destructive sibling conflict and the development of conduct problems in young boys. *Developmental Psychology, 36,* 44–53.

Gardner, R. (1983). *Frames of mind.* New York: Basic.

Gardner, R. A., (1975). *Talking, feeling, and doing game.* New York: Creative Therapeutics.

Gardner, R. A. (1984). Counseling children in stepfamilies. *Elementary School Guidance & Counseling, 19*(1), 40–49.

Gardner, R. A. (2002). Mutual storytelling. In C. A. Schaefer & A. Cangelosi (Eds.), *Play therapy techniques* (2nd ed., pp. 276–280). Northvale, NJ: Jason Aronson Publishing.

Garfield, S. L. (1994). Research on client variables in psychotherapy. In A. E. Bergin & S. L. Garfield (Eds.), *Handbook of psychotherapy and behavior change* (4th ed., pp. 190–228). New York: John Wiley.

Garfinkle, E. M., & Morin, S. F. (1978). Psychologists' attitudes toward homosexual psychotherapy clients. *Journal of Social Issues, 34,* 101–112.

Garmezy, R. (1991). In A. L. Berman & D. Jobes. (1991). *Adolescent suicide: Assessment and intervention.* Washington, DC: American Psychological Association (p. 106, 152).

Garner, D. (2002). *Eating Disorder Inventory–2(EOI–2).* Psychological Assessment Resources. Lutz, FL.

Garnet, K. E., Levy, K. N., Mattanah, J. J. F., Edell, W. S., McGlashan, T. H. (1994). Borderline personality disorder in adolescents: Ubiquitous or specific? *American Journal of Psychiatry, 151,* 1380–1382.

Garnets, L., Hancock, K. A., Cochran, S. D., Goodchilds, J., & Peplau, L. A. (1991). Issues in psychotherapy with lesbians and gay men: A survey of psychologists. *American Psychologist, 46,* 964–972.

Gartner, R. B. (1995). The relationship between interpersonal psychoanalysis and family therapy. In M. Lionells, J. Fiscalini, C. Mann, & D. Stern (Eds.), *Handbook of interpersonal psychoanalysis* (pp. 793–822). New York: Analytic Press.

Ge, X., Brody, G. H., Conger, R. D., Simons, R. L., & Murry, V. M. (2002). Contextual amplification of pubertal transition effects on deviant peer affiliation and externalizing behavior among African American children. *Developmental Psychology, 38*(1), 42–54.

Geldard, K., & Geldard, D. (1997). *Counseling children: A practical introduction.* Thousand Oaks, CA: Sage Publications.

Geller, B., Fox, L. W., & Clark, K. A. (1994). Rate and predictors of prepubertal bipolarity during follow-up of 6- to 12-year-old children. *Journal of American Academy of Child and Adolescent Psychiatry, 33,* 461–468.

Geller, B., Sun, K., Zimmerman, B., Luby, J., Frazier, J., & Williams, M. (1995). Complex and rapid cycling in bipolar children and adolescents: A preliminary study. *Journal of Affective Disorders, 34,* 259–268.

Gelso, C. J., Fassinger, R. E., Gomez, M. J., & Latts, M. G. (1995). Countertransference reactions to lesbian clients: The role of homophobia, counselor gender, and countertransference management. *Journal of Counseling Psychology, 42,* 356–364.

Gencoz, T., Voelz, Z. R., Gencoz, F., Pettit, J. W., & Joiner, T. E., Jr. (2001). Specificity of information processing styles to depressive symptoms in youth psychiatric inpatients. *Journal of Abnormal Child Psychiatry, 29*(3), 255–265.

Gentry, C. S. (1986). Social distance regarding male and female homosexuals. *Journal of Social Psychology, 127,* 199–208.

Gershon, J. (2002). A meta-analytic review of gender differences in ADHD. *Journal of Attention Disorders, 5*(3), 143–154.

Gerstel, C. J., Feraios, A. J., & Herdt, G. (1989). Widening circles: An ethnographic profile of a youth group. *Journal of Homosexuality, 17,* 75–92.

Giaconia, R. M., Reinherz, H. Z., Silverman, A. B., & Pakiz, B., Frost, A. K., & Cohen, E. (1995). Traumas and posttraumatic stress disorder in a community population of older adolescents. *Journal of the American Academy of Child and Adolescent Psychiatry, 34,* 1369–1380.

"Giant steps for autistic kids: Play therapy helps children overwhelmed by sounds and touch." *Maclean's, 111:* 66.

Gilligan, C. (1982). *In a different voice: Psychological theory and women's development.* Cambridge, MA: Harvard University Press.

Gilligan, C. (1994). In a different voice: Women's conceptions of self and morality. In B. Puka (Ed.), *Caring voices and women's moral frames* (pp. 1–37). Cambridge, MA: Harvard University Press.

Ginsberg, G. S., & Schlossberg, M. C. (2002). Family-based treatment of childhood anxiety disorders. *International Review of Psychiatry, 4*(2), 143–154.

Gittelman, R., Mannuzza, S., Shenker, R., & Bonagure, N. (1985). Hyperactive boys almost grown up: Psychiatric status. *Archives of General Psychiatry, 42,* 937–947.

Gittelman-Klein, R. (1988). Childhood anxiety disorders. In C. J. Kestenbaum & D. T. Williams (Eds.), *Handbook of clinical assessment of children and adolescents* (Vol. II., pp. 722–742). New York: New York University Press.

Glick, I. D., Clarkin, J. F., Spencer, J. H., Haas, G. I., Lewis, A. B., Peyser, J., DeMaine, N., Good-Ellis, M., Harris, E., & Lestelle, V. (1985). A controlled evaluation of inpatient family intervention. *Archives of General Psychiatry, 42,* 882–886.

Gold, J. M., Carpenter, C., Randoloph, C., Goldberg, T. E., & Weinberger, D. R. (1997). Auditory working memory and Wisconsin Card Sorting Test performance in schizophrenia. *Archives of General Psychiatry, 54,* 159–165.

Goldfried, M. R. (2002). A cognitive-behavioral perspective on termination. *Journal of Psychotherapy Integration, 12*(3), 364–372.

Goldman, S. J., D'Angelo, E. J., & DeMaso, D. R. (1993). Psychopathology in the families of children and adolescents with borderline personality disorder. *American Journal of Psychiatry, 150,* 1723–1726.

Goldman, S. J., D'Angelo, F. J., DeMaso, D. R., & Mezzacappa, E. (1992). Physical and sexual abuse histories among children with borderline personality disorder. *American Journal of Psychiatry, 149,* 1723–1726.

Goldsmith, H. H., Buss, K. A., & Lemery, K. S. (1997). Toddler and childhood temperament: Expanded context, stronger genetic evidence, new evidence for importance of environment. *Developmental Psychology, 33,* 891–905.

Goldsmith, H. H., Gottesman, H., & Lemery, K. S. (1997). Epigenetic approaches to developmental psychopathology. *Developmental Psychopathology, 9,* 493–498.

Goldstein, M. J. (1992). Commentary on "Expressed emotion in depressed patients and their partners." *Family Process, 31,* pp. 172–174.

Goleman, D. (1995). *Emotional intelligence.* New York: Bantam Doubleday Dell.

Goodman, A. (1989). The depression of the narcissistic personality. *Contemporary Psychotherapy Review, 30,* 259–266.

Goodman, G. S., Rudy, L., Bottoms, B., & Aman, C. (1990). Children's concerns and memory: Issues of ecological validity in the study of children's eyewitness testimony. In R. Fivush & J. A. Hudson (Eds.), *Knowing and remembering in young children* (pp. 249–284). Cambridge, England: Cambridge University Press.

Goodwin, F. K., & Jamison, K. R. (1990). *Manic depressive illness.* New York: Oxford Press.

Goodwin, R. (1989). Infantile autism: A syndrome of multiple primary deficits? *Journal of Autism and Developmental Disorders, 19,* 409–424.

Goodyer, I., Wright, C., & Altham, P. (1990). The friendships and recent life events of anxious and depressed school-aged children. *British Journal of Psychiatry, 156,* 689–698.

Gopaul-McNicol, S. (1995). Examining psychotherapeutic and psychosocial factors in working with immigrant families. *Journal of Social Distress and the Homeless, 4*(2), 143–155.

Gotlib, I. H.; & Hammen, C. L. (1992). *Psychological aspects of depression: Toward a cognitive-interpersonal integration.* London: Wiley.

Gottlieb, M. C. (1993). Avoiding exploitive dual relationships: A decision-making model. *Psychotherapy, 30*(1), 41–48.

Graham, J. R. (1990). *MMPI-2: Assessing Personality and Psychopathology.* New York: Oxford University Press.

Gray, C. (1995). Teaching children with autism to "read" social situations. In K. A. Quill (Ed.), *Teaching children with autism: Strategies to enhance communication socialization.* Albany, NY: Delmar.

Gray, C. (1996). Social stories and comic strip conversations: Unique methods to improve social understanding [Videotape]. Arlington, TX: Future Horizons.

Greenberg, H. S., & Keane, A. (2001). Risk factors for chronic post-traumatic stress symptoms and behavior problems in children and adolescents following a home fire. *Child and Adolescent Social Work Journal, 18*(3), 205–221.

Greenberg, L. S. (2002). Termination of experiential therapy. *Journal of Psychotherapy Integration, 12*(3), 358–363.

Greenson, R. R. (1965). The working alliance and the transference neurosis. *Psychoanalytic Quarterly, 32,* 155–179.

Grier, W. H., & Cobbs, P. M. (1980). *Black rage.* New York: Basic Books.

Grimmer, A., & Tribe, R. (2001). Counseling psychologists' perceptions of the impact of mandatory personal therapy on professional development—an exploratory study. *Counselling Psychology Quarterly, 14*(4), 287–301.

Grolnick, W. S., & Farkas, M. (2002). Parenting and the development of children's self-regulation. In M. H. Bornstein (Ed.), *Handbook of parenting* (Vol. 5). Mahwah, NJ: Lawrence Erlbaum.

Grolnick, W. S., Kurowski, C. O., & Gurland, S. T. (1999). Family processes and the development of children's self-regulation. *Educational Psychologist, 34*(1), 3–14.

Gross, D., Fogg, L., & Tucker, S. (1995). The efficacy of parent training for promoting positive parent-toddler relationships. *Research in Nursing and Health, 22,* 15–25.

Gross, D., Fogg, L., Webster-Stratton, C., Garvey, C., Julion, W., & Grady, J. (2003). Parent training of toddlers in day care in low-income urban communities. *Journal of Consulting and Clinical Psychology, 71,* 261–278.

Guntrip, H. (1975). My experience of analysis with Fairbairn and Winnicott: How complete a result does psycho-analytic therapy achieve? *International Review of Psycho-Analysis, 2,* 145–156.

Guzder, J., Paris, P., Zelkowitz, P., & Feldman, R. (1999). Psychological risk factors for borderline pathology in school-age children. *Journal of the American Academy of Child and Adolescent Psychiatry, 38,* 206–212.

Gysbers, N. (1999). *Missouri Comprehensive Guidance Program.* Columbia, MO: Instructional Materials Laboratory.

Haas, L. J., & Malouf, J. L. (1989). *Keeping up the good work: A practitioner's guide to mental health ethics.* New York: Professional Resource Exchange.

Hadwin, J., Baron-Cohen, S., Howlin, P., & Hill, K. (1997). Does teaching theory of mind have an effect on the ability to develop conversation in children with autism? *Journal of Autism and Developmental Disorders, 27,* 519–537.

Hagiwara, T., & Myles, B. S. (1999). A multimedia social story intervention: Teaching skills to children with autism. *Focus on Autism and Other Developmental Disabilities, 14,* 82–95.

Hall, A. S., Lin, M-J. (1995). Theory and practice of children's rights: Implications for mental health counselors. *Journal of Mental Health Counseling, 17*(1), 63–80.

Hall, T. M., Kaduson, H. G., & Schaefer, C. E. (2002). Fifteen effective play therapy techniques. *Professional Psychology: Research and Practice, 33*(6), 515–522.

Hamm, J. V. (2002). Do birds of a feather flock together? The variable bases for African American, Asian American, and European American adolescents' selection of similar friends. *Developmental Psychology, 36,* 209–219.

Hammen, C., & Rudolph, K. D. (1996). Childhood depression. In E. J. Mash & B. A. Barkley (Eds.), *Child psychopathology* (pp. 153–195). New York: Guilford Press.

Hampton, R. (1991). Child abuse in the African American community. In J. Everett, S. Chipungu, & B. Leashore (Eds.), *Child welfare: An Africentric perspective* (pp. 220–246). Rutgers, NJ: Rutgers University Press.

Handelsman, M. M., & Martin, W. L. (1992). Effects of readability on the impact and recall of written informed consent material. *Professional Psychology: Research and Practice, 23,* 500–503.

Hardy, K. W., & Laszloffy, T. A. (1992). Training racially sensitive family therapists: Context, content, & contact. *Families in Society, 73,* 364–370.

Harris, M. P. (Ed.) (2000). *School experiences of gay and lesbian youth: The invisible minority.* New York: Harrington Park Press.

Harrison, C., & Sofronoff, K. (2002). ADHD and parental psychological distress: Role of demographics, child behavioral characteristics and parental cognitions. *Journal of the American Academy of Child and Adolescent Psychiatry, 41,* 703–711.

Harwood, R. L. (1992). The influence of culturally derived values on Anglo and Puerto Rican mothers' perceptions of attachment behavior. *Child Development, 63,* 822–839.

Harvard Mental Health Letter. (2002). Depression in children: Parts I & II.

Harvard Mental Health Letter. (2002). Treatment of bulimia and binge eating, *19*(1).

Hauck, M., Fein, D., Waterhouse, L., & Feinstein, C. (1995). Social initiations by autistic children to adults and other children. *Journal of Autism and Developmental Disorders, 25,* 579–595.

Hawley, K. M. & Weisz, J. R. (2003). Child, parent, and therapist (dis)agreement on target problems in outpatient therapy: The therapist's dilemma and its implications. *Journal of Consulting and Clinical Psychology, 71,* 62–70.

Hayes, J. A., & Gelso, C. J. (1993). Male counselors' discomfort with gay and HIV-infected clients. *Journal of Counseling Psychology, 40,* pp. 86–93.

Hazler, R. J. (1996). *Breaking the cycle of violence: Interventions for bullying and victimization.* Bristol, PA: Accelerated Development.

Hazler, R. J. (1997). Bystanders: An overlooked factor in peer-on-peer abuse. *Journal for the Professional Counselor, 11,* 11–21.

Hazler, R. J. (1998). Promoting personal investment in systemic approaches to school violence. *Education, 119,* 11–21.

Hazler, R. J., & Carney, J. V. (2000). When victims turn aggressive: Factors in the development of deadly school violence. *Professional School Counseling, 42*(2), 105–112.

Heiney, S. P. (1991). Sibling grief: A case report. *Archives of Psychiatric Nursing, 5*(3), 121–127.

Helms, J. (1984). Toward a theoretical explanation of the effects of race on counseling: Black/White interactional model. *The Counseling Psychologist, 12,* pp. 153–165.

Henderson, P. (1994). Counseling children of parents with severe mental illness, *School Counselor, 42*(2), 147–154.

Henderson, P. A. (1987). Terminating the counseling relationship with children. *Elementary School Guidance & Counseling, 22*(2), pp. 143–148.

Hendrix, D. H. (1991). Ethics and intrafamily confidentiality in counseling with children. *Journal of Mental Health Counseling, 13*(3), 323–333.

Henggeler, S. W. (1999). Multisystemic therapy: An overview of clinical procedures, outcomes, and policy implications. *Child Psychology and Psychiatry Review, 4*(1), 2–10.

Herek, G. M. (Ed.). (1998). *Psychological perspectives on lesbian and gay issues: Vol. 4. Stigma and sexual orientation: Understanding prejudice against lesbians, gay men, and bisexuals.* Thousand Oaks, CA: Sage.

Herman, J. L., & Schatzow, E. (1987). Recovery and verification of memories of childhood sexual trauma. *Psychoanalytic Psychology, 4,* 1–4.

Herring, M., & Kaslow, N. J. (2002). Depression and attachment in families: A child-focused perspective. *Family Process, 41*(3), 494–518.

Hersoy, L. (1985). School refusal. In M. Rutter & L. Hersoy (Eds.), *Child and adolescent psychiatry* (2nd ed., pp. 388–399). Oxford, England: Blackwell.

Hibbs, E. D., & Jensen, P. S. (Eds). (1996). *Psychosocial treatments for child and adolescent disorders: Empirically based strategies for clinical practice.* Washington, DC: American Psychological Association.

Hill, A. J. (1993). Pre-adolescent dieting: Implications for eating disorders. *International Review of Psychiatry, 5,* 87–100.

Hill, A. J., & Pallin, V. (1998). Dieting awareness and self worth: Related issues in 8-year-old girls. *International Journal of Eating Disorders, 24,* 405–413.

Hill, C. E., & Knox, S. (2001). Self-disclosure. *Psychotherapy: Theory, research, practice, training, 38*(4), 413–417.

Hobday, A., & Ollier, K. (1999). *Creative therapy with children and adolescents: A British Psychological Society book.* Atascadero, CA: Impact Publishers.

Hofberg, K. (2001). Personal psychotherapy, training, and psychodrama. *Psychiatric Bulletin, 25*(5), 195–196.

Hops, H., Lewinsohn, P. M., Andrews, J. A., & Roberts, R. E. (1990). Psychosocial correlates of depressive symptomatology among high school students. *Journal of Clinical Child Psychology, 19,* 211–220.

Horne, A. M., & Sayger, T. V. (1990). *Treating conduct and oppositional defiant disorders in children.* New York: Pergamon.

Horvath, A. O., & Luborsky, L. (1993). The role of the therapeutic alliance in psychotherapy. *Journal of Consulting and Clinical Psychology, 61,* 561–573.

Hossain, Z., & Roopnarine, J. L. (1994). African American fathers' involvement with infants: Relationship to their functioning style, support, education, and income. *Infant Behavior and Development, 17,* 175–184.

Hudson, J. A. (1990). The emergence of autobiographical memory in mother-child conversation. In R. Fivush & J. A. Hudson (Eds.), *Knowing and remembering in young children* (p. 167). Cambridge, England: Cambridge University Press.

Huesmann, L. R., Moise-Titus, J., Podolski, C-L., & Eron, L. D. (2003). Longitudinal relations between children's exposure to TV violence and their aggressive and violent behavior in young adulthood: 1977–1992. *Developmental Psychology, 39,* 201–221.

Hughes, J. N., Cavell, T. A., & Grossman, P. B. (1997). A positive view of self: Risk or protection for aggressive children? *Development and Psychopathology, 9,* 75–94.

Human Rights Watch. (2001). Hatred in the hallways: Violence and discrimination against lesbian, gay, bisexual, and transgender students in U.S. schools. Retrieved from *http://www.hrw.org/reports/2001/uslgbt/toc.htm* on June 16, 2003.

Hundert, J., Cassie, J., & Johnston, N. (1988). Characteristics of emotionally disturbed children referred to day treatment, special class, outpatient, and assessment services. *Journal of Clinical Child Psychology, 17*(2), 121–130.

Hurth, J., Shaw, E., & Izeman, S. G. (1999). Areas of agreement about effective practices among programs serving young children with autism spectrum disorders. *Infant and Young Child, 12,* 17–26.

Hutchinson, R. L. (1990). Termination of counseling with children: Punishment or reward? *Journal of Mental Health Counseling, 12*(2), 228–231.

Hymel, S., Bowker, A., & Woody, E. (1993). Aggressive versus withdrawn unpopular children: Variations in peer and self-perception in multiple domains. *Child Development, 64,* 879–896.

Hymel, S., Rubin, K. H., Rowden, L., & LeMare, L. (1990). Children's peer relationships: Longitudinal predictions of internalizing and externalizing problems from middle to late childhood. *Child Development, 61,* 2004–2021.

Ialongo, N., Edelsohn, G., & Kellam, S. G. (2001). A further look at the prognostic power of young children's reports of depressed mood and feelings. *Child Development, 72*(3), 736–748.

Ialongo, N., Edelsohn, G., Werthamer-Larsson, L., Crockett, L, & Kellam, S. (1994). The significance of self-reported anxious symptoms in first-grade children. *Journal of Abnormal Psychology, 22,* 441–455.

Ialongo, N., Edelsohn, G., Werthamer-Larsson, L., Crockett, L., & Kellam, S. (1995). The significance of self-reported anxious symptoms in first-grade children: Prediction to anxious symptoms and adaptive functioning in fifth grade. *Journal of Child Psychology and Psychiatry, 36,* 427–437.

Ievers, C. E., Drotar, D., Dahms, W. T., Doershuk, C. F., & Stern, R. C. (1994). Maternal child-rearing behavior in three groups: Cystic fibrosis, insulin-dependent diabetes mellitus, and healthy children. *Journal of Pediatric Psychology, 19,* 681–687.

Ingersoll, S., & LeBoeuf, K. (1997). Reaching out to youth out of the education mainstream. *Juvenile Justice Bulletin,* 1–11.

Isley, S. L., O'Neill, R., Clatfelter, D., & Parke, R. D. (1999). Parent and child expressed affect and children's social competence: Modeling direct and indirect pathways. *Developmental Psychology, 35,* 547–560.

Ivey, A. E. (1986). *Developmental therapy: Theory into practice.* San Francisco: Jossey-Bass.

Ivey, A. E. (1991). *Developmental strategies for helpers: Individual, family, and network interventions.* Pacific Grove, CA: Brooks/Cole.

Ivey, A. E. (1999). *Developmental therapy.* North Amherst, MA: Microtraining Associates.

Ivey, A. E., Rigazio-DioGilio, S. A., & Bradford-Ivey, M. (1991). The standard cognitive developmental interview. In A. E. Ivey (Ed.), *Developmental strategies for helpers: Individual, family, and network interventions.* Pacific Grove, CA: Brooks/Cole.

Jackson, D. D. (1965). The study of the family. *Family Process, 4,* 1–20.

Jackson, S., & Bosma, H. A. (1992). Developmental research on adolescence: European perspectives for the 1990s and beyond. *British Journal of Developmental Psychology, 10*(4), 319–337.

James, W. H., West, C., Deters, K. E., Armijo, E. (2000). Youth dating violence. *Adolescence, 35,* 455–465.

Jenkins-Hall, K., & Sacco, W. (1991). Effects of client race and depression on evaluation by white therapists. *Journal of Social and Clinical Psychology, 10,* 322–333.

Johnson, B. D., Franklin, L. C., Hall, K., & Prieto, L. R. (2000). Parent training through play: Parent-child interaction therapy with a hyperactive child, *Family Journal: Counseling and Therapy for Couples and Families, 8*(2), 180–186.

Johnson, M. K., & Foley, M. A. (1984). Differentiating fact from fantasy: The reliability of children's memory. *Journal of Social Issues, 40,* 33–50.

Johnson, V., & Pandina, R. J. (1991). Effects of family environment on adolescent substance abuse, delinquency, and coping styles. *Journal of Drug and Alcohol Abuse, 17,* 171–188.

Kafantaris, V. (1995). Treatment of bipolar disorder in children and adolescents. *Journal of the American Academy of Child and Adolescent Psychiatry, 34,* 732–741.

Kagan, J. (1984). *The nature of the child.* New York: Basic Books.

Kagan, J., Reznick, J. S., & Snidman, N. (1988). Biological bases of childhood shyness. *Science, 240,* 167–171.

Kaminski, K. M., & Garber, J. (2002). Depressive spectrum disorder in high-risk adolescents: Episode, duration, and predictors of time to recovery. *Journal of the American Academy of Child and Adolescent Psychiatry, 41*(4), 410–418.

Kann, R. T., & Hanna, F. J. (2000). Disruptive behavior disorders in children and adolescents: How do girls differ from boys? *Journal of Counseling and Development, 78,* 267–274.

Kaplan, L. M., & Reich, W. (1991). *Manual to diagnostic interview for child and adolescents–revised (DICA-R).* St. Louis, MO: Washington University.

Karno, M., Jenkins, J. H., de la Selva, A., Santana, F., Telles, C., Lopez, S., & Mintz, J. (1987). Expressed emotional and schizophrenic outcome among Mexican American families. *Journal of Nervous and Mental Disease, 175,* 143–151.

Kashani, J. H., & Orvaschel, H. (1988). Anxiety disorders in mid-adolescence: A community sample. *American Journal of Psychiatry, 145,* 960–964.

Kashani, J. H., & Orvaschel, H. (1990). A community study of anxiety in children and adolescents. *American Journal of Psychiatry, 147,* 313–318.

Kaslow, N. J., Deering, C. G., & Racusin, G. R. (1994). Depressed children and their families. *Clinical Psychology Review, 14,* 39–59.

Kaslow, N. J., & Racusin, G. R. (1994). Family therapy for depression in young people. In W. M. Reynolds & H. F. Johnston (Eds.), *Handbook of depression in children and adolescents: Issues in clinical child psychology* (pp. 345–363). New York: Plenum Press.

Kaslow, N. J., Rehm, L. P., & Siegel, A. W. (1984). Social-cognitive and cognitive correlates of depression in children. *Journal of Abnormal Child Psychology, 12,* 605–620.

Kaslow, N. J., Smith, G. G., & Croft, S. S. (2000). Families with young children: A developmental-family systems perspective. In W. C. Nichols & M. A. Pace-Nichols (Eds.), *Handbook of family development and intervention* (pp. 189–207). New York: Wiley.

Kaufman, J., Birmaher, B., & Brent, D. (1997). Schedule for affective disorders and schizophrenia for school-age children–present and lifetime version (K-SADS-PL): Initial reliability and validity data. *Journal of the American Academy of Child and Adolescent Psychiatry, 36,* 980–988.

Kaufman, J., Birmaher, B., Brent, D., Rao, U., Flynn, C., & Moreci, P. (1997). Schedule for affective disorders and schizophrenia for school-age children–present and lifetime version: Initial reliability and validity data. *Journal of the American Academy of Child and Adolescent Psychiatry, 40,* 27–35.

Kazdin, A. E. (1987a). *Conduct disorders in childhood and adolescence.* Newbury Park, CA: Sage.

Kazdin, A. E. (1987b). Treatment of antisocial behavior in children: Current status and future directions. *Psychological Bulletin, 102,* 187–203.

Kazdin, A. E. (1989). Developmental psychopathology: Current research, issues, and direction. *American Psychologist, 44*(2), 180–187.

Kazdin, A. E., & Mazurick, J. L. (1994). Dropping out of child psychotherapy: Distinguishing early and late dropouts over the course of treatment. *Journal of Consulting and Clinical Psychology, 62*(5), 1069–1074.

Kearney, C. A., & Silverman, W. K. (1990). A preliminary analysis of a functional model of assessment and treatment for school refusal behavior. *Behavior Modification, 14,* 340–366.

Keat, D. B. (1990). Change in child multimodal counseling. *Elementary School Guidance & Counseling, 24*(4), 248–262.

Keat, D. B., II. (1996). Multimodal therapy with children. *Psychotherapy in Private Practice, 15*(2), 63–79.

Kegan, R. (1982). *The evolving self.* Cambridge, MA: Harvard University Press.

Keith-Spiegel, P. C., & Koocher, O. (1985). *Ethics in psychology: Professional standards and cases.* New York: Random House.

Keller, M., Beardslee, W., Dover, D., Lavori, P., Samuelson, H., & Klerman, G. (1986). Impact of severity and chronicity of parental affective illness on adaptive functioning and psychopathology in children. *Archives in General Psychiatry, 43,* 930–937.

Keller, M. B., Hirschfeld, R. M. A., Demyttaraene, K., & Baldwin, S. (2002). Optimizing outcomes in depression: Focus on antidepressant compliance. *International Clinical Psychopharmacology, 17*(6), 265–271.

Keller, M. B., Lavori, P., Wunder, J., Beardslee, W. R., Schwarts, C. E., & Roth, J. (1992). Chronic course of anxiety disorders in children and adolescents. *Journal of the American Academy of Child and Adolescent Psychiatry, 31,* 595–599.

Kenardy, J., & Ball, K. (1998). Disordered eating, weight dissatisfaction, and dieting in relation to unwanted childhood sexual experiences in a community. *Journal of Psychosomatic Research, 44,* 327–337.

Kendall, P. C. (1994). Treating anxiety disorders in children: Results of a randomized clinical trial. *Journal of Consulting and Clinical Psychology, 62,* 100–110.

Kendall, P. C. (Ed.). (2000). *Child and adolescent therapy: Cognitive-behavioral procedures* (2nd ed.). New York: Guilford Press.

Kennedy, E., Spence, S. H., & Hensley, R. (1989). An examination of the relationship between childhood depression and social competence amongst primary school children. *Journal of Child Psychology and Psychiatry, 30,* 561–573.

Kernberg, P. (1997). Personality disorders. In J. Weiner (Ed.), *American Academy of Child and Adolescent Psychiatry textbook of child and adolescent psychiatry* (3rd ed., pp. 515–533). Washington, DC: American Psychiatric Press.

Kershner, J. G., Cohen, N. J., & Coyne, J. C. (1996). Expressed emotion in families of clinically referred and nonreferred children: Toward a further understanding of the expressed emotion index. *Journal of Family Psychology, 10,* 97–106.

Kestenbaum, C. J. (1983). The borderline child at risk for major psychiatric disorder in adult life. In K. R. Robson (Ed.), *The borderline child* (pp. 49–82). New York: McGraw-Hill.

King, R., & Noshpitz, D. (1991). *Pathways of growth: Essentials of child psychiatry* (Vol. 2). New York: Wiley.

Kitchener, K. S. (1988). Dual role relationships: What makes them so problematic? *Journal of Counseling and Development, 67,* 217–221.

Kobasigawa, A. (1974). Utilization of retrieval cues by children to recall. *Child Development, 45,* 127–134.

Kohlberg, L. (1981). *The philosophy of moral development.* New York: Harper & Row.

Kong, Y., Hu, Y., & Sun, M. (2001). Behavioral problems and quality of life in children with asthma. *Chinese Journal of Clinical Psychology, 9*(3), 216–217.

Korchenderfer, B. J., & Ladd, G. W. (1997). Victimized children's responses to peers' aggression: Behaviors associated with reduced versus continued victimization. *Development and Psychopathology, 9,* 59–73.

Kotler, L. A., & Walsh, B. T. (2000). Eating disorders in children and adolescents: Pharmacological therapies. *European Child & Adolescent Psychiatry, 9*(Suppl 5), 1108–1116.

Kovacs, M. (1992). *Children's depression inventory manual.* North Tonawanda, NY: Multi-Health Systems.

Kovacs, M., & Pollock, M. (1995). Bipolar disorder and comorbid conduct disorder in childhood and adolescence. *Journal of the American Academy of Child and Adolescent Psychiatry, 34,* 715–723.

Kovalenko, P. A., Hoven, C. W., Wu, P., Wicks, J., Mandell, D. J., & Tiet, Q. (2000). Association between allergy and anxiety disorders in youth. *Australian and New Zealand Journal of Psychiatry, 35*(6), 815–821.

Kraemer, S. (1994). The promise of family therapy. *British Journal of Psychotherapy, 11*(1), 32–45.

Kreilkamp, T. (1989). *Brief intermittent therapy.* Philadelphia: Brunner-Routledge.

Kurasaki, K. S., Sue, S., Chun, C-A., & Gee, K. (2000). Ethnic minority intervention and treatment research. In J. F. Aponte & J. Wohl (Eds.). *Psychological intervention and cultural diversity* (2nd ed., pp. 234–249). Boston: Allyn & Bacon.

Kutcher, S., Marton, P., & Korenblum, M. (1990). Bipolar disorders in a community sample of older adolescents: Prevalence, phenomenology, comorbidity, and course. *Journal of the American Academy of Child and Adolescent Psychiatry, 34,* pp. 454–463.

LaFountain, R., Garner, N., & Boldosser, S. (1995). Solution-focused counseling groups for children and adolescents. *Journal of Systemic Therapies, 14*(4), 39–51.

Lahey, B. B., Loeber, R., Quay, H. C., Frick, P. J., & Grimm, J. (1992). Oppositional defiant and conduct disorders: Issues to be resolved for DSM-IV. *Journal of the American Academy for Child and Adolescent Psychiatry, 31,* 539–546.

Lahey, B. B., McBurnett, K., & Loeber, R. (2000). An attention deficit/hyperactivity disorder and oppositional defiant disorder developmental precursors to conduct disorder. In A. J. Sameroff, M. Lewis, & S. M. Miller (Eds.), *Handbook of developmental psychopathology* (2nd ed., pp. 431–446). New York: Kluwer.

Laitinen-Krispijn, S., Van Der Ende, J., Hazebrock-Kampschreur, A. A. J. M., & Verhulst, F. C. (1999). Pubertal maturation and the development of behavioural and emotional problems in early adolescence. *Acta Psychiatrica Scandinavica, 99*(1), 16–25.

Lamborn, S. D., Mounts, N. S., Steinberg, L., & Dornbusch, S. M. (1991). Patterns of competence and adjustment among adolescents from authoritative, authoritarian, indulgent, and neglectful families. *Child Development, 62,* 1049–1065.

Landreth, G. L. (2002). Therapeutic limit-setting in the play therapy relationship. *Professional Psychology: Research and Practice, 33*(6), 529–535.

Landreth, G., Baggerly, J., & Tyndall-Lind, A. (1999). Beyond adapting adult counseling skills for use with children: The paradigm shift to child-centered play therapy. *Journal of Individual Psychology, 55*(3), 272–287.

Langs, R. J. (1982). Countertransference and the process of cure. In S. Slipp (Ed.), *Curative factors in dynamic psychotherapy* (pp. 538–548). Los Altos, CA: Lange Medical Publications.

Larson, R. W. (2001). How U.S. children and adolescents spend time: What it does (and doesn't) tell us about their development. *Current Directions in Psychological Science, 10*(5), 160–164.

Larzelere, R. E., Dinges, K., Schmidt, M. D., Spellman, D. F., Criste, T. R., & Connell, P. (2001). Outcomes of residential treatment: A study of adolescent clients of Girls and Boys Town. *Child and Youth Care Forum, 30*(3), 175–185.

Lask, B., & Bryant-Waugh, R. (Eds.). (2000). *Anorexia nervosa and related eating disorders in children and adolescents.* Florence, KY: Taylor & Francis.

Last, C. G., Francis, G., Hersen, M., Kazdin, A. E., & Strauss, C. C. (1987a). Separation anxiety and school phobia: A comparison using DSM-III criteria. *American Journal of Psychiatry, 144,* 635–657.

Last, C. G., Hersen, M., Kazdin, A. E., Finkelstein, R., & Strauss, C. C. (1987b). Comparison of DSM-III separation anxiety and overanxious disorders: Demographic characteristics and patterns of comorbidity. *Journal of the American Academy of Child and Adolescent Psychiatry, 26,* 527–531.

Last, C. G., Hersen, M., Kazdin, A. E., Orvaschel, H., & Perrin, S. (1991). Anxiety disorders in children and their families. *Archives of General Psychiatry, 48,* 928–934.

Last, C. G., Perrin, S., Hersen, M., & Kazdin, A. E., (1992). DSM-IIIR anxiety disorders in children: Sociodemographic and clinical characteristics. *Journal of the American Academy of Child and Adolescent Psychiatry, 31,* 1070–1076.

Last, C. G., Perrin, S., Hersen, M., & Kazdin, A. E., (1996). A prospective study of childhood anxiety disorders. *Journal of the American Academy of Child and Adolescent Psychiatry, 35,* 1502–1510.

Lauer, C. J., Gorzewski, B., Gerlinghoff, M., Backmund, H., & Zihl, J. (1999). Neuropsychological assessments before and after treatment in patients with anorexia nervosa and bulimia nervosa. *Journal of Psychiatric Research, 33,* 129–138.

Laursen, B., Finkelstein, B. D., Townsend, B. N. (2001). A developmental meta-analysis of peer conflict resolution. *Developmental Review, 21*(4), 423–449.

Lay, B., Blanz, B., Schmidt, M. H. (2001). Effectiveness of home treatment in children and adolescents with externalizing psychiatric disorders. *European Child & Adolescent Psychiatry, 10*(Suppl 1), 80–90.

Leasel, A. M., & Axelrod, J. L. (2001). Position of the peer group's perceived organizational structure: Relation to social status and friendship. *Journal of Early Adolescence, 21*(4), 377–404.

Lee, C. M., & Hunsley, J. (2003). Evidence-based assessment of childhood mood disorders: Comment on McClure, Kubiszyn, & Kaslow (2002). *Professional Psychology: Research and Practice, 34*(1), 112–113.

Leff, J., Wig, N. N., Ghosh, A., Bedi, H., Menon, D. K., Kuipers, L., Korten, A., Emberg, G., Day, R., Satorius, N., & Jablensky, A. (1987). Influence of relatives' expressed emotion on the course of schizophrenia in Chandigarh. *British Journal of Psychiatry, 151,* 166–173.

Lefley, H. P. (2002). Ethical issues in mental health services for culturally diverse communities. In P. Backlar & D. L. Cutler (Eds.), *Ethics in community mental health care: Commonplace concerns* (pp. 3–22). New York: Kluwer Academic/Plenum Publishers.

Le Grange, D., Eisler, I., Dare, C., & Russell, G. F. (1992). Evaluation of family treatments in adolescent anorexia nervosa: A pilot study. *International Journal of Eating Disorders, 12,* 347–357.

Leondari, A., & Kiosseoglou, G. (2002). Parental, psychological control, and attachment in late adolescents and young adults. *Psychological Reports, 90* (3, Pt. 1), 1015–1030.

Levenbach, D., & Lewak, B. (1995). Immigration: Going home or going to pieces. *Contemporary Family Therapy, 17*(4), 279–394.

Levine, C. (2000). AIDS and a new generation of orphans: Is there a role for group care? *Residential Treatment for Children and Youth, 17*(3), 105–120.

Levine, J., & Noell, D. (1995). *Interventions with bereaved children.* Bristol, PA: Jessica Kingsley.

Levy, S. E., & Hyman, S. L. (2002). Alternative/complementary approaches to treatment of children with autistic spectrum disorders. *Infants and Young Children, 14*(3), 33–43.

Lewinsohn, P. M. (1974). A behavioral approach to depression. In R. Friedman & M. Katz (Eds.), *The psychology of depression: Contemporary theory and research,* (pp. 157–185). Washington, DC: Winston-Wiley.

Lewinsohn, P. M., Hops, H., Roberts, R. E., Seeley, J. R., & Andrews, J. A. (1993). Adolescent psychopathology: Prevalence and incidence of depression and other DSM-III-R disorders in high school students. *Journal of Abnormal Psychology, 102,* 133–144.

Lewinsohn, P. M., Klein, D., & Seely, J. R. (1995). Bipolar disorders in a community sample of older adolescents: Prevalence, phenomenology, comorbidity, and course. *Journal of the American Academy of Child and Adolescent Psychiatry, 34,* 454–463.

Lewinsohn, P., Rohde, P., Seeley, J., & Fischer, S. (1993). Age-cohort changes in the lifetime occurrence of depression and other mental disorders. *Journal of Abnormal Psychology, 102,* 110–120.

Lewis, D. O., Balla, D. A., & Shanok, S. S. (1979). Some evidence of race bias in the diagnosis and treatment of the juvenile offender. *American Journal of Orthopsychiatry, 49,* 53–61.

Lewis, D. O., Feldman, M., & Barrengos, A. (1986). Race, health, and delinquency. *Journal of the American Academy of Child Psychiatry, 24,* 161–167.

Lewis, M. (1995). Memory and psychoanalysis: A new look at infantile amnesia and transference. *Child and Adolescent Psychiatry, 34*(4), 405–417.

Liddle, B. J. (1995). Sexual orientation bias among advanced graduate students of counseling psychology. *Counselor Education and Supervision, 34,* 320–331.

Liddle, H. A. (1995). Conceptual and clinical dimensions of a multidimensional, multisystems engagement strategy in family-based adolescent treatment. *Psychotherapy, 33,* 39–58.

Lieb, R. (2002). Parental major depression and the risk of depression and other mental disorders in offspring: A prospective-longitudinal community study. *The Journal of The American Medical Association, 288*(2), 148–150.

Lieberman, A. F., & Zeanah, C. H. (1995). Disorders of attachment in infancy. *Child and Adolescent Psychiatric Clinics of North America, 4,* 571–588.

Lightfoot, S., & Evans, I. M. (2000). Risk factors for a New Zealand sample of sexually abusive children and adolescents. *Child Abuse and Neglect, 24,*(9), 1185–1198.

Lincoln, A. J., Bloom, D., Katz, M., & Boksenbaym, N. (1998). Neuropsychological and neurophysiological indices of auditory processing impairment in children with multiple complex developmental disorder. *Journal of the American Academy of Child and Adolescent Psychiatry, 37,* 100–112.

Lionells, M., Fiscalini, J., Mann, C. H., & Stern, D. B. (Eds.). (1995). *Handbook of interpersonal psychology.* Hillsdale, NJ: Analytic Press.

Little, S. A., & Garber, J. (1995). Aggression, depression, and stressful life events predicting peer rejection in children. *Development and Psychopathology, 7,* 845–856.

Liu, W. M., & Clay, D. L. (2002). Multicultural counseling competencies: Guidelines in working with children and adolescents. *Journal of Mental Health Counseling, 24,* 177–187.

Llyons, J. S., Terry, P., Martinovich, A., Peterson, J., & Bouska, B. (2001). Outcome trajectories for adolescents in residential treatment: A statewide evaluation. *Journal of Child and Family Studies, 10*(3), 333–345.

Lochman, J. E. (1987). Self and peer perceptions and attributional biases of aggressive and nonaggressive boys in dyadic interactions. *Journal of Consulting and Clinical Psychology, 55,* 404–410.

Lochman, J. E., & Dodge, K. A. (1998). Distorted perceptions in dyadic interactions of aggressive and nonaggressive boys: Effects on prior expectations, context, and boys' age. *Development and Psychopathology, 10,* 495–512.

Lock, J. (2001). Innovative family-based treatment for anorexia nervosa. *The Brown University Child and Adolescent Behavioral Letter, 17*(14), 1.

Lock, J., & Steiner, H. (1999). Gay, lesbian, and bisexual youth risks for emotional, physical, and social problems: Results from a community-based survey. *Journal of the American Academy of Child and Adolescent Psychiatry, 38*(3), 297–304.

Lockhart, L. L., & Wodarski, J. S. (1989). Facing the unknown: Children and adolescents with AIDS. *Social Work, 34*(3), 215–221.

Loeber, R., & Dishion, T. J. (1984). Boys who fight at home and school: Family conditions influencing cross-setting consistency. *Journal of Consulting and Clinical Psychology, 52,* 759–768.

Loeber, R., Green, S., Keenan, K., & Lahey, B. B. (1995). Which boys will fare worse? Early predictors of the onset of conduct disorder in a six-year longitudinal study. *Journal of the American Academy of Child and Adolescent Psychiatry, 34,* 499–509.

Loeber, R., Green, S. M., Lahey, B. B., Frick, P. J., & McBurnett, K. (2000). Findings on disruptive behavior disorders from the first decade of the developmental trends study. *Clinical Child and Family Psychology Review, 3,* 37–60.

Loeber, R., Lahey, B. B., & Thomas, C. (1991). Diagnostic conundrum of oppositional defiant disorder and conduct disorder. *Journal of Abnormal Psychology, 100,* 379–390.

Loeber, R., & Stouthamer-Loeber, M. (1998). Development of juvenile aggression and violence: Some common misconceptions and controversies. *American Psychologist, 53,* 242–259.

Lofgren, D. P., Bemporad, J., King, J., Lindem, K., & O'Driscoll, G. (1991). A prospective follow-up study of so-called borderline children. *American Journal of Psychiatry, 148*(11), 1541–1547.

Loftus, E. F., & Davies, G. M. (1984). Distortion in memory of children. *Journal of Social Issues, 40,* pp. 51–67.

Lopez, S., & Hernandez, P. (1986). How culture is considered in evaluation of psychopathology. *Journal of Nervous and Mental Disease, 176,* 598–606.

Lopez, S., & Nunez, J. A. (1987). Cultural factors considered in selected diagnostic criteria and interview schedules. *Journal of Abnormal Psychology, 96,* 270–272.

Lorimer, P. A., Simpson, R. L., Myles, B. S., & Ganz, J. B., (2002). The use of social stories as a preventative behavioral intervention in a home setting with a child with autism. *Journal of Positive Behavior Interventions, 4,* pp. 53–58.

Loveland, K. A., Pearson, D. A., Tunali-Kotoski, B., Ortegon, J., Gibbs, M. C. (2001). Judgments of social appropriateness by children and adolescents with autism. *Journal of Autism and Developmental Disorders, 31*(4), 367–376.

Lowenthal, D. (2002). Case studies in confidentiality. *Journal of Psychiatric Practice, 8,* 151–159.

Lowinger, R. J., & Kwok, H. (2001). Parental overprotection in Asian American children: A psychodynamic clinical perspective. *Psychotherapy, 38*(3), 319–330.

Luborsky, E. B. (2001). "No talking!": The possibility of play. *Journal of Clinical Psychoanalysis, 10*(3–4), 445–459.

Luthar, S. S., & Burack, J. A. (2000). Adolescent wellness: In the eye of the beholder? In D. Cicchetti & J. Rappaport (Eds.), *The promotion of wellness in children and adolescents* (pp. 29–57). Washington, DC: Child Welfare League of America.

Lyons, A., & Kashima, Y. (2001). The reproduction of culture: Communication processes tend to maintain cultural stereotypes. *Social Cognition, 19*(3), 372–394.

Mace, C. (2001). Personal therapy in psychiatric training. *Psychiatric Bulletin, 25*(1), 3–4.

Mahoney, G., Robinson, C., & Fewell, R. R. (2001). The effects of early motor intervention on children with down syndrome or cerebral palsy: A field-based study. *Journal of Developmental and Behavioral Pediatrics, 22*(3), 153–162.

Mahoney, M. J. (1991). *Human change processes.* Delran, NJ: Basic Books.

Maikler, V. E., Broome, M. E., Bailey, P., & Lea, G. (2001). Children's and adolescents' use of diaries for sickle cell pain. *Journal of the Society of Pediatric Nurses, 6,* pp. 161–169.

Main, M., & Solomon, J. (1986). Discovery of an insecure-disorganized/disoriented attachment pattern. In T. B. Brazelton & M. Hogman (Eds.), *Affective development in infancy* (pp. 95–124). Norwood, NJ: Ablex.

Malik, S., Sorenson, S. B., & Aneshensel, C. S. (1997). Community and dating violence among adolescents: Perpetration and victimization. *Journal of Adolescent Health, 21,* 219–302.

Mannheim, C. I., Sancillo, M., Phipps-Yonas, S., Brunnquell, D., & Somers, P. (2002). Ethical ambiguities in the practice of child clinical psychology. *Professional Psychology: Research and Practice, 33*(1), 24–29.

Mansdorf, I. J., & Lukens, E. (1987). Cognitive-behavioral psychotherapy for separation anxious children exhibiting school phobia. *Journal of the American Academy of Child and Adolescent Psychiatry, 26,* 222–225.

March, J. S., Parker, J. D. A., Sullivan, K., Stallings, P., & Conners, C. K. (1997). The multidimensional anxiety scale for children (MASC): Factor structure, reliability, and validity. *Journal of the American Academy of Child and Adolescent Psychiatry, 36*(6) pp. 554–565.

Marcia, J. (1994). Identity and psychotherapy. In Archer, S. L. (Ed.), *Interventions for adolescent identity development* (Vol. 169, pp. 29–46). Newbury Park, CA: Sage.

Marcus, B., Vollmer, T. R., Swanson, V., Roane, H. R., & Ringdahl, J. E. (2001). An experimental analysis of aggression. *Behavioral Medicine, 25*(2), 189–213.

Marlatt, G. A. (Ed.) (1998). *Harm reduction: Pragmatic strategies for managing high-risk behaviors.* New York: Guilford Press.

Martin, F., & Farnum, J. (2002). Animal-assisted therapy for children with pervasive developmental disorders. *Western Journal of Nursing Research, 24*(6), 657–670.

Mash, E. J., & Foster, S. L. (2001). Exploring analogue behavioral observation from research to clinical practice: Useful or cost-defective? *Psychological Assessment, 13,* 454–463.

Mastrosimone, W. (1999). *Bang-Bang, You're Dead.* Retrieved from *http://bangbangyouredead.com.home.html* on June 16, 2003.

Mattejat, F., Hirt, B. R., Wilken, J., Schmidt, M. H., Remschmidt, H. (2001). Efficacy of inpatient and home treatment in psychiatrically disturbed children and adolescents: Follow-up assessment of the results of a controlled treatment study. *European Child & Adolescent Psychiatry, 10,*(5), 171–179.

Matthys, W., Cuperus, J. M., & Van Engeland, H. (1999). Deficient social problem-solving in boys with ODD/CD, with ADHD, and with both disorders. *Journal of the American Academy of Child and Adolescent Psychiatry, 38,* 311–321.

Mboya, M. M. (1995). A comparative analysis of the relationship between parenting styles and self-concepts of black and white high school students. *School Psychology International, 16*(1), pp. 19–27.

McAdams, C. R., III, & Foster, V. A. (2002). The safety session: A prerequisite to progress in counseling families with physical aggressive children and adolescents. *Family Journal: Counseling and Therapy for Couples and Families, 10,* 49–56.

McClellan, J., Werry, J. S., Ayres, W., Dunne, J., Benedek, E., Bernstein, G., Gross, R. L., King, R., Leonard, H., & Licamele, W. (1997). Practice parameters for the assessment and treatment of children and adolescents with bipolar disorder. *Journal of the American Academy of Child and Adolescent Psychiatry, 36*(10), 1578–1598.

McClellan, J. M., Werry, J. S., & Ham, M. (1993). A follow-up study of early onset psychosis: Comparison between outcome diagnoses of schizophrenia, mood disorders, and personality disorders. *Journal of Autism and Developmental Disorders, 23,* 243–262.

McClure, E. B., Kubiszyn, T., & Kaslow, N. J. (2002). Advances in the diagnosis and treatment of childhood mood disorders. *Professional Psychology: Research and Practice, 33*(2), 125–134.

McClure, E. B., Kubiszyn, T., & Kaslow, N. J. (2003). Evidenced-based assessment of childhood mood disorders: Reply to Lee & Humsley. *Professional Psychology: Research and Practice, 34*(1), 113–114.

McCullough, L., Winston, A., Farber, B. A., & Porter, F. (1991). The relationship of patient-therapist interaction to outcome in brief psychotherapy. *Psychotherapy, 28*(4), 525–533.

McDermott, J. F., Werry, J., Petti, T., Combrinck-Graham, L., & Char, W. F. (1989). Anxiety disorders of childhood or adolescence. In T. B. Karasu (Ed.), *Treatments of psychiatric disorders* (Vol. I, pp. 401–446). Washington, DC: American Psychiatric Association.

McDougall, C. (2002). Rogers's person-centered approach: Consideration for use in multicultural counseling. *Journal of Humanistic Psychology, 42*(2), 48–65.

McFarlane, A. H., Bellissimo, A., Norman, G. R., & Lange, P. (1994). Adolescent depression in a school-based community sample: Preliminary findings on contributing social factors. *Journal of Youth and Adolescence, 23,* 601–620.

McGee, G., Krantz, P. J., & McClannahan, L. E. (1984). Conversational skills for autistic adolescents: Teaching assertiveness in naturalistic game settings. *Journal of Autism and Developmental Disorders, 14,* 319–330.

McGee, R., Feehan, M., Williams, S., Partridge, F., Silva, P. A., & Kelly, J. (1990). DSM-III disorders in a large sample of adolescents. *Journal of the American Academy of Child and Adolescent Psychiatry, 29,* 611–619.

McGlashon, T. H. (1988). Adolescent versus adult onset of mania. *American Journal of Psychiatry, 145,* 221–223.

McGoldrick, M. (1993). Ethnicity, cultural diversity, and normality. In F. Walsh (Ed.), *Normal family process* (2nd ed., pp. 331–360) New York: Guilford Press.

McGoldrick, M. (Ed.). (1998). *Re-visiting family therapy: Race, culture, and gender in clinical practice.* New York: Guilford Press.

McGoldrick, M. (2002). Culture: A challenge to concepts of normality. *Culture and Normality, 1–12.*

McGoldrick, M., & Gerson, R. (1985). *Genograms in family assessment.* New York: Norton.

McGoldrick, M., Heiman, M, & Carter, B. (1993). The changing family life cycle. In F. Walsh (Ed.), *Normal family process* (2nd ed., pp. 405–443). New York: Guilford Press.

McGoldrick, M., Pearce, J., & Giordano, J. (Eds.). (1982). *Ethnicity and family therapy.* New York: Guilford Press.

McIntosh, J. L., & Kelly, L. D. (1992). Survivors' reactions: Suicide vs. other causes. *Journal of Crisis Intervention and Suicide: 13,* 82–93.

McKay, J. R., Murphy, R. T., Rivinus, T. R., & Maisto, S. A. (1991). Family dysfunction and alcohol and drug use in adolescent psychiatric inpatients. *Journal of the American Academy of Child and Adolescent Psychiatry, 30*(6), 967–972.

McKelvey, R. S., Baldassar, L. V., Sang, D. L., & Roberts, L. (1999). Vietnamese parental perceptions of child and adolescent mental illness. *Journal of the American Academy of Child and Adolescent Psychiatry, 38*(10), 1302–1310.

McKelvey, R. S., Sang, D. L., & Tu, H. D. (1997). Is there a role for child psychiatry in Vietnam? *Australian and New Zealand Journal of Psychiatry, 31,* 114–119.

McKenry, P. C., & Price, S. J. (Eds.). (2000). *Families and change: Coping with stressful events and transitions.* Thousand Oaks, CA: Sage.

McKenry, P. C., Tishler, C. L., & Kelley, C. (1982). Adolescent suicide: A comparison of attempters and nonattempters in emergency room population. *Clinical Pediatrics, 21*(5), 266–270.

McLatchie, R. (1997). Psychological adjustment and school performance of immigrant children. *Journal of Psychological Practice, 3*(2), 34–46.

McLeod, J. D., Kruttschmitt, C., & Dornfeld, M. (1994). Does parenting explain the effects of structural conditions on children's antisocial behavior? A comparison of blacks and whites. *Social Forces, 73*(2), 575–604.

McLoyd, V. C. (1990). The impact of economic hardship on black families and children: Psychological distress, parenting, and socioemotional development. *Child Development, 61,* 311–346.

McLoyd, V. C. (1998). Socioeconomic disadvantage and child development. *American Psychologist, 53,* 185–204.

McLoyd, V. C., Jayaratne, T. E., Ceballo, R., & Borquez, J. (1994). Unemployment and work interruption among African American single mothers: Effects on parenting and adolescent socioemotional functioning. *Child Development, 65,* 562–589.

McMahon, R. J., & Estes, A. M. (1997). Conduct problems. In E. J. Mash & L. G. Terdal (Eds.), *Assessment of childhood disorders* (3rd ed., pp. 130–193). New York: Guilford Press.

McNab, W. L. (1983). Anorexia and the adolescent. *Journal of School Health, 53,*(7), 427–430.

McQuaid, E. L., Kopel, S. J., & Nassau, J. H. (2001). Behavioral adjustment in children with asthma: A meta-analysis. *Journal of Developmental and Behavioral Pediatrics, 22*(6), 430–439.

Meijer, A. M., & Oppenheimer, L. (1995). The excitation-adaptation model of pediatric chronic illness. *Family Process, 34,* 441–454.

Michael, K. D., & Crowley, S. L. (2002). How effective are treatments for child and adolescent depression? A meta-analytic review. *Clinical Psychology Review, 22*(2), 247–269.

Miklowitz, D. J., Goldstein, M. J., Doane, J. A., Nuechterlein, K. H., Strachan, A. M., Snyder, K. S., & Magana-Amato, A. (1989). Is expressed emotion an index of a transactional process? Parents' affective style. *Family Process, 28*, 153–167.

Miller, C. (2001). Childhood animal cruelty and interpersonal violence. *Clinical Psychology Review, 21*(5), 735–749.

Miller, J. M. (1993). Resistance in child psychoanalysis. *Journal of Child Psychotherapy, 19*(1), 33–45.

Minuchen, S., Rossman, B. L., & Baker, L. (1978). *Psychosomatic families.* Cambridge, MA: Harvard University Press.

Mirande, A. (1991). Ethnicity and fatherhood. In F. Boznett & S. Hanson (Eds.), *Fatherhood and families in cultural context.* New York: Springer.

Mirsky, J., & Kaushinksy, F. (1989). Immigration and growth: Separation individual processes in immigrant students in Israel. *Adolescence, 24*(95), pp. 725–740.

Mol Lous, A., De Wit, C. A. M., De Bruyn, E. E. J., Riksen-Walraven, M., & Rost, H. (2000). Depression and play in early childhood: Play behavior of depressed and nondepressed 3- to 6-year-olds in various play situations. *Journal of Emotional and Behavioral Disorders, 8*(4), 249–262.

Montague, J. (1996). Counseling families from diverse cultures: A nondeficit approach. *Journal of Multicultural Counseling and Development, 24*, 37–41.

Moreau, D., & Follett, C. (1993). Panic disorder in children and adolescents. *Child and Adolescent Psychiatric Clinics of North America, 2*, 581–602.

Morena, A. B., & Thelan, M. H. (1995). Eating behavior in junior high school females. *Adolescence, 30*, 171–174.

Morita, Y., Soeda, H., Soeda, K., & Taki, M. (1999). Japan. In P. K. Smith, Y. Morita, J. Junger-Tas, D. Olweus, R. Catalano, & P. Slee, (Eds.), *The nature of school bullying: A cross-national perspective* (pp. 309–323). New York: Routledge.

Morris, R. J., & Nicholson, J. (1993). The therapeutic relationship in child and adolescent psychotherapy: Research issues and trends. In T. R. Kratochwill, & R. J. Morris, (Eds.), *Handbook of psychotherapy with children and adolescents* (pp. 405–425). Needham Heights, MA: Allyn & Bacon.

Mosak, H. H., & Maniacci, M. P. (1993). Adlerian child psychotherapy. In T. R. Kratochwill & R. J. Morris (Eds.), *Handbook of psychotherapy with children and adolescents* (pp. 162–184). Needham Heights, MA: Allyn & Bacon.

Murray, J. B. (1996). Psychophysiological aspects of autistic disorders: Overview. *The Journal of Psychology, 130,*(2), 145–159.

Murray, R. (2002). The phenomenon of psychotherapeutic change: Second-order change in one's experience of self. *Journal of Contemporary Psychotherapy, 32,*(2–3), 167–177.

Nash, M. R., Hulseley, T. L., Sexton, M. C., Harralson, T. L., & Lambert, W. (1993). Long-term effects of childhood sexual abuse: Perceived family environment, psychopathology, and dissociation. *Journal of Consulting and Clinical Psychology, 61*, 276–283.

Nathan, P. E., & Gorman, J. M. (Eds.). (2002). *A guide to treatments that work* (2nd ed.). London: Oxford University Press.

National Association of Social Workers (NASW) (1996). Code of Ethics. Washington, DC: NASW Press.

National Center for Health Statistics. (2003). *Cohabitation, Marriage, Divorce, & Remarriage in the United States.* Hyattsville, MD. US Department of Health & Human Services.

Nebbe, L. L. (1991). The human-animal bond and the elementary school counselor. *School Counselor, 38*, 362–371.

Neihart, M., & Reis, S. M. (Eds.). (2002). *The social and emotional development of gifted children.* Waco, TX: Prufrock Press.

Ness, D. E., & Pfeffer, C. R. (1990). Sequelae of bereavement resulting from suicide. *American Journal of Psychiatry, 147,* 279–285.

Neubauer, P. B. (1996). Current issues in psychoanalytic child development. *Psychoanalytic Study of the Child, 51,* 35–45.

Neumark-Sztainer, D., & Hannan, P. J. (2000). Weight-related behaviors among adolescent girls and boys: Results from a national survey. *Archives of Pediatrics and Adolescent Medicine, 154,* 569–581.

New York State Department of Health, Early Intervention Program (1999). Autism/pervasive developmental disorders: Assessment and intervention for young children (ages 0–3 years). Albany, NY: State Department of Health. Publication 4217.

Neziroglu, F., Yaryara-Tobias, J. A., Walz, J., & McKay, D. (2000). The effect of fluvoxamine and behavior therapy on children and adolescents with obsessive-compulsive disorder. *Journal of Child and Adolescent Psychopharmacology, 10*(4), 295–306.

Nigg, J. T., & Goldsmith, H. H. (1994). Genetics of personality disorders: Perspectives from personality and psychopathology research. *Psychological Bulletin, 115,* 346–380.

Nock, M. K., & Kazdin, A. E. (2001). Parent expectancies for child therapy: Assessment and relation to participation in treatment. *Journal of Child and Family Studies, 10,* 155–180.

Nolen-Hoeksema, S., Girgus, J. S., & Seligman, M. E. (1986). Learned helplessness in children: A longitudinal study of depression, achievement, and explanatory style. *Journal of Personality and Social Psychology, 51,* 435–442.

Nolin, M., Davies, E., & Chandler, K. (1995). Student victimization at school: Statistics in brief. Washington, DC: National Center for Education Statistics.

Noll, K., & Carter, J. (1997). *Taking the bully by the horns.* Reading, PA: Unicorn Press.

Nomura, Y., Wickramaratne, P. J., Warner, V., Mufson, L., & Weissman, M. M. (2002). Family discord, parental depression, and psychopathology in offspring: Ten-year follow-up. *Journal of the American Academy of Child and Adolescent Psychiatry, 41*(4), 402–409.

Oaklander, V. (1997). The therapeutic process with children and adolescents. *Gestalt Review, 1*(4), 292–317.

O'Brien, M., Margolin, G., John. R. S., & Krueger, L. (1995). Mothers' and sons' cognitive and emotional reactions to simulated marital and family conflict. *Journal of Consulting and Clinical Psychology, 59,* 692–703.

O'Brien, P., & Burnett, P. C. (2000). Counseling children using a multiple intelligences framework. *British Journal of Guidance and Counseling, 28*(3), 353–371.

O'Dea, J. A., & Caputi, P. (2001). Association between socioeconomic status, weight, age, and gender, and the body image and weight control practices of 6- to 19-year-old children and adolescents. *Health Education Research, 16*(5), 521–532.

Ogbu, J. U. (1981). Origins of human competence: A cultural-ecological perspective. *Child Development, 52,* 413–429.

Olarte, S. W. (1985). Changing gender stereotyped behavior: Role of therapist's personal disclosure. *Journal of American Academy of Psychoanalysis, 13*(2), 259–269.

Ollendick, T. H., Langley, A. K., Jones, R. T., & Kephart, C. (2001). Fear in children and adolescents: Relations with negative life events, attributional style, and avoidant coping. *Journal of Child Psychology and Psychiatry and Allied Disciplines, 42*(8), 1029–1034.

Ollendick, T. H., Yang, B., King, N. J., Dong, Q., & Akande, A. (1996). Fears in American, Australian, Chinese, and Nigerian children and adolescents: A cross-cultural study. *Journal of Child Psychological Psychiatry, 37,* 213–220.

Olweus, D. (1991). Bully/victim problems among schoolchildren: Basic facts and effects of a school based intervention program. In D. J. Pepler & K. H. Rubin (Eds.), *The development and treatment of childhood aggression.* Hillsdale, NJ: Lawrence Erlbaum.

Olweus, D. (1996). Bully/victim problems at school: Facts and effective intervention. *Journal of Emotional and Behavioral Problems, 5,* 15–22.

Ooms, T., & Preister, S. (Eds.). (1988). *Strengthening families: Using family criteria in policy making and program evaluation: A consensus report of the family criteria task force.* Washington, DC: Family Impact Seminar.

Orvaschel, H. (1995). *Schedule for affective disorders and schizophrenia for school-age children–epidemiologic version-5 (K-SADS-E-5).* Fort Lauderdale, FL: Nova Southwestern University.

Orvaschel, H., Puig-Antich, J., Chambers, W., Tabrizi, M. A., & Johnson, R. (1982). Retrospective assessment of prepubertal major depression with the Kiddie-SADS-E. *Journal of American Academy of Child and Adolescent Psychiatry, 21,* 392–397.

Osterman, K., & Kottkamp, R. B. (1993). *Reflective practice for educators: Improving schooling through professional development.* Thousand Oaks, CA: Corwin Press.

Ozonoff, S., & Miller, J. N. (1995). Teaching theory of mind: A new approach to social skill training for individuals with autism. *Journal of Autism and Developmental Disorders, 25,* 415–433.

Palmatier, L. L. (Ed.) (1998). *Crisis counseling for a quality school community: Applying Wm. Glasser's choice theory.* Philadelphia: Accelerated Development.

Papadatou, D., & Papadotos, C. (Eds.). (1991). *Children and death.* Washington, DC: Hemisphere Publishing.

Papernow, P. L. (1993). *Becoming a stepfamily: Patterns of development in remarried families.* San Francisco: Jossey-Bass.

Pardeck, J. T., & Pardeck, J. A. *Bibliotherapy: A clinical approach for helping children.* Newark, NJ: Gordon & Breach Science Publishers.

Paris, J., Zelkowitz, P., Guzder, J., Joseph, S., & Feldman, R. (1999). Neuropsychological factors associated with borderline personality disorder in children. *Journal of the American Academy of Child and Adolescent Psychiatry, 38,* 770–774.

Patterson, C. J., Kupersmidt, J. B., & Griesler, P. C. (1990). Children's perceptions of self and relationships with others as a function of sociometric status. *Child Development, 61,* 1335–1349.

Patterson, G. R., & Stoolmiller, M. (1991). Replication of a dual failure model for boys' depressed mood. *Journal of Consulting and Clinical Psychology, 59,* 491–498.

Pary, R., Lewis, S., Matuschka, P. R., Rudzinskiy, P., Safi, M., & Lippmann, S. (2002). Attention deficit disorder in adults. *Annals of Clinical Psychiatry, 14,* 105–111.

Paulson, S. E. (1994). Relations of parenting style and parental involvement with ninth grade students' achievement. *Journal of Early Adolescence, 14,*(2) 250–267.

Pazaratz, D. (2001). Theory and structure of a day treatment program for adolescents. *Residential Treatment for Children and Youth, 19*(1), 29–43.

Perez, R. M., DeBord, K. A., & Bieschke, K. J. (Eds.) (2000). *Handbook of counseling and psychotherapy with lesbian, gay, and bisexual clients.* Washington, DC: American Psychological Association.

Perkins, D. F., & Luster, T. (1999). The relationship between sexual abuse and purging: Findings from a community-wide survey of female adolescents. *Child Abuse and Neglect, 23,* 371–382.

Petarik, G., & Finney-Owen, K. (1987). Outpatient clinic therapist attitudes and beliefs relevant to client dropout. *Community Mental Health Journal, 23*(2), 120–130.

Peters, M. F. (1985). Racial socialization in young black children. In H. McAdoo & J. McAdoo (Eds.), *Black children.* Beverly Hills, CA: Sage.

Peterson, C. C. (1989). Conflict resolution strategies and adolescent identity development. *Psychology and Human Development, 2*(2), 67–75.

Peterson, Z. D. (2002). More than a mirror: Ethics of therapist self-disclosure. *Psychotherapy: Theory, Research, Practice, Training, 39*(1), 21–31.

Pfeffer, C. R., (1986). *The Suicidal Child.* New York: Guilford Press.

Pfeffer, C. R. (1990). Manifestation of risk factors. In G. Maclean (Ed.), *Suicide in children and adolescents.* Toronto: Hogrefe and Huber.

Pfeffer, C. R., Martins, P., Mann, J., & Sunkenberg, M. (1997). Child survivors of suicide: Psychosocial characteristics. *Journal of the American Academy of Child and Adolescent Psychiatry, 36,* 65–74.

Piaget, J. (1963). *The origins of intelligence in children.* New York: Norton.

Pianta, R. C., & Caldwell, C. B. (1990). Stability of externalizing symptoms from kindergarten to first grade and factors related to instability. *Developmental Psychopathology, 2,* 246–258.

Pianta, R. C., & Castaldi, J. (1989). Stability of internalizing symptoms from kindergarten to first grade and factors related to instability. *Developmental Psychopathology, 1,* 305–316.

Pierce, K., & Schreibman, L. (1997). Using peer trainers to promote social behavior in autism: Are they effective at enhancing multiple social modalities? *Focus on Autism and Other Developmental Disabilities, 12,* 207–218.

Pinderhughes, E. (1991). The delivery of child welfare services to African American clients. *American Orthopsychiatric, 61*(44), 599–605.

Pipher, M. (2002). *The middle of everywhere: The world's refugees come to our town.* New York: Harcourt.

Pledge, D. S. (1992, September). Marital separation/divorce: A review of individual responses to a major life stressor. *Journal of Divorce and Remarriage, 17*(3–4), 151–181.

Polivy, J., & Herman, C. (1993). Etiology of binge eating: Psychological mechanisms. In C. G. Fairburn & G. T. Wilson (Eds.), *Binge eating: Nature, assessment and treatment* (pp. 173–205). New York: Guilford Press.

Ponterotto, J. D. (Ed.). (1995). *Handbook of multicultural counseling.* Thousand Oaks, CA: Sage.

Pope, K. S. (2001). Security of clinical records on computers: Viruses, firewalls, and the golden rule. Retrieved August 30, 2002, from *http://kspope.com/security.html*

Pope, K. S., & Feldman-Summers, S. (1992). National survey of psychologists' sexual and physical abuse history and their evaluation of training and competence in these areas. *Professional Psychology: Research and Practice, 23*(5) 353–361.

Pope, K. S., & Morin, S. F. (1991). AIDS and HIV infection update: New research, ethical responsibilities, evolving legal frameworks, and publishing resources. In P. A. Keller & S. R. Heyman (Eds.), *Innovations in clinical practice: A source book (Vol. 10),* pp. 443–457. Brooklyn, NY: Professional Resource Exchange.

Pope, K. S., Sonne, J. L., & Holroyd, J. (1993). *Sexual feelings in psychotherapy: Explorations for therapists and therapists-in-training.* Washington, DC: American Psychological Association.

Pope, K. S., & Tabachnick, B. G. (1993). Therapists' anger, hate, fear, and sexual feelings: National survey of therapist responses, client characteristics, critical events, formal complaints, and training. *Professional Psychology: Research and Practice, 24,* 142–152.

Pope, K. S., & Tabachnick, B. G. (1994). Therapists as patients: A national survey of psychologists' experiences, problems, and beliefs. *Professional Psychology: Research and Practice, 25,* 247–258.

Pope, K. S., Tabachnick, B. G., & Keith-Spiegel, P. (1986). Sexual attraction to clients: The human therapist and the (sometimes) inhuman training system. *American Psychologist, 41*(2), 147–158.

Pope, K. S., Tabachnick, B. G., & Keith-Spiegel, P. (1987). Ethics of practice: The beliefs and behaviors of psychologists as therapists. *American Psychologist, 42,* 993–1006.

Pope, K. S., & Vasquez, M. J. T. (1998). *Ethics in psychotherapy and counseling: A practical guide,* (2nd ed). San Francisco: Jossey-Bass.

Pope, K. S., & Vetter, V. A. (1991). Prior therapist-patient sexual involvement among patients seen by psychologists. *Psychotherapy, 28,* 429–438.

Pope-Davis, D. B., Toporek, R. L., Ortega-Villalobos, L., Ligiero, D. P., Brittan-Powell, C. S., Liu, W. M., et al. (2002). Client perspectives of multicultural counseling competence: A qualitative examination. *Counseling Psychologist, 30,* 355–393.

Prange, M. E., Greenbaum, P. E., Silver, S. E., & Friedman, R. (1992). Family functioning and psychopathology among adolescents with severe emotional disturbance. *Journal of Abnormal Child Psychology, 20*(1) 83–102.

Pressly, P. K., Parker, W. M., & Jennie, J. (2001). Actualizing multicultural counseling competencies: A multifaceted approach. *International Journal for the Advancement of Counselling, 23,* 223–234.

Psychopathology Committee of Group for Advancement of Psychiatry. (2001). Re-examination of therapist self-disclosure. *Psychiatric Services, 52*(11), 1489–1493.

Puig-Antich, J., Kaufman, J., Ryan, N. D., Williamson, D. E., Dahl, R. E., Lukens, E., Phil, M., Todak, G., Ambrosini, P., Rabinovich, H., & Nelson, B. (1993). The psychosomatic functioning and family environment of depressed adolescents. *Journal of the American Academy of Child and Adolescent Psychiatry, 32,* 244–253.

Puritz, P., & Shang, W. W. L. (1998). Innovative approaches to juvenile indigent defense. *OJJDP Juvenile Justice Bulletin,* 1–8. Retrieved June 22, 2003, from *http://www.ncjrs.org/pdffiles/171151.pdf.*

Quay, H. C., & LaGreca, A. M. (1986). Disorders of anxiety, withdrawal, and dysphoria. In H. C. Quay & J. S. Werry (Eds.), *Psychopathological disorders of childhood* (3rd ed., pp. 111–155). New York: Wiley.

Quiggle, N. L., Garber, J., Panak, W. F., & Dodge, K. A. (1992). Social information processing in aggressive and depressed children. *Child Development, 63,* 1305–1320.

Rao, U., Ryan, N. D., & Birmaher, B. (1995). Unipolar depression in adolescents: Clinical outcome in adulthood. *Journal of the American Academy of Child and Adolescent Psychiatry, 34,* 566–578.

Rashid, H. (1985). Black family research and parent education programs: The need for convergence. *Contemporary Education, 56,* 180–185.

Raymond, L., Friedlander, M. L., Heatherington, L., Ellis, M. E., & Sargent, J. (1993). Communication processes in structural family therapy: Case study of an anorectic family. *Journal of Family Psychology, 6,* 308–326.

Rea, M. M., Goldstein, M. J., Miklowitz, D. J., & Weisman, A. G. (2000). Difficulty in implementing a family intervention for bipolar disorder: The predictive role of patient and family attributes. *Family Process, 39*(1), 105–118.

Reddy, K. S., Bhadramani, G., & Samiullah, S. (2002). Placement of family members by normal and neglected boys: A study of family drawings. *Social Science International, 18*(1), 72–82.

Reed, M., & Greenwald, J. (1991). Survivor-victim status, attachment and sudden death bereavement. *Suicide and Life Threatening Behavior, 21,* 385–401.

Reed, M. D. (1993). Sudden death and bereavement outcomes: The impact of resources on grief symptomatology and detachment. *Suicide and Life-Threatening Behavior, 23,* 204–220.

Reich, T., Van Eerdewegh, P., Rice, J., Mullaney, J., Kierman, G., & Endicott, J. (1987). The family transmission of primary depressive disorder. *Journal of Psychiatric Research, 21,* pp. 613–624.

Reich, W. (2000). Diagnostic interview for children and adolescents. *Journal of American Academy of Child and Adolescent Psychiatry, 39*(1), 59–66.

Reich, W. (1997). *Diagnostic interview for children and adolescents–Revised, DSM-IV Version.* Toronto: Multi-Health Systems.

Reiser, D. E., & Levenson, H. (1984). Abuses of the borderline diagnosis: A clinical problem with teaching opportunities. *American Journal of Psychiatry, 141,* 1528–1532.

Remafedi, G. (Ed.). (1999). *Death by denial: Studies of suicide in gay and lesbian teenagers.* Boston: Alyson Publications.

Rest, J. R. (1984). Research on moral development: Implications for training counseling psychologists. *Counseling Psychologist, 12,* 19–29.

Reynolds, C. R., & Richmond, B. O. (1985). What I think and feel (RCMAS). Los Angeles: Western Psychological Services.

Rich, C. L., Fower, R. C., Fogarty, L. A., & Young, D. (1988). San Diego Suicide Study: III. Relationships between diagnoses and stressors. *Archives of General Psychiatry, 45,* 589–592.

Rich, C. L., Warstadt, G. M., Nemiroff, R. A., & Fowler, R. C. (1991). Suicide, stressors, and the life cycle. *American Journal of Psychiatry, 148,* 524–527.

Richman, N., Stevenson, J., & Graham, P. J. (1982). Pre-school to school: A behavioural study. *Behavioural Development: A Series of Monographs.* New York: Academic Press.

Rice, R., Reich, T., & Andreasen, N. C. (1987). The familial transmission of bipolar disorder. *Archives of General Psychiatry, 44,* 441–447.

Ridley, C. R. (1995). *Overcoming unintentional racism in counseling and therapy.* Thousand Oaks, CA: Sage.

Rigby, K., Cox, I., & Black, G. (1997). Cooperativeness and bully/victim problems among Australian schoolchildren. *Journal of Social Psychology, 137*(3), 357–368.

Rigby, K., & Slee, P. (1999a). Suicidal ideation among adolescent school children, involvement in bully-victim problems, and perceived social support. *Suicide and Life Threatening Behavior, 29,* 119–130.

Rigby, K., & Slee, P. (1999b). Australia. In P. K. Smith, Y. Morita, J. Junger-Tas, D. Olweus, R. Catalano, & P. Slee (Eds.), *The nature of school bullying: A cross-national perspective.* New York: Routledge.

Ritter, J. (May 22, 1998). Oregon teen threatened revenge: One dead, 23 hurt in shooting at high school. *USA Today,* A1.

Roberts, M. (1998). A thing called therapy: Therapist-client counseling co-constructions. *Journal of Systemic Therapist* 17(4) 14–26.

Robertson, H. A., Kutcher, S. P., Bird, D., & Grasswick, L. (2001). Impact of early onset bipolar disorder on family functioning: Adolescents' perceptions of family dynamics, communication, and problems. *Journal of Affective Disorders, 66*(1), 25–37.

Robin, A. L., Siegel, P., Bedway, M., & Gilroy, M. (1996). Therapy for adolescent anorexia nervosa: Addressing cognitions, feelings, and the family's role. In E. D. Hibbs & P. S. Jensen (Eds.), *Psychosocial treatments for child and adolescent disorders: Empirically based strategies for clinical practice* (pp. 239–259). Washington, DC: American Psychological Association.

Robin, A. L., Siegel, P. T., Koepke, T., Moye, A. W., & Tics, S. (1994). Family therapy versus individual therapy for adolescent females with anorexia nervosa. *Journal of Developmental Behavioral Pediatrics, 15,* 111–116.

Robin, A. L., Siegel, P. T., Moye, A. W., Gilroy, M., Dennis, A. B., & Sikand, A. (1999). A controlled comparison of family versus individual therapy for adolescents with anorexia nervosa. *Journal of the American Academy of Child and Adolescent Psychiatry, 38*(12), 1482–1494.

Robinson, D. J. (2001). *Brain calipers: Descriptive psychopathology and the psychiatric mental status exam* (2nd ed.). Port Huron, MI: Rapid Psychler Press.

Robinson, N. M. (1996). Counseling agenda for gifted young people: A commentary. *Journal for the Education of the Gifted, 20,* 128–137.

Robison, L. M., Skaer, T. L., Sclar, D. A., & Galin, R. S. (2002). Is attention deficit hyperactivity disorder increasing among girls in the US? Trends in diagnosis and the prescribing of stimulants. *CNS Drugs, 16*(2), 129–137.

Robson, K. R. (Ed.) (1983). *The borderline child.* New York: McGraw-Hill.

Rofes, E. (1989). Opening up the classroom closet: Responding to the educational needs of gay and lesbian youth. *Harvard Educational Review, 59,* 444–453.

Rogosch, F., Cicchetti, D., & Aber, J. L. (1995). The role of child maltreatment in early deviations in cognitive and affective processing abilities and later peer relationship problems. *Development and Psychopathology, 7,* 591–609.

Roland, E. (1989). Bullying: The Scandinavian research tradition. In D. P. Tattum & D. A. Lane (Eds.), *Bullying in schools.* London: Trentham Books.

Rolland, J. S. (1993). In F. Walsh (Ed.), *Normal family processes* (2nd ed., 444–473). New York: Guilford Press.

Rollock, D., & Terrell, M. D. (1996). Multicultural issues in assessment: Toward an inclusive model. In J. L. DeLucia-Waack, (Ed.), *Multicultural counseling competencies: Implications for training and practice* (pp. 113–153). Alexandria, VA: Association for Counselor Education and Supervision.

Rolvsjord, R. (2001). Sophie learns to play her song of tears: A case study exploring the dialectics between didactic and psychotherapeutic music therapy practices. *Nordic Journal of Music Therapy, 10*(1), 77–85.

Ronch, J. L., & Van Ornum, W. (Eds.). (1994). *The counseling sourcebook: A practical reference on contemporary issues.* New York: Crossroad Publishing.

Roser, W., Bubl, R., Buergin, D., Seelig, J., Radue, E., & Rost, B. (1999). Metabolic changes in the brain with anorexia nervosa and bulimia nervosa as detected by proton magnetic resonance spectroscopy. *International Journal of Eating Disorders, 26,* 119–136.

Ross, D. D., Fischhoff, J., & Davenport, B. (2002). Treatment of ADHD when tolerance to methylphenidate develops. *Psychiatric Services, 53*(1), 102–110.

Rossman, B. B. R., Bingham, R. D., & Emde, R. N. (1997). Symptomatology and adaptive functioning for children exposed to normative stressors, dog attack, and parental violence. *Journal of the American Academy of Child and Adolescent Psychiatry, 36*(8), 1089–1097.

Rotatori, A. F., & Gerber, P. U. (Eds.). (1986). *Counseling exceptional students.* New York: Human Sciences Press.

Rothbaum, R., Rosen, K., Ujiee, T., & Uchida, N. (2002). Family systems theory: Attachment theory and culture. *Family Process, 41*(3), 328–351.

Ruck, M. D., Keating, D. P., Abromovitch, R., & Koegl, C. J. (1998). Adolescents' and childrens' knowledge about rights: Some evidence for how young people view rights in their own lives. *Journal of Adolescence, 21*(3), 275–289.

Rudolph, K. D., & Clark, A. G. (2001). Conceptions of relationships in children with depression and aggressive symptoms: Social-cognitive distortions or reality? *Journal of Abnormal Child Psychology, 29*(1), 41–57.

Rudolph, K. D., Hammen, C., & Burge, D. (1997). A cognitive-interpersonal approach to depressive symptoms in preadolescent children. *Journal of Abnormal Child Psychology, 25,* 33–45.

Ruiselova, Z. (1998). Relationships with parents and teachers in connection with pubertal maturation timing in girls. *Studia Psychologica, 40*(4), 277–281.

Russell, G. F. M., Szmulder, G. I., Dare, C., & Eisler, I. (1987). An evaluation of family therapy in anorexia nervosa and bulimia nervosa. *Archives of General Psychiatry, 44,* 1047–1056.

Rutter, M. (1985). Psychopathology and development: Links between childhood and adult life. In M. Rutter & L. Hersoy (Eds.), *Child and adolescent psychiatry: Modern approaches* (pp. 720–739). Oxford, U.K.: Blackwell Scientific Publication.

Rynn, M. A., Siqueland, L., & Rickels, K. (2001). Placebo-controlled trial of sertraline in treatment of children with generalized anxiety disorder. *American Journal of Psychiatry, 158*(12), 2008–2015.

Sabell, R. A. (1998). World Wide Web resources for counseling children and adolescents with disabilities. *Professional School Counseling, 2*(1), 47–53.

Sampson, R. J., Raudenbush, S. W., & Earls, F. (1997, August 15). Neighborhoods and violent crime: A multilevel study of collective efficacy. *Science, 277,* 918–924.

Sandhu, D. S., & Brown, S. P. (1996). Empowering ethnically and racially diverse clients through prejudice reduction: Suggestions and strategies for counselors. *Journal of Multicultural Counseling and Development, 24,* 202–217.

Sandoval, J. (1988). *Crisis counseling, intervention, and prevention in the school.* Hillsdale, NJ: Lawrence Erlbaum.

Santisteban, D. A., & Mitrani, V. B. (2003). The influence of acculturation processes on the family. In K. M. Chun, & P. B. Organista (Eds.), *Acculturation: Advances in theory, measurement, and applied research* (pp. 121–135). Washington, DC: American Psychological Association.

Sapienza, B. G., & Bugental, J. F. T. (2000). Keeping our instruments finely tuned: An existential-humanistic perspective. *Professional Psychology: Research and Practice, 31*(4), 458–460.

Sargent, J. (1997). Family therapy in child and adolescent psychiatry. *Child and Adolescent Psychiatric Clinics of North America, 6*(1), 151–171.

Schacher, R. J., & Wachsmuth, R. (1990). Oppositional defiant disorder in children: A validation study comparing conduct disorder, oppositional disorder and normal control children. *Journal of Child Psychology and Psychiatry, 31,* 1089–1102.

Schaefer, C. E. (2000). The therapeutic use of ball play in psychotherapy with children. *International Journal of Play Therapy, 9,* 1–10.

Schetky, D., & Green, A. (1988). In *Child sexual abuse: A handbook for health care professionals.* New York: Brunner/Mazel.

Schmidt, M. E., Demulder, E. K., & Denham, S. (2002). Kindergarten social-emotional competence: Development predictors and psychosocial implications. *Early Child Development and Care, 172,* 451–462.

Schraufnagel, C. D., Brumback, R. A., Harper, C. R., & Weinberg, W. A. (2001). Affective illness in children and adolescents: Patterns of presentation in relation to pubertal maturation and family history. *Journal of Child Neurology, 16*(8), 553–561.

Schulz, M. S., & Masek, B. J. (1996). Medical crisis intervention with children and adolescents with chronic pain. *Professional Psychology: Research and Practice, 27*(2), 121–129.

Schwartz, D., Phares, V., Tantleff-Dunn, S., & Thompson, J. K. (1999). Body image, psychological functioning, and parental feedback regarding physical appearance. *International Journal of Eating Disorders, 26,* 119–136.

Scott, J., Cully, M., & Weissberg, E. (1995). Helping the separation anxious school refuser. *Elementary School Guidance & Counseling, 29*(4), 289–296.

Seager, K. M., & Spencer, S. C. (1996). Meeting the bereavement needs of kids in patient/families—not just playing around. *Hospice Journal, 11*(4), 41–66.

Sedlak, A. J., & Broadhurst, D. D. (1996). *Executive summary of the Third National Incidence Study of Child Abuse and Neglect.* Washington, DC: U.S. Department of Health & Human Services.

Seifert, K., Phillips, S., & Parker, S. (2001). Child and adolescent risk for violence (CARV): A tool to assess juvenile risk. *Journal of Psychiatry and Law, 29*(3), 329–346.

Seguin, J. R., Pihl, R. O., Harden, P. W., Tremblay, R. E., & Boulerice, B. (1995). Cognitive and neuropsychological characteristics of physically aggressive boys. *Journal of Abnormal Psychology, 104,* 614–624.

Selekman, M. D. (1993). Solution-oriented brief therapy with difficult adolescents. In S. Friedman (Ed.), *The new language of change: Constructive collaboration in psychotherapy* (pp. 138–157). New York: Guilford Press.

Seligman, M. E. (1975). *Helplessness: On depression, development, and death.* New York: Freeman.

Seligman, M. E. P., Reivich, K., Jaycox, L., & Gilliham, J. (1995). *The optimistic child.* Boston: Houghton Mifflin.

Shaffer, D. (1988). The epidemiology of teen suicide: An examination of risk factors. *Journal of Clinical Psychiatry, 49*(9, Suppl), 36–41.

Shaffer, D., Fisher, P., & Dulcan, M. (1996). The NIMH diagnostic interview schedule for children (DISC 2, 3): Description, acceptability, prevalence, and performance in the MECA study. *Journal of the American Academy of Child and Adolescent Psychiatry, 35,* 865–877.

Shaffer, D., Fisher, P., Lucas, C. P., Dulcan, M. K., & Schwab-Stone, M. E. (2000). NIMH diagnostic interview schedule for children version IV: Description, differences from previous versions, and reliability of some common diagnoses. *Journal of the American Academy of Child and Adolescent Psychiatry, 39,* 28–38.

Sharp, S., & Smith P. K. (1991). Bullying in the UK schools: The DES Sheffield bullying project. *Early Child Development and Care, 77,* 47–55.

Sheeber, L., Hops, H., Alpert, A., Davis, B., & Andrews, J. (1997). Family support and conflict: Prospective relations to adolescent depression. *Journal of Abnormal Child Psychology, 25,* 333–344.

Shek, D. T. L. (1989). Perception of parental treatment styles and psychological well-being in a sample of Chinese secondary school students. *The Journal of Genetic Psychology, 150*(4), 403–415.

Shek, D. T. L. (1993). Perceptions of parental treatment styles and psychological well-being in Chinese college students. *Psychologia, 36,* 159–166.

Shek, D. T. L. (1995). Chinese adolescents' perceptions of parenting styles of fathers and mothers. *The Journal of Genetic Psychology, 156,* 175–190.

Shek, D. T. L. (1997). Family environment and adolescent psychological well-being, school adjustment, and problem behavior: A pioneer study in a Chinese context. *Journal of Genetic Psychology, 158*(1), 113–129.

Shek, D. T. L. (1998). Adolescents' perceptions of paternal and maternal parenting styles in a Chinese context. *The Journal of Psychology, 132*(5), 527–538.

Sheldon, K., & Datillo, J. (1997). Multiculturalism in therapeutic recreation: Terminology clarification and practical suggestions. *Therapeutic Recreation Journal, 31*(3), 148–159.

Shepherd, D. M., & Barraclough, B. M. (1976). The aftermath of parental suicide for children. *British Journal of Psychiatry, 129,* 267–276.

Sherwood, N. E., Neumark-Sztainer, D., Story, M., Beuhring, T., & Resnick, M. D. (2002). Weight-related sports involvement in girls: Who is at risk for disordered eating? *American Journal of Health Promotion, 16*(6), 341–344.

Shih, M., Pittinsky, T. L., & Ambady, N. (1999). Stereotype susceptibility: Identity salience and shifts in quantitative performance. *Psychological Science, 10*(1), 80–83.

Shirk, S. R., Boergers, J., Eason, A., & Van Horn, M. (1998). Dysphoric interpersonal schemata and preadolescents' sensitization to negative events. *Journal of Clinical Child Psychology, 27,* 54–68.

Shirk, S. R., & Saiz, C. C. (1992). Clinical, empirical, and developmental perspectives on the therapeutic relationship in child psychotherapy. *Development and Psychopathology, 4,* 713–728.

Shirk, S. R., Van Horn, M., & Leber, D. (1997). Dysphoria and children's processing of supportive interactions. *Journal of Abnormal Child Psychology, 25,* 239–249.

Shisslak, C. M., Renger, R., Sharpe, T., Crago, M., McKnight, K. M., Gray, N., Bryson, S., Estes, L. S., Parnaby, O. G., Killen, J., & Taylor, C. B. (1999). Development and evaluation of the McKnight Risk Factor Survey for assessing potential risk and protective factors for disordered eating in preadolescent and adolescent girls. *International Journal of Eating Disorders, 25,* 195–214.

Silva, T. (1996). Poverty and uneven development: Reflections from a street children project in the Philippines. *Childhood, 3*(2), 279–282.

Silver, S., & Oakes, B. (2001). Evaluation of a new computer intervention to teach people with autism or Asperger syndrome to recognize and predict emotion in others. *Autism, 5*(3), 299–316.

Silverman, W. E., & Albana, A. M. (1996). Anxiety disorders interview Schedule-r DSM-VI: Child version–Child interview schedule. San Antonio, TX: Psychological Corporation.

Simeon, J., Milin, R., Walker, S. (2002). A retrospective chart review of risperidone use in treatment-resistant children and adolescents with psychiatric disorders. *Progress in Neuro-Psychopharmacology and Biological Psychiatry, 26*(2), 267–275.

Simons, R. L., Johnson, C., Beaman, J., Conger, R. D., & Whitbeck, L. (1996). Parents and peer group as mediators of the effect of community structure on adolescent problem behavior. *American Journal of Community Psychology, 24,* 145–171.

Simons, R. L., et al.(2002). Community differences in the association between parenting practices and child conduct problems. *Journal of Marriage and Family, 64,* 331–345.

Skoc, E. E. A. (1998). The ethic of care: Issues in moral development. In E. E. A. Skoc & A. L. von der Lippe (Eds.), *Personality development in adolescence: A cross national and life span perspective. Adolescence and Society.* (pp. 143–171). Florence, KY: Taylor & Francis/Routledge.

Slesnick, N., & Waldron, H. B. (1997). Interpersonal problem-solving interactions of depressed adolescents and their parents. *Journal of Family Psychology, 11*(2), 234–245.

Slonim-Nevo, V., Sharaga, Y., & Mirsky, J. (1999). A culturally sensitive approach to therapy with immigrant families: The case of Jewish emigrants from the former Soviet Union. *Family Process, 38*(4) 445–459.

Smart, L. S., Chibucos, T. R., & Didler, L. A. (1990). Adolescent substance use and perceived family functioning. *Journal of Family Issues, 11*(2) 208–227.

Smith, C., & Nylund, D. (Eds.). (1997). *Narrative therapies with children and adolescents.* New York: Guilford Press.

Smith, K. A., Fairburn, C. G., & Cowen, P. J. (1999). Symptomatic relapse in bulimia nervosa following acute tryptophan depletion. *Archives of General Psychiatry, 56,* 171–176.

Smith, M. K. (1995). Utilization focused evaluation of a family preservation program. *Families in Society, 76*(1), 11–19.

Smith, P. K., Madsen, K. C., & Moody, J. C. (1999). What causes the age decline in reports of being bullied at school? Towards a developmental analysis of risks of being bullied. *Educational Research, 41,* 267–285.

Smith, S. C., & Pennells, M. (Eds.) (1995). *Making memory stores with children and families affected by HIV.* Bristol, PA: Jessica Kingsley.

Smolak, L., Levine, M. P., & Schermen, F. (1999). Parental input and weight concerns among elementary schoolchildren. *International Journal of Eating Disorders, 25,* 263–271.

Solantaus-Simula, T., Punamkai, R.L., & Beardslee, W. R. (2002). Children's responses to low parental mood: I: Associations with family perceptions of parenting styles and child distress. *Journal of the American Academy of Child and Adolescent Psychiatry, 41*(3), 287–296.

Sommers-Flanagan, J., & Sommers-Flanagan, R. (1995). Psychotherapeutic techniques with treatment-resistant adolescents. *Psychotherapy, 32,* 131–140.

Spees, E. K. (2002). Word movies: Strategy and resources for therapeutic storytelling with children and adolescents. *Annals of the American Psychotherapy Association, 5*(1) 14–21.

Speltz, M. L., McClellan, J., DeKlyen, M., & Jones, K. (1999). Preschool boys with oppositional defiant disorder: Clinical presentation and diagnostic change. *Journal of the American Academy of Child and Adolescent Psychiatry, 38,* 838–845.

Spence, S. H., Sheffield, J. K., & Donovan, C. L. (2003). Preventing adolescent depression: An evaluation of the Problem Solving for Life program. *Journal of Consulting and Clinical Psychology, 71,* 3–13.

Spencer, G. A., & Bryant, S. A. (2000). Dating violence: A comparison of rural, suburban and urban teens. *Journal of Adolescent Health, 6,* 302–305.

Spencer, M. B. (1990). Development of minority children: An introduction. *Child Development, 61,* 267–269.

Spiegel, J. (1971). *Transactions: The interplay between individual, family, and society.* New York: Science House.

Sprafkin, J., Gadow, K. D., & Nolan, E. E. (2001). The utility of a DSM-IV referenced screening instrument for attention-deficit hyperactivity disorder. *Journal of Emotional and Behavioral Disorders, 9,* 513–524.

Sprafkin, J., Gadow, K. D., Salisbury, H., Schneider, J., & Loney, J. (2002). Further evidence of reliability for the child symptom inventory-4: Parent-checklist in clinically referred boys. *Journal of Clinical and Child Psychiatry, 31*(4), 513–524.

Sprafkin, J., Volpe, R. J., Gadow, K. D.; Nolan, E. E. (2002). A DSM-IV referenced screening instrument for preschool: The early children. The early child inventory–4. *Journal of the American Academy of Child and Adolescent Psychiatry, 41,* 605–612.

Springer, E. A., Winzelberg, A. J., Perkins, R., & Taylor, C. E. (1999). Effects of a body image curriculum for college students on improving body image. *International Journal of Eating Disorders, 26,* 13–20.

Stark, K. D., Humphrey, L. L., Crook, K., & Lewis, K. (1990). Perceived family environments of depressed anxious children: Child's and maternal figure's perspectives. *Journal of Abnormal Child Psychology, 18,* 527–547.

Stein, A., Wooley, H., Cooper, S. D., & Fairburn, C. G. (1994). An observational study of mothers with eating disorders and their infants. *Journal of Child Psychology and Psychiatry, 35,* 733–748.

Stein, J. A., Newcomb, M. D., & Bentler, P. M. (1993). Differential effects of parent and grandparent drug on behavior problems of male and female children. *Developmental Psychology, 29,* 31–43.

Stein, K. F., & Hedger, K. (1997). Body weight and shape self-cognitions, emotional distress, and disordered eating in middle adolescent girls. *Archives of Psychiatric Nursing, 11,* 264–275.

Steinberg, L. (2001). *Adolescence* (6th ed.). New York: McGraw-Hill.

Steinberg, L., Mounts, N. S., Lamborn, S. D., & Dornbusch, S. M. (1991). Authoritative parenting and adolescent adjustment across varied ecological niches. *Journal of Research on Adolescents, 1,* 19–36.

Steiner, H., Garcia, I. G., & Matthews, Z. (1997). Posttraumatic stress disorder in incarcerated juvenile delinquents. *Journal of the American Academy of Child and Adolescent Psychiatry, 36,* 357–365.

Stern, M., McIntosh, B. J., Norman, S. L. (1998). *The emerging role of counseling psychology in health care.* New York: Norton.

Stillion, J. M. (1994). Suicide: Understanding those considering premature exits. In Corless, I. B., Germino, B. B., & Pittman, M. (Eds.), *Dying, death, and bereavement: Theoretical perspectives and other ways of knowing.* Boston: Jones & Bartlestt.

Stoeop, A. V., Weiss, N. S., McKnight, B., Beresford, S. A. A., & Coehen, P. (2002). Which measure of adolescent psychiatric disorder-diagnosis, number of symptoms, or adaptive functioning best predicts adverse young adult outcomes? *Journal of Epidemiology and Community Health, 56*(1), 56–65.

Strachan, A. M., Feingold, D., Goldstein, M. J., & Miklowitz, D. J. (1989). Is expressed emotion an index of a transactional process? II. Patient's coping style. *Family Process, 28,* 169–181.

Strachan, A. M., Leff, J. P., Goldstein, M. J., Miklowitz, D. J., & Neuchterlein, K. H. (1989). Is expressed emotion an index of a transactional process? Patient's coping style. *Family Process, 28,* 169–181.

Strauss, C. C., & Last, C. G. (1993). Social and simple phobias in children. *Journal of Anxiety Disorders, 7,* 141–152.

Strauss, C. C., Last, C. G., Hersen, M., & Kazdin, A. E. (1988a). Association between anxiety and depression in children and adolescents with anxiety disorders. *Journal of Abnormal Child Psychology, 16,* 57–68.

Strauss, C. C., Lease, C. A., Last, C. G., & Francis, G. (1988b). Overanxious disorder: Examination of developmental differences. *Abnormal Child Psychology, 16,* 433–443.

Streigel-Moore, R., & Kearney-Cooke, C. (1994). Exploring parents' attitudes and behaviors about their child's physical appearance. *International Journal of Eating Disorders, 15,* 377–385.

Streigel-Moore, R., Silberstein, L., & Rodin, J. (1986). Toward an understanding of risk factors for bulimia. *American Psychologist, 41,* 246–263.

Strober, M. (1992a). The pharmacotherapy of depressive illness in adolescence: III. Diagnostic and conceptual issues in studies of tricyclic antidepressants. *Journal of Child and Adolescent Psychopharmacology, 2,* 23–29.

Strober, M. (1992b). Bipolar disorder. In Peschel, E. & Peschel, R. (Eds.). *Neurobiological disorders in children and adolescents. New directions for mental health services, No. 54: The Jossey-Bass social and behavioral sciences series (pp. 35–38).* New York: Jossey-Bass.

Strober, M., & Carlson, G. (1982). Bipolar illness in adolescents with major depression: Clinical, genetic, and psychopharmacologic predictors in a 3–4 year prospective follow-up investigation. *Archives of General Psychiatry, 39,* 549–555.

Strober, M., Morrell, W., Lampert, C., & Burroughs, J. (1990). Relapse following discontinuation of lithium maintenance therapy in adolescents with bipolar I illness: A naturalistic study. *American Journal of Psychiatry, 147,* 457–461.

Strohmer, D. C., & Shivy, V. A. (1994). Bias in counselor hypothesis testing: The robustness of counselor confirmatory bias. *Journal of Counseling and Development, 73,* 191–197.

Sturkie, J., & Cassady, M. (1992). *Acting it out junior.* San Jose, CA: Resource Publications.

Sue, D., & Sue, S. (1987). Cultural factors in clinical assessment of Asian Americans. *Journal of Counseling and Clinical Psychology, 55,* 479–487.

Sue, D. W., & Sue, S. (1990). *Counseling the culturally different: Theory and practice* (2nd ed.). New York: Wiley.

Sue, S. (1988). Psychotherapeutic services for ethnic minorities: Two decades of research findings. *American Psychologist, 43,* 301–308.

Sue, S., Fujino, D. C., Hu, L.-T., & Takeuchi, D. T. (1991). Community mental health services for ethnic minority groups: A test of the cultural responsiveness hypothesis. *Journal of Consulting and Clinical Psychology, 59,* 533–540.

Sugai, G., et al. (2000). Applying positive behavior support and functional behavioral assessment in schools. *Journal of Positive Behavior Interventions, 2,* 131–143.

Sugarman, A. P., Nemiroff, R. A., & Greenson, D. P. (2000). The technique and practice of psychoanalysis: A memorial volume to Ralph R. Greenson. New York: International Universities Press.

Sund, A. M., & Wichstrom, L. (2002). Insecure attachment as a risk factor for future depressive symptoms in early adolescence. *Journal of the American Academy of Child and Adolescent Psychiatry, 41*(12), 1478–1485.

Sunseri, P. A. (2001). The prediction of unplanned discharge from residential treatment. *Child and Youth Care Forum, 30*(5), 283–303.

Swaggart, B. L. et al. (1995). Using social stories to teach social and behavioral skills to children with autism. *Focus on Autistic Behavior, 10,* 1–16.

Swann, A. C., Secunda, S. K., & Katz, M. M. (1993). Specificity of mixed affective states: Clinical comparison of dysphoric mania and agitated depression. *Journal of Affective Disorders, 28,* 81–89.

Swanson, J. M., et al. (2001). Clinical relevance of the primary findings of the MTA: Success rates based on severity of ADHD and ODD symptoms at the end of treatment. *Journal of the American Academy of Child and Adolescent Psychiatry, 40*(2), 168–182.

Szatamari, P., Brywon, S. E., & Streiner, D. L. (2001). Children with Asperger's disorder, autism differ. *The Brown University Child and Adolescent Behavior Letter, 17,* 4.

Takeuchi, D. T., & Uehara, E. S. (1996). Ethnic minority mental health services: Current research and future conceptual directions. In B. L. Levin & J. Petrila (Eds.), *Mental health services: A public perspective* (pp. 63–80). New York: Oxford University Press.

Tarasoff v. Regents of University of California, 551 p2d 334, 431 (Cal 1976).

Taylor, C. B.et al. (1998). Factors associated with weight loss in adolescent girls. *International Journal of Eating Disorders, 24,* 31–42.

Taylor, R. (1991). Child rearing in African American families. In J. Everett, S. Chipungu, & B. Leashore (Eds.), *Child welfare: An africentric perspective* (pp. 119–155). Rutgers, NJ: Rutgers University Press.

Taylor, R. J., Chatters, L. M., Tucker, M. B., & Lewis, E. (1990). Developments in research on black families: A decade review. *Journal of Marriage and Family, 52,* 993–1014.

Tercyak, K. P., Lerman, C., & Audrain, J. (2002). Association of attention-deficit/hyperactivity disorder symptoms with levels of cigarette smoking in a community sample of adolescents. *Journal of the American Academy of Child and Adolescent Psychiatry, 41,* 799–805.

Terr, L. (1988). What happens to early memories of trauma? A study of twenty children under age five at the time of documented traumatic events. *Journal of the American Academy of Child and Adolescent Psychiatry, 27,* 96–104.

Terr, L. (1985). Children traumatized in small groups. In S. Eth & R. Pynoos (Eds.), *Posttraumatic stress disorder in children.* Washington, DC: APA Press.

Terr, L. (1983). Time sense following psychic trauma. *American Journal of Orthopsychiatry, 53,* 244–261.

Terr, L. (1980). Personal injury to children: The court case claiming psychic traumas. In D. H. Schetky & E. P. Benedek (Eds.), *Child psychiatry and the law.* New York: Brunner/Mazel.

Thapar, A., & McGuffin, P. (1994). A twin study of depressive symptoms in childhood. *British Journal of Psychiatry, 165,* 159–265.

Thomsen, P. H. (2000). Obsessive-compulsive disorder: Pharmacological treatment. *European Child & Adolescent Psychiatry, 9*(Suppl 5), 176–184.

Thornton, C., & Russell, S. (1997). Obsessive-compulsive co-morbidity in the dieting disorders. *International Journal of Eating Disorders, 21,* 83–87.

Thuppal, M., Carlson, G. A., Sprafkin, J., & Gadow, K. (2002). Correspondence between adolescent report, parent report and teacher report of manic symptoms. *Journal of Child and Adolescent Psychopharmacology, 12*(1), 27–35.

Tickle-Degnan, L. (2002). Client-centered practice therapeutic relationship and use of research evidence. *American Journal of Occupational Therapy, 56*(4), 470–474.

Todd, R. D., Neuman, R., Geller, B., Fox, L. W., & Hickok, J. (1993). Genetic studies of affective disorders: Should we be starting with childhood onset probands? *Journal of Affective Disorders, 28,* 81–89.

Todd, R. D., Reich, W., & Reich, T. (1994). Prevalence of affective disorder in the child and adolescent offspring of a single kindred: A pilot study. *Journal of the American Academy of Child and Adolescent Psychiatry, 33,* 198–207.

Tolan, P. H., & Lorion, R. P. (1988). Multivariate approaches in the identification of delinquency proneness in adolescent males. *American Journal of Community Psychology, 16*(4), 547–561.

Tomlinson, R. K. (1991). Unacceptable adolescent behavior and parent-adolescent functioning: A comparison of healthy and somaticizing adolescents. *Family Process, 27*(3), 317–325.

Tomlinson-Clarke, S., & Camilli, G. (1995). An exploratory study of counselor judgments in multicultural research. *Journal of Multicultural Counseling and Development, 23,* 237–245.

Towbin, K. E., Dykens, E. M., Pearson, G. S., & Cohen, D. J. (1993). Conceptualizing "borderline syndrome of childhood" and "childhood schizophrenia" as a developmental disorder. *Journal of the American Academy of Child and Adolescent Psychiatry, 32*(4), 775–783.

Treuting, J. J., & Hinshaw, S. P. (2001). Depression and self-esteem in boys with attention-deficit/hyperactivity disorder: Associations with comorbid aggression and explanatory attributional mechanisms. *Journal of Abnormal Child Psychology, 29*(1), 23–41.

Tripathi, B. M., Lal, R., & Kumar, N. (2001). Substance abuse in children and adolescents: An overview. *Journal of Personality and Clinical Studies, 17*(2), 67–74.

Troiden, R. R. (1988). Homosexual identity development. *Journal of Adolescent Health Care, 9*(2), 105–113.

Tsai, L. Y. (1992). Medical treatment in autism. In D. Berkell (Ed.), *Autism: Identification, education, and treatment* (pp. 151–184). Hillsdale, NJ: Lawrence Erlbaum.

Tucker, S., Gross, D., Fogg, L., Delaney, K., & Lapporte, R. (1998). The long-term efficacy of a behavioral parent training intervention for families with 2-year-olds. *Research in Nursing and Health, 21,* 199–210.

Tung, T. M. (1980). *Indochinese patients.* Washington, DC: Action for South East Asia.

Turk, D. C., & Melzack, R. (Eds.) (2001). *Handbook of pain assessment* (2nd ed.). New York: Guilford Press.

Turner, S. M., Beidel, D. C., & Costello, A. (1987). Psychopathology in the offspring of anxiety disorders patients. *Journal of Consulting and Clinical Psychology, 55,* 229–235.

Uribe, V. M. (1988). Short-term psychotherapy for adolescents: Management of initial resistances. *Journal of American Academy of Psychoanalysis, 16*(1), 107–116.

Van der Mark, I. L., van Ijzendoorn, M. H., & Bakermans-Kranenburg, M. J. (2002). Development of empathy in girls during the second year of life: Associations with parenting, attachment, and temperament. *Social Development, Vol 11*(4), 451–468.

Van Ornum, W., & Mordock, J. B. (1990). Crisis counseling with children and adolescents: A guide for nonprofessional counselors. New York: Continuum Publishing.

Van Reekum, R., Links, P. S., & Mitton, J. E. (1996). Impulsivity, defensive functioning, and borderline personality disorder. *Canadian Journal of Psychiatry, 41,* 81–84.

Vega, W. A. (1990). Hispanic families in the 1980s: A decade of research. *Journal of Marriage and the Family, 52,* 1015–1024.

Velez, C. N., Johnson, J., & Cohen, P. (1989). A longitudinal analysis of selected risk factors for childhood psychopathology. *Journal of the American Academy of Child and Adolescent Psychiatry, 28,* 861–864.

Veltman, M. W. M. & Browne, K. D. (2001). Identifying childhood abuse through favorite kind of day and kinetic family drawings. *Arts in Psychotherapy, 28*(4), 251–259.

Venkataraman, S., Naylor, M. W., & King, C. (1992). Case study: Mania associated with fluoxetine treatment in adolescents. *Journal of the American Academy of Child and Adolescent Psychiatry, 31,* 276–281.

Verhulst, F. C., Achenbach, T. M., Althaus, M., & Akkerhuis, G. W. (1988). A comparison of syndromes derived from the child Behavioral Checklist for American and Dutch girls aged 6–11 and 12–16. *Journal of Child Psychology and Psychiatry, 29,* 879–895.

Verhulst, F. C., & Van Der Ende, J. (1992). Six-year developmental course of internalizing and externalizing problem behaviors. *Journal of the American Academy of Child and Adolescent Psychiatry, 31,* 941–950.

Vernberg, E. M., & Johnston, C. (2001). Developmental considerations in the use of cognitive therapy for post-traumatic stress disorder. *Journal of Cognitive Psychotherapy, 15*(3), 233–237.

Viesselman, J. O., Yaylayan, S., Weller, E. B., & Weller, R. A. (1993). Antidysthymic drugs (antidepressants and antimanics). In J. S. Werry & M. G. Aman (Eds.), *Practitioner's guide to psychoactive drugs for children and adolescents* (pp. 239–268). New York: Plenum.

Vitiello, B. (2001). Psychopharmacology for young children: Clinical needs and research opportunities. *Pediatrics, 108,* 983–989.

Vladimir, R., & Brubach, A. (2000). Teasing among school-aged children. (ERIC Document Reproduction Service No. 446 321). Rockville, MD: Educational Resources Information Center.

Wachtel, P. L. (2002). Termination of therapy: An effort at integration. *Journal of Psychotherapy Integration, 12*(3), 373–383.

Wagner, W. G. (1994). Counseling with children: An opportunity for tomorrow. *Counseling Psychologist, 22*(3), 381–401.

Walker, L. S., McLaughlin, F., & Greene, J. W. (1988). Functional illness and family functioning: A comparison of healthy and somaticizing adolescents. *Family Process, 27*(3), 317–325.

Walsh, F. (Ed.). (1993). *Normal family processes* (2nd ed.). New York: Guilford Press.

Wamboldt, M. A., & Wamboldt, F. S. (2000). Role of the family in the onset and outcome of childhood disorders: Selected research findings: *Journal of the American Academy of Child and Adolescent Psychiatry, 39*(1), 1212–1219.

Wang, W., & Viney, L. (1997). The psychosocial development of children and adolescents in the People's Republic of China: An Eriksonian approach. *International Journal of Psychology, 32*(3), 138–153.

Warren, S. L., Huston, L., Egeland, B., & Sroufe, L. A. (1997). Child and adolescent disorders and early attachment. *Journal of the American Academy of Child and Adolescent Psychiatry, 36,* 637–644.

Watson, A. C., & Guajardo, N. R. (2000). Talking about pretending: Young children's explicit understanding of representation. *Child Study Journal, 30*(2), 127.

Wechsler, D. (1991). Wechsler intelligence scale for children (3rd ed.). San Antonio, TX: Psychological Corporation.

Weeks, G. R. (Ed.) (1989). *Treating couples: The intersystem model of the Marriage Council of Philadelphia.* Philadelphia: Brunner/Mazel.

Weiner, M. F. (2002). Re-examining therapist self-disclosure. *Psychiatric Services, 53*(6), 769.

Weiss, B., Harris, V., Catron, T., & Han, S. S. (2003). Efficacy of the RECAP intervention program for children with concurrent internalizing and externalizing problems. *Journal of Consulting and Clinical Psychology, 71,* 364–374.

Weissman, M. M., Leckman, J. F., Merikangas, K. R., Gammon, G. D., & Prusoff, B. A. (1984). Depression and anxiety disorders in parents and children. *Archives of General Psychiatry, 41*(9), 845–852.

Weisz, J. B., Rudolph, K. D., Granger, D. A., & Sweeney, L. (1992). Cognition, competence, and coping in child and adolescent depression: Research findings, developmental concerns, therapeutic implications. *Development and Psychopathology, 4,* 627–653.

Weisz, J. R., Weiss, B., Suwanlert, S., & Chaiyasit, W. (2003). Syndromal structure of psychopathology in children of Thailand and the United States. *Journal of Consulting and Clinical Psychology, 71,* 375–385.

Weisz, J. R., Weiss, B., Wasserman, A., & Rintoul, B. (1987). Control-related beliefs and depression among clinic-referred children and adolescents. *Journal of Abnormal Psychology, 96,* 58–63.

Weller, E. B., Weller, R. A., & Fristad, M. A. (1995). Bipolar disorder in children: Misdiagnosis, underdiagnosis, and future directions. *Journal of the American Academy of Child and Adolescent Psychiatry, 34,* 709–714.

Weller, E. B., Weller, R. A., Fristad. A. F., & Rooney, M. T. (1999). *Administration manual for the ChIPS (Children's Interview for Psychiatric Symptoms).* Washington, DC: American Psychiatric Press.

Welner, A., Welner, Z., & Fishman, R. (1979). Psychiatric adolescent inpatients: A 10-year follow-up. *Archives of General Psychiatry, 36,* 698–700.

Werry, J. S. (1991). Overanxious disorder: A review of its taxonomic properties. *Journal of the American Academy of Child and Adolescent Psychiatry, 30,* 533–544.

West, M. M. (1998). Meta-analysis of studies assessing the efficacy of projective techniques in discriminating child sexual abuse. *Child Abuse and Neglect, 22*(11), 1151–1166.

West, S. A., McElroy, S. L., Strakowski, S. M., Keck, P. E., Jr., & McConville, B. J. (1995). Attention deficit hyperactivity disorder in adolescent mania. *American Journal of Psychiatry, 152,* 271–273.

Westermeyer, J. (1987). Cultural factors in clinical assessment. *Journal of Consulting and Clinical Psychology, 55,* 471–478.

Westrich, C. A. (1994). Art therapy with culturally different clients. *Art Therapy, 11*(3), 187–190.

Wetchler, J. L., Ofte-Athe, G. R. (1993). Empowering families at termination: A structural/strategic orientation. *Journal of Family Psychotherapy, 4*(1), 33–44.

White, J. H. (2000). The prevention of eating disorders: A review of the research on risk factors with implications for practice. *Journal of Child and Adolescent Psychiatric Nursing, 13*(2) pp. 76–87.

Wiesner, M., & Ittel, A. (2002). Relations of pubertal timing and depressive symptoms to substance use in early adolescence. *Journal of Early Adolescence, 22*(1), 5–23.

Wigfield, A., & Eccles, J. S. (Eds.) (2002). *Development of achievement motivation: A volume in the educational psychology series.* San Diego, CA: Academic Press.

Wilkie, C., Macdonald, S., & Highdahl, K. (1998). Community case study: Suicide cluster in a small Manitoba community. *Canadian Journal of Psychiatry, 43*(8), 823–828.

Williams, F., Coyle, A., & Lyons, E. (1999). How counseling psychologists view their personal therapy. *British Journal of Medical Psychology, 72*(4), 545–555.

Williams, J. M., & Currie, C. (2000). Self-esteem and physical development in early adolescence: Pubertal timing and body image. *Journal of Early Adolescence, 20*(2), 129–149.

Williamson, D. E. et al. (2000). Atypical symptoms of depression in a sample of depressed child and adolescent outpatients. *Journal of the American Academy of Child and Adolescent Psychiatry, 39*(10), 1253–1261.

Wilson, J. P., & Friedman, M. J. (Eds.) (2001). *Treating psychological trauma and PTSD.* New York: Guilford Press.

Wilson, K., & Ryan, V. (2002). Play therapy with emotionally damaged adolescents. *Emotional and Behavioural Difficulties, 7*(3), 178–191.

Winnicott, D. W. (1993). Transitional objects and transitional phenomena: A study of the first not-me possession. In Pollack, G. H. (Ed.). Pivotal papers on identification (pp. 139–157). London: International Universities Press.

Winzelberg, A., et al. (1998). Evaluation of a computer-mediated eating disorder program. *International Journal of Eating Disorders, 24,* 339–349.

Wise, A. J., & Spengler, P. M. (1997). Suicide in children younger than fourteen: Clinical judgment and assessment issues. *Journal of Mental Health Counseling, 19*(4), 318–335.

Wolkow, K. E., Ferguson, H. B. (2001). Community factors in the development of resiliency: Considerations and future directions. *Community Mental Health Journal, 37*(6), 489–498.

Wonderlich, S. A., Brewerton, T. D., Jocic, Z., Dansk, B. S., & Abbott, D. W. (1997). The relationship between childhood sexual abuse and eating disorders. *Journal of the American Academy of Child and Adolescent Psychiatry, 36,* 1107–1115.

Wolfe, D. A., et al. (2003). Dating violence prevention with at-risk youth: A controlled outcome evaluation. *Journal of Consulting and Clinical Psychology, 71,* 279–291.

Woody, R. H.(1991). *Quality care in mental health: Assuring the best clinical services.* New York: Jossey–Bass.

Wozniak, J, et al. (1997). Mania in children with pervasive developmental disorder revisited. *Journal of the American Academy of Child and Adolescent Psychiatry, 36*(11), 1552–1561.

Wozniak, J., Biederman, J., & Kiely, K. (1995). Mania-like symptoms suggestive of childhood-onset bipolar disorder in clinically referred children. *Journal of the American Academy of Child and Adolescent Psychiatry, 34,* 867–876.

Wrenn, C. G. (1988). The person in career counseling. *Career Development Quarterly, 36*(4), 337–342.

Wright, L. S. (1982). The use of logical consequences in counseling children. *School Counselor, 30*(1), 37–49.

Wuerker, A. K. (1994). Relational control patterns and expressed emotion in families of persons with schizophrenia and bipolar disorder. *Family Process, 33,* 389–407.

Wuerker, A. K., Haas, G. L., & Bellack, A. S. (1999). Racial and gender differences in expressed emotion and interpersonal control in families of persons with schizophrenia. *Family Process, 38*(4), 477–495.

Yalom, I. (1983). *Group therapy.* New York: Basic Books.

Yang, K. S. (1986). Effects of family factors on child behavior: A review of empirical studies in Taiwan. *Acta psychologica Taiwanica, 28*(1), 7–28.

Yauman, B. E. (1991). School-based group counseling for children of divorce: A review of the literature. *Elementary School Guidance & Counseling, 26*(2), 130–138.

Yeh, M., Eastman, K., & Cheung, M. K. (1994). Children and adolescents in community mental health centers: Does the ethnicity or the language of the counselor matter? *Journal of Community Psychology, 22,* 153–163.

Yeh, M. & Weisz, J. R. (2001). Why are we here at the clinic? Parent-child (dis)agreement on referral problems. *Journal of Consulting and Clinical Psychology, 69,* 1018–1025.

Yirmiya, N., & Sigman, M. D. (1991). High functioning individuals with autism: Diagnosis, empirical findings, and theoretical issues. *Clinical Psychology Review, 11,* 669–683.

Yorbik, O., Dikkatli, S., Cansever, A., Soehmen, T. (2001). The efficacy of fluoxetine treatment in children and adolescents with posttraumatic stress disorder symptoms. *Klinik Psikofarmakoloji Buelteni, 11*(4) 251–256.

Zametkin, A. J., & Yamada, E. M. (1999). Monitoring and measuring drug effects: Vol. 1. Physical effects. In J. Werry & M. Aman (Eds.), *Practitioner's guide to psychoactive drugs for children and adolescents* (2nd ed., pp. 69–97). New York: Plenum.

Zeanah, C. H. (Ed.). (2000). *Handbook of infant mental health* (2nd ed.). New York: Guilford Press.

Zipkin v. Freeman, 436 S. W. 2d753 (Mo.1968).

Index

TO THE OWNER OF THIS BOOK:

I hope that you have found *Counseling Children and Adolescents*, First Edition, useful. So that this book can be improved in a future edition, would you take the time to complete this sheet and return it? Thank you.

School and address: _____

_____

Department: _____

Instructor's name: _____

1. What I like most about this book is: _____

_____

_____

2. What I like least about this book is: _____

_____

_____

3. My general reaction to this book is: _____

_____

_____

4. The name of the course in which I used this book is: _____

_____

5. Were all of the chapters of the book assigned for you to read? _____

   If not, which ones weren't? _____

6. In the space below, or on a separate sheet of paper, please write specific suggestions for improving this book and anything else you'd care to share about your experience in using this book.

_____

_____

OPTIONAL:

Your name: _____ Date: _____

May we quote you, either in promotion for *Counseling Children and Adolescents*, First Edition, or in future publishing ventures?

Yes: _____ No: _____

Sincerely yours,

Deanna S. Pledge

FOLD HERE

**NO POSTAGE
NECESSARY
IF MAILED
IN THE
UNITED STATES**

BUSINESS REPLY MAIL
FIRST CLASS   PERMIT NO. 34   BELMONT, CA

POSTAGE WILL BE PAID BY ADDRESSEE

ATTN: Amy Lam

BROOKS/COLE/THOMSON LEARNING
10 DAVIS DRIVE
BELMONT, CA   94002-9801

FOLD HERE